MW00488634

PRAISE FOR
A REPUBLIC OF SCOUNDRELS

"In *A Republic of Scoundrels*, the down and dirty side of the American Revolution and its aftermath is revealed in all of its scandalous glory. Despite the mythos that surrounds the event, this book shows that the seedy underbelly of war played a critical role in shaping 'The Glorious Cause.' As much as we like to remember pride and patriotism, sometimes murder, unrest, and espionage were lurking just around the corner."

—Brady Crytzer, author of *The Whiskey Rebellion: A Distilled History of an American Crisis*

"A rogues' gallery of the shadiest, most dishonest, self-serving, and duplicitous characters who traipsed across the stage of the early American Republic. In this insightful and enjoyable anthology, Tim Hemmis and David Head have gathered together a collection of talented historians whose chapters illuminate the schemers, intriguers, and adventurers who created the new American nation. Ranging from the distasteful, to the outrageous, to the repulsive, these figures helped shape the contours and texture of the Early Republic and the course of American development for years to come."

—Ricardo A. Herrera, author of *Feeding Washington's Army: Surviving the Valley Forge Winter of 1778*

"This wonderful collection of essays highlights the exploits of the villains who helped shape the Revolutionary Era and the early American Republic. From Benedict Arnold and Charles Lee to William Blount, Matthew Lyon, James Wilkinson, Aaron Burr, and Florida's notorious Kemper brothers, the book reveals the radically different paths to becoming a notorious scoundrel. While the creation of the American Republic required the demigods we often praise, the stories featured here offer an interesting yet contradictory story of the American founding beyond the efforts of the famed founding fathers."

—Gene Allen Smith, author of *The Slaves' Gamble: Choosing Sides in the War of 1812* and co-author of *Filibusters and Expansionists: Jeffersonian Manifest Destiny, 1800–1821*

"Shines a distinctive light on the first decades of American independence. They illuminate how the same conditions—the fragility of the union, the hostility of the new nation's neighbors, the uncertainty of the people's loyalties, and the fluidity of social and cultural expectations—that struck real fear in the hearts of Washington, Hamilton, Jefferson, and Madison represented alluring opportunities for a different set of men, at no small cost to their reputations at the time and since."

—James E. Lewis, Jr., author of *The Burr Conspiracy: Uncovering the Story of an Early American Crisis*

"It took all kinds to make up the early republic. Unsurprisingly, not a few of them were better suited to Hell than halos. Welcome to a fascinating convocation of the misfits, miscreants, and chancers, who sometimes purposely—and often inadvertently—helped to build America. From the darkest days of the Revolution to Americans' early leaps across the Mississippi, these schemers and would-be empire builders impacted their times, some to become legends, and others pariahs. Taken together, as a fine cast of authors demonstrates, they truly make up *A Republic of Scoundrels*."

—William C. Davis, author of *The Greatest Fury: The Battle of New Orleans and the Rebirth of America* and *The Pirates Laffite: The Treacherous World of the Corsairs of the Gulf*

"*A Republic of Scoundrels* brings together a motley mix of fascinating, sometimes perplexing, and always entertaining individuals to paint a new portrait of the early American Republic. While none of those in this book are considered Founders, and in fact, as this book shows, they often tried to undermine the fledgling nation, their failed schemes, duplicitous acts, and otherwise untoward behavior often proved unexpectedly important to shoring up the country's foundations."

—Patrick Spero, Executive Director, George Washington Presidential Library

"A feisty romp through early American history, full of corruption, greed, and misunderstood antiheroes. The book provides an innovative approach to the clashing imperial interests feuding on the borders of the new and emerging United States. *A Republic of Scoundrels* proves that scoundrels are a timeless element in the American story, but they defined the Early Republic."

—Lindsay M. Chervinsky, author of *The Cabinet: George Washington and the Creation of an American Institution*

A REPUBLIC OF SCOUNDRELS

★ ★ ★

THE SCHEMERS, INTRIGUERS & ADVENTURERS WHO CREATED A NEW AMERICAN NATION

EDITED BY
DAVID HEAD &
TIMOTHY C. HEMMIS

PEGASUS BOOKS
NEW YORK LONDON

A REPUBLIC OF SCOUNDRELS

Pegasus Books, Ltd.
148 West 37th Street, 13th Floor
New York, NY 10018

First Pegasus Books cloth edition December 2023

Interior design by Maria Fernandez

ISBN: 978-1-63936-407-7

10 9 8 7 6 5 4 3 2 1

Printed in the United States of America
Distributed by Simon & Schuster
www.pegasusbooks.com

To the Founding Generation

CONTENTS

NOTE ON QUOTATIONS

Early American English lacked things that we would now consider essential, such as standardized spelling, punctuation, and grammar. Aside from a few silent corrections for clarity, quoted material reproduces the original language, "errors" and all, to allow an author's voice to emerge through the page.

INTRODUCTION

TIMOTHY C. HEMMIS

★ ★ ★

In the summer of 1787, as the Constitutional Convention took place in Philadelphia, General James Wilkinson journeyed to New Orleans to visit Spanish Governor Esteban Miró, ostensibly about obtaining a monopoly on trade down the Mississippi River from Kentucky. Wilkinson brought with him flour, butter, bacon, and tobacco—examples of the goods he said he hoped to trade—but it was all just a cover for what he really wanted to discuss: removing the region of Kentucky from the United States to join the Spanish Empire as a new colony. During that trip, Wilkinson enlisted in the Spanish cause and agreed to be a spy for them while serving in the United States Army. On August 21, 1787, Wilkinson presented his plan to Governor Miró.[1]

The general was confident of success. He believed free access to the Mississippi would persuade many in Kentucky to pledge allegiance to a new flag. Their loyalty would follow their crops to Spanish New Orleans. Still, Wilkinson explained, it would help to pay off several notable men of Kentucky. If "Spain can attach to her, the influential Characters among the Western Americans," Wilkinson argued, "then they [will be] able to accomplish their separation from the United

States." Wilkinson had in mind men such as Virginia Attorney General Harry Innes, Congressman John Brown, Judge Caleb Wallace, Revolutionary War veteran Isaac Shelby, Commodore Richard Taylor, and Colonel Henry Lee.[2]

Wilkinson's plot never came to fruition. Some of the leaders he targeted, such as Taylor and Lee, only wanted to break Kentucky away from Virginia, of which it is was still a part, not join a new country, while others thought the new Constitution should be given a chance before making a permanent separation. Wilkinson found his dealings with the Spanish scrutinized. One official reported to President George Washington that "a violent separation from the United States seems to be laid down as the groundwork which ever other consequence depends." And yet Wilkinson's so-called Spanish Conspiracy did not ruin his reputation. Rumors circulated, but Wilkinson was careful to conceal his true intentions and went on to enjoy a long career in the U.S. Army, maintaining the trust of multiple presidents.[3]

What does the existence of a man like Wilkinson say about the new American nation? How could he have worked against US interests while so brazenly advancing his own—and gotten away with it? Certainly, Wilkinson was skilled in the arts of deception, but he was hardly unique in the early United States. Untold numbers of men saw opportunity in the new nation—opportunity to serve themselves regardless of what the official culture said about public virtue and self-sacrifice as the lifeblood of a republic.

After all, the country was unstable at best under the Articles of Confederation, and even after it went into effect, little was known about the untested Federal Constitution. Many people doubted its strength and longevity, including the Spanish and British who believed that with correct nudging they could induce the young nation into chaos. Revolutionary America (1776–1815) was a time of fluid national identity, when attachments to the nation competed with local, regional, and state affiliations. Into the uncertain political and commercial environment stepped self-interested men who saw their chance to improve their social status, fatten their pocketbooks, and burnish their legacies. Although, like Wilkinson, their plans often failed, their actions ultimately determined how the young United States of America matured.

★ ★ ★

Today, the term "scoundrel" seems either archaic—the kind of thing wig-wearing gentlemen called each other before taking up dueling pistols—or something from the realm of fantasy, a way to describe Han Solo from the *Star Wars* universe. (A scoundrel *definitely* shoots first.) In reality, "scoundrel" was a meaningful term in the Revolutionary era. Samuel Johnson's 1755 dictionary, for example, defined scoundrel as "a mean rascal; a low petty villain." That definition implies a lot of potential meanings, and in common usage the term was certainly flexible. Some men were considered scoundrels because of their unethical commercial activities. Others because of their political schemes. Still others were labeled "scoundrels" because of the way they violated international boundaries. Some were simply criminals.[4]

The present work reveals the many ways to be a scoundrel in the Revolutionary period. Perhaps the most extreme way to earn the name was to do something which might be considered treason. To many Americans, there was no man more treasonous than Benedict Arnold. With his defection to the British Army in 1780, Arnold immediately became one of the most hated men for American patriots, erased all the heroic deeds he had previously performed on the battlefield, and forever tarnished his legacy. Aaron Burr, too, has a scandalous reputation. Though his legacy in popular culture is mostly tied to killing Alexander Hamilton, Burr was also accused of treason, standing trial for his escapades in the West which involved plans for filibustering in Mexico, waging a war against Spain, creating an independent government, launching a coup, or starting a civil war. Burr was a former vice president and popular among his followers. His scheming rocked the young republic. Other men's involvement with foreign powers was more hidden but still raised suspicions. James Wilkinson's treachery was not known until after his death in 1825, but throughout his life his rivals always suspected his treason. Yet he rose to be the highest ranking general in the army. One of Wilkinson's protégés, Philip Nolan, was also suspected of being in league with the Spanish. Over time, Nolan went from being a horse trader in Central Texas to Spanish informant to an untrustworthy American, which led to his murder in 1801.

Another extreme way to be remembered as a scoundrel was to commit murder. That's how Jason Fairbanks of Dedham, Massachusetts, gained infamy in 1801: as the killer of his would-be love, Elizabeth Fales. Early nineteenth-century America was a violent place, but the murder and Fairbanks's trial were the talk of New England because the story was about more than love gone wrong. Fairbanks's obsession with virtue and reputation drove him, paradoxically, to become a scoundrel and damage his family's legacy, a warning for a nation with a public culture similarly obsessed with virtue and reputation.

Other figures profiled in the pages that follow looked west and south and found ample opportunities for taking advantage of others. Located on the border with Spanish territory and far from the seat of the US government, the American West and the Gulf South were often an international playground for schemers who sought to make a fortune or even to carve out their own empire. William Blount, Thomas Green, and the Kemper brothers—Reuben, Nathan, and Samuel—sought ways to line their own pockets by taking advantage of their situations and positions in society. The moral flexibility of these men leaned toward their economic favor regardless of the ethics or legality of the activity. William Blount of Tennessee, for example, was a crooked senator and land speculator. He became the first person impeached in the newly formed federal government because he openly used his position to increase the value of his real estate. He was also crucial to the development of early Tennessee. Thomas Green attempted to launch an unauthorized private military attack, called a filibuster, against Spanish Natchez on behalf of the state of Georgia. Green's actions forced the national governments of the United States and Spain to take notice of the backcountry region of Natchez and the lower Mississippi River. He showed that self-serving men could dictate the policies of the nation because there really was not anything stopping them, as the Articles of Confederation were weak and ineffective. The Kemper brothers turned a personal vendetta against Spanish officials in West Florida into a bid for the region's independence. Unlike the Kempers, however, many Americans living in Spanish West Florida were happy under a foreign government. It worked for them. But the Kempers wouldn't listen and violence followed.

Americans weren't the only ones to intrigue in the borderlands. International agents worked to destabilize the region and the United States. Don Diego de Gardoqui was a Spanish agent who created disorder along the American border. Although he began his career in the United States far differently—as the Spanish minister to the United States during the American Revolution he was a diplomatic hero—he became an international scoundrel after the war. His plan: to subvert the young American Republic by persuading Americans to join the Spanish cause. Also operating in the borderlands, William Augustus Bowles, a loyalist during the Revolution, sought to create a Muskogee state in northern Florida. It would be a protectorate of Great Britain where Natives and Europeans could live together. Bowles's actions caught the attention of both the Spanish and American governments, who did not want to see a semi-independent Native state that allowed the British back into Florida after they were expelled during the American Revolutionary War.

Treachery, speculation, malfeasance, self-dealing, foreign intrigue—all these actions attracted the label of scoundrel. At the same time, the epithet was also applied by enemies for simply having the wrong background, representing the wrong people, or challenging a revered figure. Charles Lee and Matthew Lyon were deemed scoundrels by opponents, in no small part because they had the audacity to disagree. Lyon arrived in the United States as an indentured servant and became a Republican Congressman representing Vermont. Boisterous and annoying, he attracted the ire of Federalists, who saw him as an unruly immigrant scoundrel and complained he spoke too freely and too often out of turn. To Republicans, Lyon was a working-class hero and a faithful representative of his people. Although Lyon was arrested for sedition in 1798, he still won his re-election bid from a jail cell.

General Charles Lee had the misfortune to think he was just as good a general as the hallowed George Washington. And for good reason—he had been a commissioned officer in the British Army, trained in Europe, and was experienced in warfare. Yet whatever professional expertise lay behind Lee's opinion of Washington, he had the terrible judgment to make it public to the Continental Congress, a lapse of the political skills needed to preserve a reputation in the crucible of army command.

Much like today, scoundrels in the late eighteenth and early nineteenth centuries came in a variety of shapes and sizes, from traitors and corrupt politicians to spies, speculators, and outright criminals. However, during the Revolutionary era, opportunities for both happiness and mischief abounded as the young nation was in flux in its government, laws, and business ethics. Each chapter in this book highlights a self-interested and opportunistic man or group of men who helped shape the United States of America. Many of these men have been left out of the larger historical narrative because they have been overshadowed by other, more revered figures. Even more well-known men such as Benedict Arnold, Aaron Burr, and James Wilkinson have become secondary characters in the national story. *A Republic of Scoundrels* reconsiders the Founding generation and shows that they were not the monolithic group that many people revere today, but a diverse collection of self-interested and sometimes unscrupulous individuals.

★ ★ ★

A Republic of Scoundrels is organized by time and place. The first section focuses on two Continental Army generals: Benedict Arnold and Charles Lee. In "'Your Best Friends Are Not Your Countrymen': The Treason of Benedict Arnold," James Kirby Martin reexamines how Arnold went from being a patriotic hero to a treasonous pariah when he returned his allegiance to the British during the Revolutionary War.

Mark Edward Lender follows with a reassessment of General Charles Lee. In "Charles Lee: The General as a Scoundrel?" Lender suggests that Lee's reputation is contested at best. Lee's overt criticism of George Washington tarnished his reputation and labeled him a scoundrel. Both Martin and Lender demonstrate that during the American War for Independence, general officers such as Arnold and Lee felt slighted and overlooked by leadership in the Continental Army. Each man had different reactions to their perceived slights: Arnold committed treason and Lee openly questioned Washington's decision-making to members of Congress. But because Lee ultimately remained loyal, he escaped Arnold's fate of having his name become synonymous with the word "traitor," even in the present day.

Section two turns to the aftermath of the Revolution, when the new republic represented a fresh start for many men, including ones mostly out for themselves who took advantage of the uncertainty of the times as state and national governments formed and found their footing. In the third chapter, "Blount's Bunko: Private Fortune Through Public Service in the Southwest Territory, 1790–1796," Christopher Magra sheds light on the activities of William Blount and how he used his political position in the US Senate to benefit himself. Magra illuminates the crooked career of Blount, how he helped shape the new state of Tennessee, and how his scandalous actions earned him ignominy of being the first federal officeholder to be impeached. Blount was truly an American scoundrel.

In the fourth chapter, "'The Spitting Lyon': Matthew Lyon and the Federalists' Fears," Shira Lurie shows how Federalists painted a crude immigrant Congressmen from Vermont, Matthew Lyon, as a scoundrel not worthy of the office. However, not everyone agreed. Lyon fought for his constituents in an unorthodox manner, but his voters understood him and reelected him even though he had been in jail for sedition. Although Lyon is not a household name of the Founding generation, Lurie shows why he should be remembered.

The next chapter, Craig Bruce Smith's "The Devil from Dedham: Jason Fairbanks and the Failure of Manly Virtue," examines how societal norms of masculine virtue and honor pressured a young man to murder a woman who rejected his proposal of marriage in 1801. Fairbanks went to extraordinary lengths to forge a marriage certificate and force Elizabeth Fales to marry him. When she said no, he killed her. After his arrest he attempted to escape his fate, but Smith shows that, in the end, a criminal like Fairbanks was simply a scoundrel.

The next section focuses on the American borderlands. In the sixth chapter, "James Wilkinson: Schemer, Scoundrel, Solider, Spy . . . Success?" Samuel Watson reexamines the career and legacy of General Wilkinson. Watson suggests that Wilkinson was a notorious scoundrel, but much more complex than just a simple bad actor. Despite his schemes and scandals, Wilkinson was also effective as a American Army general. Watson argues that Wilkinson was a self-centered opportunist who seemed to always weasel out of trouble, but ultimately maybe he was a true American.

Jackson Pearson follows with the story of one of Wilkinson's barely remembered associates, Phillip Nolan, in the seventh chapter, "'The Mexican Traveler': Phillip Nolan and the Southwest Horse Trade." Nolan's charisma allowed him to gain passage from Louisiana into Spanish Texas to acquire horses from the Comanche and Wichita, but it also entangled him in various romantic affairs. Eventually, Nolan's activity in Texas would get him killed and forgotten until the twentieth century when he became a historical hero and martyr to Anglo-Texans. Pearson outlines why the pro-Anglo filibuster narrative around Nolan needs to be revisited in favor of the complete story.

Another story of a now unknown figure causing trouble in the borderlands is found in chapter eight. Christian Pinnen's "American Adventurers in the Mississippi Borderlands: Thomas Green and Georgia's 1785 Bourbon County Scheme in Spanish Natchez" explores Green's forgotten attempt to capture the Natchez District from the Spanish. Pinnen demonstrates that Southern planters already had expansion of slavery and manifest destiny on their minds in the 1780s. Green's activities as a filibuster stepped outside of societal norms and manipulated the United States foreign policy in the region.

Staying in the Gulf South for chapter nine, Jane H. Plummer's "Troubled Trio: The Kemper Brothers and Rebellion in West Florida, 1804" examines how Rueben, Samuel, and Nathan Kemper attempted to seize parts of West Florida from the Spanish in the early 1800s. Much like Pinnen's account of Thomas Green, Plummer demonstrates that the borderlands of the Gulf South were contested areas with little or no government to control them. Plummer further suggests that the Kemper brothers sought ways to expand American interests—seizing land, goods, and enslaved people—through unofficial force rather than diplomacy. Because of the proximity to the frontier, their unscrupulous activities were overlooked by many American officials because the Kempers promoted their agenda.

The tenth chapter, "William Augustus Bowles, the Pretender: A Tory Adventurer as a Native American Leader" by David Narrett, expounds on the life of William Augustus Bowles and his bid for an independent Muskogee state. With the Gulf South a contested backwater between two empires, the Tory Bowles sensed he had a chance to create a Native American state with the backing of the British government. He became a thorn in the side of both the Spanish and the Americans. Narrett's narrative of Bowles demonstrates how intricate borderland politics were and how activities on the fringes of the empire influenced foreign policies.

In the modern world, it seems odd that foreign policy is a word used to describe activities in the Gulf South or along the Mississippi River, but in the early republic the borderlands were areas of international contention. In the eleventh chapter, "Diego de Gardoqui: From Hero of the Revolution to Scoundrel of the Early Republic," Tyson Reeder assesses the career of Don Diego de Gardoqui as a Spanish Minister to the United States. Reeder uses Gardoqui's influence on the failed state of Franklin as a case study for how the Spanish minister sought to dislodge the West from the United States. Although a Spanish subject, Gardoqui truly was one of the many scoundrels of the early republic.

In the last chapter, "An American Scoundrel on Trial: Aaron Burr and His Failed Insurrection, 1805–1807," Timothy Hemmis explores the national drama surrounding Burr's arrest and subsequent trial in the summer of 1807. Despite Burr's ultimate acquittal, he remains one of the most infamous scoundrels in the early republic. His treason trial divided the nation. But as Hemmis shows, it could have been much worse. Burr's shadowy scheming almost caused an insurrection and possibly a civil war.

* * *

Popular Founding Fathers such as George Washington, Benjamin Franklin, Thomas Jefferson, and Alexander Hamilton have become American saints, men revered for their wisdom and self-sacrificing service to the nation. However, within the Founding generation lurked many unscrupulous figures—men who violated the era's expectation of public virtue and advanced their own interests at the expense of others. They were turncoats and traitors, opportunists and con artists, spies and foreign intriguers. The early years of the republic were full of people who placed themselves above the nation—sometimes succeeding in their plots, sometimes failing, but always shaping the young nation. This collection seeks to reexamine the Founding generation and replace the hagiography of the Founding Fathers with something more realistic: a picture which embraces the many shadows of the nation's origins.

"YOUR BEST FRIENDS ARE NOT YOUR COUNTRYMEN": THE TREASON OF BENEDICT ARNOLD

JAMES KIRBY MARTIN

★ ★ ★

Benedict Arnold was the most enthusiastic of American rebel patriots when the war with England broke out in April 1775. He was ready and more than willing to fight for what he and so many other colonists perceived as the loss of their basic liberties. Gung ho as Arnold was to go to war, a little over five years later, on September 25, 1780, he fled from his headquarters across from West Point, New York, down the Hudson River to the protective arms of British forces in New York City. His coat had changed very dramatically from blue to red. This essay will investigate why Arnold, having chosen treason once before when he took up arms against his sovereign in 1775, was now willing to commit treason a second time. Because of this switch in allegiance, he is known as one of the greatest scoundrels in American history.

On the evening of September 25, safely in the waiting hands of British forces, Arnold penned a note about his apostasy to his one-time military patron, George Washington. His "heart," he declared, was "conscious of its own rectitude" in forsaking what he considered a lost cause. Arnold knew that he had taken "a step which the world may censure as wrong." However, he had "ever acted from a principle of love to my country," which "may appear inconsistent to the world, who very seldom judge right of any man's actions."[1]

Stated differently, Arnold had convinced himself that the patriot cause was venal, bereft of integrity, and lacking in citizenry virtue, as well as being destroyed from the inside by feigned patriots whose only real goal was to serve themselves rather than the greater good of the Revolutionary community. He had concluded that "the mass of the people are heartily tired of the war" and, as a result, the once glorious cause was in its death throes, evidencing "the pangs of a dying man, violent but of a short duration." The only sensible course was to return to the British fold before the cause collapsed.[2]

Immediately, Arnold's actions backfired on him—and on his reputation. A Continental Army Orderly Book issued the next day announced that "Treason of the blackest dye was yesterday discovered." Fortunately, this potentially "deadly wound, if not a fatal stab" to the patriot cause—Arnold's plot to sell out the vital West Point defenses at so dangerous a time—had failed. Surely this "providential train of circumstances . . . affords the most convincing proof that the liberties of America are the object of . . . divine protection."[3]

Thus began a major reformulation of Arnold's character. Colonel Alexander Scammell, on duty near West Point, wondered how "an officer so high on the list of fame . . . could be lost to every sense of honor, patriotism, and his own true interest." Scammell speculated that "Arnold's bravery at Saratoga has in the eyes of his country and army, covered a multitude of his villainous actions." Clearly the explanation was a deep character flaw, namely, Arnold's insatiable greed for filthy lucre, over which he had "practiced for a long time the most dirty, infamous measures to acquire gain."[4]

The darkened image of Arnold the traitor quickly took shape. On September 30, Philadelphia's patriots held a parade with a float featuring their newfound antihero. It displayed "an effigy of General Arnold sitting" with Beelzebub "shaking a purse of money at the general's left ear, and in his right hand a pitchfork, ready to drive him [Arnold] into hell as the reward due for the many crimes which the thief of gold had made him commit."[5]

Four days later, the Continental Congress ordered that this bedeviled agent of Satan should have his name erased forever from its Army's list of general officers. Within weeks negative characterizations appeared everywhere. Arnold was a complete "scoundrel," "a mean toad eater," a false patriot who had apparently been planting his treasonous plot because, as the Marquis de Lafayette stated, he was an insidious deceiver ultimately consumed by his "rascality" of temperament.[6]

Arnold's pleas for reconciliation with the British Crown were lost in the rush of activity to trash forever his good name. Actually, Arnold was correct in his assessment that the patriot cause had reached its nadir of popular enthusiasm and support in 1779 and into 1780. What he had not calculated was that his apostasy would help rekindle the waning flames of popular support for the American cause. Though it may have been nothing more than lip service, the people cheered Washington and his Continentals even as they loudly jeered Arnold as a truly corrupted agent of the devil. As the talented general Nathanael Greene—another of Washington's stars—declared: "Never since the fall of Lucifer has a fall equaled his."[7]

★ ★ ★

Images of the "scoundrel" Arnold helped fix in place interpretations of the Revolution as a cosmic struggle between good and evil. On the American side was everything luminous protected by Divine Providence; on the British side nothing existed but darkness fostered by Satan and his demonic underworld. In this popular interpretive framework, the virtuous colonists came together as one united body when going to war in 1775 and never wavered in their willingness to give their all, even life itself, to breathe the new American Republic into existence. The tyrannical British, led by Mad King George and a corrupting Parliament, did whatever possible to keep the self-sacrificing colonists powerless in their tyrannical political regime of monarchism. George Washington, who could never tell a lie, was the epitome of selfless citizen virtue; Benedict Arnold, by comparison, was the high exemplar of self-serving vice, the ultimate apostate who for filthy lucre would do anything the British asked of him to despoil and destroy the glorious cause of American liberty.

That was how my fourth-grade teacher, stern but kindly Mrs. Helen Rand, presented the story of the American Revolution so many decades ago. I carried that impression through high school and into college, where flaws in the "all good" versus "all bad" interpretation started to become obvious. In graduate school at the University of Wisconsin, my academic mentor, the late Merrill Jensen, a superb scholar with significant books to his credit, made the essential point that writing and, ultimately, interpreting history begins, methodologically speaking, with open-minded research of extant evidence in the archives.[8]

Thinking about a new project to research several years after graduate school, I recalled those fourth-grade lessons. Why not, I decided, investigate the twists and turns of Benedict Arnold's life? Was he really that bad? Was he nothing more than just a rascally, toad-eating scoundrel? If so, why all the fuss? As I dug into the surviving records, I was also reading published books about Arnold. Virtually all of them addressed one dominant question: Why treason? The standard approach was to look backward through the prism of the moment treason became public (September 25, 1780) to compile incidents and stories—too often made up—that would explain how and why this no-account traitor tried to ruin the Revolution. In doing so, these writers found ways to downgrade and belittle Arnold's impressive array of battlefield accomplishments in fighting for the patriot cause, often nearly giving his life trying to win American independence.

The highly productive nineteenth-century historian Jared Sparks (1789–1866) set the tone for virtually all later Arnold biographies. In 1835, he published *The Life and Times of Benedict Arnold*. Sparks featured a childhood full of mischief, including little Benny climbing trees and strangling baby birds, spreading glass along the sidewalks so kids going to school would cut up their bare feet, and showing off by riding the paddle wheel at the local grist mill as it spun round and round—all evidence of a mean-spirited, self-absorbed adult in the making.

Certainly, too, Arnold's military career was tainted in numerous ways. Read, for example, Sparks's chapter about the rebel withdrawal from Canada during the springtime of 1776. The title is "Arnold censured for the seizure of goods in Montreal." The obvious implication is that the bad boy, now an adult, was stealing these goods, a clear misrepresentation of what was actually going on (see ahead for Arnold's dealings with Colonel Moses Hazen, a former British Army officer). In sum, the book concludes, Arnold was a horrible person living among a special generation of fully committed and united patriots whose selfless virtue always characterized their behavior.[9]

Sparks saw the devil at work but did not push the satanic theme. More modern writers were also less enamored of the devil's explanatory power, but Arnold's lust for money remained a crucial variable, as did the alluring influences of his teenage wife, Peggy Shippen.

Arnold's first wife, Margaret Mansfield, died unexpectedly in 1775 at thirty years of age. Arnold had scant time to look for a new spouse during the Canadian campaign that followed in 1776, or during the critical Saratoga campaign of 1777 when he played a starring role in defeating a British–Hessian Army under the command of General John Burgoyne. Arnold was seriously wounded in his left leg, a debilitating injury he suffered from the rest of his life. Unable to ride a horse, Arnold was assigned by Washington to the post of military governor of Philadelphia upon the British evacuation of that city in June 1778.

There Arnold met beautiful Margaret "Peggy" Shippen. She had developed friendships with such notable British officers as Major John André, who became the adjutant general of the British Army. Once married in 1779, Shippen, supposedly a closet loyalist, used her seductive, Eve-like charm to convince her heroic husband to go for the gold and glory that awaited them upon returning his allegiance to the British. By this interpretation, a traitorous correspondence between Arnold and André, facilitated by Shippen, opened the pathway to treason.[10]

Thus, the great betrayal rested on a devilish young Arnold whose love of money was insatiable. Later he fell under the influence of his second wife, who, with her expensive tastes, helped to seduce him again into betraying a cause always above reproach in its self-sacrificing character.

John Brown, a patriot lawyer and sometime soldier from Pittsfield, Massachusetts, seemed to be prescient when he declared in 1777, over three years before Arnold's apostasy, that his "character was not worth a sixpence." Brown, who hated Arnold for various personal reasons noted ahead, did not stop there. He went on to declare that "Money is this man's god; and to get enough of it, he would sacrifice his country." As such, Brown supposedly knew long before others what a natural-born, obviously complete scoundrel that Benedict Arnold really was. Case closed. Maybe, yes? Or, more likely, case not closed at all.[11]

★ ★ ★

Unfortunately, Brown's characterization of Arnold only resonates as long as commentators present his words out of context. Brown was just one of a number of Revolutionaries who were themselves self-absorbed patriot scoundrels most interested in serving themselves. For various reasons, Arnold and Brown were not getting along during the months when the war started in 1775. Both were enthusiastic patriots. While Arnold was organizing his Second Company of Footguards in New Haven, Connecticut, Brown made a hazardous journey from western Massachusetts all the way north to Montreal in Quebec Province. His mission was to determine if British subjects in this French-dominated but recently conquered colony might join the patriot cause. During his journey, Brown met notorious Vermont land-grabber Ethan Allen, the boisterous head of the Green Mountain Boys. They promised to work together should war break out.

When musket balls started flying at Lexington and Concord on April 19, Arnold, in his turn, activated the Footguards and marched them off to join thousands of other rebel enthusiasts ready to challenge British forces in Boston. Along the way, Arnold explained to an acquaintance returning from Boston that valuable artillery pieces could be had at Fort Ticonderoga and Crown Point, located on the western shoreline of Lake Champlain. This gentleman proceeded to Hartford where he helped gain funds to pay for a party of adventurers to travel north, capture the fort, and seize heavy weaponry in the area. Cutting through the story, Ethan Allen emerged as the leader of this band of rebels that included John Brown and another Pittsfield resident, a heavy drinking tavern keeper named James Easton.

On the evening of May 9, Allen, Easton, Brown, and some two hundred or more Green Mountain Boys gathered at Hand's Cove along Lake Champlain's eastern shore in Vermont territory. They were getting ready to cross the lake and overrun the lightly defended fort when out of nowhere Benedict Arnold, of all unexpected people, rode up. He showed his Massachusetts colonel's commission, declaring that he outranked Allen, who had no commission. Arnold, however, brought no fighters with him. The Boys insisted they would only follow their trusted leader, Allen. After much squabbling, the convenient solution was to accept Allen and Arnold as joint commanders.[12]

What was the significance? Less than a month into the war, the supposedly arm-in-arm patriots were already squabbling over matters of rank and leadership. Such wrangling would continue throughout the War for Independence. Despite the national myth of universal harmony, the reality was that the Americans were never one happily united family at any point during their Revolution. In gross numbers, amounting to 2.5 million colonists in 1775, including slaves but not Indigenous peoples, major divisions existed. On one side, about 25 percent of the people might be described as fervent patriots; on the other side was another 25 percent or so who were committed loyalists to the Crown. In the middle were the largely uncommitted neutrals who avoided taking sides unless military actions from either side threatened their personal security in some way. They might be called rebels or loyalists for a day or weeks or months depending on circumstances of the moment.[13]

Further dividing the rebel populace was ceaseless infighting over matters of reputation, recognition, and personal honor. In 1777, John Adams, then a Massachusetts delegate serving in the Continental Congress, was "wearied to death with the wrangles between military officers, high and low. They quarrel like cats and dogs. They worry one another like mastiffs, scrambling for rank and pay like apes for nuts." Rancor among the rebels, especially involving many of their most prominent leaders, was more common than working harmoniously together to defeat the British.[14]

An early outburst of patriot acrimony grew out of the seizure of Fort Ticonderoga and focused on Arnold. A thoroughgoing self-promoter, Allen was the protagonist. He did not like sharing the command with Arnold and wanted to make sure he alone received full credit for the victory. Rather than focusing on documenting the available artillery pieces, Allen turned the Boys loose to plunder whatever might be worth taking back home, not including the ninety gallons of rum they happily consumed on the premises.

Even as the Boys got drunk and hassled Arnold—apparently two of them even fired their weapons at him—Allen had after-action reports prepared to share with rebel political bodies. While bragging about himself and praising his key subordinates, including Easton and Brown, he neglected to mention Arnold. "Colonel" Easton, as he now styled himself, carried one of the reports to the Massachusetts Provincial Congress. In presenting Allen's report, he could not help but mention that Arnold, the man in their employ, had acted rashly and almost ruined everything before the alleged savior Allen intervened and saved the day.[15]

Allen's bad-mouthing of Arnold's activity reached all the way to the Second Continental Congress, which had just started meeting in Philadelphia. The Green Mountain Boys leader selected his "able counselor" John Brown to carry his good news report to the delegates. Unexpectedly, Brown walked into a trap, since neither he nor Allen had any idea that the delegates wanted to prevent further warfare and were anxious to reconcile differences with the king and Parliament. Suddenly, Brown's story changed. Now it was the always-impetuous Arnold who had taken command with the likes of the ever-sensible and cautious Allen trying to restrain him. In reaction, Congress voted to have all patriot troops pull back from Ticonderoga until further notice. Reconciliation was what the majority of delegates "so ardently wished for," not openly rebellious acts from hotheads like Arnold. But if there were self-serving scoundrels in the telling of what actually happened in taking Ticonderoga, overwhelming evidence exposes them as Ethan Allen, James Easton, and John Brown.[16]

As for Arnold, many delegates now viewed him as a potential troublemaker, not to be taken seriously as a sensible, trustworthy leader. As for Allen, he no longer mattered, despite his endless braggadocio. That summer the Green Mountain Boys repudiated him as their leader in favor of the less noisome Seth Warner. As the summer progressed, Allen volunteered to join the campaign to bring Quebec Province into the rebellion. With little thought—but much bravado—he tried to capture Montreal with a small force in November 1775. He failed miserably, partially because his putative ally John Brown held back at the last minute a supporting force that might have given Allen a fighting chance to earn great personal glory as the conqueror of this major Canadian community. Instead, the British defenders shipped Allen off to England where he lingered in prison before being exchanged for British POWs in 1777 and returned to New York. Allen received a colonel's commission, but no one among the patriot leaders was foolish enough to offer this unwise blowhard, in so many ways a real scoundrel, another command.[17]

Easton and Brown, however, remained painful thorns in Arnold's flesh. With Allen and the Boys gone from Ticonderoga, Arnold did an impressive job getting this strategic area ready for the expected invasion from Canada. In early July, his reward was personal humiliation when the Massachusetts Provincial Congress dumped Arnold from command in favor of, at best, a competent Connecticut militia colonel named Benjamin Hinman. Why? Massachusetts wanted to shift the burden of paying all the expenses for the troops now gathered at Ticonderoga onto neighboring Connecticut, which the latter colony reluctantly accepted, so long as a Connecticut officer was in charge. Ironically, while Arnold was from Connecticut, his colonel's commission came from Massachusetts.

Thus, Arnold had to go. A double irony arose in the process of removal when Arnold objected and refused a subordinate assignment under Hinman: he found himself replaced at the head of his own regiment by James Easton as its colonel, with Brown selected to serve as its major. As for Arnold, he was to return east and settle his accounts with the Massachusetts Provincial Congress, which later stiffed him for what he had spent out of his personal funds. One might legitimately ask: Who were the real scoundrels in these less-than-harmonious patriot dealings?[18]

Arnold began his patriot military adventures anew in August 1775, but not before he returned home to New Haven to deal with the death of his first wife, Margaret. Once he had convinced his sister Hannah to take care of his three sons, he headed back to Massachusetts hoping to settle his accounts. There he managed to meet with the new Continental Army commander in chief, George Washington. Having been stuck with some loser general officers appointed by the Continental Congress, Washington was on the lookout for real military talent, and he had heard about the excellent leadership Arnold had provided at Ticonderoga and Crown Point before being so gracelessly dismissed. Washington decided this eager patriot had the capacity to lead a detached force through the main wilderness to capture the capital City of Quebec in order to bring that province into the rebellion.[19]

The campaign to conquer Quebec Province began. Two armies proceeded north. One of them was Arnold's. The other bivouacked in the Ticonderoga region and sailed north across Lake Champlain to capture Montreal before moving to take Quebec City, unless Arnold's troops had already accomplished that mission. Joining the Champlain side was the Easton/Brown regiment. On November 13, the rebel column under Brigadier General Richard Montgomery captured Montreal.

During the British retreat down the St. Lawrence River, the Easton/Brown regiment managed to block and capture some vessels with British officers aboard. Word soon began to spread that these two patriots led the way in rifling through the officers' private baggage, grabbing as plunder whatever goods they wanted.

Whether true or not, the story reached Arnold outside Quebec City. On the last day of December in 1775, he and Montgomery combined their forces in a desperate attempt to seize the walled city. Disaster followed. Montgomery was killed and Arnold was seriously wounded in his left leg. With Montgomery gone, Arnold was now in charge of what was left of the invading rebel force.[20]

Arnold performed admirably in maintaining a form of siege operations, but as Major Brown's superior officer, he thought it only fair to call this prickly officer to account. On February 1, 1776, he wrote a letter to Congress regarding a claim by Brown that Montgomery had earlier promised him a colonelcy. However, Arnold indicated Montgomery had reversed his decision when he found out about the "unbecoming" report that Easton and Brown "were publicly impeached with plundering the . . . baggage" of the captured British officers. Arnold, as a brigadier general now outranking Easton and Brown, turned the matter over to Congress, since "he could not, in conscience or honor promote him [Brown] . . . until these matters were cleared up."[21]

It would have been wiser for Arnold not to expose Easton, and especially Brown, to such public scrutiny. Each reader will have to consider whether Arnold was acting impartially as a superior officer or just being vindictive toward two men who had more than once acted inharmoniously toward him. Regardless, the personal honor and reputations of Easton and Brown were now on trial, and they were more than unhappy about it.

Once out of Canada, Brown was so self-consumed that he traveled to Congress in Philadelphia to demand Arnold's arrest. Further, he conjured a list of thirteen written charges against Arnold for his allegedly illicit actions while in Canada, not the least of which was "for endeavoring to asperse your petitioner's character, in the most infamous manner." To their credit, the delegates eventually exonerated Arnold in regard to all of Brown's accusations. As John Adams wrote to his wife, Abigail, he was sorry to see so worthy a general officer "basely slandered and libeled" by the likes of Brown."[22]

★ ★ ★

As the rebel pullback from Canada continued, the story line became even more contentious. In June 1776, Arnold, who was now in command at Montreal, arranged with friendly merchants to buy on credit and ship war-related provisions southward to help support the retreating patriot force. He ordered Colonel Moses Hazen, a former British officer who had finally decided to side with the rebels, to guard these goods. However, Hazen, who did not like being subordinate to a rebel upstart now in command over him, refused the order. As a result, the goods lay exposed on the bank of a river and, as Arnold wrote, the "great part" of them were "stolen or plundered" by desperate, starving patriot soldiers evacuating southward toward Lake Champlain.[23]

Arnold had every right—and duty—to write up Hazen on grounds of insubordination. He called for court-martial proceedings, expecting this prideful colonel to be severely disciplined or, perhaps, even sacked from Continental military service. Instead, he got the exact opposite. Hazen heartily joined in the bad-mouthing of Arnold that Easton and Brown had been chirping about for months. Hazen helped throw Arnold's charges of thievery back at him: General Arnold had actually stolen all the exposed supplies for his own personal benefit.

The court-martial proceedings against Hazen began at Ticonderoga in late July 1776 and turned into a fiasco. Eventually, the hearing board exonerated Hazen of any wrongdoing while condemning Arnold for his lack of respect for them as a panel of judges. Arnold could not believe that implications of his possible thievery were being whispered about rather than the actual issue—the extent of Hazen's insubordination. To say the least, he was not happy about this outcome.

Hazen got away, appearing like an innocent victim—which he was not—while further planting the seed of Arnold's alleged thievery in Montreal. Hazen went on to perform mostly ordinary service in leading the Continental Army's 2nd Canadian Regiment, also known as "Congress's Own," for the rest of the war. Arnold, for his part, was so angry with the less-than-respectful hearing panel of field grade officers that he challenged any of them to a duel for needlessly—and intentionally, from his point of view—smearing his good name. The panel members, in turn, bad-mouthed Arnold far and wide while demanding that Horatio Gates, then in command at Fort Ticonderoga, arrest and incarcerate him. Readers can decide who the scoundrel was, or the scoundrels were, in this heated controversy, which took place when the real focus should have been on preparing to ward off the expected major invasion of British forces from Canada.[24]

Military reality caused General Gates to act "dictatorially" and ignore the officers' demand to punish Arnold. He wrote to John Hancock, then serving as the president of Congress, and explained that "Arnold's temper" had pushed him past "the precise line of decorum" to be expected "toward a court martial," as had the officers' panel, which had shown "too much acrimony" as well. To arrest and discipline Arnold would have been a major mistake, Gates stressed, because the "United States must not be deprived of that excellent officer's service at this important moment."[25]

Gates was thinking pragmatically. He needed Arnold's seafaring skills much more than what his complaining field grade officers could offer in defending the lake and Fort Ticonderoga. Arnold was directing the building of a patriot naval fleet that would sail northward on Lake Champlain to resist the massive British–Hessian troop movement sailing south out of Canada, which finally got underway in early October. "Commodore" Arnold commanded the patriot fleet in challenging superior British naval power at the Battle of Valcour Island on October 11 and at Split Rock two days later. The upshot was that the British force, so impressed, if not stunned, by the show of patriot naval strength displayed by Arnold and his soldier-sailors, would only scout the patriot defenses at Ticonderoga before retreating into Quebec Province for the winter season.

Although many praised Arnold's performance, some patriot whiners, as usual, were ready to spread negative commentary across the land. One such commentator was General William Maxwell, an inconsequential former British officer who had moved to New Jersey in his youth and later became colonel of the 2nd New Jersey Regiment. In a letter to his state's governor, William Livingston, Maxwell, who was at Ticonderoga that autumn, unloaded on Arnold. The commodore was "our evil genius to the north" who "has, with a good deal of industry, got us clear of all of our fine fleet." He went on to claim, falsely, that "by all impartial accounts" the patriot fleet "was by far the strongest." By allowing so many of his vessels to be destroyed, Arnold's "pretty piece of admiralship" left Fort Ticonderoga undefended, another false statement. Just to finish this smear piece, Maxwell asserted that those in the army whom he knew held no higher "opinion of his abilities by land than water."[26]

Maxwell's ad hominem attack reflected the derogatory comments of Moses Hazen and the panel of field grade officers, who, along with Easton and Brown, were out to destroy Arnold's reputation. Dr. Lewis Beebe of Connecticut, who had married a sister of Ethan Allen and was a close friend of Brown's, joined the anti-Arnold parade while they were all retreating from Canada. He castigated Arnold, who in his "superior wisdom" had placed the bedraggled retreating troops on half rations, not considering that food supplies were very dangerously low. Apparently, it would have been better to let some men starve while other troops gorged themselves. Beebe went on to "heartily wish some person would try an experiment upon" Arnold "to make the sun shine through his head with an ounce ball; and then see whether the rays come in a direct or oblique direction." So much for harmony and unity of patriot purpose during critical moments when the likes of Arnold were doing their best to save the cause of liberty from complete collapse.[27]

While Arnold focused his efforts that spring and summer on blocking the British invasion from Canada, both Easton and then Brown made a beeline to Philadelphia. Satisfying their bruised egos was apparently more important than continuing to serve and fight in the northern theater. Congress finally exonerated Easton in an unexpected way. After some Massachusetts creditors caught up with him in Philadelphia and had him incarcerated for not paying long overdue debts, the delegates took pity, recognized Easton as a colonel in the Continental service, and awarded him full back pay to July 1775. Brown screamed repeatedly to the delegates how Arnold had so unfairly denied him a promised promotion in rank, let alone unjustly charging him with stealing from the British officers' baggage when Brown, like Easton, was the real thief. As with Easton, Congress conceded by awarding him a promotion to lieutenant colonel including back pay dated to November 1775.

Both men demanded courts of inquiry to clear their presumed good names. The delegates advised them to travel back to Albany and make arrangements for hearings with the Northern Department commander, Major General Philip Schuyler. They did so, but to their disappointment Schuyler was more focused on defending the Lake Champlain region than worrying about sensitive officers' claims to sullied honor. Further, Schuyler wanted to protect Arnold, who was essential to stopping the British advance, rather than satisfy these two complainers who had contributed nothing to defending Lake Champlain that summer.

Easton grumbled but mostly gave up on his personal campaign and returned home to Pittsfield, Massachusetts. There he revived his tavern business and dealt, apparently successfully, with his pressing creditors. He thus brought an end to his less-than-spectacular stint of Continental military service. Brown, however, refused to accept Schuyler's ruling. He developed a laser-like focus on what he thought was the best way to contribute his talents to the patriot cause: doing everything in his power to destroy Arnold's reputation.[28]

As for Arnold, while preparing for naval combat on Lake Champlain he received a clear warning about the denigrating commentary from Easton and Brown happening behind his back in Philadelphia. Samuel Chase, a Congressional delegate from Maryland who had visited Montreal during the rebel collapse, sent this startling warning: "Your best friends are not your countrymen." Chase appreciated that Arnold could not defend himself before Congress while campaigning in the northern theater. "I cannot but request all persons to suspend their opinion, and to give you an opportunity of being heard," Chase wrote.[29]

By the time Arnold was in a position to defend his service record, Congress had already acted negatively toward him by not approving his well-deserved promotion to major general. The chain of denial led back to John Brown and, of all people, Horatio Gates, among other anti-Arnold complainers. Schuyler told Brown to seek out field commander Gates, Arnold's immediate superior officer, to pursue the retrieval of his supposedly "asperse[d]" honor through court-martial proceedings. Brown followed up by sending his thirteen charges calling for the "arrest" of Arnold for the latter's endless "crimes" during the Canadian campaign. Gates, who had repeatedly spoken in glowing terms about Arnold's invaluable service in the defense of Lake Champlain, agreed to share Brown's litany of complaints with Congress.[30]

A reasonable question is to ask why Gates would give Brown yet another opportunity to continue his rant against Arnold. The answer lies in Gates's own ambitions. Having served as Washington's adjutant general when Congress first established the Continental Army in June 1775, Gates repeatedly maneuvered for an independent line command. Washington thought of him as a capable staff officer but had come to believe Arnold was the real fighter among those general officers who survived the Canadian campaign. In early December 1776, the commander in chief selected Arnold over Gates to go east and help take charge of Continental and militia forces gathering to resist the British incursion into Rhode Island and possibly elsewhere in New England.

Suddenly Arnold, who had made Gates look so good in the defense of Lake Champlain, became a threat to that general's own career advancement. Why? Because Arnold, Gates's junior in rank, had been favored by Washington, who assigned this independent command to Brigadier General Arnold over higher-ranked Major General Gates. The latter gentleman was not happy, to say the least. When he reached Washington's headquarters in eastern Pennsylvania after traveling south from Ticonderoga in December 1776, Gates denounced Washington's plan to attack Trenton on Christmas evening, then declared himself sick and continued his southward journey all the way to Baltimore, where apparently the best doctors were available—and where the Continental Congress was now meeting to escape the British threat to Philadelphia.[31]

Gates had already committed to hand over Brown's thirteen written charges to the delegates while also hinting that Washington was about to make a foolish move in attacking the British–Hessian outpost stronghold in Trenton. The New England delegates admired Gates, so when Washington's campaign succeeded, they chose to forget this prediction of disaster. However, a number of them remembered both Brown's summertime visit and now had his written charges to reinforce possible doubts about Arnold's service to the cause of liberty.

Given the animosity directed toward him, we need to inquire: What was Benedict Arnold thinking about the levels of appreciation toward his service as the year 1776 progressed? He expressed his own frustrations and injured feelings, even before his brilliant defense of Lake Champlain at Valcour and Split Rock, when he wrote to Gates at Ticonderoga while sailing northward toward Canada. "I cannot but think it extremely cruel when I have sacrificed my ease, health, and a great part of my private property, in the cause of my country," he wrote to Gates, "to be calumniated as a robber and thief—at a time, too, when I have it not in my power to be heard in my own defense."[32]

★ ★ ★

As 1777 dawned, the open condemnation against "evil genius" Arnold from such self-serving patriots as Easton, Brown, Hazen, Gates, and Maxwell clearly worked against Arnold's promotion to major general. Because of the wrangling over rank and seniority among Continental officers, Congress had earlier voted that general officer promotions should be based on merit, seniority in rank, and the number of troops raised from each state. On merit, Arnold was clearly the most deserving, and he was the senior brigadier, but Connecticut already had two major generals. In what was a political logroll, Congress promoted five men inferior to Arnold in military rank and merit to major generalships.[33]

Washington could not believe that the delegates had snubbed Arnold, but did not want to directly question Congress's superior authority in general officer appointments. Instead, he sent a following pointed message to his Virginia colleague, delegate Richard Henry Lee. "Surely a more active—a more spirited, and Sensible Officer, fills no department in your Army," Washington stated. The commander in chief expressed his "uneasiness" that Arnold, because he was "the oldest Brigadier," would resign from the "Service under such a slight."[34]

Washington tried to console Arnold by telling his fighting subordinate about "some mistake" by Congress. Both he and Arnold knew better. The latter, in turn, did not resign immediately but asked for permission to travel to Philadelphia to clear his good name. He also wrote a letter to Gates asking for his support but never heard back from this supposed mentor. Over time he began to realize that Gates was no longer his friend.[35]

Returning home to New Haven in mid-April, Arnold became involved in driving a large British raiding force out of eastern Connecticut. Arnold repeatedly risked his life in skirmishes at Ridgefield and Compo Hill, the result of which was that an embarrassed Congress gave him a new horse to replace the one that he was riding during one of these small, bloody actions.[36]

As a further reward, the delegates accorded him the promotion to major general they had so shortsightedly denied him two months earlier—but they refused to restore his seniority in rank in relation to the five men promoted over him. Even though Arnold had once again proven himself a heroic fighter, Congress was not going to let him, Washington, or anyone else question their absolute authority over the military. What the delegates did not want to admit was that they had engaged in a political trade in naming the new crop of major generals. Adhering to principles of protecting civilian authority over the military was, at most, a secondary consideration for these gentlemen-politicians.

Delegate John Adams thought Congress should at least acknowledge Arnold's undoubted courage by casting a special medal celebrating his actions in driving the British invaders from Connecticut. On one side of the coin would be the enemy "firing at General Arnold, on horseback, his horse falling dead under him, and he deliberately disentangling his feet from the stirrups and taking his pistols out of his holsters before his retreat." Then on the backside, Arnold "should be mounted on a fresh horse, receiving another discharge of musketry, with a wound in the neck of his horse."[37]

But there was to be no medal for Arnold. Such recognition from Congress would have represented an embarrassing admission of logrolling rather than serving the cause of liberty. Nor would the delegates relent on the seniority point when Arnold traveled to Philadelphia. He was not out to puff himself up and denigrate others in the mold of Easton, Brown, and also Gates for that matter. Even though correcting his position in rank was a small point, as a gentleman of proven commitment to the cause, not doing so was a slap at his personal honor. He did have some support among the delegates but not enough to restore his seniority. With each state getting one vote, the delegates officially voted against his request for a return to his full respect as a worthy patriot in August 1777.

This point of personal honor may seem silly today, but it was no small matter during the Revolutionary era. Arnold was not exceptional in caring about his reputation as a resolute patriot. The gentleman's code of that era demanded he protect his reputation. Washington wrote that Arnold would not "continue in the Service under such a slight," being that he was "the oldest brigadier." Arnold proved the point when he delivered a letter to Congress on July 11 resigning his commission. He stated that he still wanted to "enjoy my highest ambition, that of being a free citizen of America," but he could not continue to serve "in my present disgraceful rank in the army. . . . Honor is a sacrifice that no man ought to make, as I received [it] so I wish to transmit [it] inviolate to posterity."[38]

What Arnold did not know was that Washington, in referencing Burgoyne's invasion which began in June 1777, informed Congress that he needed "an Active—spirited Officer" to travel north as soon as possible and assist in delaying, perhaps even defeating, this large, well-equipped British–Hessian army. Surely many delegates thought he would call for Gates, who was then hanging out around Philadelphia looking for a high-level command assignment. Washington, unlike Congress, knew real talent and specifically called for his fighting general, Benedict Arnold, to ride north as soon as possible in resisting the Burgoyne invasion.[39]

Now, if Arnold had been a true scoundrel at this point, he would have ignored Washington's plea and sulked all the way home to New

Haven. Instead, he ignored his resignation, at least temporarily, and heeded Washington's call to further Continental service. Arnold rushed northward to Albany and well beyond. He met up with General Philip Schuyler and began a fierce—and effective—delaying campaign to slow the advance of Burgoyne's superior numbers.

Just before mid-August, Arnold agreed to lead a column of Continentals westward along the Mohawk River to help drive off a diversionary enemy force that was part of the Burgoyne invasion. He did so with aplomb when lower ranked officers refused the assignment and he succeeded, through some military trickery, in convincing the enemy force comprised of British Regulars, loyalists, and Indians under their commanders, Barry St. Leger and Chief Joseph Brant, to abandon their siege of Fort Schuyler (normally called Fort Stanwix) and flee back into Canada. Arnold had acted boldly, even though he would learn that the overly sensitive Congress had voted to deny him his seniority status.[40]

As he returned down the Mohawk River, Arnold received word that Congress had removed Schuyler from the Northern command in favor of none other than Horatio Gates. He now knew Gates had joined in the denigration of him before Congressional leaders, especially among the New England delegates who thought Gates was an oracle of brilliant military thinking. Arnold had good reason not to trust Gates as the final phases of the Saratoga campaign played out.

During September and into October, these two leaders showed how not to get along in the face of the enemy. Gates preferred to stay in a fixed position and let Burgoyne's British and Hessian troops attack the American defenses on Bemis Heights. Arnold wanted to go on the offensive. Gates, supported by his chief aide, a thoroughgoing scoundrel named James Wilkinson, cut Arnold out while making key tactical decisions. Arnold, supported by former Schuyler aides now on his staff, grew angry with Gates's slights. In the end, Gates stayed back from the actual combat on September 19 and then again on October 7. Arnold rushed forward, the second time without Gates's permission. Burgoyne was all but entrapped, had no choice except to retreat northward, and officially surrendered at the town of Saratoga (today's Schuylerville) in grand ceremonies on October 17, 1777.[41]

★ ★ ★

The Battles of Saratoga represented a significant turning point both for the course of the American Revolution and for Benedict Arnold. In reaction to the defeat of Burgoyne's army, leaders in France, including King Louis XVI and Foreign Minister Charles Gravier, the Comte de Vergennes, decided the time had come to openly support the Revolution through formal treaties along with formal diplomatic recognition of the new American nation. With the approval of the Franco-American alliance in early 1778, French military support in the form of land troops, naval forces, weaponry, and related war matériel proved invaluable in carrying the American patriots forward to winning independence.[42]

Unfortunately for Arnold, the second Saratoga battle, on October 7, proved to be personally disastrous. With or without Gates's approval, he led the way in breaking through the British line. Near dark, he charged into a redoubt at the extreme right end of British defenses. A flurry of Hessian gunfire greeted both Arnold and his horse. The dying animal collapsed to the ground with its full weight coming down on Arnold's left leg—the very limb so seriously wounded during the failed attempt to capture Quebec City on the last day of 1775. Possibly a Hessian musket ball ripped into this same left leg before the horse's weight further crushed it.

Living until June 14, 1801, Arnold never really recovered, physically or psychologically, from this horrible moment. As he lay on the ground writhing in pain and as they hauled him in a wagon from the Saratoga battlefields some thirty miles south to a military hospital near Albany, his near-delirious thoughts projected something worse: growing disillusionment with the patriot cause. The right word for his disheveled mental state was complete embitterment—to the point that the cause was no longer worthy of his selfless support.

He had been unfairly treated at places like Fort Ticonderoga, Montreal, Quebec, Lake Champlain, and even Philadelphia. But the problem stretched to supposedly high-minded patriots. The cast was extensive and were personified by such self-serving characters as Ethan Allen, James Easton, John Brown, Moses Hazen, Horatio Gates, William Maxwell, and various civilian leaders in the Continental Congress. As Arnold lay in his hospital bed with a wooden cast strapped around his shattered leg, he felt that he had been a fool. As he wrote more than once, he had fought, bled, and given all short of life itself; he had shared his personal wealth but was not fairly repaid. And his reward for his selfless service were a host of damning charges, ranging from wasting a fleet on Lake Champlain to stealing goods while retreating out of Canada. From his perspective, these patriots were the antithesis of his best friends. Rather, they were a bunch of scoundrels.

The insults and personal attacks continued as Arnold recovered from his physical wounds, but mentally he had had enough. He was now asking himself why he should continue to support the patriot cause. After so many brilliant military accomplishments, he doubted whether he should keep giving so much of himself when too many self-serving patriots kept treating him with both contempt and disrespect. After all, the thought kept coming back to him that "your best friends are not your countrymen."[43]

A telling exchange of messages occurred in early 1778 when Arnold was still bedridden at the hospital in Albany. He received a warm, encouraging letter from George Washington who expressed genuine concern about Arnold's health. The commander in chief stated his "earnest wish to have your services [in] the ensuing Campaign" and promised him "a Command which, I trust will be agreeable to yourself and of great advantage to the public." The commander also officially informed his fighting general that at long last Congress had restored his seniority in rank over those officers promoted over him. Washington hoped Arnold would accept this overdue correction in status as the restoration of his legitimate claim to properly earned seniority status.[44]

That was not to be the case. Arnold waited more than a month before responding to Washington's encouraging letter. When he did, he complained that his wounded leg was not healing properly because of "some loose splinters of bone remaining in the leg, which will not be serviceable, until they are extracted." Then Arnold made a highly revealing statement: "It is my most ardent Wish to render every Assistance in my Power," he wrote, "that *your* Excellency may be enabled to finish the arduous Task, *you* have with so much Honor to *yourself* and Advantage to *your* country, been so long engaged in, and have the Pleasure of seeing Peace and Happiness restored to *your* Country on the most permanent Basis" (emphasis added).[45]

The tenor of this unusual compliment to Washington's selfless service is obvious. Mentally at least, Arnold was clearly separating himself from the patriot cause. Too many times his countrymen had attacked his reputation. Like his shattered limb, the pain of these endless petty insults were now consuming him. Enough was enough. For Arnold, henceforth it was Washington's cause, but not necessarily his own. He would become like the others who had besmirched him, serving himself and his family first, the cause of liberty second but only if it served his own best interests as he would now define them.

Arnold no longer thought in terms of victory but of restoring the peace and happiness that once characterized Washington's country. Actively fighting for the cause became a matter of getting something of personal value in return. By May 1778, he had enough energy to travel, in great pain, to Valley Forge. What began was a two-year slide, mostly downhill, to September 25, 1780, the day he fled his West Point headquarters and publicly returned his allegiance to the British Empire. In his descent, he angrily turned against the very cause he had so successfully sustained in so many ways, especially during the Saratoga campaign. He became what he most hoped not to be—an apostate known everywhere as a true scoundrel, a most hated man of treason.[46]

Arnold's enemies fared much better. Gates became the declared hero of Saratoga and received a rarely given Congressional medal honoring his supposed bravery, even though he was never really near the actual fighting. Ethan Allen accomplished little to nothing in the war but is famously known for words he never uttered, supposedly capturing Fort Ticonderoga in the name of the Great Jehovah and the Continental Congress. John Brown died in October 1780 when he rushed into a small battle near the Mohawk River. He was acclaimed a hero, ignoring his rashness and the needless deaths of the good men who followed him into their graves. Moses Hazen remained cantankerous. He denounced and even sued anyone who dared question his honesty or authority. Congress eventually tried to pacify him by appointing him a brigadier general, a statement of their limited judgment.

As for Arnold, who questioned the world's likely condemnation of him the night he returned his allegiance to the British, he became the ultimate antihero, just as I was first taught back in the fourth grade. What I learned along the way with further study and archival research was that Arnold lived in a less-than-perfect world in which many patriot scoundrels existed.

The Revolutionaries did not represent one big, happy family, but a quarrelsome bunch that helped turn Arnold into a likeness of them. In response, he finally gave up on the cause of liberty, which marked him as one of the greatest historical scoundrels of all time. History is full of irony, and for Arnold, it was that his best friends were not his countrymen. Nor were the British for that matter. Circumstances morphed this heroic fighter into a historical pariah, passed down to us as Benedict Arnold, "*vile, treacherous, and leagued with Satan.*"[47]

CHARLES LEE: THE GENERAL AS SCOUNDREL?

MARK EDWARD LENDER

★ ★ ★

Major General Charles Lee is one of the Revolution's most complex figures. By turns erratic, vain, volatile, and even crude, Lee was also intelligent, brave, scholarly, and politically interesting. He has been tarred by his friendship with critics of George Washington, by a revelation of supposedly treasonable correspondence while a prisoner of war, and by his court-martial after the Battle of Monmouth. As a result, there is no historical consensus on Lee, and the legacy of the Continental Army's second-ranking officer remains a source of controversy among historians who have struggled to understand him. Was he a misunderstood patriot? Or, as his detractors insist, a self-serving opportunist? Could he have even been a traitor? Indeed, apart from Washington and perhaps Benedict Arnold, no military figure of the Revolution was as controversial as Charles Lee. So, who was this man? And more to the point for this essay—was he a scoundrel?[1]

★ ★ ★

Lee was born in 1732 near Chester, England, to a family of middling gentry but with politically influential relations. Charles's father was Colonel John Lee and his mother, Isabella Bunbury, was the daughter of Sir Henry Bunbury, Baronet. Charles had a difficult youth. He and his sister, Sidney, were the only two of seven siblings to survive childhood, and his mother never warmed to her only remaining son. Charles considered himself physically unattractive and lacked the social graces of English gentry; apparently he liked his dogs better than he liked most people. Still, as the son of a family with connections, Charles began life with advantages. Well-educated at home and abroad, he learned several languages and passionately read the classics, military history, Shakespeare, and the radical works of Jean-Jacques Rousseau. The future general was a man of the Enlightenment, comfortable in the realm of ideas.[2]

Charles Lee's father commanded the 55th Regiment of Foot, and in 1746 Lee joined the regiment as a teenaged ensign. In 1754 he sailed for America, where he saw rugged duty during the French and Indian War. The following year the 55th Foot was cut up at Edward Braddock's disastrous defeat at Monongahela, although Lee survived the debacle. Lee subsequently campaigned at Louisbourg, Fort Ticonderoga, Fort Niagara, Montreal, and finally on a mission west of Fort Pitt. By the end of the war, Lee was a battle-hardened captain with a record the envy of any professional soldier.

America fascinated Lee. He enjoyed the towns, the people, and the scenery, and he briefly took an Iroquois consort who bore him twins. The Iroquois called him Ounewaterika, which roughly translated as "boiling water, or one whose spirit never sleeps." The moniker was apt, for Lee emerged a complex and volatile individual. He could be genial with friends, but also brusque and arrogant; he thought nothing of castigating the foibles of senior officers, caring little when his views became known. Lee developed a reputation for "pugnacity and hot-headedness," and after one altercation an army surgeon actually tried to kill him. We do not know what sparked the incident, but we can easily imagine some insulting or sarcastic remark on Lee's part as the source of the trouble. In 1760 when he sailed for home, Lee ranked as one of Britain's most unconventional junior officers.[3]

Upon his return Lee sought promotion to major. He petitioned the king, and friends importuned George III on his behalf. But promotion came slowly, no doubt partly because his acid pen had irritated too many ranking officers. Lee finally advanced when he transferred to the 103rd Foot, and in 1762 Major Lee accompanied his regiment to Portugal, a British ally, to resist a combined French and Spanish invasion. Here he met General John Burgoyne. On October 7, Burgoyne gave Lee a British–Portuguese detachment, including fifty men of the 16th Light Dragoons, and in a daring night attack Lee routed the Spanish at Vila Vehla. The action effectively stymied the invasion, and the grateful Portuguese made him a colonel. Portugal, however, saw Lee's final service as a redcoat. In 1763, with the end of the Seven Years' War, the 103rd Foot disbanded and Lee retired on half-pay.

With no place on the British roster, for the next eight years Lee led the life of a military vagabond. He spent considerable time in the service of King Stanislaus Poniatowski of Poland, who made Lee a major general. Lee's travels, for Stanislaus and otherwise, took him far afield. His itinerary included Constantinople, the Russo–Turkish War in the region of modern Romania (where he was an observer with the Russian army), Hungary, Austria, Italy (where he killed a man in a duel), and France. He was nothing if not well-traveled.

Despite continuing entreaties, however, Lee found no place in the British army, although in 1772 he was promoted to lieutenant colonel on the inactive list. He was bitter, still volatile, and his political views only exacerbated his resentments. Lee identified with Britain's liberal Whigs and he publicly approved of America's resistance to imperial policies. Then in 1770 his politics blended with his frustrations, and he published a biting satire of George III. It was an act typical of the impetuous Lee, but hardly a judicious step for a man hoping for preferment. He simply could not control his temper. Burgoyne, who had maintained "a certain style of friendship" with Lee, saw his uncontrollable temper as the major impediment to Lee's efforts to get back into a red coat. "His disappointments in preferment," Burgoyne told Lord North, "arose from the indiscretion of his discourse and writings," including Lee's satire of "the King himself." In the land of his birth, Lee's career was finished.[4]

Like many Englishmen with dimmed expectations at home, Lieutenant Colonel Lee (retired) looked to America. Through the advice of an old army friend, Horatio Gates, who had settled in Virginia, in 1774 Lee purchased some 3,000 acres with a modest house near the modern town of Leeville (named in his honor) in what is now West Virginia. He called the estate Prato Verde (now Prato Rio). Lee made influential acquaintances including Richard Henry Lee, George Mason, Thomas Jefferson, and George Washington. Many Americans found the transplanted Englishman—with his grasp of ideas, radical sympathies, and well-traveled background—a fascinating character. Indeed, when Lee joined the patriot cause, he was "perhaps the most cosmopolitan of the revolutionaries," as Phillip Papas has observed. "No other American revolutionary, except maybe Benjamin Franklin, was as worldly as Lee."[5]

Lee was indeed a revolutionary. As the imperial crisis deepened, Lee was among the first patriots to call for outright independence. No doubt some of this ardor derived from his lingering bitterness toward those who, in his eyes, had thwarted his advancement in the British Army. But Lee's radicalism was sincere; his views were too consistent over time to admit of mere opportunism in his new country.[6]

Lee rose quickly in the patriot military. His credentials as a patriot and soldier justifiably impressed Congress, and the delegates commissioned him as a major general. Lee ranked only behind Washington and Artemus Ward, and with Ward's early resignation Lee became second-in-command. Lee may have believed he deserved the chief command, but he worked capably with Washington around Boston as rebel forces besieged the city. He tried to reestablish contact with Burgoyne, then trapped in the city with the British Army. Nothing came of the effort, and Burgoyne considered his former subordinate an "incendiary" driven by vanity. After Boston, Washington sent Lee to the South, where he helped frustrate a British invasion of Charleston. He then traveled back north and arrived in New York in October 1776 in time to assist in the losing defense of the city. After the Battle of White Plains in October, Washington left Lee in command of a detachment near the battlefield while he led the main army on its retreat across New Jersey.[7]

At this point Lee's volatility reemerged. Critical of Washington's leadership—and the commander in chief had made his share of mistakes, including the debacle at Fort Washington on November 16—Lee unburdened himself in letters to Colonel Joseph Reed, the army's adjutant general and Washington's former military secretary, and to Major General Horatio Gates. Washington inadvertently saw the letter to Reed, but in the press of events he did nothing. Then Lee crossed the line between criticism and insubordination. In early December, with his army moving toward the Delaware River, Washington urged Lee to join him as quickly as possible. Lee disobeyed. He refused to hasten, even after Washington sent preemptory orders to move. Lee was convinced Howe would not drive on Philadelphia, as Washington feared, but would stop for the winter in New Jersey. Lee wanted to remain behind, rally the militia, then fall on Howe's rear. Events proved Lee right. The British did stop, and the militia did rally, but it was no excuse for not following direct orders. Washington, trying to hold his army together, was bewildered by the conduct of his second-in-command. The last thing the patriot army needed was a showdown between its two senior generals.[8]

Fate spared that trauma. On December 12, with his troops encamped west of Morristown, Lee rode some three miles to White's Tavern near Basking Ridge, where he spent the night attended by a small guard (one historian has insinuated he was also attended by the Widow White, but the story is likely a calumny). The next morning, a mounted British patrol learned of Lee's presence and captured the general, still in his nightshirt. The horsemen were from none other than the 16th Light Dragoons, a detachment of which Lee had led to victory in Portugal. It is doubtful the irony was lost on Lee as the dragoons led him away.[9]

★★★

Lee was a prisoner for almost sixteen months, from mid-December 1776 to early April 1778, when he was freed on parole. Yet even in captivity he stirred his share of drama. Alarmed patriots, who considered Lee a hero, were genuinely concerned for his safety. The British saw Lee as a half-pay officer taken in arms against the king; that was treason, a capital offense. The British kept him in close confinement in New York, but Congress demanded Lee be accorded prisoner of war status with accommodations normally allowed senior officers. Failing that, British prisoners in patriot hands would pay the price. Howe relented, and Lee found himself comfortably situated aboard HMS *Centurion* in New York harbor. He was allowed to write to friends, members of Congress, Washington, and others; he even wrote to his servant in Virginia requesting fresh clothes, books, and his dogs (including, one assumes, his favorite Pomeranian, Spado). Eventually Lee enjoyed the liberty of the city, and he socialized openly (and suspiciously, in the view of some historians) with British officers. It was a captivity a world apart from American enlisted prisoners and junior officers confined relatively nearby—and dying in droves—on rotting prison hulks.[10]

Of all his writings in captivity, Lee's most extraordinary missives never reached patriot eyes. In the mid-1850s George H. Moore, librarian at the New-York Historical Society, announced the discovery of a Lee manuscript dated March 29, 1777, in a British collection the society had acquired. The document, certainly in Lee's hand, was addressed to the "Royal Commissioners"—that is, to Lord Richard Howe and Sir William Howe—and received by one Henry Strachey, secretary to the Howe brothers in their roles as peace commissioners. In his epistle Lee proposed a "Scheme for Putting an End to the War"—a plan to defeat the Revolution. The Scheme called for the Crown to seize the Hudson River-Lake Champlain Valley line, take Philadelphia, and seal off ports from Annapolis, Maryland, to Newport, Rhode Island. This, Lee claimed, would spark a loyalist rising and end the rebellion in two months. To say the least, Moore's discovery of Lee's Scheme was startling.[11]

Why did Lee write such a letter? Was he a scoundrel? Conclusions differ. Moore was the first to comment. In 1858 he emphatically insisted that Lee was a traitor and presented his findings in a paper, "The Treason of Charles Lee." The title neatly summarized his conclusions. John Alden, however, one of Lee's principal modern biographers, conjectured the captive general's plan was a ruse, with Lee intending to send Howe on his (eventually) pointless campaign into Pennsylvania. Philip Papas sees no disloyal intent and finds there is simply no evidence to support any definitive conclusion. He can only suggest that Lee, frustrated with his captivity and worried about a trial for treason, sought to curry favor with the Howes. Other historians are having none of this. For Dominick Mazzagetti the issue is clear: Lee had given up the American cause and turned-coat; worse, Lee supposedly lived in fear of discovery, which influenced all his subsequent actions, particularly at the Battle of Monmouth. Christian McBurney assigns no motive to Lee's action, but reasonably points out that by any legal definition of treason Lee was certainly guilty, no matter what his intentions may have been.[12]

Yet no author arguing for actual treachery on Lee's part has produced definitive evidence to sustain the charge. And no reputable study of Howe's Pennsylvania campaign sees Lee's hand in British planning. There is no evidence to suggest Howe or anyone else took the captive general's plan seriously; indeed, there is no indication that Strachey ever bothered to show the manuscript to the Howes. Perhaps it was misfiled and forgotten in the rush of events as Sir William launched his 1777 campaign. We just do not know. If this seems improbable, the fact remains that there is no evidence that the Howes—or *anyone* in a position to affect British military operations—ever laid eyes on Lee's document. No British military or civil official mentioned it during or after the war. Amid all the post-defeat finger-pointing among the British officers who served in America, as well as the Parliamentary and public furor over Sir William's conduct, *someone* would have said something about the treason of the rebels' second-ranking general. The British said plenty about Arnold's later change of coat, but nary a word about Lee's plan to defeat the rebellion.[13]

Besides, if Lee wanted to switch sides, he had ample opportunity to do so. Why did he remain with the Americans, for example, after his 1776 frustrations with Washington's leadership (and, as we will see, his differences with the commander in chief only grew in 1778)? Mazzagetti points to other correspondence between Lee and the British as further evidence of collusion. But if Lee saw himself as a go-between in brokering a peace, he was hardly discreet; he made no secret of his acquaintance with British officers, including Burgoyne. True, he wrote openly to anyone he wished—a bad habit for a senior officer and perhaps a mark of arrogance. But it was not necessarily that of a scoundrel or traitor. If Lee was some sort of conspirator, he was a rank amateur; compare his conduct with that of Benedict Arnold, who knew how to conduct a conspiracy. We are left with the question of why Lee composed his Scheme. John Shy, in a masterful essay on Lee, may have hit close to the mark: Lee did it "perhaps simply to become a participant again instead of a bystander." Lee's aide-de-camp, Otway Byrd, points to the same conclusion; he once told the general "I know you would rather write than be idle." Perhaps the Iroquois were closer yet—maybe it was all another manifestation of the one "whose spirits are never asleep." We can say this: For whatever reason Lee composed his Scheme, the document was neither a prelude to disloyalty nor an influence on the conduct of the war.[14]

★ ★ ★

Of course, had patriots learned of Lee's plan they would have considered him a traitor. But they never set eyes on the scheme, and American concern for Lee was about getting him back. After months of wrangling, the British agreed to trade Lee for captured Royal Brigadier Richard Prescott. On April 5, 1778, the major general was released on parole, still technically a prisoner of war and thus barred from returning to active duty. But as long as he did nothing "contrary to the interest of his Majesty or his government," Lee was a free man.[15]

While he could not have known it at the time, Lee's release led directly to professional oblivion and personal trauma. Lee had little sense of how much military and political affairs had changed since his capture in late 1776. He missed the political attacks Washington had endured over late 1777 and early 1778 (the Conway Cabal), the army's reorganization at Valley Forge, and the new personnel in the commander in chief's "family," including the rise of such men as the Marquis de Lafayette, Friedrich Steuben, and Nathanael Greene. In short, he lacked "situational awareness," which today's US military defines as a skill that allows one to "comprehend the critical elements of information about what is happening." Situational awareness is, simply put, "*knowing what is going on around you.*" Lee seemed at a complete loss in 1778.[16]

Shortly before his parole, Washington assured Lee he was anxious to have him back. If Washington harbored hard feelings from 1776, he buried them; with a new campaign in the offing—the British would evacuate Philadelphia in mid-June—it was no time for discord. On April 5 an honor guard met Lee when he rode into Valley Forge, and that evening he dined with General Washington, his wife, Martha, and senior officers. In this cordial atmosphere Lee left to visit Congress in York and then to sojourn to Prato Verde. On his travels he assumed his relationships with the officer corps, including the commander in chief, were fine. He was wrong.[17]

In York, Lee met with Henry Laurens, president of the Continental Congress. To Laurens, Lee seemed ill at ease with Washington's leadership, hardly an impression to leave with one of the commander in chief's strongest political supporters. In a follow-up letter Lee expressed his gratitude for all Congress had done to arrange his exchange, and he assured Laurens that his relationship with Washington was "well." But then, in an utterly tactless passage, he added, "I am persuaded (considering how he is surrounded) that he [Washington] cannot do without me." That was an astonishing message to a man whose son—Lieutenant Colonel John Laurens, a close aide to Washington—was one of those "surrounding" the general. Laurens warned his son he was leery of Lee, and if Lee had thought to befriend the congressional president, he had failed miserably.[18]

Laurens was not the only one uneasy with Lee. Even one of Lee's admirers, Congressman Thomas Burke of North Carolina, wondered at Lee's standing in the army. "That some Officers," Burke groused, "wish not for the release of General Lee because his enterprising disposition and martial genius will be a strong contrast to their want of both." Burke was exaggerating, but while many officers were happy to see Lee back, there was no mistaking an undercurrent of skepticism as well. Nathanael Greene sounded a cautionary note. He allowed that Lee was a fine officer, but he feared the "junto"—Washington's critics of the Conway Cabal, many of whom admired Lee—would try to "debauch and poison his mind" against Washington. Greene confessed he thought "no great good" would come of Lee's return.[19]

Concern over the "junto" was real. If Washington felt secure enough in his job by May, he, his army, and political allies had taken the Cabal seriously—and the Virginian and his inner circle held grudges. Lee had been a prisoner during the Cabal, but early in the war he had been friendly with some of Washington's most virulent critics. These included such notable sitting or former congressional delegates as Benjamin Rush, Samuel Adams, and James Lovell, and in the army Major Generals Thomas Mifflin and Horatio Gates. Upon his exchange Lee resumed contacts with some of these individuals as if nothing had happened while he was gone. As far as most of the officer corps was concerned, associating with Washington's adversaries was the same as being one. Lee was simply oblivious to what in fact was a seismic change in the Revolution's political universe. His correspondence with Rush told the tale. It was "hard to say," he wrote, which side had blundered the most thus far in the war, and while he saw affairs looking up for the rebels he added, "Upon my Soul it was time for fortune to interpose or We were inevitably lost." Thus, Lee went his way seemingly unconcerned with perceptions others might have of the company he kept or of what he might say.[20]

Lee certainly misread the commander in chief. Lee visited Congress twice while traveling to Virginia and back. Both times, without informing Washington, he took it upon himself to lobby on behalf of army reforms and for his own promotion. Lee sought promotion to lieutenant general, claiming that had he stayed in Europe, the Poles, the Portuguese, or the Russians would have promoted him. He also pointed out that during his captivity many Continental brigadiers had advanced to major general, while he remained in grade. Lee understood making such a request solely on his own behalf would have seemed self-serving, but he believed the army needed the higher rank: Lieutenant General. Major Generals usually led divisions, and when the army needed formations of more than a division—Lee referred to "wings" (the modern term would be "corps")—Washington could assign a major general from one of the divisions to command the wing. This meant a division might go into action under someone other than its usual commander, which Lee thought invited confusion. In a larger army with standing wings, the idea would have made sense. Even Washington admitted it had merit. But that wasn't the point—Lee had circumvented Washington. He had gone over the head of his commanding officer, without permission.[21]

And there was more. In addition to importuning for promotion, Lee assailed Congress with a plan for army reorganization—with an accompanying strategic vision. He informed Washington only in a communication from York of April 13. The major general explained he had been thinking about "how to form an army in the most simple manner possible." His recommendations carried the fulsome title, "A Plan for the Formation of the American Army in the least Expensive Manner possible, and at the same Time for rendering their Manoeuvers so little complex that all the Essentials may be learnt, and practiced in a few Weeks." The plan was, Lee wrote, "a hobby horse of my own training," and he was "so infatuated with it that I cannot forebear boasting its excellencies on all occasions, to Friends or Enemies." Then he begged pardon: "You must excuse me therefore if I could not refrain from recommending the Beast to some members of the Congress."[22]

Washington received the plan too late to suggest that such a presentation directly to Congress was utterly inappropriate. Washington's comments on the "Plan," however, were brief and jocular. He hoped Lee's "hobby horse" would not be a "limping . . . jade." It was clear Washington had not taken Lee's plan the least bit seriously.[23]

What had Lee proposed? And why had Washington reacted so blithely? At first glance one would have thought the proposal would have infuriated the commander in chief. It began with a jab at Inspector General Friedrich Steuben. The tactics of Europe, Lee wrote, were impractical, and he "lamented" Steuben's efforts to adapt them, even in simplified form, for Continental use. Instead, what America needed was simplicity in tactics and organization. Men "drawn from their Ploughs have little Time for dressing [in ranks]," he advised, and if they were "servilely kept to the European Plan, they will make an Aukward Figure, be laugh'd at as a bad Army by their Enemy, and defeated in every Recontre which depends on Manoeuvres." Lee wanted Americans to stand on the defense and wear down an enemy forced to come after them: "Harassing and impeding can alone Succeed." Taking the offensive in open combat against British professionals, he warned, was "talking Nonsense" and "Insanity."[24]

From a strictly military point of view, Lee's plan was interesting. The implication was that the national army essentially would be a uniformly organized and trained militia with no more than a small corps of regulars. His plan was a recipe for protracted small-unit warfare, a conflict in which militias would avoid set-piece engagements and whittle away the king's army over time. It would be a guerilla war.

However, theoretical merits of the "Plan" were beside the point. The proposal was completely out of step with Washington's vision for the army. Indeed, Lee's preference for a protracted defensive war fell on deaf ears generally. Most patriots now wanted a Continental Army that could stand and *fight*. Lee's ideas were simply out of date, and if the commander in chief dismissed them, it was a sign of how sure Washington was of his footing in Congress, at least on this point. Indeed, most delegates waxed enthusiastic about Steuben's training program. All the "Plan for the Formation of the American Army" accomplished was to signal the degree of difference between Lee's thinking and that of the commander in chief. Some of Lee's contemporaries saw this. In her history of the Revolution (1805), Mercy Otis Warren, who personally knew many leading patriots, wrote with some sympathy for Lee. Before his capture, she observed, "the American army was too justly considered by him, an undisciplined rabble." Upon his release, however, he failed to appreciate the "great improvements in the art of war" achieved during his absence. John Shy summed it up: during his captivity "the war seemed to have moved beyond Charles Lee."[25]

At this point, however, Washington had had enough. By directly approaching Washington's political superiors, Lee was out of line, and the now-offended Washington let him know. He wrote Lee explaining his communications with Congress on matters of army organization, officer ranks, and probable British intentions. Then he got to his real point: Washington would "always be happy in a free communication of your sentiments upon any important subject relative to the service," but he insisted any such communications "come directly to myself." The general was clear that there was to be no more ignoring your superior officer and vetting ideas or requests directly to Congress or to anyone else. "The custom," he continued, "which many officers have, of speaking freely of things . . . is never productive of good, but often of very mischievous consequences." It was a tactful reproof, but a reproof nevertheless, and a reminder of who was commander in chief.[26]

During Lee's travels, Washington completed the formal prisoner exchange and Lee returned to active duty at Valley Forge on May 21. Washington gave him one of the army's five divisions—a responsible command—but Lee quickly generated friction. Given the details of his "hobby horse," it is no surprise that he remained opposed to Steuben's efforts, and he wanted the inspector general's authority curtailed. By definition, this also meant he disagreed with Washington's vision of the Continental Army as a professional force—no small difference of opinion. Given Washington's dismissal of Lee's plan, Lee should have known better. The commander in chief was having none of this, and he reminded the army that Steuben's drill was official orthodoxy; there was no going back. One has to wonder at Washington's private reaction to Lee's obstinacy on the matter—and at Lee's judgment.[27]

Other more personal, less tangible qualities also distanced Lee from army peers. Indeed, his attitude upon his return to duty was a bit cavalier. In the aftermath of congressional debate over army reorganization and post-war officer pensions, Congress ordered all officers to swear a new loyalty oath. On June 9, Washington arranged to personally administer the oath to Lafayette and Lee. The young Frenchman swore routinely, but not Lee. Instead, Lee gladly renounced allegiance to George III, but announced he had some "scruples about the Prince of Wales." Most witnesses took the remark as a typical bit of Lee's irreverence. Nevertheless, Washington, who had worked long and hard with Congress on behalf of the status of the officer corps, was anything but pleased. Again, evidently this was lost on General Lee.[28]

There was also Lee's personal conduct: he was not genteel. He was famously careless about his appearance, once sitting down unshaven and bedraggled to breakfast with General and Martha Washington.

His conduct the night before allegedly was worse. According to Elias Boudinot, the army's commissary general of prisoners who had helped arrange Lee's exchange, Lee had secreted "a miserable dirty hussy" into his room. As Lee's room was next to Martha Washington's sitting room, the situation was potentially very awkward. Correspondence with Horatio Gates reflected a similar casualness toward gentility. Gates boasted to Lee that his son, Robert, had drunk himself silly and contracted a venereal disease. Lee thought it was splendid and bespoke a manly youth. Lee was no more a reprobate than many officers of the era. But such sentiments were foreign to Washington; one cannot imagine the commander in chief applauding the conduct of Robert Gates. Nor did he expect those in his circle to feel differently in such matters. Like Washington, most of these men, as well as many other officers, were highly conscious of their dignity as officers and gentlemen. Lee frequently was not.[29]

Did all this make Charles Lee a scoundrel? It would depend on who you asked. But there would have been quite a few contemporaries happy to label the man "difficult" or "unpredictable"—Washington probably among them. Armies have always been composed of disparate individuals, and personalities differ. Officers with differences could and did function as professional associates. Such was the case with Generals Lee and Washington. On important matters—personal, political, and military—the gulf between them was considerable, and despite mutual expressions of affection in their correspondence, they were never close friends. At Valley Forge in June 1778 much of this was unspoken. But there is no question potential flashpoints existed that made it easier for Washington and those around him to break with Lee. Few things are inevitable in history, but it is not going too far to say there are things that are or were *likely*. Even without benefit of hindsight, a rupture between Washington and Lee was certainly one of them—it just was not *quite* time.

★ ★ ★

On June 28, 1778, a Continental advanced force under Lee engaged the British Army near the village of Monmouth Courthouse (also known as Freehold) in New Jersey. It was a battle Lee did not want to fight. Sir Henry Clinton had evacuated Philadelphia on June 18, and on the 24th, Washington, who had given chase from Valley Forge, paused his pursuit to convene a council of war. The subject: What to do about Clinton. Lee, with support from a number of officers, argued for letting Clinton go. Why risk the army, he asked, when the British were leaving New Jersey anyway? Why not await French intervention while preserving American strength? He maintained that a victory in New Jersey would mean little, while a defeat could do irreversible harm. Hawks, notably Greene, Anthony Wayne, and Lafayette, agreed that fighting a general action would be unwise, but they insisted on striking a blow. "If we suffer the enemy to pass through New Jersey without attacking," Greene warned. "I think we shall . . . regret it." He continued, "People expect something from us and our strength demands it." Greene made a political argument aimed at restoring popular faith in Washington and the army after the disappointments of 1777. "I am by no means for rash measures, but we must preserve our reputation," Greene concluded. Washington agreed, ultimately ordering a vanguard of some 4,500 troops toward Clinton.[30]

After a series of false starts, including Lee's initial reluctance to lead the vanguard, on June 27 Lee took command of this force, then posted at Englishtown, about five miles from the British in and around Freehold. Late that day, Washington met with Lee and his chief subordinates, and everyone later agreed that the commander in chief wanted Lee's men to advance early on June 28. But Washington issued no specific orders on how, or even if, to attack. Wayne, who disliked Lee, admitted he never heard Washington "give any particular orders for the attack." Lee reasonably concluded that his orders were discretionary and that he was to govern his conduct according to events. He told his officers exactly that. Lee had Washington's promise, however, to support the vanguard with the main army.[31]

Lee marched around 7:00 A.M. on Sunday, June 28. His initial advance was hesitant, impeded by conflicting intelligence and unfamiliar terrain, but battle was joined just after 10:00 A.M. as Lee attempted to encircle what he thought was a British rearguard. He hoped to bag the lot without risking a major battle—exactly the kind of blow Washington preferred. But a surprised Lee halted his movement when Clinton responded with a massive counterattack. Wayne wanted to stand and fight, but Lee correctly judged that such a course would have been suicidal. Conducting an orderly retrograde as the British came on, Lee eventually directed his men toward good defensive ground on Perrine's Hill, well west of Freehold. He intended to stand there until Washington brought up the main army.

Approaching Perrine's Hill from Englishtown, Washington was alarmed to discover the vanguard retreating. Riding forward, he met Lee about 1:00 P.M. Lee honestly expected a compliment on his skillful retrograde. Instead, Washington curtly "desire[d] to know, sir," as Lee recalled, "the reason—whence arises this disorder and confusion?" "Confounded," Lee was momentarily lost for words, flustered by Washington's tone and the commander in chief's insistence that Lee should have pushed his attack. That a stand near Freehold would have been foolish made no difference; nothing Lee could have said would have mattered. Bewildered, Lee tagged along as Washington rode forward to reconnoiter.[32]

The Washington–Lee confrontation is embedded in American folklore, with supposed witnesses embellishing the incident over the years. Lafayette and Brigadier Charles Scott were classic examples. As old men their accounts had Washington enraged—the Frenchman remembering him calling Lee a "damned poltroon." Scott recalled Washington swearing "till the leaves shook on the trees, charming, delightfully. Never did I enjoy such swearing before or since. Sir, on that memorable day, he swore like an angel from Heaven." It was all nonsense. Neither man was remotely close enough to hear anything said by either Washington or Lee. No one, including Lee, made any such claims during Washington's lifetime, and Lee's court-martial transcript accurately reflected only a blunt exchange between the army's two senior commanders, an occasion dramatic enough to need no after-the-fact embellishment.[33]

As Washington confronted Lee, the British advance continued. Washington recognized the gravity of the threat and, cooling off, ordered Wayne with some 900 men into a wood to the right of the British approach, and he tasked Lee with organizing a holding action west of Wayne's position. Washington then rode back to form the main army on Perrine's Hill while Lee and Wayne feverishly prepared for combat. Wayne ambushed the redcoats as they marched past his position, but a prompt counterattack drove Wayne reeling from the woods and down the road toward Perrine's Hill. Lee formed up behind a hedgerow directly in front of the British advance. The hedgerow offered little cover—musket balls and bayonets could easily penetrate it—but at least the Continentals could form a line. They also had artillery support, as Henry Knox had come forward to join Lee and take charge of the guns retreating with Lee's infantry. The fighting was brutal but short. Continentals and redcoats exchanged fire and bayonet thrusts only feet from one another as Lee and Knox watched from a knoll behind the hedgerow. The mayhem lasted no more than ten minutes before Lee realized the British were gaining the upper hand. Redcoats who had routed Wayne were working around Lee's left and the 16th Light Dragoons were closing on his right. Flanked on both ends of his line, Lee again directed an orderly retrograde toward Washington's position. It had been a desperate defense, but Lee and Wayne had bought time necessary for the commander in chief to put the main army into a solid defensive posture.

In small but sharp actions the Battle of Monmouth continued until sundown. The engagement was a tactical draw and Clinton's army withdrew safely, ultimately to positions in and around New York. The Continentals performed well—even the British admitted as much—and Washington won hosannas from virtually all patriots for his leadership. But the retreat from the hedgerow ended Lee's battle. Exhausted, he followed his depleted vanguard back to Englishtown. Monmouth saw his last combat—although other conflicts began almost immediately.

Lee's ambiguous position in the officer corps now became apparent. His differences with Washington, his loose tongue, and his abrasive personality had made too many enemies, who now sharpened their knives. Lee's morning retreat gave rise to sniping from Washington's partisans; rumors circulated questioning Lee's competence, courage, and even his loyalty. His association with Washington's erstwhile critics now came back to haunt him. Washington's friends saw Monmouth as a chance to settle scores with the Cabal once and for all, and Lee would pay the price. Elias Boudinot wrote Alexander Hamilton that "Every Lip dwells on his [Washington's] Praise for even his pretended friends (for none dare to acknowledge themselves his Enemies) are obliged to croak it forth." Hamilton and fellow Washington aide John Laurens assiduously spun the Monmouth story favorably for the commander in chief. Laurens wrote his influential father casting aspersions on Lee's conduct, and Hamilton did the same with anyone who would listen. The spin was consistent: Washington had won the day, and only Lee's retreat had prevented Clinton's destruction. The public got the message.[34]

The attacks by Hamilton, Laurens, and others amounted to character assassination. Lee had fought well at Monmouth and his fate had more to do with personalities and politics than the battlefield. Despite his battlefield exchange with Lee there is little indication that Washington envisioned any post-battle action against him. But Lee, offended at the circulating gossip, wrote two snarky letters to Washington insisting on a court-martial to clear himself of rumored misconduct. Washington complied, and Lee stood accused on three counts: failing to attack on June 28 "agreeable to repeated instructions;" leading "an *unnecessary*, *disorderly*, and *shameful retreat*;" and disrespect toward the commander in chief in his post-battle letters. The first two charges were ridiculous, but Lee certainly had been disrespectful to Washington. That finished him. "Under the circumstances," John Shy has noted, "an acquittal on the first two charges would have been a vote of no-confidence in Washington." That was impossible; thus the guilty verdict on all counts was no surprise, although the court deleted "shameful" from the second count. The court suspended Lee from the service for a year and Washington forwarded the verdict to Congress.[35]

The delegates were in no hurry to deal with the hot-button matter, and the delay provided time for partisans of Washington and Lee to lobby for their favorites. There was plenty of acrimony, and Lee's plight garnered considerable sympathy. But on December 5, Congress resolved to sustain the verdict. What choice was there? Could Congress risk the army's welfare to offer justice to one man? Either Lee or Washington had to go—and it was *not* going to be Washington. But the vote was not unanimous: of the twenty-three delegates, seven believed Lee had been wronged. Lee's disgrace virtually silenced public criticisms of the commander in chief. Rather than accept his suspension, Lee resigned in disgust. *C'est la guerre.*[36]

True to his character, Lee did not go away quietly. He remained in touch with friends in and out of the army and occasionally commented on current affairs. In 1779, he even wrote to archenemy Anthony Wayne complimenting him on his dramatic coup at Stoney Point. He still had men willing to defend his reputation, but there was no further chance of his taking up arms for the Revolution. In 1782 he decided to sell his land in Virginia, and he was in Philadelphia on that errand and other business when he died of an unspecified fever. Patriot luminaries in the city, in and out of uniform, attended his funeral. Even then, however, Lee got in something of the last word. Never a partisan of zealous religion, he was laid to rest in Christ Church–Episcopal, having left instructions in his will that he "desire[d] most earnestly, that I may not be buried in any church or churchyard within a mile of any Presbyterian or Anabaptist meeting-house; for since I have resided in this country, I have kept so much bad company when living, that I do not chose to continue it when dead." It was classic Charles Lee.[37]

★ ★ ★

We end where we began: Was Charles Lee a "scoundrel"? If we use Samuel Johnson's definition of the word (not a bad benchmark, as Johnson's famous *Dictionary* would have been familiar to Lee's generation—and probably to Lee) the answer is still hazy. As hostile historians have unendingly reminded us, in many ways Lee was not a likeable individual. But in actual fact that did not necessarily make him a "rascal" or a "low petty villain." Those words imply a deliberate shiftiness or even dishonesty, and those things Lee was not. He *was* socially and politically obtuse, astonishingly so. Lee does deserve some credit for consistency: from the early days of his military career, he was volatile, obstinate, temperamental, and opinionated, all characteristics he carried with him into the Continental Army. He did not lack self-esteem. In fact, he generally thought he was smarter than most. His problem was that he could not help letting others know as much. These were (and are) *not* traits likely to win many friends.[38]

We go back to "situational awareness:" the ability to recognize what is going on around you. In a self-confidence that often crossed the line to arrogance, Lee simply "didn't get it," especially with Washington. As a subordinate officer—even as a senior general—you did *not* consort with your commanding general's critics, let alone go behind his back to his political superiors, and expect him to trust you. You certainly did not commit your criticisms or differences to paper, at least not in tactless language. Nor did you casually ignore his standards of personal conduct or decorum. Lee did all of these things, oblivious to the feelings of others or of possible consequences. Even if his conduct carried no malevolent intent—and I do not think it did—his persona was such that he simply could not see beyond his own opinions and habits. The views of others didn't register. This was not the outlook of a scoundrel who acted deliberately or dishonestly, but perhaps of a narcissist who acted because that was just who he was. Who really knows? In the opinion of John Shy, it would take a psychiatrist to figure out Lee, and it's hard to argue with that.[39]

However, we need to revisit the matter that has most dogged Lee's reputation: his conduct at Monmouth. Did his performance on June 28, 1778, deserve the obloquy so many contemporaries—and historians—heaped upon him? Lee, like most of Washington's senior lieutenants, was a competent but hardly inspirational leader. Yet few critics who have faulted his decisions at Monmouth have suggested convincingly what he might or should have done differently. Should he have devised a specific plan before advancing? *How*, given the frequently changing intelligence on the enemy situation? Did Lee fail to gather sufficient intelligence on the British before attempting his advance? If he had waited until Clinton's movements were fully clear, the redcoats would have been long gone—well out of reach of the blow Washington wanted Lee to strike. Should he have maintained better control of his command during the morning? Of course. But *how*, given the terrain and distance realities of the battlefield, the necessity of making decisions on the spot, and the state of field communications? Should he have stood and fought as Wayne wanted? It would have been suicidal given vastly superior British numbers. Was there another viable line he could have held short of Perrine's Hill? No critic has remotely suggested where. Had Lee tried to fight somewhere east of the hill, Clinton would have been delighted. With few exceptions, Lee's critics have glossed over or ignored these questions. Did Washington relieve him of command? No—the commander in chief had Lee fight a holding action while Washington rallied the army on Perrine's Hill. Nor has Lee received sufficient credit for buying the time Washington needed to position his main line on the hill. To dislike Lee is one thing—there were plenty of reasons—but to demean his conduct on June 28 smacks more of armchair generalship than credible history. It was only Lee's intemperate and foolish post-battle insolence to Washington that led to his court-martial; it was *not* his performance in command.[40]

Historians have been trying to comprehend Charles Lee for some 250 years. Strong opinions on the man's nature and character abound, but there is no consensus. However, there is a final observation on Lee I think we can make with some certainty: To the extent historians may still be interested in Major General Charles Lee in *another* 250 years, there will be strong opinions on the man—but still no agreement.

BLOUNT'S BUNKO: PRIVATE FORTUNE THROUGH PUBLIC SERVICE IN THE SOUTHWEST TERRITORY, 1790–1796

CHRISTOPHER MAGRA

★ ★ ★

North Carolina legislator William Blount received great news in the summer of 1790. President George Washington had appointed him as the first territorial governor of the Southwest Territory, the area east of the Mississippi River and south of the Ohio River which Congress had carved out of the region won from Britain in the treaty ending the American Revolution. Blount was a fellow Federalist and had friends in high places. Receiving his commission, Blount expressed his gratitude for the trust placed in him. The office made him feel a "very perfect Sense of the Honor," he told Washington and Secretary of State Thomas Jefferson, and he vowed "with a firm Determination" that he would "perform the duties of it to the best of [my] Abilities." This was the response Washington and Jefferson wanted to hear, and Blount knew it.[1]

To his close personal friends and family, Blount communicated a more pecuniary sentiment. Blount revealed that his federal appointment was "of great importance" to his family's business of buying and selling western lands, or "our Western speculations." He explained "the Salary is handsome, and my Western Lands had become so great an object to me that it had become absolutely necessary that I should go to the Western Country, to secure them and perhaps my Presence might have enhanced their value. I am sure my present appointment will."[2]

Blount's term as governor went according to plan. Between the time he took up his post in August 1790 and when he left office once the Territory became the state of Tennessee in 1796, Blount accumulated over two million acres of land, making him one of the largest landowners in the United States. His land holdings dwarfed the 50,000 acres George Washington owned. Blount was a scoundrel through and through, and his chicanery played a pivotal—but largely overlooked—role in the westward expansion of the United States.[3]

Because he possessed most of the vices and few of the virtues of the other Founding Fathers, there has not been much scholarship on Blount or his role in expanding US borders. What is more, recent histories of westward expansion have shifted attention away from elite white men and toward important larger trends associated with the proliferation of slavery and the promotion of racial ideas and the practice of settler colonialism. Emphasizing these important topics has necessarily led to less light being cast on individuals such as Blount. To date, there has only been a single biography of Blount. As a result, the extent to which American imperialism was predicated upon Blount's machinations remain little understood.[4]

William Blount used the power of elected office to expand the United States farther west. He did not do this for the glory of the new nation. He did not work toward the common good for all his constituents. Instead, Blount sought public office and abused various government positions to promote his own self-interests. He fought to be the first and the only governor of the Southwest Territory. He convinced people he was the man for the job. Blount then played a leading role in the formation of the state of Tennessee. All this public work enabled him to become one of the largest landowners in the United States. Investigating Blount's political machinations and entrepreneurial manipulations helps us come to terms with the ways in which the individual abuse of power moved national boundaries during the formative years of the American Empire.

★ ★ ★

William Blount was an unscrupulous land speculator. He believed in bribery. On one 1782 land deal, Blount instructed his brother to "stand behind the Curtain" and use "Bribery or any other Way it will be best" to secure a large profit margin. He was not above lying to get what he wanted. He bought real estate on the condition that he had to settle three hundred families on the land within three years. Blount instructed an unnamed associate to "keep up a Report of as many being about to go as you possibly can whether true or not." Blount invented ghost purchasers to enable his own firm to secure legal title to more western land than the law allowed in 1784. He explained to his associates that they should "make use of any Names, fictitious ones will do I suppose . . . You need not fear, but I can find the People to transfer their Rights to the Company." He hoarded supplies during the Revolutionary War and sold them dearly to his needy neighbors, which earned the scorn of his kin. Blount's cousin informed him, "I wonder truly how many poor sons of bitches with tears in their eyes have I seen . . . coming from your place." Blount also deliberately canceled prior treaties with Indigenous people to open more lands for speculation and settlement. And Blount was the first federal employee to be impeached for conspiring with foreign governments in an unbelievable scheme to raise the value of his own real estate.[5]

Blount's obsession with buying and selling large amounts of western land began in North Carolina, where he was born in 1749. Blount learned the business from his father, a wealthy land speculator, and grew up investing in real estate. The Blount family even sent agents to

Europe to sell land in North America on their behalf. Blount and other affluent North Carolina landowners initially wore Loyalist clothes at the start of the American Revolution because they stubbornly believed this was the best way to preserve their property rights. But, Blount soon realized, the British government was not going to safeguard his right to buy and sell real estate. If he switched sides and fought for independence, however, he would be better positioned to gain access to western territories freed from British regulations. So he put on a Patriot uniform.

The conversion allowed Blount to win a seat in the North Carolina legislature, and to purchase property confiscated from Loyalists at a discounted rate. His newfound patriotism further paved the way to participate in the Revolutionary War as paymaster for North Carolina troops. During his service, Blount lost $300,000 which the state of North Carolina had allocated for its soldiers' payroll. Where did the money go? No one knows.[6]

The big prize for Blount was the western land of the newly independent state. Before the ink dried on the 1783 peace treaty, Blount proposed a bill to allow the North Carolina government to print £100,000 in paper currency to stimulate speculation in western lands controlled by the state. Blount then proposed another bill to "amend" western lands previously reserved for North Carolina veterans of war, creating a new way for speculators to get rich. Blount targeted an older system that promised to pay soldiers in land instead of wages. Blount's proposal first expanded the number of veterans who could claim land on the frontier to include anyone from North Carolina who had served in the American armed forces for two years, allowing many more people to claim western lands. Blount then changed what land was set aside for veterans to claim, choosing an area that was more difficult to access and less desirable for farming. Blount's proposal also added bureaucratic hurdles that lengthened the amount of time it took for veterans to actually settle on their land. The goal: make it more likely that poor veterans would claim western lands and then, rather than settling it themselves, sell it to speculators for pennies on the dollar. Blount's proposal became law and North Carolina set aside, or "reserved," a total of 2,789,224 acres in what is today East Tennessee for these veterans.[7]

Blount saw veteran land grants not as a reward for military service in the cause of American independence, but as a land grab for speculators. While William Blount was getting these bills passed into law, he had his younger brother John Gray Blount, also a North Carolina legislator, present a bill that opened for sale all the western lands North Carolina claimed between the Appalachian Mountains and the Mississippi River, minus the military reserve and a small reservation for Indigenous people between the Tennessee and Big Pigeon Rivers. All prior treaties with Indigenous people were declared null and void, as they had sided with the British and lost the war.[8] These Blount bills stripped Indigenous peoples of their land and collectively flung the West open to speculators. The Blount family then made 2,760 entries in North Carolina's land office for plots on the frontier.[9]

William Blount purchased 50,000 acres of land inside the military reserve, land he got cheap from desperate veterans. Blount secured a further 60,000 acres of other western lands in one deal, and 365,000 acres in another. He bought an enormous 300,000 acre tract of rich farmland within the great southern bend of the Tennessee River. Owning so much land came with a hefty tax bill, but Blount had that covered: he paid the taxes in credit—illegally—instead of in cash. Blount admitted the "thirst" speculators such as himself had "for a Piece of the Tennessee land." He made no effort to hide his motives. "The Object" of the business, he said, was "private Emolument."[10]

And yet these initial land purchases did not fulfill Blount's ambitions. He had an insatiable desire to accumulate more and more land. He came to believe that his best chance to buy and sell even more real estate was to have the North Carolina legislature cede these lands to the federal government, which was headquartered far away and unable to watch what locals were up to.

The problem was how to convince state sovereignty-minded North Carolina legislators that ceding western lands to the federal government would be good for the state. Blount found a way in with the help of James Cole Mountflorence, a fellow legislator and notorious land speculator. North Carolina had not paid its quota of the national debt as required under the Articles of Confederation, and it was in arrears to the tune of $19 million. North Carolina could cede western lands to the federal government to pay off a portion of this debt. This cession further reduced state land taxes, and it shifted oversight of western lands away from nearby North Carolina to the federal government in New York City. It relocated regulatory power out of the hands of people familiar with the Southeast. The lack of close scrutiny made it safer for speculators to operate in the region. Moreover, having western lands in federal hands increased the value of those lands, as buyers believed, rightly or wrongly, that the federal government was better positioned to defend settlers and negotiate with hostile Indigenous people. Blount and Mountflorence "labored strenuously" in 1788 to get other North Carolina legislators to agree to cede western lands to the federal government. Ultimately their "joint efforts were crowned with success."[11]

Blount had another reason for wanting the federal government to control western lands. He knew Congress would need a new governor for the region, as the federal government had already established the Northwest Territory with its own governor. Blount had been in the federal Congress in 1787 and witnessed the Northwest Ordinance become law. He saw the power given to federal officials to make treaties with Indigenous people and pave the way for settlers. Blount coveted this power. His friend Hugh Williamson reported that by the end of March 1790 Blount was "assured" he would be appointed as governor of the lands North Carolina ceded to the federal government. This was before Congress formally accepted the ceded lands on April 2.[12]

Blount's assurance seems remarkable at first glance. He was not alone in seeing wealth in western lands. Nor was he the only one to realize the potential for profits associated with governing this territory. Powerful men vied for the governorship of the area initially named "The Territory of the United States South of the River Ohio."[13]

Virginia was the wealthiest, most populous state. Virginians were some of the most politically powerful people in the United States. Patrick Henry was a Founding Father and a land speculator who wanted to put one of his friends in charge of the territory North Carolina ceded. Henry believed this placeman would pave the way for dispossessing Indigenous people, surveying and purchasing real estate, and selling lands to settlers, who he would transport into the region. This would have made Henry richer than he already was. Thomas Jefferson supported Henry's candidate. Jefferson was a fellow Virginian and a land speculator, and he was a man who did not miss out on many opportunities.

Anthony Wayne was a wealthy landowner in Pennsylvania. His military service as an American general in the Revolutionary War took him to Georgia, where he defeated Great Britain's Indigenous allies. He served in the Georgia House of Representatives after the war and wanted to be the new governor of the Southwest Territory. He called this region an "immense and valuable country" that was "vastly superior" to any other part of North America for land speculation.[14]

The settlers living in the western lands, legally and illegally, put John Sevier forward as their candidate for governor. They petitioned Congress to say that "no other man upon the Continent, the President of the United States not excepted, can give as general satisfaction to the People of this Country in that office." Sevier was Blount's friend and business partner in various land speculations.[15]

Blount worked extremely hard to fight these rivals, even Sevier. He wrote to Congressmen to openly solicit their aid in getting him the governorship. He had Congressmen write to other Congressmen on his behalf. One of Blount's friends, Congressman Hugh Williamson, even lobbied President George Washington for Blount. "It is true that Mr. Blount has a considerable Quantity of Land within the ceded

Territory," Williamson acknowledged. And yes that meant he had a vested business interest in the region. But Washington need not be concerned by Blount's possible conflict of interest. "He must be the more deeply interested in the Peace and Prosperity of the new Government," precisely because he owned land there. Williamson admitted that he, too, owned "some Land" in the region, but that made him just as "anxious to see it prosper" as Blount. These lobbying efforts combined with Blount's patriotic military service in the Revolutionary War and his Federalist voting record won over Washington. The president named Blount the first governor of the newly minted Southwest Territory and superintendent of Indian Affairs for the Southern department on June 8, 1790.[16]

Blount and his cronies cackled with glee. Williamson was "relieved from any anxiety respecting our Western Territory." By "our Territory," he meant the lands speculators had purchased with the intention of selling to settlers. "I am now only to consider how the current of Migration shall best be turned towards the Tennessee Government," Williamson wrote. If they could get a lot of European settlers to purchase these lands, then "the value of our land may be improved or increased." Another supporter similarly rejoiced: "I conceive it a great point gained to our landholders, that the business of an Indian boundary will fall into the hands of a man, of all others the most proper." Blount was "the most proper" person to move Indigenous people off their land because he had years of experience nullifying preexisting treaties. Blount was ecstatic about the federal appointment. He marveled "at it myself." Not because governing the Southwest Territory meant a chance to honor previous treaties with Indigenous people and to create lasting peace between the United States of America and Native Americans. No, no. That was not William Blount. He wanted the US to expand farther and farther west. Nor was his desire for the glory of the fledgling nation. That was not Blount, either. Blount explained to his brother precisely what amazed him about being named governor: "I think it of great Importance to our Western Speculations."[17]

★ ★ ★

The new governor sold some of his enslaved people to settle outstanding debts. Then, taking one of his slaves with him to act as manservant, he travelled to Alexandria, Virginia, to take the oath of office. It was administered by James Iredell, a fellow North Carolinian and an original Supreme Court justice, on September 20, 1790. It was there that he learned of the full extent of his powers as governor. Blount's commission as Indian Affairs superintendent made him responsible for any and all activities involving Indigenous people in the Southwest Territory. He could appoint all civil officers, from constables up to his own secretary, and he could appoint all military officers except generals, though he could nominate those candidates directly to the president. Vested powers in hand, Blount headed into what is today Tennessee to govern and to profit. But mostly the latter.[18]

In late fall 1790, Blount appointed important settlers such as Andrew Jackson, John Sevier, and James White to various political offices in the Southwest Territory. He travelled to four nearby counties in the Territory that held around 28,000 settlers and read his new commission aloud to those who wanted to hear. Then Blount and Sevier hatched a get rich quick scheme.

In 1783, North Carolina had put Sevier in charge of distributing Revolutionary military certificates, or pay vouchers, for the state's veterans, who were supposed to receive the vouchers in lieu of back wages they were owed. Once in hand, the veterans could choose to cash them out or hold onto them while they accrued interest. But Sevier had kept the certificates—all of them—for seven years, just waiting for an opportunity. In 1790, Blount learned that Alexander Hamilton had made it a point as the nation's first Secretary of the Treasury to pay these certificates back in full, with interest. Whoever held them now stood to make a handsome profit.

Blount told Sevier to hold on to the certificates until he could arrange for his brother John Gray Blount to purchase them from

North Carolina. They could write fictitious soldiers' names onto the blank certificates. The purchase would then provide ownership to the conspirators. While John Gray was illegally borrowing money from the North Carolina Treasurer, a close personal friend, Blount formally issued the certificates by postdating them, selling them all to his brother at 1783 prices, and changing the wording to reflect Hamilton's Assumption Act of 1790. Doing this made the certificates function as though they had been issued to veterans in 1783, sold at some unspecified time to John Gray, and now they were worth full face value plus interest. It was only his first month as governor, and William Blount was already making money off the backs of veterans.[19]

In 1791, Blount schemed to take away lands previously reserved for Indigenous people. He used his power as governor and Indian Affairs superintendent to call for a gathering of Native American leaders on the banks of the Holston River near James White's fort. He told these leaders that he wanted to forge a new peace treaty. The real reason for the meeting, Blount informed Secretary of War Henry Knox, was to "disregard the treaty of Hopewell" previously made between the federal government and the Cherokee, Chickasaw, Choctaw, and Creeks in 1785 "and form an entire new treaty." The Treaty of Hopewell had reserved nearly all the Southwest Territory for Native Americans. Blount wanted Indigenous leaders to agree to abandon the Hopewell agreements and cede additional lands to the governor. Blount told Knox he believed the leaders would accept these harsh terms in exchange for an "annual stipulation of a thousand dollars." Not by coincidence, the land Blount had in mind for cession was land he had already sold to 300 settlers.[20]

Blount decided to shock and awe the Indigenous people into accepting his terms. He had workers erect an enormous open-air canopy tent near the Holston River. Sitting in a large chair underneath the canopy and dressed in fancy clothing, sword, and an oversized martial hat, Blount, flanked by all his newly appointed civil and military officers, had a master of ceremonies formally announce each Indigenous leader one by one and escort them under the canopy into his presence.

Once they had all been introduced, Blount announced the true purpose of the meeting: the Native Americans must cede land to the governor. This made the Indigenous leaders angry, as they had been duped into believing the meeting was for a new peace treaty. They insisted that the settlers were treaty-breakers. Blount responded by pointing out that all the lands east of the Mississippi River belonged to the US government by right of conquest in the American Revolution. Then he lied and said that the federal government no longer wished to reserve lands for Indigenous people.[21]

This lie did the trick. Indigenous people were not awed by Blount's marquee. Nor were they satisfied with an annual stipend of $1,000. But the lie that the United States government wanted their land convinced enough people to relent and agree to terms. It seemed plausible, and they risked losing everything if they refused. In the Treaty of Holston, Indigenous leaders ceded all land east of the Clinch River to white settlers.[22]

The treaty benefited Blount in several ways. He did not have three hundred angry settlers demanding their money back. He could now legally sell other lands he owned in the region. A peace treaty with multiple Indigenous leaders looked impressive to Knox and Washington. Blount seemed to have guaranteed peace, for a time at least. Plus, this diplomacy raised land prices, which made Blount more money.

But Blount wanted even more. According to Indigenous complaints to the federal government in the wake of the treaty, Blount approached multiple Indigenous leaders throughout the treaty negotiations trying to buy additional lands for himself on the side. They refused on the basis that these lands were common hunting grounds for the Cherokee, Chickasaw, Choctaw, and Creeks. Blount was stymied, despite having abused his position in the negotiations to try to conduct business as a private citizen.[23]

Blount informed Jefferson about his success negotiating the Treaty of Holston. It had "extinguished" the "Indian claim" to lands south of the French Broad River—a waterway that straddles the border between Tennessee and North Carolina today—and paved the way for white settlement in the region and eventual statehood for Tennessee. It also meant wealth for land speculators, especially well-positioned entrepreneurs such as Blount.[24]

The federal government ratified Blount's treaty into law, but Jefferson, Knox, and Washington were unhappy with the governor's work. Knox believed the treaty would have "pernicious effects." According to Knox, "the Cherokees would complain, and with justice, that all the assurances given by the new government . . . were deceptions, and calculated to ensnare them." For his part, Jefferson expressed to Blount "my anxiety" over the precise borders between lands reserved for the Cherokee and the lands settled by whites in the Southwest Territory and in North Carolina. Jefferson was so anxious about these borders in part because he did not want settlers encroaching on Native American reservations and stimulating conflict that could result in costly wars. The federal government did not have much revenue, and the army and navy had been almost entirely demobilized after the Revolutionary War. "It imports highly to the people within your government to conform to the articles of the treaty against hunting or settling on the Indian lands," the secretary of state told Blount in no uncertain terms. Jefferson informed Blount that he was aware the governor was personally responsible for settling "three hundred families" on 300,000 acres of land in what is today East Tennessee "without right or license." In another letter, Jefferson reminded Blount of the "necessity" to "promulgate immediately such parts at least of the treaty lately made with the Cherokees, as are interesting to our citizens."[25]

Jefferson had a grand vision for the West. He wanted a constant flow of settlers into frontier spaces to resolve the boundary dispute with Spain in the Southwest in the United States's favor. Jefferson also promoted westward expansion to guarantee the future of an agrarian social order that would ultimately preserve American republicanism. Jefferson and other American leaders believed they could make this

American vision come to life, because "all the lands" between the Mississippi River and the Appalachian Mountains were "subject" to the "disposal" of Congress. This federal sovereignty meant only Congress had the "right" to grant lands in this region.[26]

Jefferson wanted to prevent individuals from selling western lands that now belonged to Congress. He also felt it was necessary to prevent speculators from selling western lands that Congress had reserved for Indigenous people. Jefferson had speculated in real estate development companies before. He was very familiar with buying and selling western lands. He understood that problems were going to arise as people pushed West. Jefferson's plan to deal with settler infringement on Native American land rights was to "purchase" the "right of occupation" from Indigenous people if problems ensued. However, these purchases took time and money, and there were no guarantees of success. Blount wanted something else. He wanted the political power to buy and sell western lands fast.[27]

Blount's desire for power and Jefferson's vision for the West came to a head over a census. Jefferson wanted an official census of the Southwest Territory in order to begin the formation of a representative government in the area. He believed this was the first step toward democracy on the frontier. Blount did his best to avoid a census for the people in his territory, because it was the first step toward democracy on the frontier. A census would help make it possible for people to elect an assembly for the region. Blount wanted all power unto himself.

Blount tried to obstruct Jefferson's plans. On one occasion, he had his secretary, Daniel Smith, write to Jefferson about an unfortunate delay. They were having difficulty determining the boundaries of the territory, as Blount "has been unable to take the bearings of the mountains marking the eastern Territorial boundary because of his attendance at the Cherokee treaty [Treaty of Holston]." Later, Blount sent another man in his place to talk about the border with Jefferson in Philadelphia. The secretary of state was not pleased. But Blount got what he wanted—wasted time and no census. Blount then took a leave of absence for the entire month of October 1791. The repeated delays frustrated Jefferson. Privately, Blount boasted to a friend that "the People of the Territory and myself are unanimous in agreeing to have no General Assembly." He managed to put off the formation of a territorial legislature until 1794.[28]

Fully ensconced in his position as governor of the Southwest Territory, Blount used his public office to restrain business competitors and encourage his own private ventures in 1792. He fought off efforts on the part of other land speculators to survey and obtain legal title to lands in what is today East Tennessee. He ordered Andrew Jackson, whom Blount had appointed attorney general, to forcefully prosecute anyone who violated the boundaries of the Holston Treaty. At the same time, the governor ordered his own surveyor, James Robertson, to "Lay as many of the Warrants within the present Indian Bounds as you can, taking Care to avoid disputes in the Titles, but in case you cannot find good land within the Boundary and have got Surveys without the Bounds already made, then let such locations rest as they are." In other words, Blount authorized his men to do the very thing that he had ordered Jackson to prosecute. The difference, of course, was that Blount was in power.[29]

At the height of his power in 1793, Blount learned that Robert Morris, former Superintendent of Finance in the Articles of Confederation government and one of the richest men on the continent, had sold an enormous amount of western land to a group of Dutch investors. The profits Morris made from this single transaction changed Blount's approach to land speculation. In addition to purchasing a variety of smaller plots, Blount began looking to replicate Morris's monster deal. He sent agents to London, Amsterdam, and Paris to explore European interest in large land sales. He had western lands surveyed and mapped for the express purpose of marketing real estate to overseas investors and settlers. And he began asking friends for "the Names of sundry People who owned large quantities of land." Blount explained that he desired "to purchase the lands." He frankly admitted that he wanted "to purchase to sell again to immediate profit . . . a large body laying together near the settlements say from sixty thousand to hundred thousand acres . . . such a tract I believe I would sell to an advantage in Europe to people of large capital." He even sold some of the enslaved people he owned in North Carolina to generate a portion of the funds to buy this real estate.[30]

Primed with knowledge, capital, and political authority, in 1794 Blount set about buying and selling more and more land in the territory he governed. According to a grand jury in North Carolina, Blount used fictitious names to fraudulently purchase 105,000 acres of western lands. At the same time, Blount used public funds and government employees to map his holdings in the Southwest Territory. He planned to use these maps to market his holdings. Then, during his time in office, he purchased an additional 409,000 acres in the Territory for sale to overseas investors.[31]

When Blount finally consented to allow people to elect representatives to a general assembly in the Southwest Territory in 1794, he did so for one reason. He needed extra voices to convince the federal government to declare war on the nearby Creek Nation who had allied with Spanish settlers in Florida to dislodge Blount and other settlers from the Territory, panicking investors, scaring off potential settlers, and depressing land values. Blount deliberately timed the first meeting of the delegates for February 24 to ensure Congress would still be in session. "I call the persons elected to represent the several counties together at so early a period," he wrote, so a strong message could be laid "before Congress in the present session." He was certain the delegates would join him in petitioning Congress for war. He was right about this petition, but he was wrong that the federal government would listen to the chorus of frontier voices.[32]

Jefferson, Knox, and Washington rejected the call for war with the Creeks out of fear of conflict with Spain. In response, Blount began to campaign for an end to the Southwest Territory and promote statehood for Tennessee. He did not do this out of any nationalism. He was not in it to expand the United States, though that is what happened. Nor did Blount desire statehood for the good of the people living in his region. Blount did not have better angels. He believed that the only way to protect his huge land holdings from Native American assaults, and the one path to prevent declining real estate values, was to create a state that would have the power to regulate its own internal affairs. "The Creeks must be humbled before you can enjoy Peace and I fear that wished for Period will never arrive until this Territory becomes a State and is represented in Congress," he explained. "For this and other Reasons I am dearly determined that it is the true Interest of this Territory to become a State as early as possible and I hope that will be the Opinion of the Majority of the People." To "humble" Indigenous people meant to kill a number sufficient to secure their obeisance. If this was not enough, then Blount believed they should be wiped from the face of the Earth. He wanted a military force "sufficient to humble if not destroy the Creek Nation, and thereby give Peace to the Southwestern Frontiers." By "peace," Blount meant the protection of private property, especially his own. Blount used the Knoxville newspaper, private meetings with influential people, and correspondence to campaign for Tennessee statehood to benefit his own burgeoning land business.[33]

By 1796, when Tennessee became the sixteenth state in the union, William Blount owned outright or was invested in 2,660,335 acres of land, mostly in the West. Being governor of the Southwestern Territory had been very good to Blount.[34]

★ ★ ★

Though no longer governor of the new state, Blount still wanted a government position from which to protect his empire. He became one of the first senators to represent Tennessee in Congress. The greatest threat remained attacks from Indigenous peoples across the region which were encouraged by the Spanish, who wanted to hem in American expansion. Blount came to believe the best way to defend his vast holdings was to instigate a British invasion of North America. A war against Spain would redirect Spanish and Native hostilities away from Blount's lands. Blount conspired with British agents—while a US senator—to make the invasion happen. When the details came to light, Congress erupted. Federalists condemned Blount as a traitor and initiated impeachment proceedings, the first in the nation's history. Blount escaped removal by resigning his office. Returning to Tennessee, he passed his final days convinced he had done everything he could to promote landed interests, especially his own.

William Blount grew up in North Carolina dreaming of buying and selling large amounts of western lands. He viewed political office as a means to achieve those ends. And he came to equate Indigenous dispossession and genocide with stable land values. Blount used and abused the power of the offices he held to become one of the largest landowners in the United States. He worked every angle to make sure the price of western lands did not decrease, including trying to get the federal government to wage war against Indigenous peoples. A thorough scoundrel, his self-interested machinations also produced the state of Tennessee.

"THE SPITTING LYON": MATTHEW LYON AND THE FEDERALISTS' FEARS

SHIRA LURIE

★ ★ ★

When the Federalists, the party in support of the Washington and Adams administrations in the 1790s, imagined the new republic's most obnoxious, repulsive, and lowly scoundrel, their minds likely turned to Matthew Lyon. An Irish immigrant and former indentured servant who ended up in Vermont, Lyon advanced quickly during the nation's early years, amassing property, founding manufacturers, and starting a newspaper for the opposition party, the Republicans.[1] Lyon's humble beginnings, tireless criticism of the government, and influence over his readers marked him as the type of foreign upstart and outspoken radical that the Federalists most dreaded in American politics. When Lyon won a seat in the House of Representatives in 1797, their worst fears of the havoc an unruly immigrant could wreak were realized. He mocked the president, brawled on the chamber floor, and spat in a colleague's face. He was imprisoned for sedition—then won reelection from his jail cell. Congressional Federalists tried, and failed, three times to expel Lyon from the House for his outrageous behavior.

In one sense, Lyon's story is a familiar one about the established upper class's anxieties regarding new-moneyed men who capitalized on the opportunities for political and social status opened by the American Revolution. While elites welcomed a degree of social mobility inherent in republicanism, they worried about the instability of unbridled advancement, especially in politics. The nation was too young and vulnerable for its leadership to be entrusted to just any lucky riser. The American experiment would not last long if "a man who is only fit 'to patch a shoe,' attempts 'to patch the state,'" explained one Federalist. Indeed, previous studies of Matthew Lyon often depict him as representative of these changes and challenges. "He is an early example of the self-made man who embraced the politics of democracy while challenging the control exercised by the social and economic elite," explains one biographer.[2]

But the Federalists' hatred of Lyon ran deeper than mere class anxieties—he struck at the very heart of their vision for the politics of the new republic. The Federalists believed that the success of government by the people required the right kind of leadership. After all, the principle of popular sovereignty meant government would fall if it lost the citizenry's confidence and approval. Only a well-educated, well-bred elite should be trusted to govern. "The people are turbulent and changing; they seldom judge or determine right," observed one man to Secretary of the Treasury Alexander Hamilton. "The rich and well born" must therefore hold "a distinct, permanent share in the government." By properly serving the public good, elite officials would earn the deference of the citizenry needed for a stable and peaceful society. The survival of the republic required that the best people served in government and acted in a way that garnered popular respect and obedience.[3]

But Lyon confounded this elitist vision at every turn. He ridiculed the Federalists' attempts to instill respect and deference as pompous and monarchical. He drummed up popular disapproval of the government and claimed that the wealthy could not be entrusted with power. On more than one occasion, he caused pandemonium on the floor of the

House of Representatives, leading violence and chaos to replace the somber decorum the Federalists hoped would reign. Worst of all, he proved that the citizenry responded to this type of leadership. Whenever the Federalists mocked Lyon's antics and declared him unfit for office, they only increased his popular appeal. Thus, Lyon's success did not just mark the rise of unpolished "new men," but also, and more troublingly, it revealed a citizenry who happily empowered brutes like him.

Lyon proved that the United States would not be the republic the Federalists envisioned. If not quite a republic of scoundrels, then at least one that was less hierarchical, deferential, and orderly than they hoped. One in which even the most obnoxious immigrant could win a seat in Congress. One in which even outrageous and seditious behavior did not disqualify him from office. One in which even the "best sort" could not tame a Lyon.

★ ★ ★

Lyon's life in North America began humbly. He left his home country of Ireland in his early teens and sailed to the colony of Connecticut as an indentured servant in 1764. After completing his indenture, he purchased some land from the colonial government of New Hampshire. However, his holding lay in territory contested by New Hampshire and New York—both governments had granted deeds to the same plots. After the King's Privy Council ruled that the land belonged to New York, the colonial legislature warned all those holding New Hampshire grants that they had to purchase new titles from New York or face eviction. Outraged, many of the New Hampshire landowners, including Lyon, formed their own government and militia. Called the Green Mountain Boys, they resisted any attempted evictions and eventually declared independence from Britain, forming the state of Vermont.[4]

Lyon fought in the Continental Army in the War of Independence, during which he expanded his holdings by buying surrendered

Loyalist property. After the war, he continued to amass new land and established several mills and manufactures. By the early 1790s, Lyon's personal wealth had ballooned considerably. As the national political scene began to fracture into Federalists and Republicans, Lyon seemed to have all the makings of a potential Federalist. "When the struggles commenced between aristocrats and democrats, I had wealth, high political standing, an established character, and powerful connections," he later reflected to a friend. However, "[my] nature, reflection and patriotism led me to take the Democratic side." In particular, Lyon detested the aristocratic lawyers who populated the Federalist party. He bristled at their affection for elites over ordinary citizens, and he despised their affinity for Britain over Revolutionary France. By entering the political fray, Lyon hoped to become "the representative of the commercial, agricultural, and manufacturing interests in preference to any of their law characters." In other words, he would be the voice of hardworking people.[5]

To promote the Republican cause in his home state, Lyon started his own newspaper in the spring of 1793. "I was surrounded by newspapers containing high toned British doctrines," he later wrote, and so, lacking investors, he spent $1,000 of his own money to create the *Farmers' Library*. "By this means the Republican doctrines were scattered through the Northern States," he boasted. The paper circulated domestic and foreign news, with particular attention to developments in France's revolution. It took especial aim at Federalist politicians as "a set of gentry" who "consider the science of government to belong naturally only to a few families." Rather than the reflexive deference preached by the Federalists, Lyon encouraged his readers "to watch over the government; look over their rules; examine their conduct." He hoped this close scrutiny would reveal Federalist elitism and mismanagement, and so inspire support for the Republicans and, eventually, his own bid for a seat in Congress.[6]

In Vermont, Lyon ran for the House of Representatives unsuccessfully three times before finally securing a victory in 1797. In his campaigns, he positioned himself as the hardworking everyman, distinct from the corrupt elites of the Federalist party. "Experience has taught the people of Vermont, that these professional gentlemen are inclined to stand up for the claims of landlords, landjockies, and overgrown landjobbers, in preference, to the poorer sort of people," he asserted in the *Farmer's Library*. He regularly accused his opponents of joining with "a set of aristocrats" in Congress to tax "the hard-earnings of the industrious part of the community" to engross the treasury and enhance the government's power. Instead, "appoint a person to Congress, who despises those . . . appendages of hereditary tyranny," he implored the people of Vermont. They acquiesced in the winter of 1797 after a run-off election won him a majority of nearly four hundred votes.[7]

Once in Congress, Lyon wasted no time in undermining the Federalist vision for American politics. He began his tenure with a refusal to participate in the Congressional procession to President Washington's residence, which he described as "vain adulation." He put forward a motion, subsequently passed, that those who did not wish to wait upon the president be excused. In doing so, Lyon ridiculed the pomp and monarchical trappings with which the Federalists tried to instill respect for the new government. While others scoffed, Lyon explained that "he had spent a great part of his life amongst a people whose love of a plainness of manners forbids all pageantry." He pointed out that "he had no objection to gentlemen of *high blood*" participating, but preferred not to engage in the spectacle. Hence, he positioned himself as a common man and true republican, devoted to political equality and serving the public good. His colleagues came off as silly aristocrats who fawned over the president and wasted time on ridiculous ceremony.[8]

The Federalist press quickly publicized Lyon's contrariness. "The Lyon of Vermont," one paper claimed, "differs considerably from the African lion, is much more clamorous and less magnanimous." The paper referenced Lyon's resolution and "uneasiness at *going with the crowd*." It claimed that his fellow Congressmen "do not hesitate to declare, they think him a most extraordinary beast." Indeed, Albert Gallatin, a Republican Congressman from Pennsylvania, wrote to his wife that the Federalists in Congress viewed "Lyon as a low-life fellow" and had made "a habit of saying very hard things" about him. But Lyon likely shrugged off these aspersions. He was uninterested in forging friendly relations with the Federalists, as his next exploit made clear.[9]

★ ★ ★

On January 30, 1798, House members chatted casually as they waited for a vote count. The speaker of the house, Jonathan Dayton, wandered over to Lyon and struck up a conversation about popular opposition to the new stamp tax in Vermont. Lyon turned the discussion to Connecticut. Raising his voice so it would carry through the chamber, he began making derisive comments about that state's representatives. Lyon asserted that the Connecticut men "were pursuing their own private views, without regarding the interests of the people," that they had "deceived" their constituents and "acted in opposition to the interests and opinion of nine-tenths" of them, and that they were "seeking offices" for personal profit. Lyon boasted that if he were to start a newspaper in Connecticut to combat Federalist misinformation, within half a year the residents would turn on their current representatives. Roger Griswold, a Connecticut Federalist, fired back from his seat, "If you go into Connecticut, you had better wear your wooden sword"—an insulting reference to Lyon's punishment for cowardice during the War of Independence. Lyon, not hearing him, continued his rant. Griswold then rose from his seat and strode over to Lyon. He grabbed Lyon's arm, leaned into him, and repeated the insult. Lyon spat in his face.[10]

The Federalists immediately moved that Lyon be expelled for "disorderly behaviour" due to his "violent attack and gross indecency" against Griswold. The House then referred the matter to a Committee on Breach of Privilege, making Lyon the first Congressman investigated for misconduct in the House of Representatives. The committee endorsed the resolution, stating that Lyon's conduct "was highly indecorous, and unworthy of a member of this House." For the following two weeks, the House debated the matter. The Federalists, for their part, insisted on expulsion as the only way to salvage the body's damaged reputation. He must be removed from Congress, one Federalist said, "as citizens removed *impurities* and *filth* from their docks and wharves." If they failed to do so, they would allow Lyon to debase the entire institution. As another Congressman put it, "the outrage committed by him bid defiance to order and decorum, tended to degrade the members of that House from the rank of men, and to reduce them to a level with the meanest reptile that crawled upon the earth." A third Federalist claimed that "no well-bred, well-disposed man could keep company with him . . . If he must be a legislator, it should be in a part of the world where all decisions were made by *spitting* and *scratching*." During the debate, Lyon defended his actions by pointing out that the House was not in order when the altercation occurred and so had no business investigating it. As for his conduct, Lyon justified his actions as a legitimate defense of his honor. "I never did receive injuries with impunity," he affirmed, "nor did I come here to do so." In the end, the resolution won fifty-two yea votes to forty-four nay votes, but it fell short of the two-thirds majority required for expulsion.[11]

The Federalist press then took up the fight, none more enthusiastically than William Cobbett, the editor of *Porcupine's Gazette*. Cobbett relayed the "filthy conduct of this spitting hero" to his readers, careful to remind them that Lyon was "an Irishman, and a furious democrat" elected by the "*enlightened* republicans of Vermont." Dripping with sarcasm, Cobbett wrote of Lyon's "*decent* conduct . . . so highly honourable to democracy" in "*spit[ting]* the nauseous slime from his jaws in the face of ROGER GRISWOLD." Elsewhere, Federalist editors shared the joke of a new, strange creature called the "spitting LYON of Vermont" whose "faculty of Spitting" led naturalists to conclude that he was of a "mongrel breed" who needed to be caged. Even in their correspondence, Federalists insisted that "the spitter Lion is a great beast." The *Federal Gazette* published a pretend advertisement for "A Treatise on the Polite Accomplishment of Spitting, &c, by Matthew Lyon." In their mockery, the Federalists aimed to demonstrate Lyon's unfitness for public office. He behaved like a brute, not a member of Congress. One writer suggested Griswold should "resolve to beat this fellow daily" since "surely Mr. Griswold should never sit again with him as an equal and gentleman." Griswold took the advice.[12]

On February 15, just a few days after the House had failed to expel Lyon, Griswold strode into the chamber carrying a freshly purchased hickory walking stick. He walked over to Lyon, who was seated with his head down over his desk and so did not see Griswold approach. Griswold called Lyon "a scoundrel," raised the stick high above his head, and brought it down on his foe. He continued to rain down blows as a startled Lyon struggled to get out from behind his desk. Once free, Lyon tried to grab Griswold, but Griswold kept him at bay with an unrelenting barrage of strikes. Lyon ran for the fireplace behind the speaker's chair and grabbed the tongs kept there. He tried to strike Griswold's head with them, but Griswold parried the blow with his stick. The men then wrestled to the floor. Griswold pinned Lyon and landed a few punches before onlookers tore the two apart and the speaker called the House to order.[13]

Like the previous Federalist editorials, Griswold's attack painted Lyon as beneath his office. As historian Manisha Sinha has observed, the early American honor code required that gentlemen sort insults between them through the ritual of duelling. To beat someone with a cane instead marked them as an inferior—a form of violence reserved for the correction of women, children, servants, and enslaved people. Indeed, Federalist newspapers described the attack with the language of "chastisement" and "discipline." The Rutland *Herald*, for instance, commended Griswold for "bestow[ing] merited chastisement on the brute who dared to enter the society of civilized men." By punishing Lyon for his unruly behavior, Griswold publicly shamed him as an unequal and unsuited to government.[14]

The following day, the House considered a resolution expelling both Griswold and Lyon for "violent and disorderly behaviour." Several Republicans rose in Lyon's defense, claiming he had been the victim of the attack and the Federalists clearly had a vendetta against him. "We are still hunting the Lyon," Gallatin lamented to his wife, "and it is indeed the most unpleasant and unprofitable business that ever a respectable representative body did pursue." Once again, the Committee of Privileges investigated, but this time recommended both members be allowed to stay, though it did not provide a rationale. The House voted seventy-three to twenty-one in favor of the committee's recommendation. Lyon, once again, escaped expulsion.[15]

The press, of course, spread news of the event far and wide. Republicans commented that Griswold accosting Lyon without warning and while he was unarmed revealed "a most cowardly spirit." Clearly, they contended, Lyon was an "honest, independent, and manly supporter of the liberties and interests of the people, [who had roused] the vengeance of the aristocratic faction." But the Federalists insisted that Griswold carried out a legitimate and necessary defense against an unworthy foe. "Mr. GRISWOLD, who was determined to be the avenger of his own honor and who could never find *Lyon* at the city Coffee-House, or any other resort of gentlemen, was determined to take vengeance on him wherever he was to be found," the *Columbian Centinel* explained. The Federalists emphasized the legitimacy of Griswold's actions by pointing out the care and deliberation with which he delivered the blows: "he humanely avoid[ed] as much as possible to strike [Lyon's] head," when he "could have beaten him to atoms." All in all, they blamed Lyon for stirring up trouble and undermining the House's decorum. Griswold's actions were a natural consequence of allowing unruly men into the legislature.[16]

★ ★ ★

Amid the fallout from the fight, the divide between the Federalists and Republicans grew even starker over a series of French naval attacks on American shipping, an event known as the Quasi-War. President John Adams sent envoys to France to negotiate a peaceful end to the conflict, but they returned home without a deal. The publication of their dispatches, termed the XYZ Affair, exposed French demands for a sizable bribe before beginning negotiations. The revelation turned public opinion against France and their Republican allies. The Federalists used this momentum to pass new taxes and measures aimed at putting the nation on a war footing. The Sedition Law (1798) proved to be one of the most controversial of these policies since it criminalized any false criticism of the government and its officials. The Republicans denounced the law as a blatant effort to silence critics, but the Federalists defended it as a necessary safeguard for government at a time of heightened national security risk. Lyon decried it as the Federalists' attempt "to have all your follies, your absurdities and your atrocities buried in oblivion . . . to shut the mouths of all but sycophants and flatterers" and to maintain through censorship their grip on power.[17]

These developments colored the 1798 midterm campaign in which the Federalists looked to widen their majority and, hopefully, unseat Lyon. To this end, *Spooner's Vermont Journal* published a vicious letter attacking him. The anonymous author accused Lyon of "protruding yourself into business and company for which you are totally unfit." It was only through "bribery, forgery and corruption" that Lyon had won a seat in Congress and, once there, his behaviour "would disgrace even a *savage*." What was more, he and the other Republicans opposed the Federalists in a plot to weaken the government so France could take control. Only "an absolute idiot," concluded the author, would re-elect such an "infernal rascal and traitor."[18]

Lyon fired back in a letter of his own. The writer, he said, "must have drawn his foolish, monarchical doctrine from the speeches of the Connecticut members in Congress." He accused the writer of, like other Federalists, fanning the flames of anti-French feeling to justify enlarging the executive branch's power. As for his criticism of the Federalists, Lyon refused to blindly support a president and party who did not serve the public good. "When I see every consideration of the public welfare swallowed up in a continual grasp for power, in an unbounded thirst for ridiculous pomp, foolish adulation, or selfish avarice," he wrote, "I shall not be their humble advocate." That did not make him a traitor and conspirator, but rather a patriot.[19]

However, Lyon was not content to limit his reelection campaign to the partisan press. Having returned to Vermont from Philadelphia, he aimed to re-energize Republican sentiment on the ground. To do so, he made use of a letter written by fellow Republican Joel Barlow in which Barlow criticized President Adams and the Federalists' war preparations. "The misunderstanding between the two governments (France and the United States), has become extremely alarming," Barlow wrote. "Confidence is completely destroyed, mistrusts, jealousy, and a disposition to a wrong attribution of motives, are so apparent, as to require the utmost caution in every word and action that are to come from your Executive." The president's misjudgment of the French was so egregious, Barlow mused, that he wondered why Congress had not committed Adams to a "mad house." Lyon carried the letter throughout his campaign travels and read it aloud to all who would listen. He used it to drum up anti-Federalist feeling and squash any lingering fears from the XYZ Affair.[20]

The Federalists saw in these activities the chance to silence Lyon once and for all. Just a few weeks before the midterms, the federal court in Vermont indicted him for violating the Sedition Law. The court deemed Lyon "a malicious and seditious person, and of a depraved mind and wicked and diabolical disposition" who "deceitfully, wickedly, and maliciously contriv[ed] to defame the Government of the United States . . . and to bring the said Government and President into contempt and disrepute." The court based the charges on Lyon's piece in *Spooner's Vermont Journal* and his dissemination of Barlow's letter. Both aimed to weaken public confidence and trust in government with "false, feigned, scandalous, and malicious matters." Thus, Lyon became the first person charged under the new Sedition Law.[21]

He surrendered to authorities and pled "not guilty" the next morning in a Rutland court. At the ensuing trial, Lyon tried to claim that the Sedition Law was unconstitutional, but the court rejected the argument. Witnesses for the prosecution attested to the fact that Lyon "had extensively used the [Barlow] letter for political purposes, and in doing so had frequently made use of language highly disrespectful to the administration." Representing himself, Lyon argued that since the law was unconstitutional, the court had no jurisdiction to prosecute him. In addition, as the Sedition Law criminalized only false criticisms of the government, he maintained his innocence since the accusations he had made against the president were true. To prove this point, Lyon boldly called the presiding judge, William Paterson, as a witness for the defense. In his examination, Lyon asked the judge whether he had "observed [the president's] ridiculous pomp and parade" on the occasions when the two had dined together. When Paterson replied in the negative, Lyon pressed him, asking if the president's table had "more pomp and servants there, than at the tavern at Rutland?" Paterson refused to reply. With this unconventional move, Lyon undermined the seriousness of his trial and, once again, made the Federalists look foolish. He also demonstrated the Sedition Law's flaw in pivoting on truth, which, in this instance, was subjective.[22]

In his charge to the jury, Judge Paterson instructed that this case was not about the constitutionality of the Sedition Law, as Lyon had tried to claim. Rather, the jury simply had to judge whether Lyon had violated the law as it currently existed. After an hour's deliberation, the jury returned and pronounced Lyon guilty. At his sentencing the following morning, Lyon explained that recent economic misfortunes had left him unable to pay a heavy fine. Unmoved, the judge chastised Lyon for breaking the law, particularly as a congressman. "No one, also, can be better acquainted than yourself with the existence and nature of the act," he declared. And so, "a fine alone" would be insufficient. Instead, he sentenced Lyon to four months imprisonment, along with a heavy fine of $1,000, plus court costs. "This sentence was unexpected to all my friends as well as myself," Lyon wrote later. "No one expected imprisonment." Indeed, it likely concerned many Republicans that the Federalists were willing to jail one of their political enemies for his outspoken criticism.[23]

As it turned out, the Federalists could not have provided Lyon with a better platform for his reelection campaign. Their repeated attempts to delegitimize him only made Lyon a more compelling figure to his constituents and the partisan press. From jail, Lyon penned plaintive accounts of his mistreatment that Republican newspapers circulated throughout the country. "This cell is the common receptacle for horse-thieves, money makers, runaway negroes, or any kind of felons," he reported. "It is about 16 feet long by 12 wide, with a necessary in one corner, which affords a stench about equaly to the Philadelphia docks, in the month of August." The cell had no light except for a small, glassless window that made for frigid nights. Still, Lyon claimed that he shared his plight not for pity, but as a warning: "I never thought myself fit for a martyr, but I bear what they put upon me with a degree of cheerfulness, in hopes the people of the United States will profit by the lesson." Lyon knew his imprisonment would shock the nation and paint the Federalists as tyrants and cowards.[24]

Republican and Federalist newspapers spun Lyon's situation for their own purposes. Republican printers described Lyon as "the first sacrifice on the altar of the Sedition Bill" and a frightful sign of prosecutions to come. But the Federalists scoffed at Lyon's lamentations and mocked his false suffering. His "nasty cell or hole as he calls it," wrote one paper, "is a room in one of the most elegant houses in town." Another claimed that Lyon was "in good spirits, and better health than he was in previous to his confinement." As ever, his motives for spreading untrue tales of suffering were obvious: "It is presumed that he published those notorious falsehoods for the sole purpose of making the public believe that cruelty and inhumanity are added to his confinement in order to gain partizans to the Democratic cause." But they felt optimistic that it would not work. Rather, the Federalists hoped

Lyon's imprisonment would convince "the lately deluded clan of this filthy reproach to humanity" to abandon him. Of course, the opposite occurred. In a widely published letter, Lyon's friend Steven T. Mason informed him that his description of his imprisonment "will tend more to open the eyes of our fellow citizens than all the speeches of all the republican orators in the last two sessions of congress."[25]

Indeed, that January, Lyon received word that the western district of Vermont had reelected him, making him the first (and, as of this writing, only) person elected to Congress from jail. Lyon wrote a letter, later published in Republican newspapers, thanking the voters and once again excoriating the Federalists: "Although two judges and thirty jurymen have been found to declare your representative guilty of evil intentions, more than three thousand five hundred enlightened freemen have declared him NOT GUILTY." The only crimes he had committed, Lyon maintained, were "refusing to sacrifice [his constituents'] sacred trust to the views of those who wish to see a luxurious court." He would return to Congress as committed as ever to serve the common man and challenge his opponents' elitism.[26]

The Federalists, despite a significant midterm victory, lamented Lyon's triumph. "Tho' depriv'd of his seat at present, [he] will once more disgrace the Council of a great Nation," bemoaned one Federalist editor. Another pondered whether Congress would honor him with a "*new carpet* to *spit upon*." Federalist papers revived their charges that Lyon was a "vile beast," "King of all Beasts," and, as one paper asserted, the king of "beastiality." But most of all, the Federalists were distraught that the voters of Vermont could stand to re-elect Lyon. "How lost to decency [are] the servile advocates of such an animal!" declared the *Spectator*. Elsewhere, editors commented that Lyon made the perfect representative for "the *lowest* class of citizens," those "who may want an advocate for sedition," and Vermont's "ill manners, seditious dispositions, low intrigues and Irish league of insurrection." The Federalists felt deeply troubled at what Lyon's reelection revealed about their fellow countrymen.[27]

Despite his electoral victory, Lyon remained in jail, which put his constituents in the odd situation of having elected a representative who could not, at present, represent them in Congress. Several thousand people attempted to remedy this in a petition addressed to the president asking him to pardon Lyon. In it, they insisted that any claims of a Republican preference for France were false and that neither they nor Lyon posed a danger to the United States. They asked Adams to address the "disagreeable situation" in which "the man who is our legal Representative, who has by no means lost our confidence, is confined in a dreary and uncomfortable prison, and at a time when his service will soon be requisite in the National Legislature." After learning it was his constituents, and not Lyon himself, who petitioned for a pardon, Adams refused, stating that "penitence must precede pardon." The Republican printers grumbled about this hard line and told their readers that such authoritarianism was "what ye are to expect from the hand of power." Lyon served his entire four-month sentence and, with the help of some fundraising, paid his fine.[28]

Upon his release that February, he enjoyed a hero's welcome. Republicans in Bennington greeted him with two songs written in his honor and a speech extolling his bravery and patriotism. "I heartily congratulate you on your escape from the fangs of merciless power," proclaimed the speaker. "You have been deprived of social comforts, but your spirits have evidently surmounted your trials." As Lyon travelled to Philadelphia, Republicans elsewhere likewise celebrated him. The Federalist press mocked these displays. "Immediately on his arrival he received the adorations of all the Democrats, of our country, who were not averse to partake of his saliva," scoffed one editor. But Republican excitement could not be dampened as Lyon triumphantly returned to the capital.[29]

His reception in Congress was not as warm. Lyon had barely sat down at his desk before Federalist Congressman James A. Bayard of Delaware presented a resolution for Lyon's expulsion based on his prior conviction of "a crime not only affecting the members of this House, but the whole community, as its consequences go to the subversion of government." Republicans, of course, clamored to Lyon's defense. In doing so, they once again denounced the Sedition Law and warned of a troubling precedent if the Federalists succeeded in purging their political enemies from the legislature. As Gallatin explained, if the resolution passed, then "every member who shall write anything which is contrary to the opinion of a majority of this House, whether what he writes be founded in truth or not will be liable to be expelled, in order to purify the House." For the third time, Lyon narrowly avoided expulsion. The forty-nine to forty-five vote in favor failed to reach the required two-thirds majority.[30]

In the end, Lyon's second term progressed more quietly than his first and he quickly turned his attention to the presidential election of 1800, a critical referendum on President Adams and the Federalists. During the campaign, Lyon toured Republican candidate Thomas Jefferson's home state of Virginia. Everywhere he went, people flocked to him, eager to glimpse the infamous "Spitting Lyon" and hear him extol the virtues of Jefferson and the Republicans. "Being just out of prison, I was looked at a martyr," Lyon later recalled, "and every word [I said] had weight." Yet again, he made plain the Federalists' miscalculation—their attempts to silence Lyon only ended up amplifying him.[31]

The Republicans won the election, although a tie in the Electoral College between Jefferson and his running mate Aaron Burr forced the contest into the House of Representatives. The House deadlocked between the Federalists, who favored Burr, and the Republicans, who backed Jefferson. After thirty-five successive ties, a breakthrough for Jefferson finally occurred. Since the state of Vermont fell last alphabetically, Lyon enjoyed the poetic justice of casting the final vote for Jefferson. Although, perhaps, he had signalled the Federalists' impending defeat long before.[32]

★ ★ ★

Throughout his many tangles with the Federalists, Lyon proved repeatedly that their brand of elitism was incompatible with a democratic republic. He revealed the inconsistencies of their pomp and ritual with the political equality embedded in republicanism. He questioned whether the high-born were truly best suited to govern. He showed that Congress was not a sacred and enlightened chamber isolated from the ugliness of the real world. He argued that citizens should scrutinize and criticize those in power, not blindly obey them.

More fundamentally, he made manifest the Federalist nightmare lurking beneath the surface of popular sovereignty. If anyone could hold political office, it was possible that the "wrong sort" would attain power. If the people chose their rulers, there would always be the chance they would choose poorly. Lyon showed not only the kind of havoc the unpolished could wreak, but also, and more troublingly, that the citizenry would elect (and re-elect) him. The problem with the Federalist vision for a hierarchical and deferential republican politics was that it required that the people acquiesce. And sometimes they did not.

The Federalists could not defeat Lyon, and perhaps their failure carries a warning for our own time. The attempt to weaken one's distasteful political opponents through ridicule, mockery, and expressions of outrage did not work then, and it does not work now. Too often, such tactics just enhance these individuals' popularity. Instead of looking down on them and their supporters, we might do better to seriously and humbly contemplate the nature of their appeal. And so, confront the real America, scoundrels and all.

THE DEVIL FROM DEDHAM: JASON FAIRBANKS AND THE FAILURE OF MANLY VIRTUE

CRAIG BRUCE SMITH

★ ★ ★

On August 8, 1801, prisoner Jason Fairbanks was led through the doors of the sweltering First Parish Church Meeting House in Dedham, a growing Massachusetts market town of some two thousand people, twelve miles southwest of Boston along the Charles River. Standing about six feet tall, Fairbanks's right arm dangled lifelessly beneath the dark blue topcoat resting on his shoulders. Slightly concealed by strands of dark hair, tears trickled down his pale, pockmarked face. The packed audience stared at Fairbanks and his "unwell" and "weakly" appearance. Days before, this same "throng of anxious spectators" had overwhelmed Dedham's courthouse, creating a scene "never before witnessed in this place" and necessitating a move to the more spacious meetinghouse. This day's proceedings were the culmination of an event that had gripped the minds and tongues of New Englanders for months: the death of Elizabeth Fales.[1]

They had met in the fall of 1796 at a singing class in the very same First Parish Church Meeting House. Jason Fairbanks was the youngest son of a respectable Dedham family; he had ambitions to be accounted a gentleman, despite having lost the use of his right arm and being dismissed from the prestigious Wrentham Academy, his expected gateway to Harvard College. Elizabeth Fales was a "self-taught" lover of music and literature from another long-established Dedham family who lived about a mile away. He was seventeen. She was thirteen.

In the following years, their friendship blossomed into something more—or so Fairbanks thought. Fales was "infinitely engaging" and her beauty was like "the Grecian Helen" of Troy, an observer said. True, her family was cool to Fairbanks's suitability as a match, but in New England marriages for love dated to Puritan times, becoming more common in the youth-empowering days after the Revolution. In Fairbanks's mind, Elizabeth Fales was destined to be his wife.[2]

On May 18, 1801, Fairbanks determined to make the union happen. With a forged marriage certificate and a small knife in his pocket, Fairbanks waited for his beloved in Mason's Pasture near their homes, where Fales had agreed to meet, not knowing he had already hired a carriage to spirit them to Wrentham, Massachusetts, seventeen miles away.[3]

A shriek broke the silence. Cries of "O dear!" rang out. Fales, covered in blood, fell to the ground. Fairbanks, also bleeding, stumbled towards the Fales's house. Fairbanks presented an awful sight with thirteen wounds that, he told her family, he had inflicted himself in a frenzy of grief. Elizabeth, he swore, had killed herself.

At roughly 2:15 P.M., Elizabeth's father and uncle discovered her lying in the brush, blood soaked but alive—barely. She asked for water. It was too late. Within a half hour, she was dead. A doctor's examination revealed the extent of her trauma: forearm slashed, chest riddled with eleven stab wounds, throat sliced. Between the shoulder blades was a four-inch "mortal wound" cutting fatally close to the spine. Fairbanks claimed it was a botched double suicide, using the same penknife. Not believing the explanation, authorities arrested Fairbanks and charged him with murder. The trial caused a sensation across the country and across centuries.[4]

Murders in northern states were rare at the turn of the nineteenth century, since "homogeneity and continuity within the population" kept it (supposedly) "virtually impossible." Elizabeth Fales's death caused a scandal throughout Massachusetts, while news of Fairbanks's trial reached President Thomas Jefferson. It popularized the sale of trial records and made Fairbanks notable enough to have his wax figure displayed throughout New England alongside one of George Washington in a traveling exhibit. The incident was so infamous that the *New York Times* and the *Saturday Evening Post* reported on it into the twentieth century. "No trial in our Courts of Justice," reported the *Columbian Centinel* in 1801, "has excited so much sympathy and horror: and nothing perhaps in history, or fiction, exceeded the remarkable facts which gave it rise."[5]

But beyond the long-lasting spectacle, the death of Elizabeth Fales and the trial of her would-be lover highlights the role of virtue, community standards, and post-Revolution generational divides. With Fairbanks the only witness, the trial—in both the court of law and in the court of public opinion—turned on the question not simply of what happened but of weighing reputations.

Reputation, or character, was tied to one's virtue and honor. Virtue traditionally was linked to morality, and honor to reputation. The American Revolution democratized and joined these concepts into a collective ethical ideal of the greater good. But older notions of personal honor, impacted by social status, remained. Honor and its trappings always had a communal component. It was not enough for one to deem themselves honorable; the community had to agree. As Massachusetts-born patriot and president John Adams put it, society expected citizens to exercise "hardy manly Virtues." Did Jason Fairbanks possess a reputation for hardy, manly virtues? Then maybe he told the truth about what happened in Mason's Pasture, however unlikely. Or was he a scoundrel who of course would also be a murderer?[6]

Previously, scholarship on this case has focused on real and imagined connections to politics or sentimentalist fiction. This chapter offers a narrative interpretation of republican virtue lost. Confusion over Fairbanks's motive/psyche, gaps in the sources, and conflicting evidence makes the account admittedly speculative. No one can definitively answer what happened and why. But there is a possible solution: that the saga of Fairbanks and Fales (and the broader suspicion of Dedham) was linked to a failure to uphold societal expectations of republican virtue in the wake of the American Revolution. The reader is invited to investigate the clues.[7]

★ ★ ★

Jason Fairbanks was born in Dedham on September 25, 1780 (by coincidence the same day as Benedict Arnold's treason). Dedham was a growing market town of some two thousand people, twelve miles southwest of Boston along the Charles River. Though overshadowed by Boston, Dedham was a patriot stronghold during the Revolution. Its people had supported colonial resistance "with great unanimity" since the Stamp Act (1765). One resident joined the 1774 Suffolk Resolves committee, which formalized Massachusetts's opposition to Parliament following the Coercive Acts (1774). By May 1776, the town meeting "unanimously" resolved to support independence. More than 650 Dedham men served in the Revolution, accounting for "virtually the entire male population."[8]

As the youngest of the six children of Ebenezer Fairbanks and Prudence Farrington Fairbanks, Jason was only a baby when the war ended, and he grew up surrounded by family who fought for liberty. Jason's father, brothers, uncles, and cousins had answered the Lexington Alarm as minutemen, repulsed the British at Bunker Hill, and served throughout the war. Second cousin Captain David Fairbanks was elected to lead a militia company, and Jason's sister married Captain Eliphalet Pond. "The muster was almost a family reunion," writes historian Robert Gross, "All joined together not so much by a chain of command as a complex network of kinship."[9]

The young Jason was "beloved" by his family and doted upon by his brother Ebenezer Jr. and sister Prudence, both in their twenties and already raising their own families when Jason came along. The same age as his nieces and nephews, Jason viewed his eldest brother and sister more as his parents than as siblings—Prudence even suckled him. For Jason, the legacy of the Revolution was always present. Imagine the tales Uncle Israel and brother Ebenezer Jr. shared of their march to Lexington and Concord as the family crowded around the hearth. Perhaps the anonymous Needham signal rider was even transformed into Paul Revere? Against the sounds of a roaring wood fire, Israel could have regaled the awed Fairbanks children of his engaging the retreating British Army in Menotomy. Uncle Benjamin could relive Bunker Hill and waiting until he saw the "whites of their eyes." It's not hard to picture Jason playing soldier on the common, where the militia mustered and drilled. There was a chance of some future war or service as a militiaman. As recently as 1786, the Dedham militia proved its valor and national loyalty by suppressing Shays' Rebellion, a western Massachusetts farmers' revolt. Similar bravery seemed to be Jason's destiny.[10]

But as Jason grew up, his age emerged as a key source of anxiety. He had missed out on the Revolution, the most important event in the lives of his family and community. It was a common predicament for the post-Revolutionary generation, those too young to have taken part in the war or who were born immediately afterwards. They were saddled with an insurmountable legacy. As historian Lorri Glover said of these youths, "they knew all the ways they might fail to live up to the expectations of the revolutionary age, but how could they ever succeed? How could even the most virtuous, accomplished, and dutiful children match the reputations of their fathers, the founders?"[11]

If Jason Fairbanks hoped to claim his share of his family's military glory, those dreams ended in 1792 when he suffered a permanent disability after receiving a smallpox inoculation. Amidst an epidemic, the Dedham town meeting voted for a "general inoculation," which included introducing a weakened—but live—form of the virus for the body to learn to defeat and provide future immunity. The twelve-year-old Fairbanks developed a virulent case. Treated with mercury, which exacerbated the illness, he lost the use of his right arm. By coincidence, that same year Congress and President Washington established a national militia that barred anyone not "able-bodied." Fairbanks could never serve his nation.[12]

Determined not to be thought idle, a deadly sin in Massachusetts dating back to the Puritans, Fairbanks embarked on a different path to manly virtue. He was to be a gentleman, enrolling at the Wrentham Academy. Most students attended a local public school. It was no small endeavor for a farmer's son to attend a private academy; it flaunted the family's perceived status. Adding pressure, they declared him destined for Harvard College. Attending college would protect Fairbanks against accusations of idleness, unmanliness, and immorality that might accompany his disability. For as President John Adams wrote to Harvard's students in 1798, espousing praise for "honor" and shame for "dishonor," "the studious youth of this country, in all our universities, could not fail to be animated with the intrepid spirit of their ancestors." Fairbanks could look for inspiration to Dedham's other Harvard-educated gentlemen: Dr. John Sprague (Massachusetts Constitutional Convention of 1779 delegate), Rev. Dr. Thomas Thatcher of Dedham's Third Parish (Constitutional ratifying convention delegate), and the Ames brothers ("manly" eloquent lawyer-turned-US-Congressman Fisher and Son of Liberty and physician Nathaniel).[13]

An academy did not necessarily lead to a gentleman's status, however. It could be the fast track to college or a cheap alternative. Dartmouth graduate and author Thomas Green Fessenden, for example, mocked the academy strategy to win gentility. "Though father say he can't afford/To make a grand college-learn'd lad o'me,/ He'll pay Indian corn for my board,/ And send me a month to an academy," Fessenden laughed. Moreover, the Dedham community did not take kindly to social climbers or academies. Their public school (founded in 1649) was good enough. Opposition to academies occurred throughout New England, historian Mark Boonshoft suggests, because towns feared a usurpation of local power to produce an aristocratic class. In 1827, Erastus Worthington echoed the sentiment that "heretofore many individuals have viewed the advantages of a good education in no other light than that of conferring a dangerous superiority over their neighbors." But this fear of a neighbor's "superiority" was not only tied to education.[14]

Since its founding in 1636, Dedham was known for its "fully developed social structure," based on "rank, quality, deserts [worthiness] and usefulness either in the church or commonwealth." Yet in the new United States, the concept of rank, or unearned status, and birth-based hierarchy was met with open suspicion. The greater good of the nation, the state, or the town was what mattered. But older notions survived. Though professing to believe in "equality" and reject "hereditary distinctions," the Fairbankses, among Dedham's earliest residents, reveled in lineage and family honor. A turner and wheelwright, ancestor Jonathan Fairbanks was an original signer of the "Dedham Covenant," a town charter, in 1636 and built the family's timber home (which still stands as the oldest of its type in Massachusetts). While only of middling status, Ebenezer Jr. labeled others as "inferior individuals."[15]

Fairbanks's climb up the social ladder via his education at Wrentham ended suddenly. Struck by "nervous headaches," he was forced to withdraw. A classmate thought the headaches were an excuse. Dismissing any "invisible" affliction, the classmate, writing anonymously but calling himself a "gentleman," said the headaches were a result of Fairbanks's immoral "excesses." Whatever the cause of his affliction, Fairbanks came back a changed man, and not in a good way. Having tasted the life of a genteel scholar, many academy students like Fairbanks refused to perform manual labor when they returned home. Author Thomas Fessenden mocked the self-anointed "young gentlemen" and stereotyped them as "apt to suppose themselves to be personages of too much consequence." Academy graduates expected to "crowd themselves into the learned profession," he complained, "without any of the requisite qualifications." Luckily, Fairbanks's brother-in-law Eliphalet rescued him from working with his hands, promptly offering him a job as a writer at the Office of the Register of Deeds. But poor health struck again. Lockjaw and "bleeding of the lungs, cough, and hectic fever" quickly shattered "a thousand brilliant prospects for his riper years."[16]

Unable to work and living in his parents' house, Fairbanks remained trapped in an extended childhood. He resorted to fighting with young men to prove himself. But even women and children bested him in strength. As Fairbanks's eighteen-year-old niece, Sukey Davis, recalled, "he had a scuffle with a [four-year-old] little boy, about going to school . . . the boy refused to go, and got away from him." Davis, who also tussled with Fairbanks, said she could "hold him [off] very easy" and that Fairbanks was "fatigued" for "several hours" afterwards.[17]

Lacking in manly physicality, Fairbanks retreated into books to play the gentleman. Fairbanks read vigorously, largely about history, politics, and philosophy. He was probably among the "studious" "few" that rented or purchased books from Nathaniel and Benjamin Heaton's print shop (before Herman Mann took over). The limited titles on the shelves included *American Independence*, *The Life of Thomas Paine*, *The Memoirs of General Heath*, and Baron von Steuben's *Regulations* (required reading for militia officers)—all reminders of the Revolution, and his own shortcomings. One local book garnered national attention. Herman Mann's *The Female Review*, a biography of decorated Revolutionary veteran Deborah Sampson (Gannett) who lived nearby in Sharon. She had served in the Massachusetts's Regiment's light infantry disguised as a man. Sampson's story was heralded as an "unprecedented achievement o[f] *female heroism* and *virtue*" by the *Columbia Minerva*. Sampson maintained the peak traits of two sexes. She remained chaste, kept her female "virtue," and displayed "manly" courage and patriotic spirit. Did Fairbanks read the book? Who knows, but he certainly knew her story—and how it highlighted his failures.[18]

★ ★ ★

As Fairbanks cast about for a future, he met Elizabeth Fales in singing class. The two bonded over a love of music and novels. Fairbanks's romantic intentions were obvious. Fales's sentiments were less certain. Her mother and sister Polly denied any attraction. Others disagreed, speaking of the pair meeting several times a week. Only days before her death, it was alleged during the trial, she had stayed overnight with Jason "in his own apartment, without witness . . . until the day dawned." Fairbanks bragged to his family that he had proof of her love: letters he grandiosely held to his heart before conspicuously and conveniently burning them in the fireplace.[19]

Fairbanks said he was shown "the greatest respect" by her relations for a time—allowing him to appear to be a gentleman. That was until he made a snide comment about the drinking habits of the suitor of Elizabeth's sister Clarissa. Then the Faleses accused Fairbanks of circulating an unfavorable poem about Mrs. Fales. Suddenly, Elizabeth stopped seeing him. Fairbanks cried sabotage. Her family denied it, but an idle man with no prospects was not any parent's first choice.[20]

Fairbanks's chances took another hit when his family's reputation suffered in the shadow of national politics. In 1798, Jason's uncle Benjamin was arrested for sedition after Democratic-Republicans raised a Revolutionary-style liberty pole in town meant to protest President Adams's Sedition Act of 1798, which barred falsely speaking against the government during the undeclared Quasi-War with France. Federalists labeled the "Dedham Jacobin pole" a clear "rallying point of insurrection and civil war." After his arrest, Benjamin Fairbanks claimed he had been led astray. Surprisingly, Fisher Ames, only months after leading Dedham's "Federalist Fourth of July," vouched for Benjamin Fairbanks's character. Benjamin had fought at Bunker Hill and was thus "a zealous friend of the cause of our revolution," Ames contented. As a result, Benjamin was imprisoned for only six hours and fined five dollars. But to outsiders the affair marked Dedham a "Republican stronghold," and Judge John Lowell (a former Revolutionary militia major and Massachusetts representative) associated the event with Shays' Rebellion, reminding Benjamin that "in 1786 he would have been committed to close gaol." Still, reputation mattered in Dedham and the incident marred the Fairbanks name. It may have also soured the Fales family on a connection with them.[21]

About the same time, Elizabeth Fales fixed her gaze on a mysterious Mr. Sprague. Little is known about this rival, including his first name, but her father, Nehemiah Fales, called him "Mr.," implying a gentleman. This admirer was probably a distant relation of Dr. John Sprague, an old acquaintance of Declaration of Independence signers Robert Treat Paine and John Adams, who owned a "beautiful" manor house in town. This suitor probably represented everything that Fairbanks wished to be. But after a brief "attentive" period, Sprague left for New York and married another woman—leaving Fales "a great deal disturbed." Equally shaken, Fairbanks vowed to "have no more to do with her."[22]

The vow did not last. In early 1801, Fairbanks reignited his marriage quest. The intervening years had neither improved Fairbanks economic prospects nor enhanced his social status. His poor health continued. In May, fresh off a home confinement hacking up blood, Fairbanks made a fatalistic conclusion. He "did not think he should live three months" and wanted to marry now to validate his worth and his manhood. He had, he said, "waited long enough." Marriage was the one thing he could do to finally prove he was an independent man. Fairbanks fixed on Elizabeth Fales as the means to his goal, regardless of the consequences. The day before the fatal encounter, Fairbanks told his friend Reuben Farrington that he would "violate her chastity, or carry her to Wrentham, to be married." Since the colonial era, New England men "often tried to frame their threats or acts of violence as disciplinary acts," according to historian Anne Lombard. Apparently, it wasn't the first time Fairbanks had made such horrifying comments. Perhaps that's why Farrington dismissed it as "only in fun."[23]

On May 18, 1801, Fairbanks waited for Fales in Mason's Pasture. She had no sense of doom as she strolled toward their prearranged meeting. A short time later, she lay dying in the brush. On May 20, Fales's casket was marched through the streets by two thousand people, practically the entire town, in "the greatest funeral procession" Dr. Ames ever witnessed. The next day, Fairbanks, now suffering from tetanus, was carried from the Fales's second-floor bedroom where he was recovering to the local jail. He would stay there for over two months awaiting the grand jury. The question lingered: Was it murder or suicide?[24]

★ ★ ★

Period literature primed the public with tales of seduction, female stereotypes, "hysterics," and suicide. In July, the *Columbia Minerva* featured the story of Patty Shoals who "cut her throat in a most shocking manner" because of a fortune-teller's prediction. Local memory also recalled Dedham visitor Faith Trumbull Huntington (Connecticut governor Jonathan Trumbull's daughter and painter John Trumbull's sister) becoming "delusional and despondent" over her separation from her husband during the Siege of Boston in 1775. She later hanged herself. These tales intertwined in the minds of Dedham residents, which added to the confusion, as did *Columbia Minerva* editor Mann calling Fales's death not a murder but a "MELANCHOLY CATASTROPHE!"[25]

On August 4, Justice Robert Treat Paine, Continental Congressman and Declaration signer, arrived at the Dedham Supreme Judicial Court. He felt that only "allegiance to country" and "devotion to government" could "prove" the post-Revolutionary generation "worthy of the rights they inherit from their high-minded ancestors." Murder, he believed, was contrary to "social duty." Junior judges Simeon Strong (the Massachusetts governor's cousin) and Thomas Dawes Jr. (son of the patriot of the same name) assisted. The twenty jurors, all "very respectable men," charged Fairbanks with murder. Two days later, Justice Francis Dana joined the others in opening the trial at the First Parish Church Meeting House, presiding from just below the pulpit.[26]

As expected, Fairbanks pled not guilty. At first glance, the task for each side seemed straightforward. Though Fairbanks's threats against Fales were impossible to ignore, his disability suggested he was physically unable to commit the crime. For the defense to make him appear weak and feeble threatened his masculinity, damaging his character, which was the best guarantee he had acted virtuously. But to make him appear too physically strong, too masculine, made it seem more likely he could kill. The prosecution faced the conundrum in reverse: attack his character and he would appear weak—and incapable of murder.[27]

In the crowd for all three days of the trial was floundering, alcoholic lawyer Thomas Boylston Adams, recently and begrudgingly returned to Massachusetts. If anyone understood the burdens of lineage, it was the parentally chastised youngest son of former President Adams and little brother of future President Adams. Thomas had previously fled to Philadelphia, in part, to escape his familial legacy, ever wondering, "if the sons are worthy of their Sires." In self-imposed exile, he "hope[d]" that "the father's soul survives" in patriots' "descendents & heirs." Someone more sympathetic to the struggles of the post-Revolutionary generation could not be found.[28]

Attorney General James Sullivan might have sympathized with Fairbanks. Sullivan came from a military family, but while his brothers, including a general and two captains, led men during the Revolution, a childhood accident kept him "confined" to his home and left with a limp and epilepsy. Unlike Fairbanks, however, he went on to great things, becoming a lawyer, a judge, and a Continental Congressman. He judged Fairbanks for not measuring up.[29]

At trial, Sullivan attacked Fairbanks for his "indulged and idle life." Fairbanks's academy education was the root since "he had been kept at school more than laboring lads commonly are." Sullivan believed Fairbanks was in "rebellion against" society. He had "seclude[d] [himself] from the rest of the community" and cared only for his "own corrupted and depraved opinion." Fairbanks was lacking next to his community, the Revolutionary generation, and his country. In line with Dedham sentiments, an elitist education was a vice. The Democratic-Republican Sullivan believed in preserving the "*republicanism*" birthed from "our glorious *revolution*" by guarding against "an unreasonable indulgence of a disposition to avarice, and ambition, groundless jealousies, a criminal supineness in public concerns, or an unpardonable inattention to the modes of education." Sullivan labeled Fairbanks as an unvirtuous outsider.[30]

Meanwhile for his defense, Fairbanks chose Harvard-educated attorneys Harrison Gray Otis and John Lowell Jr. For them the case was primarily about defending Fairbanks's honor against the "unjust principles," "airy fantasies," and "torrent of prejudice, against" his "most unblemished character." "His reputation" was "what is perhaps dearer" than "his life," the defense asserted. Their genteel portrayal of their client matched Fairbanks's self-imagined persona. Otis, a future Boston mayor, was the nephew of patriot author Mercy Otis Warren and Sons of Liberty member James Otis Jr., while Lowell was the son of the same Judge Lowell who sentenced Benjamin Fairbanks. Fairbanks picked these Federalist lawyers to undercut any stain from Uncle Benjamin's conviction or Democratic-Republican leanings. They cast Fairbanks as a gentleman of "irreproachable character" born into "a respectable family." They praised his republican characteristics: "exemplary virtues" and "early education, under virtuous preceptors."[31]

Fairbanks was a gentleman who must defend his character. He was not driven by "lust," for if he had wanted to use "seduction or force," the defense insisted, he had "infinitely" better opportunities. Slathering on heaping doses of victim blaming and character assassination, Fairbanks's lawyers said that Fales had kissed him (on the hand), stayed out with him alone at night, and even "deceived her mother"—implying her virginity was thanks only to Fairbanks's virtue, "purity and delicacy."

Stressing her youth, the defense called Fales a "love-sick girl" whose "head [was] filled with melancholy and romantic tales." Her "inconsiderate" suicide was the sentimental hysterics of the "softer sex." It was brought on by "phrenzy and despair," after the defendant's admission that he could never support them. Fearing the shame of returning to her parents, she took her own life. Fairbanks's suicide attempt, on the other hand, was manly and brave. He could not be guilty since "villains, capable of executing base crimes, are very rarely heroic."[32]

The defense attempted to explain away Fairbanks's threats as "light and trifling banters, as frequently occur in rustic scenes." However, the explanation cast Fairbanks as less "delicate and refined," which called into question his status as a gentleman and the entire defense. There also was no attempt to answer important questions. Why had Fairbanks hired a coach to Wrentham if he was calling off the wedding? If he was overcome by instantaneous, "heroic" grief, why move thirty feet before taking up the knife?[33]

When Sullivan made his closing argument, he targeted Fairbanks's "birth and education." Puffed up by his parents' "undue indulgences" Fairbanks was nothing but an "idle man," a "burden to society" driven by a false pride that he "erroneously called honor." The argument played into Dedham's prejudices against unmerited social climbers and un-republican self-aggrandizement. "Our public schools, maintained at the common expense, give almost equal advantage to every class of people," Sullivan said. "The poor and the rich man's sons meet there upon a footing of perfect equality." The Revolution ensured this was not a deprived generation, but one who could advance upon "perfect equality," Sullivan told the jurors. Fairbanks disrupted this new order.[34]

Looking at the evidence in the case, Sullivan highlighted Fairbanks's "dishonourable proposal" to marry Fales or take her by force. When rebuffed by Fales "with a virtuous indignation," Fairbanks "became enraged" and attempted to rape her, a perverse assertion of manliness. The defensive wounds found by the medical examiner confirmed that Fales died "in the defense of her honor." Fairbanks's physical disability was no barrier to committing the crime, according to Sullivan. In fact, it was a cause. Finding himself unable to rape her, Fairbanks was humiliated by "the imbecility of his strength" and driven to the most dishonorable act possible—he stabbed her in the back. Fairbanks's wounds, the so-called suicide attempt, was an example of his "low cunning."[35]

With closing statements concluded, the justices charged the jury, and the prosecution caught a break: Fairbanks could be found guilty, the justices said, even if he did not plunge the knife into Fales, but had only provided the knife, or simply stood by. There was an obligation to preserve life. At about ten o'clock on a Friday night, the jury of Norfolk County men began their deliberations. They were deciding more than the facts. The case was just as much about post-Revolutionary standards of virtue.[36]

We'll never know exactly what the twelve jurors debated as they were sequestered overnight, but at least ten were Revolutionary veterans, including the foreman, Brigadier General Eliakem Adams. Adams, then forty-five, started his career as a nineteen-year-old volunteer with the Lexington and Concord alarms. He once court-martialed a major for using "indignant & abusive language & gestures" that had "the intention of disaffecting the minds" of his fellow officers. Adams was a man who had committed himself to serving his country when he was younger than the accused. He expected proper conduct and punished those who corrupted others.[37]

At eight o'clock the next morning, General Adams rose from his pew and spoke: "guilty." The verdict entered, Judge Dana took roughly two hours to excoriate Fairbanks—he was "unworthy," "barbarous," and "savage"—and then pronounced a sentence of death. Fairbanks would be hanged, by this point in Massachusetts's history "an outsider's punishment." With the stroke of a gavel, Dana's sentence became a statement and the case a morality tale fit for fiction. For a moment, Dedham was the pinnacle of American scandal and Fairbanks the epitome of an American scoundrel.[38]

★ ★ ★

As Fairbanks awaited his fate, some family and friends still believed his story. Hoping to rescue an innocent man, Ebenezer Fairbanks, Jason's brother, along with two cousins, Reuben Farrington (the friend who'd heard the awful threat about forcing Fales), and two other friends broke into the Dedham jail early on the morning of August 18 and whisked him north toward Canada.[39]

National scrutiny and judgment fell upon Dedham. "Dedham," said Dr. Ames, is "doom'd to destruction for escape of Jason Fairbanks." He recognized that guilt would engulf the whole town. The memory of the government sending in troops to squash Shays' Rebellion was fresh. But there were also the crying eyes at Fairbanks's sentencing. Was something rotten in Dedham?[40]

The press thought so. Vermont's *Federal Galaxy* blamed the Fairbanks family. The paper reported a rumor that Ebenezer Sr. rewarded the jailbreakers with $1,000, the latest example of the "false fondness" that had destroyed their son's virtues.[41]

The prisoner's flight called into question the virtue, reputation, and loyalty of Dedham—casting its people as accomplices. Fairbanks's escape suggested that Dedham was circumventing the law due to a false belief of his innocence or a wicked conspiracy. "The stain of blood is upon the land," read the notice passed around Dedham. The town promptly fired their jailer to combat this "stain" on their honor. Nearly the entire town was "highly indignant at this interference with the course of law." They pledged to provide their alibis, volunteer their homes for search, and "omit no exertion to apprehend the fugitive and his accomplices." The honor of the town was at stake and "No honest man's eyes must sleep."[42]

Thanks to a thousand-dollar bounty placed on Fairbanks's head, funded by public donations (largely from Bostonians), he was caught on August 23 in Skeensborough (now Whitehall), New York, on the shores of Lake Champlain, while waiting for a ferry to St. John's, Canada. To the chagrin of Dedham, Fairbanks was not apprehended by townsmen, robbing them of the chance to counter its implication in his crimes.[43]

Fairbanks was transported to Boston and he appeared before Governor Caleb Strong on August 31. Strong was, like Fairbanks, "very feeble" in his youth and plagued by eye problems that left him nearly blind as an adult. Unlike Fairbanks, Strong had overcome his physical limitations and risen to governor as "one of the most diligent and industrious men living." Though "a man known for his compassion," Strong had none for Fairbanks. The governor scheduled Fairbanks's hanging for September 10 in Dedham.[44]

The Dedham townspeople demanded the opportunity to "vindicate" themselves from accusations of "corruption." Virtually every Dedham man pledged to personally guard Fairbanks around the clock and at his own expense for Dedham's honor. The escape had proven them personally and collectively deficient in the eyes of the nation. Fairbanks remained in Boston; Dedham was no longer trustworthy. But Strong still wanted the town to watch him die.[45]

Again languishing in jail, Fairbanks prepared a last statement, later published as *Solemn Declaration of the Late Unfortunate Jason Fairbanks*. What emerged was a sensational story of star-crossed lovers driven to a clandestine courtship. Fairbanks finally revealed why Fales ended her life—he told friends that they had sex. Horrified that Fairbanks had told their intimate secret to others, that he had "*possessed her person*"—Fales plunged the knife into "her breast and body." Her screams froze him in "a cold state of insensibility" and he then "immediately seized the cruel knife which had robbed me of all my fond heart held dear!" He stabbed himself again and again, "only leaving off," he said, "when I believed all was over for me!" He was Romeo, taking his life at the sight of his fallen Juliet. The story still did not square with the evidence—he hadn't stabbed himself immediately, for example—and it contradicted his prior respect for Fales's chastity, though his lawyers had insinuated other indiscretions. Instead, nearing death, Fairbanks chose to fulfill his earlier threat to "sacrifice her character, by violating her chastity."[46]

After nearly two weeks in prison, Fairbanks awoke on September 10 for the final time. The hangman's cart had arrived to carry him back to Dedham. Two calvary companies and an additional infantry detachment escorted the prisoner, an extravagantly unnecessary guard that revealed Boston authorities' ongoing suspicions of Dedham.[47]

In 1823, William H. Sumner, Governor Strong's aide-de-camp, insisted to retired President Adams that only the militia "could have hung Jason Fairbanks." He asked rhetorically: who could have executed him "without its aid?" Certainly not the people of Dedham, his tone implied.[48]

Any mistrust of the town didn't stop over seven hundred carriages rattling from Boston through neighboring Roxbury and along Spring Street toward Dedham for macabre entertainment. The unprecedented number of spectators overwhelmed the pastoral town. By the late afternoon, a crowd of over 10,000, "more people than ever were in Dedham before at once," gathered on the town common to watch the first execution in county history. The public hanging was a carefully choreographed drama of revenge and vindication "nurtured by the patriotic pride many Americans of the early republic felt in their governmental institutions."[49]

At a quarter to three in the afternoon, echoing the time of Fales's death, Fairbanks ascended the gallows. In a display of familial shaming and town vengeance, the platform was "constructed from a tree cut from the old Fairbanks place." Brutally symbolic, the murderer with ancestral pretensions was killed by his family tree.[50]

Ever playing the tragic "unaffected" hero, the condemned "conducted" himself "with a remarkable degree of composure." In a stroke of marketing genius, his last words were, "All that I have to communicate is already written in my Declaration"—soon to be on sale. He wasn't a poetic match for Nathan Hale, but his words echoed for years. With a final theatrical flourish, Fairbanks signaled the hangman with the drop of a handkerchief. But shattering any romanticized pretense, it took an agonizing twenty-five minutes before "justice" was concluded.[51]

The noose offered no finality. Days later, Dr. Ames, who could not bear to watch the execution, gasped in shock, "Some yet pretend to think Jason innocent!" Lowell, for one, remained a believer and gave up his legal practice over "the shock of his failure to save" his client.[52]

The Sunday following the hanging, Rev. Thatcher attempted to thwart this line of thought and turned the tragedy into a morality tale. "Are there any among us," he asked the congregation of the Third Parish, "who, will not be awakened from levity and vice, to a sense of religion and virtue?" For in a "moment" the guilty "falls from his reputation, wealth and honor, to disgrace, poverty and public scorn."[53]

Fairbanks did not die with the "fortitude" of a "truly virtuous man," continued Thatcher. He was only mimicking the "gentle dignity" and "manly firmness" of executed officer-spies Hale and John André. Fairbanks possessed only "superficial qualities." The firstborn son of a Revolutionary officer, Rev. Thaddeus Mason Harris of the Congregational Society and Church in Dorchester, agreed with Thatcher: "nothing is more disagreeable than an arrogant, haughty, overbearing young man," the inverse does "honor to society."[54]

Thatcher invoked the Revolution; Fairbanks was not "a patriot bleeding on the scaffold for vindicating the rights of his country; or a hero crowned with glory expiring on a bed of honor." He was not a martyr, like hanged twenty-one-year-old patriot-spy Hale (a one-time Dedham visitor—featured in a 1799 Mann publication) whose "only regret [was] that I have but one life to lose for my country." Likewise, an anonymous biographer enshrined patriots above the unworthy killer. "The Shades of our Beloved Washington, Warren . . . Montgomery, Prescott . . . and Hancock," "the Saviors of our Country" cast as demigods were "feasting on Nectar and Ambrosia" because of their "merits" not their birth. "Fairbanks's Shade," lost to virtue, burned in hell.[55]

Still, Thatcher recognized with great foresight "so extraordinary was it in itself—*so mysterious in its causes* . . . it will excite not merely admiration, but skepticism in posterity." The tale and the cult of innocence would live on for centuries.[56]

Promoted from the gallows, Fairbanks's innocence was publicized in three widely circulated editions of the *Solemn Declaration of the Late Unfortunate Jason Fairbanks* in 1801. Headlined by Jason's alleged declaration, the remainder was a "corrective" biography written by Ebenezer Jr. (supposedly with an anonymous "gentleman" to give it more gravitas). It featured themes of familial reputation and cast the execution as a dishonor, an "injury, insult and degradation," delivered by "inferior individuals." His motivation was straightforward: "I seek for myself and my relations that redress which our character demands, and which it is my duty to obtain."[57]

The family's lineage was central. "The reputation of my late brother's family is implicated in his disgrace," and to not defend the family's honor was to risk the reputation of "the *ascending* as well as the *descending* line." Dishonor was higher than "the laws of the state," for it was "yet the customs of society, working corruption of blood through all its roots and branches."[58]

Dr. Ames believed the *Solemn Declaration* "disgusts almost everyone," especially the disgrace of posthumously turning Fales into "a whore." But not everyone agreed. Thomas Adams, though unwilling to side with "that Monster Fairbanks," accepted why readers "were so firmly persuaded of his innocence." He later mused to his brother John Quincy, "The barriers, which time has been So long struggling to raise between virtue & vice, between honor and degeneracy, between such as are praiseworthy and of good report and such as are polluted with all manner of detestable crimes." Criminals were becoming celebrities, and their romanticized memoirs sensations. Still, they typically included a confession. Fairbanks stood for the unrepentant.[59]

To shield Dedham from dishonor, Worthington and Mann omitted Fairbanks and Fales from town histories. But it didn't silence the tale. One outlandish rumor cast Jason as the illegitimate child of the "illicit amour" between patriot lawyer (and future Massachusetts Speaker of the House) Perez Morton and his sister-in-law Fanny Apthrop—the pair had a daughter. An 1844 collective murderers' biography remarked, "there is, to this day, doubt in the minds of many, respecting the guilt of Fairbanks."[60]

On the murder's centennial anniversary, Mary Caroline Crawford, noting reputation and status, reported for the *New England Home Magazine* that "his family and many other worthy citizens of Dedham believed and kept believing to the end of their lives that the girl committed suicide, and that an innocent man was punished for a crime he could never have perpetrated." A 1918 letter to the *Dedham Transcript* editor called the evidence "entirely circumstantial"; it was time to "lift the dishonor from the grave." As late as the 1990s, Ethel Freeman, curator of the Fairbanks House, remained "highly defensive" of her ancestor Jason Fairbanks. Family honor was still at stake nearly two centuries later.[61]

In life, Jason Fairbanks tried to measure up to his peers and his family against the backdrop of Revolutionary memory. By failing, he blackened not only his own reputation but marred his entire family. The Fairbanks–Fales saga, though frequently cast as political or sentimental, was one that illustrated the limitations of post-Revolutionary society and that early republican trials extended beyond simply judging guilt—it was about assessing character, virtue, and reputation. Yet in a cruel ironic twist, Jason became better known than the ancestors he strove to emulate, leaving his descendants the burden of contending with the lasting memory of a scoundrel.

General James Wilkinson. Portrait by Charles Willson Peale, 1797. *Courtesy of Independence National Historical Park Collection.*

Colonel George Morgan. Portrait by Matthew Pratt, undated. *Courtesy of Washington County Historical Society, in Washington, Pennsylvania.*

Colonel Benedict Arnold. Portrait by Thomas Hart, 1776. *Courtesy of S. K. Brown Collection at Brown University.*

General Charles Lee. Engraving published by C. Shepard, 1778. *Courtesy of The New York Public Library Digital Collections.*

Aaron Burr. Portrait by James Van Dyck, 1836. *Courtesy of The New York Public Library Digital Collections.*

William Blount. Etching by Albert Rosenthal, 1886. *Courtesy of The New York Public Library Digital Collections.*

LEFT: William Augustus Bowles. Mezzotint by Joesph Grozer, 1791. *Courtesy of National Portrait Gallery, Smithsonian Institution.* BELOW: Matthew Lyon–Roger Griswold Brawl. Cartoon by unknown artist, 1798. *Courtesy of Library of Congress.*

ABOVE LEFT: "The Arrest of Aaron Burr." Engraving by unknown artist, ca. 1850. *Courtesy of The New York Public Library Digital Collections.* ABOVE RIGHT: "Parade of Burr's Force." Engraving by James Langridge, ca. 1876. *Courtesy of The New York Public Library Digital Collections.* BELOW: "The Trial of Aaron Burr." Illustration from *McClure's Magazine*, 1902. *Courtesy of The New York Public Library Digital Collections.*

ABOVE: George Morgan Monument, Canonsburg, Pennsylvania. *Photo by Timothy C. Hemmis.* RIGHT: Philip Nolan Monument, Rio Vista, Texas. *Photo by Timothy C. Hemmis.*

Proposed State of Muskogee Flag A. Design by William Augustus Bowles, ca. 1791–1792. *Courtesy of Library of Congress.*

Proposed State of Muskogee Flag B. Design by William Augustus Bowles, ca. 1791–1792. *Courtesy of Library of Congress.*

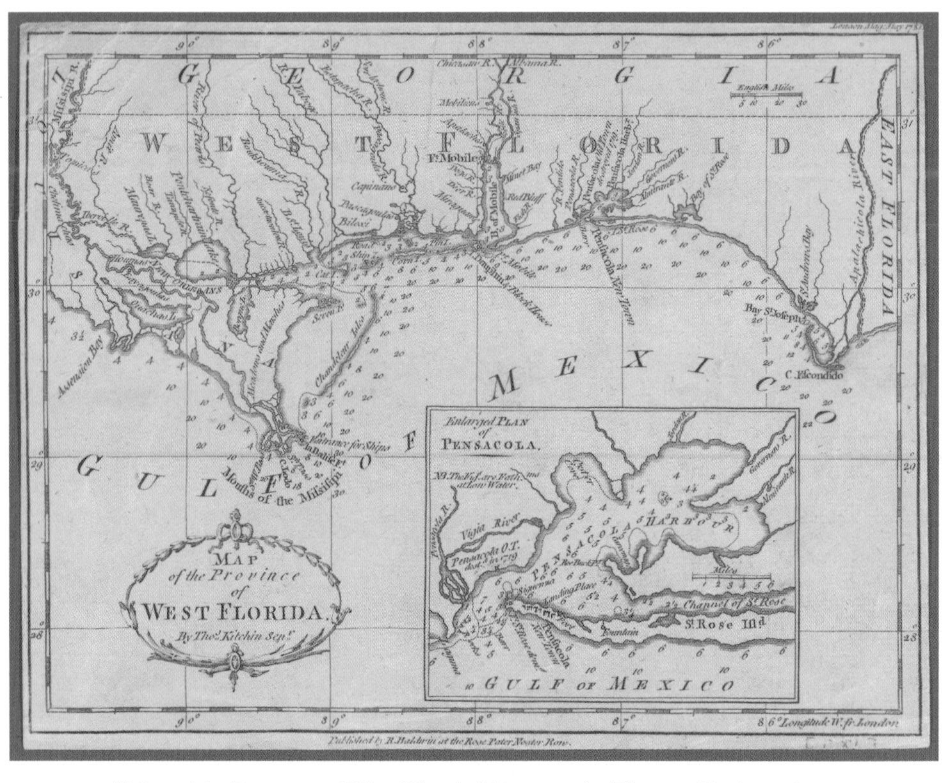

"Map of the Province of West Florida." Drawing by Thomas Kitchin, 1781.
Courtesy of The New York Public Library Digital Collections.

JAMES WILKINSON: SCHEMER, SCOUNDREL, SOLDIER, SPY . . . SUCCESS?

SAMUEL WATSON

★ ★ ★

James Wilkinson is notorious as the American general who spied for Spain in the early republic. As a scoundrel, he was that and much, much more: he plotted to replace the army's commander, Anthony Wayne, in the 1790s and went a long way with Aaron Burr's scheming in the West a decade later. Yet Wilkinson also served as the army's commanding general and the nation's leading diplomat in the western borderlands for more than a decade as the nation's territory multiplied.

International man of mystery? The most interesting man in the world? No doubt Wilkinson would have enjoyed either moniker, depending on the circumstances and his audience. Circumstances and audience were everything to Wilkinson, who certainly seems to have been the most morally flexible man in the world. Yet even Wilkinson's flexibility was uncertain and contingent. Though thoroughly self-centered, he still had to work with others to reach his selfish goals. Wilkinson played many roles and became a man of many parts.

Opportunist and entrepreneur, James Wilkinson rose quickly, suffered setbacks, then rose again, approaching the top of the power structure of the national state in the early United States as the army's de facto commanding general from 1797 until 1812. When the War of 1812 began, he was entrusted (for the third time) with the defense of New Orleans, the nation's most vulnerable target, and was then placed in command of a crucial offensive against Canada. How could he gain and retain such power, such authority, when contemporaries and biographers have been certain he was a scoundrel? Are we really to believe that this man—labeled "the finished scoundrel" and "an artist in treason"—fooled Presidents George Washington, John Adams, Thomas Jefferson, and James Madison, along with so many other members of the Founding generation? And not simply once, or twice, or in a moment of desperation, but consistently for more than two decades? Either dismissing Wilkinson would have been very embarrassing for the nation's leaders, or four consecutive presidents saw something useful in him.[1]

Despite the near consensus of biographers and historians about Wilkinson's dubious ethics, a surprising number of questions remain. Most studies of Wilkinson focus on his actions and how contemporaries judged him. But these studies have done little to assess the results of Wilkinson's scheming. After all, Wilkinson never committed overt treason. He did not levy war against the United States or aid its enemies in time of war. So full of ambiguities, paradoxes, and even ironies, Wilkinson was indeed an international man of mystery. With those paradoxes and his shifting connections to the United States, Spain, and American frontiersmen, perhaps he *was* the most interesting man in the world, at least in the western world of the United States, its borderlands, and its frontiers. Perhaps the most interesting man in the world was indeed the man to command the army, to lead much of the nation's diplomacy in the borderlands, to expand and consolidate its power and control in a West contested not only by the international competition of the United States, Britain, Spain, and France, but by private American, British, and French citizens and subjects, and dozens of Native American polities.

Wilkinson's formal occupation, which gave him official status and a position of such influence, was soldier. Morally and ethically, he was a scoundrel, finished in the arts of duplicity and the practices of deceit. That deception was doubly manifested in his spying for and against Spain. Indeed, anyone whose knowledge might yield special insight or value became a target for Wilkinson's espionage and lies. Wilkinson spied in order to scheme; he served himself or served others in order to serve himself.

Was he also a success? Every biographer and historian, even those mentioning Wilkinson only in passing or to provide color, condemns his character. As a professor at the United States Military Academy, I can hardly ignore, much less applaud, the amorality of this "tarnished warrior," regardless of whether his actions reached the level of treason. I could spin an exciting tale of the finished scoundrel, the artist in treason, yet others have done so with more journalistic flair or legal indictment. But Wilkinson's story is more than a colorful tale or a lesson in lawbreaking. It is more than an occasion for headshaking, more than an anomaly in our vision of wise founders. Wilkinson's story must go beyond the morality tale to help us understand the early national borderlands and civil-military relations.[2]

In doing so, I will argue that the conjunction of Wilkinson's position and his self-interest ultimately led him to remain loyal to the United States, and that he was a successful diplomat, advancing US interests, for two crucial decades. His business ventures and scheming encouraged a wide array of commercial connections in the new nation's southwestern borderlands. These helped to foster American trade through New Orleans, which was essential to encouraging and sustaining western settlement at a time when Spain had closed the Mississippi and some leading Americans were willing to give up access to New Orleans. He was an effective diplomat with Native Americans, with influential French creoles in Missouri, and indeed with Spain, even more so because he represented, and in practice directed, American military power. He could play good cop and bad cop. And when push came to shove, he sided with the United States against Aaron Burr in 1806, and more widely, against the filibusters and separatists he had flirted with and sometimes encouraged since the 1780s.

Wilkinson seemed motivated equally by desires for luxury and for influence, for being in the know, for being sought after. Such influence required scheming, and indeed speculating, which encouraged spying. Deciding that the security of a US commission and continued command of the U.S. Army outweighed an uncertain future under Burr, Wilkinson quickly resolved the Sabine boundary crisis that threatened war with Spain. Three times—along the Mississippi River in 1797, in New Orleans in 1803–1804, and along the Sabine River in 1806—Wilkinson performed a crucial role in defusing friction with Spain to US advantage. Pompous and irascible, he stirred civil-military and potentially local-national tensions in Detroit, New Orleans, and St. Louis, but he played a key part in attaching the creole populations of New Orleans and St. Louis to the United States. Wilkinson was always in debt, and after 1806 we see little success except in evading investigations that threatened to expose his work for Spain. However, the first thirty of his forty active years were usually both personally and nationally successful.

This essay surveys Wilkinson's life of deceit, which featured four major intrigues or conspiracies between the 1770s and the early 1800s, roughly one per decade, in addition to his intermittent employment by Spain. As we go, we must explain his rise, his personal success, the opportunities and problems that motivated and facilitated his scheming and deceit, and his impact on the early republic and its neighbors.

★ ★ ★

Born the son of a Maryland planter in 1757, left propertyless due to his father's death in debt in 1764, he was taken in by a relative who afforded him a medical education in Philadelphia. He quickly joined the Revolution, becoming a captain at eighteen. Wilkinson's energy, education, and pleasant manner, acknowledged by all, made him an ideal staff officer, and he served as an aide to several of the top patriot generals between 1775 and 1777: Nathanael Greene at Boston, Benedict Arnold in Canada, and Horatio Gates at Saratoga. Each staff position brought him to the attention of a new patron, and George Washington recommended him for lieutenant colonel at nineteen. Gates chose Wilkinson as his chief of staff, which meant Wilkinson got to deliver the news of the victory at Saratoga to Congress. Being the bearer of such good news propelled Wilkinson to brevet brigadier general at the age of twenty.

Yet his early success led to ethical and political entanglements, and the first evidence of Wilkinson the scoundrel emerged. The rigid honor culture of the aspiring gentlemen who served as Continental Army officers made it difficult to have more than one patron at a time, and Wilkinson clearly had his eye on the main chance. He essentially traded his connection to Arnold for a more advantageous tie to Gates. It was a shrewd decision. But Wilkinson made mistakes as well. While carrying messages for Gates after Saratoga, Wilkinson's fondness for sociability got the better of him. He let slip word of the communications between Gates and Inspector General Thomas Conway, in which Conway suggested replacing Washington, who had been unable to hold New York or Philadelphia, with Gates—the origins of the so-called "Conway Cabal." The revelation was unintentional, and Wilkinson was not a player in the intrigue himself, but he tried to wiggle his way out of suspicions of disloyalty from either camp, misleading both Washington and Gates. Though Wilkinson did not exactly lie in explaining his conduct, he was tripped up by omissions. Trying to bluff his way out when called to account and angered by what he saw as betrayal by his former patron, he sought to vindicate his honor by issuing no less than three challenges to Gates. (Only one duel was actually fought, without injury.)

Condemned on all sides as a result of his prevarications in the Conway controversy, Wilkinson resigned from the army in 1778.

The same year, he married Ann Biddle, a member of the wealthy, prestigious Biddle family of Philadelphia. Wilkinson might have settled into business in Philadelphia. His denunciation of Arnold for fraud was well-received there and he was able to purchase a large Loyalist estate (seized by the state of Pennsylvania) at a discount, but the Biddles proved unwilling to pay the never-ending debts his now-lavish lifestyle incurred. Wilkinson reentered the army in 1779 as clothier general, in charge of supplying uniforms, but he neglected his duties to enjoy the social whirl of Philadelphia and resigned again in 1781. Hard-pressed by wartime inflation and uninterested in managing a farm, Wilkinson had to seek new fields for his ambition. Like so many others, he headed west.

★ ★ ★

While Wilkinson neither expressed a desire to be president nor entertained the fantasy of becoming "emperor of the west" like Aaron Burr, he shared the thirst for distinction so pervasive among many citizens of the early republic. Many Americans asserted a national identity rooted in the supposed simplicity of a frontier society, but few truly sought to trade cities or plantations for the long hunts of Daniel Boone. Instead, the expanding frontier was a place to build new cities and plantations, new sources of wealth and distinction. The opportunities promised by the West depended on a person's ability to take advantage of contingencies. One could gain influence and prosper by getting in on the ground floor, gaining land or helping others to do so by protecting their gains and advancing their trade. Whatever happened in the East, the West always promised more.

Thus it was that Wilkinson began his career as a political and economic entrepreneur in Kentucky, then a part of Virginia, in the autumn of 1783. He had no connections west of the Appalachian Mountains but he experienced immediate success, using his charm, education, and exaggerated military reputation to gain leadership among his fellow settlers. The proceeds from the sale of his Philadelphia estate, combined with investments from his brothers-in-law and from partners he had met in the army, enabled Wilkinson to set up a store in the fledgling village of Lexington, at the end of a trail from Virginia, to supply new settlers. Within three months of his arrival, he bought nearly 13,000 acres and claimed 18,000 more on the future site of Louisville. By 1786, he had built a warehouse to store tobacco, which provided credit in a region without banks. Having developed a network of supporters, Wilkinson entered politics, winning election to a series of conventions that sought to make Kentucky independent from Virginia, which provided little support for its westernmost counties.

The key issue for white Kentuckians was free access to New Orleans, then controlled by Spain. Otherwise, shipping their crops and goods east across the Appalachian Mountains would be prohibitively expensive. Settlers' access to the port could be gained in several ways: through alliance with and pressure from the United States, alliance with or submission to Spain, or even with Britain. In 1786, Wilkinson recognized that John Jay, the US emissary negotiating a commercial treaty with Spain, might give up access to New Orleans to win access to other Spanish ports. In response, Wilkinson argued for a Kentucky independent not just of Virginia, but of the United States.[3]

To entertain breaking from the United States was not treachery in the first days of the nation. Americans had rebelled against Britain to be free from British rule, not necessarily to establish the United States we know today. The Constitution, still in the future at the time, was intended to cement the union among the states that had won independence from Britain, but Americans believed the only true union was a union of interests. Under these circumstances, Wilkinson was not the only American to play the field. He found kindred spirits in fellow Kentuckians Benjamin Sebastian, John Brown (Kentucky's congressional delegate and future senator), and Harry Innes (a future federal judge).

Seeking independence, or alliances with European powers, required the sort of diplomatic agility Wilkinson had developed doing business in a cash-poor economy and an extension of the flexible ethics he had demonstrated during the Conway Cabal. Diplomacy is often duplicity, or scheming, or speculation. Creative ambiguity and possibility are central to them all—appealing to others' visions, rather than to an exclusive certainty, to predict opportunities for them, rather than asserting a single predictable outcome. Thus, Wilkinson could threaten that the Kentuckians could seize New Orleans by themselves, then warn the Spanish of a settler expedition rumored against the town of Natchez. That treachery toward some of his fellow citizens (who did not launch the assault) helped gain him credit with Spanish officials, furthering his goal of gaining access to New Orleans both for himself and Kentucky. In 1787, Wilkinson took a convoy of boats downriver without Spanish authorization, but he persuaded a series of officials to allow him to proceed and trade in the Crescent City. There he found the governor of Louisiana, Esteban Miró, eager to build a community of Americans loyal to Spain as a bulwark against further American expansion. Frontier luminaries such as George Rogers Clark, Daniel Boone, and George Morgan would take up such offers to swear loyalty to Spain in exchange for access to Spanish land, to say nothing of a later generation of Texans.

Wilkinson next pursued a larger deception against his fellow Americans. Since the United States (then engaged in debating whether to ratify the Constitution) did not seem interested in pursuing access to the port of New Orleans (whether through treaty or conquest), he felt Kentucky had to seek Spanish protection in order to do so, so he recommended Spain force the issue by closing the Mississippi to the United States. He followed this a day later by transferring his personal allegiance to Spain: "the policies of the United States having made it impossible for me to obtain [his] desired end [access to New Orleans] under its Government . . . The motives of my conduct are the real advantage [that access to New Orleans] of the country [Kentucky] in which I dwell." But that calculation could change if rumors of western disaffection caused the United States to provide more support.[4]

Wilkinson returned to Kentucky in 1788 still advocating its independence from the United States, but the tide had shifted. Indeed, the Spanish government in Madrid opened trade through New Orleans, dooming separatist projects, and prohibited further aid to them. Wilkinson lost a ship to river ice and was unable to pay those who had consigned goods to him for sale in New Orleans. Losing ground in Kentucky, in 1789 he leapt into explicit Spanish service. He offered to provide Louisiana Governor Miró with a list of Kentuckians to bribe and requested a Spanish commission, still trying to sell Miró on the benefits of a Kentucky independent of the United States. Miró thought Wilkinson was more useful as an American, however, and began to consider paying him to warn of American assaults—a spy, rather than a Spanish officer. Wilkinson responded by reporting on a British agent seeking to foment such attacks—yet (anonymously) sent the British governor of Canada advice (to encourage disunion in Kentucky) much like that he gave Spain! Wilkinson sought to create options and opportunities, not foreclose them.[5]

The unruly autonomy of settlers who had fought a separatist revolution meant that threats continued to emerge against New Orleans, giving Wilkinson further opportunities to ingratiate himself and puff up his potential value. He advised the Spanish to seek the allegiance of the potential South Carolina Yazoo Company settlement at Muscle Shoals, then hinted that Indians should be sent to attack it. (Plagued by debt, the settlement never occurred.) Early in 1790, Wilkinson encouraged the Spanish to send Native warriors against US surveyors on the Tennessee River, leading to the death of six soldiers. Whatever his intentions, this time Wilkinson's double-dealing resulted in American deaths.[6]

The year 1790 brought more financial losses for Wilkinson in the river trade, but war with Indigenous peoples north of the Ohio River gave him a new opportunity for self-aggrandizement. In 1791, he led a Kentuckian expedition against the Kickapoo, and that August he asked to reenter the growing U.S. Army. Despite rumors of his Spanish connections, President Washington chose to commission him, first as lieutenant colonel, then as brigadier general and second-in-command of the new Legion of the United States, behind only Major General Anthony Wayne. Washington aimed to attach Kentucky, which became the fourteenth state in 1792, more firmly to the nation. As Washington later explained when recommending Wilkinson's promotion to major general in 1799, "to hold a post of such responsibility would feed his ambition, soothe his vanity, and by arresting discontent" retain his loyalty. While Wilkinson had failed badly as Revolutionary clothier general, he was far from the only Continental officer to neglect logistics, and he had not actually supported or engaged in the Conway Cabal. Given Wilkinson's political stature in Kentucky, Washington chose to overlook his ethical shortcomings.[7]

Here was a potential turning point. Spain began paying Wilkinson just months later. Wilkinson was the ultimate compartmentalizer, and only the risk of committing an overt physical act of treason caused him to reconsider his double-dealing. One practical, and perhaps psychological, advantage of his perpetual rumormongering was to avoid that point and keep everything in potential. He could avoid making a final choice that required him to act. Advocating Kentucky's separation from the United States, for example, did not mean separation would occur—it was an option to pressure the United States. When circumstances shifted, Wilkinson could drop that option. When he needed to enhance his importance to Spain he could reassert it, which he did in hints dropped and rumors spread in 1794 and 1795 about western discontent over the whiskey tax and demands for free navigation of the Mississippi. As one historian observes, he used "the resources of each position [American soldier, Spanish spy] to enhance his performance and value in the other." The key was to never commit to overt action.[8]

The new general hoped most for "Bread & Fame." Fame was slow in coming after the defeat of the northwestern Indians in 1794, and

Wilkinson's constant worry was money. In 1792, Wilkinson began receiving a pension from Spain worth $2,000 a year plus expenses, which he inflated. Just after that, he sold what became Frankfort, the first state capital, supposedly for 300,000 pounds of tobacco. Yet all that tobacco (which was probably never realized) and interests in as many as 75,000 acres across Kentucky did not satisfy his debts. Wilkinson could compartmentalize anything, and he probably saw Spain as simply another source of bread. He explained his new commission in the U.S. Army to the Spanish as motivated by "my private interest, the Duty which I owe to the Country I live in [Kentucky, and the West more generally], & the aggrandizement of my family."[9]

His $104 a month army salary did little toward these goals, yet the resources and connections provided by national institutions made them valuable assets for entrepreneurs in the West. Had they not, would Wilkinson have remained in the army? He was a political leader in Kentucky during the 1780s, but a political career meant constant competition. The national standing army, however, was one of the most stable institutions available for individuals, despite widespread criticism that it was an authoritarian, unrepublican institution, liable to misuse by ambitious schemers. While the army was small, and subject to congressional appropriations and oversight, its more senior officers enjoyed substantial career security. It was centrally directed—one did not compete for business, election, or political appointment. Promotion was very slow, but Wilkinson got in early, near the top.[10]

In 1792, the thirty-five-year-old Wilkinson faced only a single, older superior—Wayne. After his political success and economic failure in Kentucky, Wilkinson became increasingly envious of others, especially Wayne, who he relentlessly sought to undermine, both within the army (fostering factions among the officer corps) and in charges sent to congressmen and to the War Department. Wilkinson's troublemaking concerned Washington and Secretary of War Knox, who sought a cohesive army and hoped to avoid congressional criticism but raised no real red flags. Infighting among military officers was common (remember the Conway Cabal), and Wilkinson performed effectively during and after the defeat of the northwestern Indian confederation at the Battle of Fallen Timbers. When Wayne died in 1796, Wilkinson was the army's senior officer. His initiative and military competence were evident, and as commanding general he would no longer clash with a military superior. Wilkinson's ties to Spain were only rumored (though widely so) at the time. As a result, President Adams, who displayed little interest in the frontier army amid the Quasi-War with France in the Atlantic, felt no urgent reason to replace the Kentuckian, which would draw condemnation from Westerners and embarrass Adams's fellow Federalists who had first commissioned him. Wilkinson had forged ties to anti-administration Jeffersonians in Congress during his attacks on Wayne, giving him options on both sides. Adams was hardly one to incur the opprobrium of purging the commanding general on what his enemies would portray as partisan grounds—an act that might have revived Jeffersonian criticism of the army, just after it had been reauthorized by Congress. [11]

Yet Wilkinson was restless. He was never satisfied with his influence. And he feared exposure. What would the Spanish do if he cut off communications? Playing so many conflicting roles must have made it enormously difficult to make a final decision to end any of them. Risk was the price of influence. The result was a perpetual standoff between Spain and the general: each side wanted to use the other, so neither wanted to permanently cut ties. Wilkinson began sending occasional reports to the Spanish governor of Louisiana in 1792. These were vintage Wilkinson: long-winded, exaggerating, self-inflating, full of rumor and thus possibility, but fundamentally the speculations of an opportunist and entrepreneur. Ultimately, his dealings with Spain were fraudulent efforts to profit from its anxiety about American expansion. His prescriptions were prosaic, often obvious, "replete with gratuitous advice and sweeping . . . generalizations," information easily discovered or publicly available. [12]

Wilkinson recommended establishing Spanish posts at obvious places. He criticized his superiors, from Wayne to the War Department to George Washington, to tease the possibility he might yet trade his US commission for a Spanish one. But he never did so. Nor did he reveal secret US movements against Spain (perhaps because there were none) or ever advocate US concessions to Spain. Though he would be required to register as an agent of a foreign power today, he was hardly an agent of influence. In essence, Wilkinson provided the Spanish with a digest of open-source information, rather than secrets, and they kept him on because his services were cheap in comparison with his future potential. But he ultimately betrayed any larger hopes they may have had of him. Indeed, his greatest value to the Spanish was probably for the governors of Louisiana to help justify their requests for larger budgets: a pawn in maneuvers among Spanish officials for preference within the Spanish empire.

Overt war with Native Americans ended in 1794 with Fallen Timbers and Tennessee victories over the Cherokee. Tensions with Britain ended with the Jay Treaty ratified the followed year. France defeated Spain in 1795; Spain was forced to become a French ally and Britain's enemy; with the U.S. Army free to turn south, Spain surrendered the eastern bank of the Mississippi down to Florida in the Treaty of San Lorenzo (Pinckney's Treaty) of 1796. Thus, as commanding general of the army after 1796, Wilkinson was primarily concerned with administration (personnel and logistics) and diplomacy. The small army stationed on the frontiers which Congress reauthorized in 1796 had little connection to the large forces (the "New," "Additional," and "Provisional" armies) raised by the Federalists in 1798 and 1799 for a possible war with France (or to coerce Jeffersonian Republicans the Federalists thought sympathetic to France), which the Republicans condemned. The general did correspond extensively with Alexander Hamilton, second-in-command of those "new armies," about organization, discipline, and doctrine, further demonstrating his military experience and competence. Diplomatically, his efforts were as multifaceted as ever, but he upheld and advanced US authority. For example, in 1797 he alienated many of the British merchants at Detroit by declaring martial law to reduce desertion from the fort there, but the dispute faded when he moved on to Natchez, where Spain had evacuated its fort in accordance with Pinckney's Treaty, to help ensure US control over what became the Mississippi Territory.[13]

Much as he had done with the Yazoo Company in 1790 and George Rogers Clark in 1793, Wilkinson in 1797 blocked Zachariah Cox's filibuster (an illegal expedition against territory at peace with the United States) to Muscle Shoals (territory held by Indigenous people), acts that encouraged more stable international relations. In 1798 Wilkinson took advantage of the war between Britain and France to conjure a huge conspiracy for Spanish officials, possibly linked to their British enemies, extending from Pennsylvania to Georgia, but this rumor or revival of the previous year's William Blount conspiracy was probably as much a means of putting pressure on the Spanish to complete their evacuation of the Mississippi Territory as an effort to aid his foreign paymasters. Indeed, the threats and opportunities presented by international borderlands intrigues never ceased: Wilkinson and Hamilton themselves discussed attacking Spanish Florida, perhaps in conjunction with Britain.

The suppression of filibusters and the Whiskey Rebellion, combined with the Jay and Pinckney treaties, broke the back of frontier separatism and Spanish resistance to US expansion during the mid-1790s. The massive projection of force against the Whiskey Rebels in 1794 suggested strict new boundaries for frontiersmen to act on their dissatisfaction with the national government centered on the Atlantic seaboard, while the Anglo-American peace brokered by the Jay Treaty in 1795 left Spanish Louisiana and Florida vulnerable to American power. In 1794, before Fallen Timbers, Wilkinson had suggested Spain make another effort (the second "Spanish conspiracy") to separate Kentucky, but he quickly shifted to pressuring Spain to make concessions (to fulfill Pinckney's Treaty) while still holding the potential to provide information. Diplomacy—like speculation, scheming, and espionage—would have meant nothing had the United States lacked a reliable military force to occupy new territory. Filibusters and western rebels never proved able to do so on their own. The advance of the national standing army down the Mississippi under Wilkinson's command meant the end of the western separatism of the 1780s and '90s. With the possible exception of Aaron Burr, separatists of the Jeffersonian and Jacksonian eras would plot the seizure of foreign lands—over which the United States could easily assume control, if close enough geographically—rather than the secession of those within the United States.

★ ★ ★

As the nineteenth century dawned, Wilkinson and the army faced a new party in power with Thomas Jefferson in the Executive Mansion. But the commanding general had already forged links to Republicans with his attacks on the Federalist Wayne, and it does not appear that there was any significant consideration of replacing him. As it turned out, few Republicans, much less prominent ones, wanted to serve in the frontier army during peacetime. Yet for all their condemnation of standing armies, the Jeffersonians had quickly come to accept a small standing force stationed on the frontier to threaten or defend against Britain, Spain, and Native Americans. Despite widespread fears of civil war during the Federalist mobilization of 1798 (with the Alien and Sedition Acts, the New, Additional, and Provisional armies, and the military repression of Jacob Fries's rebellion against taxation) and the election of 1800, the new administration proved capable of distinguishing between the frontier force and the partisan Federalist one. To ensure independent judgment in selecting officers for retention or dismissal, Jefferson left Wilkinson on the frontier, pressuring Creeks and Choctaws to cede land in return for cancelling their debts in 1802 and 1803, rather than bring him to Washington to advise on the cuts to the army made in 1802.[14]

Coming in 1803, Wilkinson's next major assignment to accompany new Louisiana governor William C. C. Claiborne to accept France's surrender of New Orleans demonstrates Jefferson's trust in Wilkinson—and the limits of US leadership. Jefferson could have chosen someone else. There were many notable (and Republican) Revolutionary War veterans and men who had led frontier militias against Native Americans during the 1790s, but most of the former were aging while the latter had been even more undisciplined than Wilkinson in pursuing western autonomy or launching expeditions unauthorized by the national government. Wilkinson, after all, had never actually led military forces contrary to federal authority. Claiborne was only thirty years old, with just two years of borderlands experience as governor of the Mississippi Territory. After a decade at the top of the army, experienced in diplomacy accepting the Spanish evacuation of Natchez (and in so many other ways), Wilkinson was the figure (or fig leaf) of stability in the transfer of New Orleans to the United States.

New Orleans provided Wilkinson with the chance to reconnect with the Spanish, who he accused of failing to pay his pension for a decade. (For whatever reason, they had not communicated actively for nearly five years.) At New Orleans he composed a new set of recommendations for Spain: Spain should strengthen its defenses (surprise!) and trade its claims to West Florida for the vast west bank of the Mississippi. Here, as in other instances, Wilkinson, perhaps intentionally, reflected thinking common among American leaders. Many American policymakers saw a foreign Florida as a great vulnerability, and they saw New Orleans as the great prize of the Louisiana Purchase, not the immense territory west of the Mississippi. Once again, Spain paid Wilkinson for divulging what any American leader would have told them for free and in public. The general demanded $20,000 (ten years' pension) from Spain, and was given $12,000—apparently his last payoff, though he would later send an agent to Mexico seeking compensation. Wilkinson continued passing information to the Spanish for several years, talking up the potential for American aggression in order to enhance his own value, but without providing anything secret. As one historian put it, "one is unable to note any real service that he rendered" to Spain. At the same time, Wilkinson sent extended reports to President Jefferson showing his knowledge and value while hinting at expansive western opportunities.[15]

★ ★ ★

As Wilkinson approached his fiftieth year, he had already been involved in three great intrigues: incidentally in the Conway Cabal; as a leader in Kentucky separatism in the 1780s and 1790s; and his plot to replace Anthony Wayne. Mixing constant ambition tinged with vast envy, the psychology of a gambler, a yearning to be in the know and at the center of action, and a perpetual inability to balance his books, Wilkinson could never settle into his role as merely the army's chief administrator. Wilkinson found his fourth great intrigue in 1806, thanks to a schemer even more notorious than himself: Aaron Burr.

That year presented a double crisis, international and domestic, in the Southwest, which came to a head for Wilkinson near the Sabine River in western Louisiana early that autumn. Wilkinson had just arrived to command the US troops and Louisiana militia concentrated there in a dispute over the boundary between Louisiana and Spanish Texas. Was the boundary the Sabine, as the US said? Or the Arroyo Hondo twenty miles to the east, as Spain insisted? The possibility of war hung in the balance and expansionist Jeffersonian rhetoric, along with Louisiana Governor Claiborne, seemed to encourage a fight. Despite the potential for hostilities, Wilkinson had delayed relocating to the Sabine for several months as he lingered in St. Louis, where Jefferson had appointed him territorial governor (while still commanding general of the army) in 1805. Wilkinson's wife, Ann, was suffering from an ultimately terminal illness, and the general had gotten himself entangled with Burr.

Wilkinson and Burr had met several times in 1804 and 1805 and carried on a correspondence. As it shaped up, Burr's plot, like Wilkinson's borderland intrigues of the 1790s, mixed different options to appeal to different audiences. Option one: Burr and his followers would inspire the West to rebel and secede from the United States, then ally with Spain. Option two: Burr and his followers would inspire the West to rebel and secede from the United States, then attack Mexico, perhaps in alliance with Britain or France. Option three: Burr and his followers would seize the banks in New Orleans to fund their operations, then attack Mexico and establish an independent state. Option four: Burr and his followers would attack Mexico, hinting that Jefferson approved the incursion. Who would "the followers" be? They might be Wilkinson's army, Burr's purported array of volunteers, or both (either of which might include state or territorial militia). The border crisis presented an ideal pretext to ignite a war with Spain, which Burr, and perhaps Wilkinson, could turn to their advantage. Many questions remained unanswered. Would the army follow Wilkinson in the first three options? Would the Burrites ultimately return to US loyalties, turning over any land they conquered to make a larger United States? As Stephen King wrote, everything's eventual.[16]

The Jefferson administration had received information about Burr's schemes throughout 1806 but, worried about the allegiance of Wilkinson and the army, had not acted.[17] Burr's allies also distrusted Wilkinson. Hoping to spur the general to join (or stick with) Burr, Jonathan Dayton, recently US senator, told Wilkinson he might be dismissed from the army's command, implicitly through a reduction in the army, though that must have seemed unlikely given the trust Jefferson had previously demonstrated in Wilkinson and the president's discussion of tensions with Spain in his most recent annual message to Congress. For once Wilkinson felt compelled to make a final choice: he turned on Burr and embraced his duty to the United States. Wilkinson ended the border crisis by anticipating instructions from Jefferson to agree with his Spanish counterpart to establish a "neutral ground" between the Sabine River and the Arroyo Hondo, a step the more belligerent Claiborne might have been slower to take. Wilkinson wrote to Jefferson unmasking Burr's plot and took his troops to New Orleans to halt Burr. Declaring martial law in the city, the general had several of Burr's associates and their lawyers arrested, and in February 1807 an army officer detained Burr as he fled through Mississippi. These were irrevocable steps. Whatever the substance of Burr's plans—fewer than a hundred volunteers actually appeared, suggesting Burr's force was a mirage completely dependent on Wilkinson's army for physical power—Wilkinson had defeated them.

It is not hard to see why. The general might have manufactured a border incident to start a war with Spain, but he surely knew his force was far too small to seize Texas, much less Santa Fe or Mexico as Burr's scheme envisioned. Wilkinson spoke of needing 30,000 troops to do so—how would these be supplied in such thinly populated regions? By turning on Burr, the general further ingratiated himself with Jefferson, who hated Burr, securing his position as an American general (and gaining reimbursement for many inflated expenses). If the United States went to war with Mexico, Wilkinson could still lead the army—and he could still demand money from Spain for information, as always. As Jefferson observed to Madison, "I never believed W. would give up a dependance on the government under whom he was the first [commanding general], to become a secondary & dependant on Burr." On the other hand, had he joined Burr in attacking Mexico, Spain would surely have exposed him, perhaps finally ruining his reputation.[18]

Wilkinson miscalculated his gains and could not shake free of controversy. The 1808 military buildup against Britain enabled the president to appoint two more generals, which for Wilkinson's enemies had the benefit of diluting his control over the army. Spain does not seem to have paid him again, and many congressmen were convinced he had been part of the Burr Conspiracy, a traitor almost to the last. The result was a series of three investigations: two congressional and a military court of inquiry that Wilkinson (bluffing) demanded in hopes of clearing himself. Instead it further damaged his reputation, though he retained his position. Amid all this controversy, James Madison, succeeding Jefferson, sent the general, still the government's premier expert on the Southwest, back to New Orleans in 1809 to command the troops concentrated to defend it against Britain.

This time—for the first time—Wilkinson's command proved disastrous. While pursuing a new wife in New Orleans, Wilkinson failed to attend to the health of the nearly 2,000 troops stationed outside the city, where 127 died of disease. Following War Department orders, he moved the force to a new location that proved no healthier, and another 634 soldiers died. It was the army's most deadly peacetime disaster. Court-martialed at his own request in 1811, Wilkinson again escaped when Madison confirmed, albeit "with regret," the verdict of innocence rendered by a jury of officers long acquainted with the general, though Madison shouldered some of the blame for his War Department's penny-pinching and the order to move a mass of sick troops in mid-summer.[19]

Wilkinson's decline continued during the War of 1812. He was superseded at the top of the army's command by the generals appointed for the war, though he was again sent to New Orleans to supervise the city's defense. Rehabilitation appeared nigh when he led the seizure of Mobile from the Spanish in 1813, but a new disaster followed, this time far to the north. Defeats along the Canadian border led a desperate Madison to send Wilkinson to command the US offensive against Montreal that fall, but by this time Wilkinson had finally exhausted his vast reserves of energy and was taking laudanum to relieve pain. What might have been his opportunity to command in battle devolved into a dilatory advance, defeat by better-trained British troops, and an ignominious retreat. Wilkinson was relieved from command. Though he escaped sanction at a court-martial in 1815, he was dismissed from the army in the reduction in force that year. Out of the army at last, Wilkinson spent his last decade writing his three-volume memoirs and seeking new business opportunities in Mexico, where he died in 1825.

★ ★ ★

How can we assess Wilkinson's career, beyond simply denouncing his moral turpitude? Results matter. Though we cannot separate Wilkinson from the many other causal forces at work, he was intimately involved in three crucial questions faced by the early republic and its citizens: allegiance, international security and territorial expansion, and civil-military relations. Amid all his chicanery and deceit, Wilkinson did not commit overt treason, at least under the narrow definition applied to Aaron Burr by Chief Justice John Marshall: he did not levy war against the United States, or aid or abet a nation at war with the United States. Still, to say Wilkinson never committed treason is a low standard. After all, his scheming led to the deaths of six US soldiers when he advised Spain to send Indigenous warriors to threaten army surveying parties in 1790.[20]

Declaring martial law in 1807 alienated many people in New Orleans, but it ensured Burr's failure. He rejected Spanish overtures for western secession in the mid-1790s, once Fallen Timbers and the suppression of the Whiskey Rebellion had shown the power and determination of the new federal government and pointed toward the satisfaction of western demands in Pinckney's Treaty. Most importantly, we should remember that the American revolutionaries themselves were separatists: forming new states had ample precedent, and just as scholars argue that Jefferson assumed western separatists would ultimately return to the fold, Wilkinson probably saw separatism as a threat to use while pursuing support for western interests, whether from Spain or the United States—or indeed from both. Ultimately, Wilkinson helped win and maintain control of the Mississippi and Missouri Rivers as well as New Orleans and Louisiana—the objectives Westerners, and in the long run most Americans, sought.

In the realm of international relations, Wilkinson repeatedly advanced US expansion without war. He both reflected and enhanced the manifold uncertainties and opportunities of the borderlands in the early republic, where white population growth promised US dominance in the future, but there was a much closer balance of power amongst US, European, and Indigenous forces on the ground at the time. Yet he ultimately betrayed Spanish interests more than he betrayed American ones. The American filibusters and rumors of British expeditions he reported to Spanish officials never came to much, and probably worried the Spanish as much as they helped protect Spanish security.

Wilkinson served effectively in four expeditions that mattered: Fallen Timbers to defeat the Ohio Indian resistance in 1794; Natchez to secure the transfer of Spanish forts in 1798; New Orleans to secure the city's handover in 1803; and the Sabine River in 1806, ultimately to make peace with Spain. The United States never went to war with Spain, and as commanding general Wilkinson three times advanced US territorial expansion while maintaining peace. He negotiated large cessions of Creek and Choctaw land (considered a success for the United States at the time, however we see it now). Though accused by Wayne of communicating with the British during the Legion's advance, it seems most likely that Wilkinson fed them his usual platitudes, perhaps amounting to disinformation. If spying means the betrayal of valuable secret information rather than exaggerated rumors, well-known facts, and obvious motives, interests, and tendencies, James Wilkinson was not a very good spy. His reports helped ambitious Spanish officials trying to advance policy initiatives much more than they helped Spanish policy.

Wilkinson's impact on civil-military relations appears similarly muddled, but was again ultimately, if paradoxically, positive. The military is built on discipline, and Wilkinson's actions often undermined that discipline, but across world history subordination within military institutions has often proven easier to enforce than subordination to civilian authorities. Passing by the quarrels of the Revolution, which were less civil-military crises than disputes over command between ambitious generals, we can and should fault Wilkinson for undermining Wayne (an outstanding commander), but Wilkinson and the Legion fought effectively, and the clash was restrained by the need to appeal to the civilian executive and Congress. It is a sad commentary that Wilkinson seemed the only candidate for commanding general in 1797, but a small army hidden away on the frontier attracted few prominent leaders. The general certainly served the Federalists and their administrations effectively. Most important, he promptly subordinated himself to the new Jefferson administration, an example followed by the officers he led despite their near-universal appointment by Federalist administrations after several years of partisan tension that sometimes seemed to threaten civil war. The Federalist-appointed officer corps made no opposition to its reduction in 1802 and advanced rather than frustrated Republican territorial expansion during the succeeding decade. While job security may be the best explanation for this acceptance of the new administration and its policies, Wilkinson set the right example. The same was true, however laggardly, in his choice of the government over Burr, and in maintaining peace rather than unconstitutionally precipitating war with Spain. His declarations of martial law in Detroit and New Orleans were limited and local at a time when US government and sovereignty were incompletely established and the laws that today govern military aid to the civil power largely unformed. One should hardly label Wilkinson a model of civil-military relations, but there were much worse possibilities.

On closer examination, each of Wilkinson's scandals appears, in retrospect, less than the sum of its parts. He did not engage in the Conway Cabal—which was after all a struggle over command, not treason. His false accusations against Anthony Wayne were insubordinate and divided the officer corps—they threatened to replace the army's highly capable commander with a barely tested Wilkinson, which would have been a loss for the nation—but this was an unscrupulous bid for power, not treachery against the United States. Wilkinson's support for an independent or Spanish-allied Kentucky at a specific point in time does not mean that he wanted Kentucky or the West to become or remain permanently separate from the United States—as his reversal during the 1790s and his repudiation of Aaron Burr demonstrate.

Wilkinson can be labeled expansionist, booster, confidence man, huckster—opportunist, soldier, speculator, entrepreneur, scoundrel—but maybe he was just a true American?

"THE MEXICAN TRAVELER": PHILIP NOLAN AND THE SOUTHWESTERN HORSE TRADE

JACKSON PEARSON

★ ★ ★

On April 15, 1954, monument designer Eric Adams joined a small crowd along Highway 174 near Blum, Texas, to watch a historical marker he had donated be erected in honor of a mysterious figure from the state's past: the "early-day explorer, horse wrangler and accused spy, Philip Nolan." Placed on the supposed site of Nolan's grave, the 2,000-pound monument summarized Nolan's life, from his birth in Ireland to his death at the hands of the Spanish in 1801. "Nolan's death," the marker read, "aroused a wave of indignation that led to the Independence of Texas." Newspaper writers covering the event lamented that the exact reasons for Nolan's presence in Texas "remain a mystery . . . a mystery probably buried with Nolan under the big live oak tree."[1]

The monument, grave, and media coverage of the unveiling added to the intrigue of Philip Nolan's life, but also sought to specifically tie him to a whitewashed history of Texas that tainted the state's historical memory. To these monument raisers, Nolan represented the beginnings of an Anglo-American Texas. He was a white filibuster who foreshadowed the days ahead.

Contrary to the marker's declaration and its twisted historical memory, there was a specific reason for Nolan's presence in Texas: horses. He completed four horse-trading expeditions between 1791 and 1801 that coincided with the development of Eli Whitney's cotton gin and the eventual expansion of cotton production in the United States and Spanish Louisiana. The horses driven by Nolan to planters transformed the physical landscape of plantations as they tilled fields for cotton cultivation. Nolan was not the first person to conduct these forays, but his political connections to high-ranking officials, including James Wilkinson and Thomas Jefferson, gained him notoriety that eluded others who undertook similar efforts. After Nolan's death, the continued surge in horse trading illustrates this point.

The privately funded monument represented a culmination of historical myth building surrounding Philip Nolan which began in 1863 when American novelist Edward Hale used Philip Nolan's story as his inspiration for "The Man without a Country," which became a best-selling American short story. Hale's tale shared the story of a man who undertook adventurous expeditions to Texas as a means to spread American ideals and ensure American expansion. Hale's story romanticized Nolan. He used the horse trader's name for his protagonist and merged some details of Nolan's life with the main character of the story. Hale's Nolan espoused patriotic ideals and American identity through his adventures to Texas before being charged with treason and imprisoned on a ship, never allowed to step foot on his country's soil again. Hale's short story brought Nolan to a national audience when *The Atlantic Monthly* carried the story, leading numerous other newspapers to reprint it. Hale later claimed that he mistakenly used Philip Nolan for his character, but his novel began the process of concealing and morphing the historical memory of the actual Philip Nolan. To curb his fictional liberties, Hale later published *Philip Nolan's Friends*, which only expanded the aura of his fictional character with his affirmation of Nolan's supposed patriotism. Hale's fictional image of Nolan has continued to predominate, despite the lone substantive biography, *Philip Nolan and Texas: Expeditions to the Unknown Land* by Maurine T. Wilson and Jack Jackson, which illustrated Nolan's commercial intentions but left some aspects of his life intentionally vague.[2]

Contrary to later memory, however, Nolan was more than a simple man of mystery. He was a critical player in the Southwest's economy, helping to lay the groundwork for an acceleration of commerce that followed the American acquisition of Louisiana in 1803. Contrary to the avowed patriot of literature, Nolan sought to enhance his own fortune. He tested international boundaries, cultivated relationships with high-ranking officials, and ventured where others feared to go. He constructed a geographic network of credit, animals, and land that connected markets from Kentucky to Natchez to the Southern Great Plains. Ultimately, Nolan's life illustrated how the expansion of commercial networks and personal relationships connected both humans and animals across and beyond the limits of geopolitical borderlines.[3]

★ ★ ★

Philip Nolan was born in Belfast, Ireland, in 1771 to Philip Nolan and Isabell Connelly. When he arrived in America is unclear, but he purportedly had two sisters living in Maryland in the 1780s, and he may have landed there around that time. After his arrival, the young Nolan developed a relationship with General James Wilkinson and his family. Precisely when historians may never know, but both Wilkinson and Nolan refer to the early establishment of the relationship in the 1780s. It is probable that Nolan met Wilkinson in either Maryland or Kentucky as a teenager. Nolan later lived with the Wilkinson family for at least two years in the period between 1786 and 1790. Wilkinson described Nolan as "a child of my own raising." Nolan referred to Wilkinson as his "friend and protector of my youth." Nolan must have received a good education because of the articulate expression and graceful script evident in his letters. Zebulon Pike, upon reviewing Nolan's diary and letters in 1807, called Nolan "not only a gallant gentleman, but an accomplished scholar." Perhaps Nolan learned from the teachers and tutors Wilkinson hired for his own children. Wilkinson certainly trusted Nolan. He went to work as Wilkinson's primary bookkeeper in 1790 at the age of eighteen. As for his physical attributes, a miniature portrait depicts him with dark hair, dark eyes, fair complexion, and a youthful facial composition with rounded features. He appears to have possessed a slightly rounded frame. American surveyor Andrew Ellicott described the twenty-five-year-old Nolan as "well known for his athletic exertions and dexterity in taking wild horses." Wilkinson also testified to Nolan's strength. "He could take a sack of two thousand dollars, with one hand, from off a mule or horse, and carry them with the utmost ease, into a house," Wilkinson recalled.[4]

Philip Nolan entered Wilkinson's sphere of influence just as the famed double agent concocted his treacherous scheme with Spanish Governor Esteban Rodriguez Miró. In 1788, Wilkinson received permission to ship tobacco from Kentucky to New Orleans, where it could be sold at a nearly 400 percent price increase, in exchange for Wilkinson providing intelligence related to American geopolitics and separatist agitation in Kentucky. It seems likely that Nolan worked as a boatman, assistant clerk, and shipping agent for Wilkinson immediately following the establishment of the partnership. In 1789, Nolan was named as an assistant to Wilkinson's partner, Daniel Clark Jr., in New Orleans. In 1790, Wilkinson made Nolan his principal agent in New Orleans. Nolan "has lived two years in my family and I have found him honorable, discreet, courageous, and active," Wilkinson wrote Governor Don Manuel Gayoso de Lemos by way of introduction. As Wilkinson's agent, Noland demonstrated his effectiveness later that year, selling a tobacco cargo for $15,850.00. During this period, Nolan traveled annually to New Orleans, shipping and selling tobacco before returning to Kentucky with the profits.[5]

Wilkinson's scheming failed to prosper. "My situation," he told Nolan in March 1791, "becomes hereby more painful and distressing and my fate more uncertain: my misfortunes make me a profitless connection." He outlined the dissolution of property to satisfy some of his creditors in Kentucky. Wilkinson paid each creditor hogsheads of tobacco that he had not yet shipped to New Orleans. Nolan's intimate knowledge of Wilkinson's dire financial situation led him to consider alternative enterprises. Nolan had developed close relationships with Spanish Governor Esteban Rodriguez Miró and, especially, future governor Francoise-Louis Hector (Baron de Carondelet). These relationships probably informed Nolan of large herds of wild mustangs which roamed the Southern Plains in the western province of Texas. Nolan conceived a plan to depart New Orleans for San Antonio, where he could acquire some of these horses before returning to New Orleans, Natchez, or Kentucky to sell them. For a man with little material backing, he believed that mustangs might provide an opportunity where money meant less than will and determination.[6]

In the summer of 1791, Nolan began preparations for his journey west. Most importantly, he needed capital to acquire mustangs on the prairies and plains. After closing accounts in New Orleans, Nolan traveled to Natchez where he exchanged promissory notes for merchandise and on August 7, 1791, sold a male slave named Charles to John Ballinger for $300 to further supplement his funds. Nolan's goal was to acquire several thousand dollars' worth of merchandise that he could then trade with Native American tribes in exchange for horses. After acquiring the trade goods, Nolan departed Natchez and traveled to Nacogdoches, Texas, in September 1791. Nacogdoches guarded the Camino Real to Mexico City and represented the first town in Spanish Texas where he would have to present his passport to cross provincial lines. Nolan's first foray began with a dud. Upon arrival, Spanish officials in Nacogdoches sequestered his trade goods. The loss left Nolan "as poor," he said, "as any Indian who roams the forest." Dejected, he set out for the plains. "Disappointed, distressed, tired of civilization, and all its cares," he wrote, "I was about to abandon it forever."[7]

A two-year sojourn on the Southern Plains followed, during which Nolan spent extended time with both Comanche and Wichita tribes. He likely traveled to the heart of Comanchería, in the present-day Texas panhandle and eastern New Mexico near the headwaters of the Canadian and Red Rivers. Nolan learned the basics of local spoken languages as well as an Indigenous sign language that allowed him to communicate with different tribes. Nolan also befriended John Lucas Talapoon, a trader of Indigenous background who had become fluent in the sign language while making deals with other Indigenous peoples and with whites. He traveled with Nolan on several future expeditions. During this period, Nolan probably learned and perfected techniques to capture wild mustangs. His initial plan had centered on trading merchandise for horses before selling them at higher prices to turn a profit; however, the loss of his trade goods in Nacogdoches forced Nolan to learn alternative methods to acquire horses.[8]

Nolan learned at least two methods to capture wild horses. One method is the traditional roping method. A mustanger rides a fast horse alongside an unsuspecting mustang and ropes it around the neck before tying the rope to his own horse's saddle. The rider and his horse then run alongside the roped horse until the rider stops his own horse and causes a violent jerk of the roped horse that throws it up in the air and onto its back. At this point, the rider mounts the dazed horse and rides it until it tires. The wild mustang might then be considered partially broken and fit for market. British astronomer Francis Baily later commented on Nolan's prowess in roping horses and complimented Nolan's dexterity in lassoing a fleeing horse.

A second method, employed by Comanche tribes and later Mexican cowboys, required three teams of riders and the construction of a large circular pen with a funneled entry. The pens were usually built from available materials and took advantage of the local physical environment. Riders would construct the pen in the vicinity of several large herds. A group of riders would then herd the horses and begin to guide them toward the pen. As the herd approached the pen, a second group of riders would ride alongside the opposite side of the herd and help guide the herd into the funneled entry. As the herd entered, a final group of riders closed the pen, and the herd began its circular stampede inside the pen. This method often resulted in an extremely high mortality rate upwards of 75 percent of the animals based on local observations. How often Nolan utilized this method is unclear, but he undoubtedly participated in its execution during his stay with Comanche tribes. With his mastery of communication skills and horse wrangling techniques, Nolan's first expedition proved to be an advanced education in mustanging on the Southern Plains.[9]

Nolan returned to New Orleans in late summer 1794 with fifty horses, shocking officials who greeted him "as a person risen from the dead." Nolan returned from the plains for two reasons, he told Wilkinson. "I could not altogether Indianfy my heart," he wrote, before adding the simple reality: "I was debtor." Indeed, Nolan's financial situation remained tenuous for the remainder of his life. The initial number of fifty horses did not generate a large windfall for Nolan. Based on later sales data, Nolan probably sold the horses for an average price of fifty dollars per horse for estimated total of $2,500. Given his two-year absence, this amount did not satisfy Nolan's creditors. This first expedition underlined a theme that defined the remainder of Nolan's life. Each horse-trading venture promised to repay some of his creditors, but he found himself mired a vicious cycle: he completed ventures to repay old debts before taking on new debt to fund the next venture.[10]

Nolan soon returned to Texas with a second passport approved by Louisiana Governor Baron de Carondelet on September 9, 1794. The second venture strengthened his burgeoning commercial network in both San Antonio and Nacogdoches, where he developed relationships with Antonio Leal, a landowner near Nacogdoches; Antonio's wife, Gertrudis de los Santos; and Jesse Cook, an Anglo-American who helped maintain Nolan's horse herds near Nacogdoches. At some point,

Gertrudis, who was nearly twenty years older than Nolan, became Nolan's mistress and the two renewed each other's company every time Nolan visited Nacogdoches. As a result of these developments, this second trip proved far more successful. Nolan drove 250 horses back to New Orleans in January 1796 where he sold an unspecified number of the horses. Nolan departed New Orleans by early February, bound for Natchez.

After his arrival in the town on the banks of the Mississippi River, Nolan authored romantic overtures that revealed both his romantic interests and his socioeconomic aspirations. Frances "Fanny" Lintot had captured Nolan's fancy. Her father, Bernard Lintot, was one of the preeminent planters in the region, and her older sister, Catherine, had married Stephen Minor, another preeminent planter and governor of Natchez during the final years of Spanish authority. Lintot and Minor were both tied to Spanish Louisiana Governor Gayoso, and Lintot often served as the courier between Minor and Gayoso. Nolan wrote Lintot seeking permission to court his daughter. "I love your daughter Fanny and I can no longer innocently join your social circle without your express permission," he wrote. "If you would think me worthy [of] encouragement I shall have a new spur to industry." Lintot's precise response is uncertain, but it is clear that the family initially objected to the courtship and Nolan's request was denied. Nolan supposedly wondered "how many ponies Lintot wanted for his daughter?"[11]

After having his request to court Fanny denied, Nolan then attempted to drive an unknown number of the herd to Frankfort, Kentucky, almost eight hundred miles to the northeast of New Orleans. This horse drive was not the only reason for Nolan to undertake a trip to Kentucky. It provided a convenient cover for another more clandestine purpose. In May and June 1796, Nolan rekindled his connection with his mentor, James Wilkinson. He helped Wilkinson arrange another payment from Spanish officials in New Orleans. Nolan and Thomas Power, a Spanish agent, agreed to transport $9,000 to Wilkinson in Kentucky via the Mississippi River. Nolan planned to travel overland while driving horses to Kentucky before meeting Power on the Ohio River where Nolan would take the money to Wilkinson's home. Daniel Clark Jr. reported that Nolan and Power hid the money in sugar and coffee barrels to evade detection. Wilkinson later testified that this was a false account made up by his political rivals, Daniel Clark Jr. and Andrew Ellicott. However, historians now know this was a secret payment for Wilkinson. Nolan's important role in arranging delivery of the payment cannot be understated. Wilkinson's story describing Nolan's physical strength may have emanated from this trip: he saw Nolan lift a bag containing $2,000 of his bribe money with one arm![12]

While Nolan did successfully deliver the payment to Wilkinson, his horses did not fare as well. Disease depleted much of his stock and he arrived in Frankfort with only forty-two horses. In addition to the money generated, Nolan's first two horse-trading expeditions established valuable relationships in Texas with both Indigenous people and local European Americans. It also represented Nolan's first successful horse drive to Kentucky which served to whet the appetite for more horses and cement Nolan's reputation as the "mexican traveler."[13]

Nolan's journey to Frankfort, Kentucky, in 1796 entailed more than simply selling horses and delivering secret payments to General Wilkinson's home. In October and November 1796, Nolan sold two tracts of land in Indiana to help raise funds for a third expedition. He then acquired $3,4150.50 worth of merchandise in exchange for promissory notes at merchant John Hunt's firm in Lexington. The goods acquired in Kentucky now tied credit in Lexington to Nolan's mustang operations. In January 1797, Nolan and his two flatboats loaded with merchandise began their return to Natchez. Perhaps fortuitously, they rendezvoused with American surveyor and Southern Boundary Commissioner Andrew Ellicott near the confluence of the Mississippi and Ohio Rivers. The two men shared numerous conversations as they traveled down the Mississippi River to Natchez where Ellicott planned to survey the Spanish–American boundary as outlined in the 1795 Treaty of San Lorenzo. Nolan had recently completed a map of the western territories and asked Ellicott to help improve his cartographic skills. He reported that Ellicott instructed him in basic knowledge of astronomy and cartography and even demonstrated how to use tools for conducting longitudinal and latitudinal measurements during his next foray to Texas. Their interactions left a very favorable impression on Ellicott who believed that Nolan was "strongly attached to the interests and well-being of our country."[14]

Nolan's association with Andrew Ellicott drew the ire of Governor Gayoso. Gayoso and other officials had long held suspicions of Anglo-Americans whom they deemed untrustworthy. Gayoso and Baron de Carondelet had previously warned Spanish officials of "the wandering spirit and the ease, with which [Americans] procure their sustenance and shelter, quickly form new settlements." Rugged Americans, he said, needed little support. "A carbine and a little maize in a sack are enough for an American to wander about in the forests alone for a whole month." Baron de Carondelet surmised that "if such men succeed in occupying the shores of the Mississippi or of the Missouri . . . nothing that can prevent them from crossing those rivers and penetrating our provinces on the other side." Nothing could stop them, the baron worried. "Since those provinces are in great measure wilderness, no obstacle can be opposed to them." These statements reflected concerns that enterprising individuals like Nolan posed a grave threat to the provinces of Florida, Louisiana, and Texas. Nolan lamented that Gayoso now believed him to be ready to take arms against Spain or even be unfaithful to the crown. To demonstrate his continued loyalty, Nolan declared, "I am a Spaniard and that the part I have already ailed was with a view to promote the interest of both countries." Nolan promised his sentiments of attachment and esteem be with the Spanish. Encouraged by his own actions and seemingly intent on utilizing his promises of loyalty in pursuit of another passport, Nolan proposed to Gayoso that he sponsor his plan to trade by sea with the province of Texas. Nolan insinuated to Gayoso that it may have the potential for a lucrative and silent partnership. While Gayoso maintained a leery view of Nolan and rejected the proposed partnership, he nevertheless gifted him a sextant to help him complete a more accurate map of the plains on his next mustanging venture.[15]

★ ★ ★

In the summer of 1797, Nolan prepared for his third expedition, receiving a new passport to enter Texas from Baron de Carondelet in search of horses. This time, Nolan planned to barter for horses rather than capturing them as he had done in the past. He secured $2,400 worth of trade goods by forming a partnership with Natchez merchant John Murdoch and supplied another $7,000 of merchandise himself for a total of $9,400 of merchandise. Assembling a party of traders—their packhorses burdened with small barrels full of Natchez goods—Nolan headed west. He was optimistic. "We muster twelve good rifle," he reported, "and there is but one coward of the party." His confidence was warranted. The venture turned out to be the most successful yet. It took a year and a half, but Nolan acquired 2,500 horses. After leaving 1,500 mustangs in Nacogdoches with his associates, he returned to Natchez, 1,000 horses in tow, in November 1799.[16]

Nolan's growing reputation for horse trading caught the eye of important men outside the Southwest. Thomas Jefferson heard about Nolan's expeditions and was fascinated. "It is sometime since I have understood," Jefferson wrote Nolan, "that there are large herds of horses, in a wild state, in the country West of the Mississippi, and have been desirous of obtaining details of their history in that state." Jefferson, ever curious, wanted Nolan to tell him more about the region's fauna, as well as Indian sign and spoken languages. Later, Jefferson asked Nolan to address the Philosophical Society in Philadelphia. His knowledge of horses must not be lost to the world, Jefferson wrote. With Nolan away when Jefferson's letter arrived, Daniel Clark Jr., a New Orleans merchant and former mentor to Nolan, responded to Jefferson. "You judge right in supposing him to be the only person capable of fulfilling your Views," Clark wrote, "as no Person possessed of his talents has ever visited that Country to unite information with projects of utility." Impressed, Jefferson promised that if Nolan should "decide to try the market of Virginia" he would "be very happy to become a purchaser of one of his finest horses." Wilkinson later tried to arrange a visit for Nolan to Monticello. Jefferson had two Italian busts arriving via New Orleans and Wilkinson hoped Nolan might deliver them. In May 1800, Nolan was said to be preparing to head east, with Clark Jr. telling Jefferson that Nolan "has by this time or will shortly set off for Virginia with a number of horses." Nolan never arrived. In September 1800, Wilkinson apologized to Jefferson for Nolan's failure to appear, but he offered no reason for Nolan's change in plans. It is unclear why Nolan did not visit Jefferson at Monticello. It seems that in the spring of 1800 Nolan had become preoccupied with two developments. One was personal—he finally married Fanny Lintot in December 1799. The other was geopolitical. Spanish officials had become suspicious of his expeditions and began to believe Nolan might have more sinister aims than simply trading for horses.[17]

At the same time as Nolan's communications with Jefferson, Nolan's romantic life proved very complicated. During his third expedition, Nolan resumed his affair with Gertrudis de los Santos. Historian Noel Loomis speculated that the continued affair signified an inseparable romance existed between the pair. In contrast, historian Jack Jackson asserts that Nolan did not limit his womanizing to one individual. Afterall, Nolan had fathered a daughter, Maria Josefa, with Gertrudis Quiñones of San Antonio in 1798. These relationships show that Nolan developed a romantic interest in each location of his larger mustang operations. Feelings aside, each romantic relationship also represented a web in his larger geographic network. The only location in Nolan's Mississippi-Texas network lacking a romantic affair was Natchez. This soon changed after the end of his third horse-trading expedition. It seems Nolan's recent business successes and his developing connection with the Sage of Monticello helped clear obstacles that had previously impeded his prospective relationship with Fanny Lintot. Local friends of Philip and Fanny supposedly provided space for the aspiring couple to continue their courtship until Bernard Lintot finally relented and allowed the couple to marry. Fanny was not aware of Philip's other romantic relationships. On December 24, 1799, William Dunbar oversaw the marriage of Philip Nolan and Frances Lintot. Nolan's marriage culminated an almost four-year romantic interest. The newlyweds probably received a dowry from her father Bernard as evidenced by the "$2,000.00 of Mexican coin" given to Fanny's sister Maria after her marriage to Samuel Steer. The dowry and Nolan's recent economic windfall enabled the newlyweds to move to a ranch outside of Natchez in St. Catherine's district near where Nolan had previously pastured horses.[18]

With a wife and a home, Nolan registered his brand for the first time at the Adams County Courthouse. He then contemplated expanding his operation with the help of his new father-in-law Bernard Lintot, proposing they invest in a "horse-boat" to transport animals up the Mississippi River. Nolan sought a fifteen-to-twenty-year exclusive right of navigation from Spanish and American officials for the venture. He believed Natchez provided an ideal place for outfitting such a boat as the town laid on the direct road from Natchitoches. The Natchitoches Road represented the most direct route to import horses from the west and then export them directly to Kentucky and Ohio. During this period, the demand for horses also correlated to the rapid increase in cotton production in the Natchez area. In 1794, Natchez produced approximately 36,000 pounds of cotton. By 1800, Natchez growers produced 1.2 million pounds of cotton a year. Horse prices rose with this increased demand for animal power, and Nolan was poised to take advantage. Nolan held a sale in Natchez on April 24, 1800, selling twenty-eight horses for a total of $1,860.04, an average price of $66.43 per horse. His customers included many of Natchez's elite citizens, such as John Minor, a wealthy planter and Stephen Minor's brother; William Kenner, a Natchez planter; William Brown, a wealthy planter; Thomas Wilkins, a planter; merchant Patrick Connelly; and also his present and future partners John Henderson and David Fero. Nolan sold his horses for a range of prices, from the cheapest, a white horse sold to Thomas Jackson for $42, up to a black gelding sold to John Minor for $91. Nolan's third expedition had finally earned a profitable return for the seasoned traveler. For the first time in his life, Nolan seemed to have established a permanent home base. His marriage to Fanny and the possession of over 1,500 horses provided a viable investment in mobile commodities, which promised to further improve his financial standing.[19]

★ ★ ★

As Nolan planned to undertake a fourth expedition to Texas, changes to Spanish leadership removed Nolan's political connections. Gone were the largely sympathetic figures Gayoso and Carondelet and in their place were Texas Governor Pedro de Nava, Interim Louisiana Governor Sebastian Calvo de la Puerta y O'Farrill (the Marqués de Casa Calvo), and Concordia Commandant José Vidal, who all sought to limit foreign intrusions into Spanish territory. Increased geopolitical tensions between the United States and Spain must be considered within a larger framework. Ellicott's survey of the 31st parallel and increased Anglo-American migration to western territories unnerved Spanish administrators. Marqués de Casa Calvo, Nava, and Vidal all shared concerns that the United States might attempt either an official or unofficial armed incursion into Spanish Louisiana. Suspicious of Nolan's fluid loyalties, they tried to prevent him from entering Texas. In fact, Pedro de Nava issued an arrest warrant for Nolan on August 8, 1800, even before he departed Natchez. Nolan understood that these geopolitical changes might negatively affect his horse-trading enterprise and urged his associate in Nacogdoches, Jesse Cook, to drive his horses from Texas to Natchez before Spanish officials could seize them. Unfortunately for Nolan, Cook never completed the task. Unbeknownst to Nolan,

Spanish officials arrested Cook at the Rapides Post in Spanish Louisiana in September 1800 and confiscated hundreds of Nolan's horses that were being driven by Cook to Natchez.[20]

Despite the setbacks, Nolan continued preparations for a new expedition. He financed the purchase of some $9,100 in merchandise, borrowing from local merchants in Natchez for the goods he needed to trade for horses, and contracted twenty-eight men to accompany him, including eighteen Americans, seven Spaniards (including mistress Gertrudis de los Santos's brother José), and two enslaved Black men. David Fero and Mordecai Richards agreed to serve as the second- and third-in-command of the expedition. Nolan planned to lead the group by land through Natchitoches and then on to Nacogdoches. A second group would then rendezvous with Nolan's expedition near Nacogdoches. Natchez merchant John Henderson led the second group and planned to deliver the majority of the trade goods via boat to Natchitoches where Nolan and the others could then transport the goods over land to Texas. As the expedition prepared to set off, rumors swirled that Nolan's party planned to invade Texas, not gather mustangs. It seems the increased number of mustangers reinforced Spanish suspicions that Nolan might be attempting something more sinister than acquiring horses. Concordia Commandant José Vidal, seeing a threat to the peace between the United States and Spain, urged both American and Spanish leaders to arrest the outfit immediately. American officials ignored Vidal's protest, but his warnings alerted Nolan to the potential danger of crossing into Spanish territory.[21]

The expedition left Natchez in October 1800 and proceeded north where it crossed the Mississippi River near Walnut Hills, present-day Vicksburg, Mississippi. The party encountered its first resistance near the Ouachita Post, present-day Monroe, Louisiana, where Vidal's warnings had brought out a militia patrol to arrest the expedition. After a tense meeting, Nolan altered his course, heading farther north to avoid another confrontation. Then a new problem arose. Nolan's third-in-command, Mordecai Richards, deserted the expedition and, lured by promises of land near the Rio Homochitto, passed information to Commandant Vidal. Nolan had more sinister plans than simply gathering wild horses, Richards testified. Confirming Spanish suspicions won Richards a 600-arpent tract on the Rio Homochitto as reward. Richards was not the only informant to turn against Nolan. Hannah Glasscock, resident of Louisiana, informed Spanish officials that Nolan and the expedition planned to rob government caravans on the road between Camargo and San Antonio. Spanish officials viewed these testimonies as affirmations of their suspicions toward Nolan.[22]

Unaware that Richards and Glasscock had turned informant against him, Nolan and the expedition crossed the Red River north of the Great Raft and proceeded westerly toward the Southern Plains. The informants were not the only setback to Nolan's original plan. Spanish officials arrested John Henderson and confiscated all of Nolan's merchandise at Rapides Post on the Red River, the same place where Jesse Cook had been apprehended. The expedition possessed no knowledge of this development and continued to the Southern Plains, in present-day central and western Texas. Nolan and his party followed the Red River along the present-day Texas-Oklahoma border before turning in a southwesterly direction. The party crossed the Trinity River somewhere in the vicinity of the present-day Dallas-Fort Worth metroplex before arriving at a tributary of the Brazos River near present-day Blum, Texas. The expedition constructed a blockhouse and corral before visiting Comanche and Wichita tribes for a period of at least four weeks while awaiting Henderson's arrival. After failing to receive word of Henderson's progress, the expedition returned to the blockhouse on the Brazos River tributary in February 1801 and worked to expand its footprint. The group then hunkered down for the remainder of winter.[23]

Meanwhile, Spanish officials mobilized a 150-man patrol to hunt for Nolan. Lieutenant Miguel Francisco Músquiz commanded the outfit and enlisted William Barr, a Nacogdoches trader and Nolan competitor, to serve as both a guide and translator. The group traveled for two weeks before encountering two Wichita hunters who agreed to reveal Nolan's location. On March 21, 1801, Músquiz and his men located the compound and prepared to attack at dawn. Believing Nolan would offer violent resistance from the small blockhouse and corrals, the Spanish soldiers prepared a mounted swivel gun with grapeshot. At dawn, a bearded and scraggly Philip Nolan awoke to find the Spanish force approaching the compound.[24]

After a brief parlay with the translator and Músquiz, Nolan armed himself with two rifles and two pistols, determined to fight. He urged his men to fight to the death or risk enslavement in Spanish lands, but two of the Spanish members of Nolan's party fled to the Spanish lines to avoid a fight, leaving Nolan and twelve others to face off against the much larger force. Gunfire erupted almost immediately. Nolan rapidly moved from position to position inside the compound, firing prepositioned rifles before moving to the next loaded weapon. Within mere minutes, a musket ball struck Nolan in the head. His lifeless body dropped to the ground. Some of Nolan's party immediately surrendered to the Spanish while others escaped the blockhouse and corral and took refuge in a cave. After several hours of resistance and with their ammunition depleted, the remainder of the group surrendered. By nightfall, Músquiz believed he had extinguished the American scourge from Spanish lands and prevented a threat to undermine Spanish authority in Texas.[25]

News of Nolan's death arrived in Natchez in May 1801 and quickly spread. On June 9, 1801, *The Paladium* in Frankfort, Kentucky, carried the news on its front page. Doctor Lattimore, a correspondent from Natchez declared, "it is with regret that I inform you of the death of Philip Nolan . . . In my estimation, few men are better qualified for great and hazardous enterprises than he was." Nolan's death hit Fanny hard. Far advanced in pregnancy when she learned of his fate, she seems to have suffered postpartum complications following the birth of their child, a son she named Philip, leading to her death a month later. "Corrosion of grief for unexpected fate of her late husband and advancing pregnancy," according to an obituary, caused her demise, and made an orphan of "a darling child." Nolan's death left both of his children orphaned, but it is unclear what happened to his daughter, Maria Josefa.[26]

After Nolan's death, the executorship of his estate fell to one of his chief creditors, Abijah Hunt. Abijah Hunt had established a trading firm in Natchez in 1798 as an extension of the Hunt family operations. The four brothers operated stores in Philadelphia, Cincinnati, Lexington, and Natchez. The probate accounts revealed Nolan's extensive dealings with the Hunt firm. The accounts also reinforce the commercial nature of Nolan's expeditions. His creditors ranged from Kentucky to Natchez as evidenced by the claims against his estate, and these creditors financed each venture. In total, Nolan owed the Hunts and other creditors a total of $14,093.01 for agreements made between 1796 and 1800. This accounting illustrates that Nolan acquired far more than the three pack horses' worth of supplies reported by Mordecai Richards in November 1800. Nolan exchanged promissory notes for $9,177.51 worth of merchandise in September and October of 1800 to fund his final expedition to Texas. The probate account demonstrates that the vast majority of the trade goods may have been lost when Spanish officials arrested John Henderson in November 1800. As evidenced by the accounts, Nolan's credit network directly connected the Natchez capital to the Southern Plains horse trade. Throughout his life, Nolan despised the fact that he remained a debtor unable to satisfy his creditors, which likely contributed to his decision to push on with the fourth expedition despite his loss of political connections in Louisiana and Texas.[27]

The probate account and civil lawsuits filed by Abijah Hunt also shed light on the small individual transactions that defined the horse trade and make it almost unquantifiable for modern historians. Hunt sued several individuals for payment of debts owed to the Nolan estate. These cases illustrate that Nolan's transactions occurred on small scales ranging in amount from $30 to $300. The executor organized an auction to pay off Nolan debts. Former Nolan associate John Henderson served as auctioneer in both public and private auctions for the estate. In the winter of 1801–1802, public auctions sold 145 horses and one enslaved person for a total of $5,983.75. Private sales added nine horses for a total of $409.00 for an overall total of $6,392.75. The horses sold at auction for an average of $41.51 per horse, significantly lower than the price of $66 per horse received by Nolan in the April 1800 sale. Unaccounted for in the probate records is Philip Nolan's property and horses that remained in Texas and out of reach of administrator Abijah Hunt. Over 1,500 horses never reached market. If we use data from Nolan's previous horse sales, they represented an estimated property value of between $62,267.05 at the price of $41.51 per horse and $99,000 at the price of $66 per horse. The projected profits signify the remarkable potential value of the horse trade conducted by Nolan.[28]

With the closure of Nolan's estate in 1803, the real motivations for Nolan's four horse-trading expeditions are readily apparent: they were economic rather than an Anglo-American filibuster aimed at creating an independent Texas. The expeditions reveal the growth of an interconnected regional economy that linked the Southern Plains to markets in New Orleans, Natchez, Kentucky, and the Atlantic states via goods exchanged for animals on the Southern Plains. Nolan's expeditions relied on his ability to cultivate relationships with officials in Louisiana, Texas, and beyond. Ultimately, his death occurred when those relationships ended or deteriorated. By his last expedition, Nolan no longer possessed the ability to move freely across geopolitical boundaries even if it was only for horses. For these reasons, Philip Nolan met his fate on the plains of Texas.

★ ★ ★

When Eric Adams erected the monument to Philip Nolan in 1954, the monument raisers sought to memorialize Nolan as an Anglo-American hero in the colonial period who foreshadowed the later period of Texas independence and American annexation. However, his life reveals a far more complicated historical reality. Nolan clearly displayed both enterprising actions and romantic interests less exceptional than the monument perhaps cared to acknowledge. His close association to James Wilkinson during his time as a double agent and his web of romantic relationships hint that Nolan pursued his own self-interests and ambitions before anything else. His amorphous loyalties enabled him to traverse geopolitical and cultural borders and conduct his expeditions to Texas. As demonstrated by wide-ranging business dealings and relationships, Nolan seemed at ease in a variety of locations and cultures.

Philip Nolan's four horse-trading expeditions revealed the larger geographic and economic networks that transcended geopolitical boundaries in late eighteenth- and early nineteenth-century North America. His reputation as a scoundrel during the period of the early republic depends on perspective. To Spanish officials such as Governor Gayoso, Marqués de Casa Calvo, and Pedro de Nava, Nolan morphed from a trusted informant to an untrustworthy scoundrel who could no longer be allowed in Spanish territory. His mere presence required military intervention to remove him from Spanish dominions regardless of Nolan's true intentions. Conversely, Nolan's charisma, knowledge, travels, and exploits endeared him to numerous individuals ranging from future American President Thomas Jefferson to wealthy planters such as Stephen Minor, lesser American officials like Andrew Ellicott, and even to earlier Spanish officials such as Governor Baron de Carondelet.

With these perspectives in mind, Nolan should be remembered for all his complications, not a romanticized version that incorrectly places him as a proto-Anglo-American Texan bent on siphoning off Spanish territory. He possessed more self-centric motivations and ambitions. His expeditions aimed to elevate his socioeconomic status through the acquisition of one valuable, living commodity: horses.

AMERICAN ADVENTURERS IN THE MISSISSIPPI BORDERLANDS: THOMAS GREEN AND GEORGIA'S 1785 BOURBON COUNTY SCHEME IN SPANISH NATCHEZ

CHRISTIAN PINNEN

★ ★ ★

Shortly before the end of the American Revolution, Thomas Green arrived in the Natchez District, a contested piece of territory strategically located on a bluff that controlled traffic on the Mississippi River between St. Louis and New Orleans. Originally organized by Britain as part of its West Florida Colony, Natchez was Spanish by the time Green set foot there. Spain had seized control in 1779 as part of its campaign along the Gulf Coast during the American Revolution. Green, a sixty-something Virginian and a military veteran, traveled with his adult sons and extended family alongside an additional twelve white families and several hundred enslaved Africans. Green and his fellow migrants, convinced that the way to wealth lay in the borderlands between the newly independent United States and the old Spanish Empire, greeted the Revolution's waning hostilities by moving west. Spanish Governor Francisco Bouligny knew to be wary. The new arrivals, he reported to his superiors, "may set on foot many schemes which, on account of the distance, and of the freedom they enjoy in speaking, may do the greatest harm." By the time Bouligny wrote in 1785, Thomas Green, the greatest schemer of them all, was already far advanced in his plans.[1]

Green had a voracious appetite for land and an easy conscience about slavery. He bought acre after acre in Natchez and traded person after person to fuel his dreams of wealth and moved up the social order. When Spanish authorities resisted his plans, he set in motion a plot to turn the district American. It would be a newly formed county in the state of Georgia called Bourbon County. Claiming to have official backing from Georgia, Green sought to entice Natives into a pact against Spain with promises of American support. Bullying the Spanish, Green threatened to unleash an invasion of Georgia's militia. He played a dangerous game that brought the American Republic and the Spanish Empire to the brink of conflict, all so he could profit from the lands he coveted and the enslaved people he traded to work them.

Thomas Green and his supporters represented a particular breed of adventurer who came to the lower Mississippi River Valley in the 1780s. Their moneymaking schemes unfolded in a climate of imperial uncertainty, as the United States established itself alongside an Imperial Spain and Indigenous groups along an often-ill-defined border. Their scheming reveals the haphazard approach of American states to westward expansion in the period preceding the Constitutional Convention. Settler colonizers, not the state, drove American expansion. Green almost singlehandedly destabilized the southern borderlands region. Scoundrels like Green who became agents of American expansion reveal the need to carefully evaluate how westward progress worked in the early republic.

★ ★ ★

Natchez occupied a strategic location on the Mississippi River. The most developed settlement between St. Louis and New Orleans,

Natchez was a hub for both river traffic and overland commerce; farmers' produce from across the region passed through Natchez and via the Mississippi out to the world. Home for centuries to a Mississippian people who called themselves the Théoloëls, or People of the Sun, the region produced bountiful crops grown in its fertile soil. The French empire claimed Natchez and its environs when they erected a fort and trading post in 1716. They ceded control to Britain in the 1763 Treaty of Paris at the conclusion of the Seven Years' War. Under British rule, Natchez lay in the colony of West Florida, though growth came slowly. Spain, an ally of France during the American Revolution, attacked West Florida, dislodging the British from Natchez in 1779. Although settlers at first resisted Spain's rule, by 1781 tranquility prevailed in the district, though not among the diplomats and politicians who contested Natchez's place in their nations.[2]

The Treaty of Paris failed to settle the US border with the Florida lands Spain had won from Britain, however. The United States said the 31st parallel was the new nation's southern border, following a line that ran west from the Mississippi River to the Chattahoochee River (similar to the northernmost part of today's Florida panhandle). Americans, and in particular residents of Georgia, also pointed to history. Britain's 1732 colonial charter gave Georgia rights to land extending west all the way to the Mississippi River, including Natchez. Spain, which had made its own agreement with Britain outside the British treaty with the United States, argued that the 32nd parallel was the true border. That reached as far north as present-day Vicksburg, Mississippi, and the confluence of the Mississippi River and the Yazoo River. Natchez, located at 31½° North latitude, sat squarely in the disputed zone. Having taken the district by force, Spain was not inclined to lose it.[3]

The first seven years of Spanish government in Natchez brought several changes to the district. Racial slavery rose as a major economic force, plantations grew, and Anglo-American settlers became more attracted to Spanish Natchez than they had been to British Natchez, arriving in larger numbers via the "River of Dark Dreams." They were adventurous and frequently turned into quarrelsome denizens. At the same time, the Spanish introduced their court system to the district, creating new procedures and administrative processes to be respected and followed. Yet many adventurers were determined to settle irrespective of the potential pitfalls, because wealth—or so they thought—was to be had. While prospective and current Anglo-American enslavers were busily planning their rise, the Spanish had to face the reality of maintaining a frontier settlement on the outskirts of their empire.[4]

The years 1785 and 1786, however, saw the Natchez District in grave danger of becoming the center of an armed conflict with ramifications across the Atlantic world. The United States, or rather the state of Georgia, tried to encroach on Spanish territory, and settlers in the district attempted to challenge Spanish superiority. Key to all these developments was land. The Americans desired Natchez, but the Spanish were not willing to relent. Locally, Natchez enslavers instigated schemes to expand their landholdings. Slave-owning colonizers forced the Spanish to act fast to maintain a foothold in Natchez. To keep order, Louisiana Governor Esteban Miró had to recall one Natchez governor and threaten settlers with expulsion from the district and incarceration in New Spain.

In addition, the Spanish were worried about British and American activity among the Indian Nations in the area. All three powers were constantly trying to gain the support of the most powerful Indian confederacies. An American or British alliance with either the Choctaw, Chickasaw, or Creek nations presented a formidable alliance that could spell doom for Spain's goals in the lower Mississippi valley. The fear of conflict instigated outside the confines of the district was mirrored in Natchez. "These people, removed from the oversight of the person in command, even though today they are tranquil," wrote acting governor Francisco Bouligny, "upon the slightest move on the part of America, their beloved and first country, or upon the smallest reason for discontent here, founded or unfounded, may set on foot many schemes which, on account of the distance, and of the freedom they enjoy in speaking, may do the greatest harm." Bouligny feared he had limited options to intervene. "These injuries cannot be repaired by means of spies whose information is rarely dictated by zeal, reason, or justice," he continued. "At times such information causes disturbances, making things worse than they are."[5]

Newly arrived colonists found an administration suffering from frequent turnover in leadership. Over the first decade of Spanish settlement, six men served as acting governor, with Carlos de Grand Pré holding the office twice, before the Spanish Crown found stability in 1789 with the English-speaking Don Manuel Gayoso de Lemos. Spanish authorities continuously tried to balance the demands of the enslavers in the district, the expansionist impulse of the United States, and Spanish policies to create a productive outpost, and although a governor who spoke the colonists' language improved direct communication, the great distances between the various centers of power greatly complicated efficiency.[6]

★ ★ ★

Thomas Green arrived in Natchez in 1782 under a cloud of suspicion. The Spanish questioned Green and the other new colonists in his group on the origin of the enslaved people they carried with them and found that more than a few of the enslaved Africans were stolen property. Nevertheless, the party received access to Natchez and Green soon began to dive into the local economy. Green bought and sold different properties, often on credit and likely co-financed through the barter of enslaved people, until he could settle on a plantation and town plot that suited his needs. He bought and sold several lots, including a September 14, 1782, purchase of a parcel in town with a "dwelling house" and the sale of a different lot in town on April 8, 1784. Green quickly proved himself a quarrelsome character, being sued for unpaid debts and in turn suing others to recover money he was owed. Scheming to change the region's government, in Green's eyes, might promise relief from his financial troubles and was well worth the risk.[7]

Beside the problems Anglo-American settlers caused, Louisiana Governor Miró and the Spanish Crown had to consider the larger geopolitics of North America and the Atlantic world. For example, John Jay, Secretary of Foreign Affairs, and the Spanish minister to the United States, Don Diego de Gardoqui, were in negotiations over the navigation of the Mississippi River. While these negotiations ended without a result, they played a considerable role in the Spanish policy toward the settlers in Natchez. Spain was committed to keeping the Mississippi River closed to American traffic—at least officially—and the Spanish "tried to stanch the flow of Americans into the Mississippi Valley by choking off their access to markets." The Spaniards had the right to do so under the law of nations, yet American settlers north of Spanish territory were still outraged about the measures taken by the Spanish crown. Miró had to be cautious not to ignite the smoldering threat of an open, Mississippi valley-wide rebellion against Spanish government. Therefore, he made sure not to use measures that would appear overly drastic and sought to remind the people of Natchez that they profited from the Spanish monopoly in trade and tobacco on the Mississippi River.[8]

Aware of its precarious situation in Natchez, Spain did everything it could to bind the new immigrants, including Thomas Green, to the Crown. Spain required every new immigrant to take a loyalty oath. The Spanish designed the oath especially with American immigrants in mind. Colonists had to acknowledge that they were "desirous of living in this province . . . with permission granted by the Governor." Then, they would "swear by God our Lord" with their hand on the Bible and "pledge our word of honor and promise by all means which serve to keep faith among men, in conformity with the royal order, which was read by the commandant, not to offend, directly or indirectly, nor to conspire against the Spanish nation." Colonists further agreed to subject themselves "completely to the Spanish laws, keeping faith and inviolable the orders, [and] decrees and edicts of the Kingdom and its Government." Spain tried to ensure that the new colonists understood their new role in the Spanish empire as vassals of the Spanish king, not as American citizens.[9]

Since most arrivals were American, however, the Spanish governors were uneasy with the oath alone standing between them and possible mutiny by their settlers. Bouligny introduced a militia system to the district designed to aid the Spanish by maintaining tight control and binding the social elite of Natchez to the Spanish Crown. Bouligny divided the area into three separate militia districts, with a captain for each. These captains could then "spur them [the Anglo-American inhabitants] to work and to care for their families and homes, reprehend with severity and punish with imprisonment, if it be necessary, those who, giving themselves up to vice, indulge in abandon conduct, the primary origin of all evil deeds and thoughts." The governor selected inhabitants that were trustworthy and had proven themselves as such. Most importantly, the chosen captains should be "persons of property." Bouligny hoped Anglo inhabitants who were bound to the Natchez District by their property would exercise better control over the population than the Spanish themselves. The militia also served to subdue any unrest among the growing enslaved population. Thomas Green was not part of these plans.[10]

Bouligny and the other governors of Natchez walked a tightrope. His reports to Spain were filled with actions designed to maintain control of the district. But since he was the governor, and it was his job to keep control, he had to be careful not to paint too bleak of a picture of Natchez or he would look bad to his superiors. Therefore, he usually attached a slightly optimistic judgment of the settlers to his notes. "I cannot convince myself that this [possible] opposition could be general," Bouligny wrote once, "for although I do not dare to pass a judgment as to the fidelity of these people, I am inclined to believe that they are not capable of starting a rebellion at the present time." The militia system he proposed—he hoped—further added to the disinclination of the settlers to start an insurrection, since they now were made part of the government and their leaders were raised to an even higher social position. Bouligny tried to create a steadfast tie between rich enslavers and the Spanish government that could enhance the loyalty oath.[11]

The governor carefully chose candidates for the militia captains and their subordinate officers. Adam Bingaman, one of the larger slaveowners in the area, for example, was nominated as captain or lieutenant. He was supposed to serve in the Bayou of St. Catherine. Anthony Hutchins, one of the wealthiest people in Spanish Natchez, served in the same position for the Second Creek settlement. Cato West, another major slaveowner, was the preferred choice for Cole's Creek. Along with the officers, Bouligny added several names as candidates for the additional positions, including some of Green's own adult children, but never the patriarch.[12]

By 1785, Green had shown his true colors. According to Esteban Miró, Green was never comfortable with the Spanish government in Natchez. The American was not to be bound by any oath, acting solely on his own behalf and from his own convictions. He claimed loyalty to Spain when he applied for lands in the Natchez District in 1782, yet soon after he became troublesome. Felipe Trevino, acting military commander and governor, arrested him in 1783 because Green had "given medals to Indians" and because he had "correspondence with a fugitive from Natchez who was a refugee in the Choctaw nation." Both Spain and the United States gave tribal chiefs of the Indigenous nations medals as rewards and as signs of loyalty. The Spanish feared that Green was trying to sway the chiefs of the surrounding nations to abandon their Spanish allies and join forces with the United States, or at least with the American settlers. For the Spanish, Native allies served as military buffers to the American Republic. Despite these grievous allegations, Miró overruled his governor in Natchez and released Green from prison because, he thought, "a prison sentence too severe for his crime." Miró allowed Green to leave the district and return to Georgia, where Green claimed he had to arrange the affairs of his family.[13]

Colonists like Green presented a difficult problem because Spanish officials could not simply banish them without risking the economic viability of the Natchez District. Green may have been "captious, quarrelsome, and half-witted," as Miró told his superiors, but "the rest of his family, sons and relatives, are reasonable and useful for the raising of tobacco." Despite Green's reputation as a troublemaker, his family had quickly become an integral part of the Natchez economy and the tobacco planting that sustained the district. Neither Miró, nor Trevino, nor his successor Bouligny chose to risk complete alienation of Green's extended family by acting too forcefully against Green.[14]

★ ★ ★

On February 7, 1785, the state of Georgia established Bourbon County from territory in the zone disputed between the United States and Spain. Not only did Georgia establish Bourbon County, but they also appointed leading settlers as justices of the peace, including John Bingaman, William McIntosh Jr., Benjamin Farrar—and Thomas Green. William Davenport, Nicholas Long, and Nathaniel Christmas also received commissions, even though they had never been to the district. Thomas Green had traveled to Georgia to witness the proceedings. Regardless, the three moved their families there over the next couple of months.[15]

Green soon returned from Georgia to Natchez, but once again pursued his own goals. The orders he, Davenport, Long, and Christmas received were clear: they were to go to the district and convey the nominations to the settlers selected. More importantly, upon arrival, the four men were supposed to deliver a message to the governor of the Natchez District: Georgia had established Bourbon County and the governor should voluntarily relinquish the district. If the governor should refuse to turn the district over—as he certainly would—the emissaries were instructed not to take further action until no Spanish troops were present.

As the diplomatic exchanges continued to increase in frequency and urgency, an additional problem became apparent. The Anglo settlers were not capable of speaking or writing Spanish, and their instructions, as well as the papers proving their commissions, were in English. The Spanish governors of Natchez and Miró were themselves not able to read English either. As a result, the diplomatic exchange proved complicated to say the least.[16]

Green, unperturbed, arrived in Natchez first, and he did not wait for the other three emissaries before seeking out Governor Trevino. In June 1785, Green informed the governor that he had orders from Georgia to establish Bourbon County. Before the Spaniard could draft an official response, a conflict arose among the American settlers. Richard Ellis, Tacitus Gaillard, and Sutton Banks organized a protest and authored a pamphlet against joining Bourbon County. They were unwilling to become a part of Georgia, even though Gaillard and Banks, as well as Richard Ellis's son, John, were all named justices of the peace. In fact, they called for a meeting of all citizens at which Thomas Green should explain his actions. What is more, they countered Green's plan with one of their own. The three men proposed to create a new American state, entirely separate from Georgia and free from Spain. This development was even more troubling for the Spanish. Some leading colonists were leaning toward joining Georgia while others wanted to create their own state. Both meant a loss for Spain. Even worse, Louisiana Governor Miró received a report from Alexander McGillivray, a chief in the Creek Nation, that 2,500 Americans were on their way to attack Natchez. Governor Miró had to act quickly.[17]

Louisiana Governor Miró sought answers from Trevino in Natchez. Luckily for the Spanish, Trevino revealed that Adam Bingaman had refused a commission as justice of the peace and additional unnamed colonists had also refused the commission, suggesting a lack of support for joining Georgia. "Some doubt the success of the enterprise; others do not want Thomas Green as governor, since they consider themselves by right of birth better than he," Trevino told Miró. They thought

"Thomas Green was a man of quarrelsome and wicked character and not to be trusted; that he could in no manner become governor of this territory belonging to Spain, and that the province of Georgia had no right to do this." Still, the news was not all positive. The colonists who wanted their own state "have dared," Trevino wrote, "without my consent, to call a meeting of all the inhabitants." Trevino admitted he was in no position to effectively challenge the meeting. [18]

Despite his unpopularity with the elites of the district, Green had created a dangerous split in Natchez. While the elite Anglo-American colonizers overwhelmingly rejected him, he did find some converts to his cause. Yet settlers in the town widely disagreed on a course of action. Green had arrived only three years before the creation of Bourbon County and the citizens that had lived in the district since it was a part of the British Empire thought him unworthy of becoming their leader. Issues of class and community formation became apparent. Although Green was a wealthy slaveowner, he had not yet reached a high enough social status to become a valid candidate for leadership, at least in the eyes of the wealthiest settler colonizers. [19]

Green also failed to convince some of the noncommittal colonists. Slaveowners like Adam Bingaman refrained from taking any action, either pro-Bourbon County or against the Spanish regime in Natchez. Others, like the three writers of the pamphlet—especially Gaillard—sprang into action immediately to establish their own state. Trevino found them even more dangerous. The "act of the said Jacinto Gaillard and his companions is more detestable to me than what Thomas Green has done," Trevino informed Miró. "At first sight it offered graver consequences, but I have the satisfaction of informing you that at the meeting of the war council the said Jacinto Gaillard was accused and depreciated in such manner as had been Thomas Green."[20]

Despite the reactions of most of the colonizers at the meeting, Trevino lost control over the district. Green remained on the loose, with allegations persisting that he stole enslaved people and horses in the backcountry. Although some colonists remained ostensibly loyal to

Spain, unrest from the other two parties created a tense situation. In addition, rumors began to swirl again that Georgia was sending troops to Natchez to reinforce their claim to the district. In New Orleans, Governor Miró began to fear for the integrity of Louisiana's northern border. [21]

On June 19, 1785, Miró wrote a fierce letter to Green. "Your position, your little learning, which is known, and the erratic temper that you have shown are strong reasons why I do not think the State of Georgia has given you the authority" to represent it, Miró scolded. He reminded Green, who had pledged loyalty to Spain, that he was at his mercy. "If I hesitate to order your arrest, I do so out of consideration for the State of Georgia that you so falsely represent, although I am fully authorized to do so, as you are a subject of His Catholic Majesty," Miró continued. "You obliged yourself . . . to live under our wise laws; yet you arrived here in May 1782 with all your family and without a passport." Miró insisted he had done Green a favor by allowing him into Natchez. "Having fled your country you sought to settle here," Miró wrote, "I granted you permission to do so." Miró again mentioned Green's low status. Whatever wealth he now enjoyed originated in favorable Spanish trade policies and subsidies for tobacco. Miró also chastised Green for not following proper procedure in reporting the orders from Bourbon County. "I am suspicious of you, especially as you did not come directly to me but did come to the commandant of the fort," Miró wrote. "Since the business is of such great importance, you certainly show your ignorance." Miró then summoned Green to New Orleans to explain himself. "On this day I give orders," the governor wrote, "to the commandant of the fort to aid you to come to the city of New Orleans, that you may treat with me personally." The order to appear in New Orleans served two goals: Green had to prove the validity of his documents, and he was temporarily removed from the district, thereby eliminating the leader of one faction. [22]

Green's case had immediate consequences. In addition to the sharp letter, Miró saw no other choice than to relieve Trevino of his duties.

He feared the governor had lost control of, and standing with, the citizens of Natchez. On June 20, 1785, Miró replaced Trevino with Sergeant Major Francisco Bouligny, but Bouligny did not arrive in Natchez until July 23. On June 25, Miró reported to his superior in New Spain that the problems with Green would soon be put to rest because the other three emissaries from Georgia had arrived in Natchez. Yet Miró was still worried about the independent state faction led by Gaillard, Ellis, and Banks. The situation "deserves the utmost attention to avoid the loss of the inhabitants in general of the aforementioned district," Miró wrote, "which would be very difficult afterwards to return to the flourishing state in which it is found (now) by the cultivation of tobacco." Miró's only hope was that the new governor, Bouligny, would be able to resolve the situation quickly and restore peace in the district to grow more tobacco.[23]

Bouligny was right about the influence of the three other emissaries sent from Georgia in helping to resolve Spanish problems. Arriving after Green, they were shocked to discover what he had done and how much disruption he had caused. The first to land in Natchez was Captain Davenport, who was, according to Stephen Minor, immediately besieged by the district's citizens. The people in Natchez tried to understand what exactly was going on, and it was obvious to most of them that Green was not trustworthy. Davenport and his party, including his family, were confined on the boat upon their arrival. While they were eventually allowed to come ashore, four men who accompanied him and the crew of the boat were marched "to the fort, where they were immediately confined, and obliged to sleep in the Calaboose, much inferior to our [US] Dungeons" for ten days.[24]

Throughout all of this, Davenport tried to remain uncommitted to any specific action until he had a chance to speak to the governor, or so Davenport told Minor. When they met, Davenport acknowledged that Green had commissioned himself as a colonel without the consent of the other three emissaries. Davenport began to communicate with Bouligny, yet faced consistent communication barriers because he only spoke English, whereas Bouligny and Miró spoke and wrote in Spanish.[25]

Green continued to draw much of the focus of all parties involved. In a letter to the governor of Georgia, Samuel Elbert, Davenport explained that Green had seriously overstepped his authority by beginning negotiations by himself and, in addition, had forced the Spanish on their heels. Green's actions had caused the people of Natchez to distrust any emissary from Georgia. Thomas Green clearly followed his own agenda. Governor Miró was tired of Green's games, yet still concerned with possible American military involvement in Natchez. In an early July letter to Bouligny, Miró informed the Natchez governor that while Green had left the district, he feared that Green was attempting to link up with the American troops rumored to be on their way. Miró warned Bouligny that he should be cautious and keep an eye on the people of Natchez.[26]

In August, Bouligny sent a report of his meetings with the remaining three emissaries from Georgia. According to Bouligny, Nicholas Long, not Davenport or Green, was now in charge of the delegation. Green, who had returned to Natchez sometime between July 19 and August 28, did not collaborate with the three and remained ill at home. Bouligny seems to have been comfortable with Long, since they struck up a conversation about the "vagabonds" that had been plaguing the district since Spain took over. Unwilling to settle under any government, a group of Anglo criminals haunted the Natchez Trace and proved to be a nuisance for trade and travel on the important road. Both men agreed that these "vagabonds" represented a serious threat. Long even agreed that these men should be brought to justice jointly by the United States and Spain. Bouligny must have been elated to receive this news, since those vagabonds, estimated at about five hundred, were often mentioned as an imminent threat to Spain, and it was feared that Green was trying to take command of them to lead them against the Spanish. The amicable conversation convinced Bouligny that the situation could be handled peacefully, and that future cooperation with the United States was possible.[27]

Long did his best to convince Bouligny that the United States would not take Natchez by force. However, Long also left no doubt that the Natchez District was a highly sought-after prize for the new republic. Georgia and indeed the US "would employ every means within its power to obtain this territory from Spain, because it found itself in such a position that it was impossible to do without it." According to Long, "There is no sacrifice that America would not make to obtain it from his Catholic Majesty." Bouligny believed Long and communicated to Miró that the United States favored mediation over force to obtain the district. Bouligny appears convinced that Long and Christmas, the fourth emissary, viewed the situation in Natchez and their mission in a different light then Davenport and the much-maligned Green.[28]

Sometime in late summer 1785, Green fled Natchez. He feared he would share the fate of Ellis, Gaillard, and Banks, who had all been imprisoned because they lacked the cloak of diplomatic legitimacy. Green remained in the Chickasaw Nation until at least November 1785, at which date the governor of Georgia informed the scoundrel that his request for compensation had to undergo debate in the Georgia legislature. Green's sons, conversely, remained in Natchez. Green tried to stay in Indian territory, but was eventually captured and sent to a prison in New Orleans. His wife, Martha, sought his release but fell ill and died while attempting to secure his freedom. In 1792 Green's sons petitioned the new governor of the Natchez District, Don Manuel Gayoso de Lemos, to allow their sick father to move to Baton Rouge. He was "greatly afflicted with sickness," the petition read, "and from a sense of your Excellency's tender and human disposition and through unfeigned sympathy and filial affection to their father they take the liberty with the most Humble and supplicating movements to solicit your Excellency to permit him to remove to Baton Rouge and to reside there where it probably may be more healthy and less expensive, and your memorialists as in duty bound shall ever pray." As he languished in prison, Thomas Green's dislike of the Spanish had only grown. Spanish officials felt the same way.[29]

Still, Gayoso relented. In a letter to the Baron de Carondelet, the new governor of Louisiana, he appealed for Green's removal to Baton Rouge. Since Green's children always had been "honest and peaceful people of this district," and that they were only following the law of nature in wanting to take care of their father, Green should be moved to Baton Rouge. However, Green was ordered to report to the commandant of Baton Rouge daily if he stayed there. The expenses incurred were to be paid by Green's children. Carlos de Grand Pré, the commandant who had admitted Green to Natchez in 1782, assumed the same post soon after Green's arrival in Baton Rouge and would receive his daily check-ins.[30]

In some ways, Green's journey had come full circle. Arriving in Natchez in 1782, Green set out to become a rich slaveowner and thereby move to the top of the social strata. However, Green failed to do so. He attempted to present the Natchez District to the Americans, yet he did not count on the internal resistance of his fellow enslavers nor the fault lines of Atlantic world politics. As the other three emissaries and leading Natchez planters pointed out, it was Thomas Green's countenance, his lack of proper demeanor, his brashness and bravado, and his constant scheming that caused the leading citizens to reject Georgia's plans. Colonizers like Ellis, Banks, Gaillard, Duncan, Hutchinson, Farrar, and the Minors had been in Natchez since it was an outpost of the British Empire. Ellis and his supposed co-conspirators did not reject Green's idea about a Natchez independent from Spain, yet they outright spurned Green as their superior. In the three years after his arrival, Green must have made more enemies than friends among the planter elite, and neither his wealth nor his American commission changed the opinion of Natchez's future leadership class. His sons, however, were able to assimilate. Spanish officials viewed them as important tobacco growers, and Bouligny held them in high enough regard to offer them posts in his proposed militia. Even though Thomas Green was not able to carve out a position for himself in Natchez, he succeeded in establishing his family in the district. Once the Americans received Natchez in 1798, Green's star rose one more time. He became a magistrate of the Mississippi Territory and in that function married Andrew Jackson to Rachel Donaldson. However, he did so on his son's plantation, signaling that although his family was well established, his personal wealth never recovered.[31]

The story of the other emissaries is relatively quickly told. In 1786, the United States Congress passed a resolution "strongly disapproving the course which the state of Georgia had pursued." A day later, John Jay submitted the resolution to Gardoqui, who immediately passed this information on to Bernardo de Gálvez, Viceroy of New Spain. However, this information was not instantly available to Miró or Bouligny because it would only arrive in Louisiana as fast as the quickest ship could make the voyage. Miró then sent letters to Bouligny and ordered the three emissaries to leave the district. If not, they faced the threat of arrest and trial by the Spanish crown.[32]

By this point, emissary Long had already left the district. Receiving a passport to the Cumberland from Bouligny, he departed October 16 after sending Miró the emissaries' final letter. Long disagreed with the strong wording of the letter and no longer believed in the possible success of their mission. Christmas and Davenport acknowledged the order and promised that they would leave within a week. Davenport only requested that his pregnant wife and his thirteen-year-old child could stay behind until the traveling conditions would be better. Christmas and Davenport left Natchez on December 11, and the Bourbon County affair appeared to be over.[33]

Yet Davenport remained in the area among the Indian nations surrounding Natchez. Until at least mid-1787, Davenport attempted to intervene with the Chickasaws and Choctaws, as did Green. Davenport's presence in the area continued to cause alarm among the Spanish and their subjects. For example, on July 25, 1786, David Smith warned Colonel Tacitus Gillyard "there are five hundred men now embarking for this Post and a party of Indians commanded by Captain Davenport ready to start down." By September 1787, however, Davenport appeared to have met his fate. Miró reported that Davenport and some of his companions had been murdered. Davenport had become one of the vagabonds the Spanish were constantly worried about, but it did not serve him well. [34]

* * *

Thomas Green encapsulates the problems of westward expansion in the early American Republic. As individual states jostled for power in the Articles of Confederation government before the passing of the great land ordinances, individual adventurers like Green drove foreign policy in the lower Mississippi valley. Posing as agents for individual states and the government of the United States, they pushed the diplomatic patience of the Spanish to the brink and caused the American government more than a little discomfort. The periphery, in essence, dictated foreign policy to the center through the actions of rogue colonial agents like Green. Understanding what drove men like him, and how they sought to exploit the liminal status of places like Natchez, shows how weak both the Spanish and the American empires were as they allowed a few men to dominate international events. [35]

TROUBLED TRIO: THE KEMPER BROTHERS AND REBELLION IN WEST FLORIDA, 1804

JANE H. PLUMMER

★ ★ ★

The Kemper brothers—Reuben, Nathan, and Samuel—came to Spanish West Florida hoping to start a business selling silk stockings, wig powder, and other luxuries. Instead, they ended up starting a rebellion that threatened the uneasy peace between the United States and Spain in the Gulf South. The Kempers saw opportunity not only in the region's commercial potential, but also in its uncertain geopolitical position. West Florida was located in a weakening Spanish Empire next door to an ascendent American one, and it was home to many American immigrants who the Kempers assumed were unhappy with Spanish rule and easy to manipulate to join an anti-Spanish cause. The Kempers came to West Florida determined to advance themselves, regardless of what empire stood in their way.

Born in northern Virginia, the Kempers grew up in Ohio, where they were moved by their father, a preacher, to settle near Cincinnati, around 1793. In 1799, Reuben, the eldest brother, was the first to head south to West Florida, traveling at the behest of John Smith, a member of the Ohio territorial legislature, to open a new store on the Spanish frontier. Nathan and Samuel, respectively around three and five years younger, joined him not long after.

Some thought of the Kemper brothers as "boisterous frontiersmen"; others felt they were "notorious [for their] lawless existence on the frontier." Among the three, Reuben earned a reputation as a military colonel and for "being of huge frame, loud voice, and an address that passed for affability." Among his accomplishments, "besides those of a knife and gun, was his profanity, which the men of his school pronounced unusually 'eloquent.'" Reuben Kemper "was, during most of his life, engaged in brutal, criminal acts—[and he was a] profane braggart, a whiskey-guzzling, marauding, law-defying ruffian of the border." A strong man, he stood about six feet tall, with brown hair, hazel eyes, and a face tanned from many hours outdoors.[1]

The Kempers' destination was Spanish West Florida. "West Florida" was a term initially used by the British when they acquired Florida from Spain following the Seven Years' War and divided it into two colonies, East and West Florida, with the Apalachicola River, near Tallahassee, as the border between the two. When Spain got the Floridas back following the American Revolution, they kept the division. West Florida had long been a tumultuous region and difficult to govern. At one point or another, the British, French, Spanish, and Indigenous peoples all were the most powerful authority in the region. As a result, a heterogenous group occupied the region. In the early 1800s, West Florida was divided into four districts or parishes: Baton Rouge, Feliciana, St. Helena, and St. Tammany. Today the same region is divided into eight districts or parishes: West Feliciana, East Feliciana, East Baton Rouge, Livingston, St. Helena, St. Tammany, Tangipahoa, and Washington. It is important to remember that a portion of what the Spanish called "West Florida" is in the modern state of Louisiana between the Mississippi River to the east, Pearl River to the west, the state of Mississippi to the north, and the Amite River to the south.

Together, the brothers acquired several parcels of land in the Feliciana District of Spanish West Florida and Pinckneyville, Mississippi. The Kempers lived on land owned by John Smith in the village of New Valentia in the district of Feliciana. Rough men heading to the frontier to sell fancy goods to other rough men was not such a far-fetched idea. It was a common business venture for merchants to bring hard-to-find products to the border regions and charge through the roof. Smith expected the Kempers to bring back a 100% return on his investment.[2]

Alongside enterprising merchants, the US government also kept a close eye on West Florida. In order to avoid outright war while expanding the country, the Virginia Dynasty presidents—Thomas Jefferson (1801–1809), James Madison (1809–1817), and James Monroe (1817–1825)—chose to encourage people with American allegiance to occupy borderlands and eventually usurp the established authority. They hoped the United States would in time annex the territory without waging an economically and resource-intensive war. Spanish West Florida was such a heavily contested region because whoever controlled Spanish West Florida controlled the all-important Mississippi River. As long as a foreign power owned East and West Florida, the Virginia Dynasty presidents felt the Spanish presence jeopardized America's commercial stability.[3]

However, Jefferson, Madison, and Monroe, though uneasy about their Spanish neighbor, were not willing to wage war for the Floridas. As a result of American insecurity and motivation to expand, in February 1804 Congress passed the Mobile Act, which added to the growing political tensions of the region. This act expanded American territory, claiming all the land between the Mississippi and Perdido Rivers for the United States. Using the Mobile Act as justification, the Kemper Brothers, without official assistance from the US military, attempted to overthrow Spanish authority in West Florida in the summer of 1804. They did so by kidnapping Spanish officials, destroying the property of those loyal to the Spanish, and stealing cattle and weapons from inhabitants of the region.[4]

The brothers objected to Spanish governance and thus acted to minimize their authority in the contentious borderlands of Spanish and American territories. It may be possible to attribute their actions against the Spanish presence in the Baton Rouge region to American patriotism, anti-Spanish sentiment, self-motivated greed, or a combination of several factors. Nevertheless, the Kemper brothers, regardless of their motivations, were opportunists who took advantage of the political chaos of the Gulf South region. Whether together or individually, their involvement in the 1804 rebellion that bears their name demonstrated their willingness to circumvent official authority in order to advance their personal aims. The brothers' actions, while not showcasing the feelings of their fellow frontiersmen, demonstrate a unique opportunity to show unofficial American foreign policies in the Gulf South in the early 1800s.[5]

The Kemper brothers were filibusters and scoundrels who served whatever power best suited their desired outcome. For their purposes in the early 1800s, this was the Americans. Yet the brothers were only able to become such successful filibustering scoundrels due to the combination of the declining Spanish Empire and Virginia Dynasty policies. By refusing to engage in all-out warfare and instead indirectly or directly supporting Anglo-American uprisings, the Virginia Dynasty created an environment in which the declining Spanish Empire could not be entirely effective. Since the Spanish could not completely shut down the Kemper Rebellion, it continued and expanded for several months along the Spanish–American border.

★ ★ ★

Reuben Kemper traveled to West Florida in 1799 with a budget of $12,000 to purchase goods that he and Smith had previously agreed would sell fast in the Gulf South. By March, Reuben had spent $9,500.38, and in May, Reuben and Smith headed south to set up shop in West Florida; Smith received the permission of Spanish Commandant Carlos de Grand Pré for the venture.[6]

The store opened on the Bayou Sara in Feliciana on June 1, 1799. Both Smith and Reuben Kemper believed the store would be teeming with customers. Unfortunately for Reuben, the dream never materialized, in part due to larger economic and geopolitical conditions, including inflation and concerns about Napoleon's ambitions. To encourage Reuben in the face of headwinds, Smith drew up papers for a formal business arrangement in which Reuben would remain in West Florida to sell the goods and Smith would return north.[7]

During Smith's absence, Reuben did sell items from the store, but almost all were on credit to fellow Americans in the region. Although the store was not profiting, Reuben built a social circle in the area and made several purchases for himself, including an enslaved woman and 630 arpents (about 530 acres) of land.[8]

On April 24, 1800, "citing a 4,882-peso debt to two local men as evidence of poor management," Smith dissolved, as he termed it, his "conditional partnership" with the Kempers. (One peso equaled roughly one dollar at the time.) Smith also declared that he should no longer be "held responsible for any of Kemper's dealings." Despite how Smith's reaction first appears, it was not necessarily a harsh response. It was business. They were no longer partners, but Smith retained the Kempers to liquidate the store and manage his land. Smith stayed on good terms with the Kempers, evident in Smith's decision to sell Nathan and Reuben 200 acres in 1801.[9]

With Smith headed north and no profits to show from their venture, the Kempers looked to the riverways as a new source of income. In September 1800, Reuben bought a barge he would eventually name *Cotton-Picker*. For the next two years, the Kempers utilized Smith's old store front on the Bayou Sara, where they would load timber to sell in New Orleans and Natchez. The brothers were successful in their business, yet they failed to honor their commitment to Smith. As a result, Smith petitioned the commandant of Baton Rouge and the four western districts, Carlos de Grand Pré, to have arbiters evaluate the business in hopes of settling the debt. Customs of the era allowed for each side to elect an arbiter. While Smith wanted the matter dealt with expediently, crafty Reuben Kemper delayed.[10]

By April 1803, Reuben still had not chosen a single arbiter. He believed the United States would soon rule the region and they would be more favorable to him. He suspected Smith had influence over Grand Pré, which would explain why the local commandant was attempting to settle the case instead of adhering to the custom that disputes over 100 pesos be referred to a greater authority. The delay, however, led Grand Pré to allow Smith to select all the arbiters. Not surprisingly, they found in Smith's favor. On August 20, Grand Pré ordered Reuben to pay $5,807 and turn over 240 acres of his land. Despite the verdict, the Kemper brothers refused to vacate the property and paid Smith only 200 pesos.[11]

Smith, discontented with his initial pay off, was determined to remove Nathan Kemper, the official occupant, from "his" land. On June 13, Grand Pré ordered Nathan's immediate evacuation and arrest, and he dispatched local alcalde Alexander Stirling to serve the paperwork and take Nathan into custody. Due to the tense atmosphere of the borderland, Stirling had prudent orders to arrest, but to avoid violence in the engagement. He gathered a local militia force of approximately twenty men and set out for the disputed land. After arriving, Stirling's group forced Nathan and Samuel Kemper and four others into a house on the Bayou Sara. Reuben had already departed to New Orleans to plead their case to Juan Ventura Morales, Spanish intendant of Louisiana and later West Florida.[12]

It is unclear what the "boys in the house," as Reuben Kemper called them, were trying to accomplish by refusing to comply with Stirling, though it seems likely they expected fellow Americans living in Spanish West Florida to come to their aid. The Kempers felt, as many residents of the region did, that the United States would soon rule the territory and, therefore, American loyalties would lie with their fellow citizens. However, the Kempers were sadly mistaken.

It is vital to understand the demographic composition of the region and to acknowledge Americans united not only with the Kempers but also against them. Indeed, most Americans sided against the Kempers. Nationality was simply not the defining feature of people in the region. It is revealing that Spanish officials employed Americans in the militia against the Kempers. Secure in their position, they trusted Americans to put down their fellow Americans' rebellion.[13]

As the militia surrounded the house, the "boys in the house" barricaded the doors and windows. Once armed, Nathan emerged from the house. He asked what Stirling's motivations were. Though multiple guns were fixed on him, Stirling announced he was there to arrest Nathan and evict Reuben and Samuel from the land. Samuel replied that they would not be leaving without a fight. Though backed by the militiamen, Stirling, remembering his orders to avoid a violent confrontation, retreated from the Kemper stronghold and set up a patrol under Armand Duplantier. Despite the militia's best attempts to apprehend them, the brothers escaped under the cover of darkness. They crossed the Spanish boundary into the Mississippi Territory and fled to their property in Pinckneyville.[14]

The Kemper rebels expected all the region's fellow Americans to side with them, a purely nationalistic kind of thinking that did not consider how content most Americans were with Spanish rule. As a result, the Kempers faced far stronger opposition than they expected, and as they faced a united American and Spanish force instead of simply a sparse Spanish patrol, they decided their best option was to flee to American territory.

★ ★ ★

On June 16, Samuel and Nathan returned to Bayou Sara without a clear intention other than getting revenge and causing chaos. They attacked community members they felt had insulted them, including John Mills, the founder of Bayou Sara. Nathan called Mills a "liar, Scoundrel,

& villain," as he stood armed with a pistol, rifle, dagger, and knife. Nathan accused Mills of telling people not to frequent the Kemper store. Mills did not deny it. Instead, he justified it. The brothers were acting against the government, so Mills could not in good conscience encourage people to associate with them. While displeased with this answer, Nathan did not attack. Instead he simply retreated to his house on the Bayou Sara, at which point Mills wrote to Vicente Pintado, captain of the militia and Spanish surveyor general, to inform him of the rebel's latest actions.[15]

The Kemper homestead became a hive of activity from June 16 to 18, 1804. The brothers collected weapons from local farmers. Some supplied their weapons willingly; others had to be forced. Then, in a show of bravado, the group publicly cleaned the weapons on their elevated front porch, so there would be no mistaking their intentions.[16]

Spanish Commandant of the district of Baton Rouge Don Carlos de Grand Pré offered the Kempers a deal: amnesty in exchange for immediately and permanently leaving West Florida. The brothers declined and instead issued threats. They promised raids "to burn local plantations and incite the slaves to rebellion." In the following weeks, Grand Pré and Pintado worked to keep the residents apprised of the Kempers' crimes, including murder and whippings. It is unclear if the Kempers were directly involved in all these actions, such as the murders. Since the Kempers were rebelling against the government many violent crimes in the area were attributed to them without conclusive evidence. It is not outside of the realm of possibility, yet cannot be definitively connected to the rebels. The officials maintained Spanish sovereignty and autonomy, soothing residents' fears that American forces would be occupying the area soon. They kept the Anglo-American militia on patrol, demonstrating their faith in the residents despite their different nationalities.[17]

From this point forward, the Kemper brothers' actions are discussed variously as the "1804 Kemper Raids," "Kemper Riots," or "Kemper Rebellion," reflecting the fact that although it might be difficult to characterize what happened, the Kempers were the central players. During the June 1804 raids, the Kempers and their followers assaulted Spanish residents and Anglo-Americans who supported Spanish authority. They collected resources, such as enslaved people, horses, and weapons, taking them by force from surrounding farms. Spanish authorities refused to be intimidated by those they deemed "bandits."[18]

Around 10:00 A.M. on June 19, the Kempers and their followers surrounded the patrol that had been put in place the day before. Content to intimidate, the Kempers did little besides seizing the patrol's weapons before letting everyone go. Upon his release, John Mills once again reported the incident to Pintado.

Alexander Stirling spent June 23 and 24 gathering a force of about sixty men. Then on June 25 with Alcalde Stirling's gathered forces, Grand Pré ordered the arrest of those who moved against the Spanish government, especially those who may have felt protected by the American government even in Spanish territory. As Grand Pré worked to maintain Spanish sovereignty, he decided to take swift action and take down the rebels before they gained too much support. Stirling and his forces patrolled the Kemper homestead throughout the night with the intention to arrest them in the morning. Unfortunately, the "bandits" escaped across the river to Point Coupée during the night.[19]

At this point, the primary concern for the Spanish government was not the brothers' quest for vengeance but their claims that they were supported by the American governor of Louisiana, William C. C. Claiborne. The claim cannot be substantiated. Though the Kempers were actively working to overthrow Spanish governance in the region, the degree of involvement from the American government is arguable.

The Kempers' rebellion was neither well-planned nor well-supplied. If American officials were in fact backing the rebellion, they would want it to be successful. While they could not necessarily plan the rebellion for the brothers, they could certainly provide ample weapons. Further, Reuben was likely the one with the most contact with

American forces, and he was not directly involved with his brothers at this point.

The Spanish in general were suspicious of Americans, which is not surprising along a contentious border. The Spanish were notoriously resource deficient and even though the United States was young they could threaten the undervalued Spanish colony. The Spanish were also especially aware of Americans expansionist agendas and their desire to remove foreign influences from their borders. Overall, the United States did not benefit from the Spanish presence. Specifically, Spanish Florida provided a haven for runaway slaves and was deemed a security threat by Americans, all of which the Spanish were aware of. Therefore, it would not have surprised the colonial Spanish government should American make moves against them.

Grand Pré and Pintado both believed that the Kempers had support, even if only unofficially, from American authorities in New Orleans, though the evidence neither confirms nor disproves the suspicion. Regardless of whether the Kempers had any support from the United States, Spanish officials feared they did, and that fear informed how they treated the brothers' incursions into Spanish territory.[20]

In early July, Pintado ordered the Kemper "bandits," now a group of nearly forty men, to be taken—dead or alive. Grand Pré supported this initiative as he feared the long-term consequences if the American rebels were not held responsible in the Spanish court system. The concern was magnified as it was unclear how many resources Americans expansionists were willing to put into the region to undermine Spanish authority, which was becoming precarious.[21]

The patrols Pintado ordered, mostly manned by Americans, crushed the rebel bandits. On July 5, they chased a group of the bandits to the Mississippi boundary, which, because it was an international boundary, the bandits used to escape Spanish justice. Still, the militia members shot and wounded two men before they crossed the border. They were taken into custody. Julien Poydras, magistrate and an influential American planter living in the Mississippi Territory, interrogated the captured men. The two captive bandits revealed the names of individuals within the Kempers' group, which the Spanish called "El Quadrillo de Nathan Kemper," or "Nathan Kemper's Gang." Thirty-eight names in total were provided, and some were confirmed by a network of Spanish spies in the area. Everyone on the list owned land in Spanish West Florida and at least twelve men were related.[22]

Poydras also communicated with Governor Claiborne about the Kempers and how their actions would threaten the United States' relationship with Spain. The two went on to discuss whether the Kempers should be returned to Spanish authority. "In Treaties between Nations the Subject is sometimes noticed and Special provision is made for the arrest and delivery of fugitives from justice," Claiborne explained in an August 6 letter to Poydras. "But as our Treaty with Spain contains no Stipulation of the kind the case is left to be decided by the general customs and Laws of nations." In other words, because the treaty did not specifically mandate that the Kempers be handed over to Spain, Claiborne was not going to do it. The lack of American support, however, did not stop the Spanish from hunting down the bandits themselves.[23]

Spanish Governor Vicente Folch of West Florida offered amnesty to the majority of "El Quadrillo de Nathan Kemper;" and those who accepted it were able to retain their property and reintegrate into society. The pardoning was a political move, and though a risk, Folch's gamble paid off as the Spanish maintained authority for nearly another two decades, even though the population was largely Anglo-American. The pardoned men did not revolt against Spanish authority again. To Grand Pré's credit, most of the Anglo-American population was very happy in Spanish West Florida.[24]

The Kempers, however, saw the amnesty offer as a sign of weakness. Instead of accepting Grand Pré's offer, they made plans to attack Spanish strongholds. Though it is unclear exactly who was responsible, in July 1804, arsonists attacked Vincente Pintado's house, though enslaved people of his household were able to put out the fire before it claimed the property. While there is no direct proof this threat was the work of the brothers—as a government official, Pintado angered many people—the timing is suspicious. Consequently, Pintado reestablished the patrols on all roads with particular emphasis on the Bayou Sara, where patrols had been suspended since around July 4. From the safety of American Pinckneyville, raids continued against those who opposed the Kempers. The attacks were carried out by a small group of raiders who typically stole valuable goods such as horses, enslaved people, and weapons.[25]

Since the Spanish patrols were unable to catch the Kempers, Commandant Grand Pré instead threatened to seize their land unless they surrendered. Unsurprisingly, the Kempers refused. By contrast, Governor Claiborne offered amnesty for all participants who did not return to Spanish West Florida and instead remained in their homes in American territory. Claiborne was unwilling to return the rebels to Spanish authority, but his offer maintained diplomatic relations with the Spanish by encouraging the rebels to vacate Spanish West Florida and remain in American territory permanently. The policy would essentially end the raids without requiring the Americans to face Spanish justice.[26]

Anglo-American loyalty to the Spanish government was especially indispensable once August arrived and Nathan and Samuel carried out their revolt. Prior to this point, while the Kempers were raiding and committing crimes, they do not appear to have had a master plan; their actions were driven by vengeance or American patriotism or frustration with Spanish rule or a combination of factors. Then, everything changed.

★ ★ ★

On August 7, 1804, Nathan Kemper led a group, including Samuel Kemper and Basil Abrams, a consistent friend and ally of the Kempers, as lieutenants to the Spanish–American border, where they announced their intention to win independence for the so-called West Florida Republic. Then they raised a blue flag with white and blue stripes and two stars. Their declaration was believed to be written by Edward Randolph, a friend and ally of the Kempers who also worked as a merchant with Daniel Clark. "We the undersigned inhabitants of that part of Spanish dominions called West Florida," it read, "have resolved to throw off the galling yoke of tyranny and become freemen by declaring ourselves a free and independent people, and by supporting with our lives and property that declaration." The group anticipated capturing Baton Rouge and turning it over to the United States. Though earlier the bandits attacked Spanish supporters and stole supplies, they now turned to something new: a willingness to attack Spanish officials directly—and by extension, attack Spanish rule itself.[27]

The group left Pinckneyville and headed for St. Francisville and then to their destination, Baton Rouge. Along the route, they targeted the Spanish officials who had previously caused them so much trouble. They seized Pintado, again torching his house and leaving his cotton gin in flames. They kidnapped Alcalde John O'Connor, whose property was left untouched. Both men had surrendered without a fight, but Alexander Stirling, next on their list, resisted. As the rebels rapidly progressed through town they displayed their flag proudly, violently opposing any force that attempted to resist them and collecting weapons where possible. The group truly believed they would be victorious. Continuing toward Baton Rouge and their ultimate target, Commandant Grand Pré, the gang took several other hostages along the way. Before they could arrive, however, a West Florida resident named John Mears raised the alarm, allowing Grand Pré to be ready. Grand Pré told the Baton Rouge garrison commandant of the potential danger and ordered additional patrols to the area.[28]

For two days, those fighting for West Florida's independence were able to oppose Spanish forces. On August 8, 1804, Nathan offered to exchange his hostages, including O'Connor, Pintado, and Stirling, for the prisoners Spanish authorities had apprehended from the June raids. Grand Pré denied this offer, correctly believing that none of the hostages were in genuine danger, not even Pintado. If Grand Pré had engaged with the bandits by considering the prisoner swap, he would ultimately be recognizing the bandits as an equal. Grand Pré likely did not want to set that type of precedent, especially in a frontier society. By refusing to engage, Grand Pré was certainly gambling, yet this wager again paid off in his favor. At this point, recognizing defeat was likely, the rebels withdrew from the outskirts of Baton Rouge to Bayou Sara, where the three brothers would be reunited.[29]

Reuben was not directly involved in this plot and likely unaware of it, as he was in New Orleans from late June through late August to testify in a court case. Nathan and Samuel believed there was little to lose in Spanish West Florida and their raid could only accelerate American occupation. Like most older brothers, Reuben wanted to protect his younger brothers, but he needed to manage his own agenda, too. Reuben, although anti-Spanish, is unlikely to have approved of his brothers' plan as it would complicate the lawsuit against Smith should the revolution prove unsuccessful. Since Reuben was absent he was not entirely sure of his brothers' actions; however, he wrote hostile letters to Stirling encouraging him to leave the younger Kempers alone.[30]

Contrary to his initial reluctance, however, Reuben joined his brothers' group in early August and attempted to recruit Feliciana residents to the cause. The records are not entirely clear why Reuben became actively involved in the dwindling rebellion at this point. Perhaps he wanted to support his brothers' agenda, or he also believed he had little left to lose in Spanish West Florida. Nonetheless, on August 9, the rebels were forced to retreat to Mississippi, where they released their prisoners, Pintado, O'Connor, and Stirling. As the Spanish were unwilling to negotiate and the bandits had limited resources, they had no other option than to retreat to American territory. Although the rebels were no longer in the district, Grand Pré hoped to catch and prosecute the rebels, so he proceeded with caution, calling for recruits from Feliciana and continuing proactive security measures, such as patrols.[31]

With their bid for independence at an end, the Kempers tried to negotiate peace. On August 16, Daniel Clark, good friend of the Kempers and well-known land speculator, met with Grand Pré on their behalf. Clark presented a letter, written by Nathan Kemper and signed by the rebel leaders, that proposed a deal: their voluntary disarmament in exchange for a full pardon. Grand Pré, confident he had the upper hand, denied their request. The invaders sought peace, he suspected, because they feared the military force he had mustered, and they wanted to cut their losses and at least retain their land. Grand Pré had few illusions they had any regard for Spanish authority. As a result, on August 20, the Kempers returned to the Mississippi Territory, where they faced no consequences from American authorities. As the Kempers had broken no American laws, they were free in US territory. Additionally, US officials ignored Spanish authorities demands for their return. The brothers went on to new ventures. Samuel opened a pub in Pinckneyville. Nathan developed a local plantation. Reuben, by contrast, tried to keep the rebellion alive. He traveled to the Bahamas and attempted to raise British support for their cause. Reuben became increasingly anti-Spanish after his court case with John Smith. While he was not directly involved in the 1804 rebellion, he never forgot how the Spanish treated him or his brothers.[32]

In early September 1805, Reuben got the renewal of hostilities he sought, though not in a way he expected. Having returned from the Bahamas and staying with Nathan in Pinckneyville, Reuben was grabbed by a Spanish force and spirited across the river to Spanish territory. According to Nathan, the assailants, wearing disguises, broke into his house and "seized his brother Reuben, and dragged him out at the door; after a struggle, during which they had beat him with a club, and so choked him that he had barely power to say, I surrender." Then, before Nathan could defend himself or his wife and child, the Spanish were dragging him out of the house as well. Despite the commotion, he heard one of the masked men say, "if the bitch utters another word, put her to death." Nathan called out for his wife several times before they were wrenched off his property. He never heard her reply.[33]

Reuben's testimony corresponded with Nathan's, although he also emphasized their location inside Mississippi Territory, placing them on American soil and therefore under American law. Additionally, Reuben identified members of the party sent to round up the Kemper brothers, singling out several enslaved persons of his enemies and even some men Reuben had once deemed friends.[34]

The Spanish also descended on Samuel Kemper's home that same night. "The outer door burst open," Samuel swore in an affidavit. "The door of the bedroom was then forced, and a blow made at the bed with a double-barrelled gun." Samuel described how he was seized, "thrown on the ground, and a rope was tied around his neck by which he was dragged about one hundred and fifty yards." Not long after the raids, the three brothers, now reunited under the watchful eyes of the masked men, found themselves on their way to Commandant Grand Pré.[35]

The armed band had been sent by Spanish Captain Solomon Alston, and it included Spanish, Anglo-American, and Black men. Once the brothers were back in Spanish territory, the Spanish militia put them on a pirogue headed for Baton Rouge. With all three brothers bound to one another, the river voyage was initially uneventful. As they approached Point Coupée, located in US territory, they began to yell for help, successfully catching the attention of an American, Dr. John Fowles, who alerted the commandant of the garrison, Army Lieutenant William Wilson.

Wilson stopped the vessel, then turned the brothers over to the local army commander at Fort Adams, where a judge interviewed the brothers. The brothers made sure their tale was known by all, including Governor Claiborne's father, Virginia Congressmen John Claiborne, who relayed a letter discussing the Spanish not honoring their border with the United States. By entering US territory to capture the Kempers, if under official Spanish order, this kidnapping violated the international border between Spain and the US. As a result, American officials feared the Kemper brothers' abduction was part of a larger Spanish plot.[36]

When confronted with the Spaniards' action, Grand Pré claimed he was completely unaware and the men were acting on their own. He promised to investigate the matter, while reminding American officials of their own unofficial actions in Spanish West Florida. Whether Grand Pré was truly ignorant can never be proven, although it's certainly true that the Kempers' capture would have assisted Grand Pré's efforts to calm the West Florida districts. It is possible Grand Pré's administration knew the benefits the Kempers' capture would reap for the colony, and how for diplomatic reasons an official such as Grand Pré could not be involved. Therefore, those close to him acted on his behalf if not on his direct orders. At the same time, it is also possible pro-Spaniards were simply acting on their own agenda, infuriated by the Kempers and everything they stood for. The Kempers attacked many people, stole many resources, and as a result, their enemies were numerous.[37]

Just as Grand Pré claimed not to be aware of any designs against the Kempers in 1805, US officials kept a studied distance from the Kempers' activities. American officials certainly did not dissuade the actions of those involved. The Kempers resided in Pinckneyville after the rebellion without any fear of being turned over to the Spanish, despite repeated requests by the Spanish government. Spanish official Marquis de Casa Calvo, for example, urged Claiborne to tell authorities in Mississippi that they must not "give refuge to any of the rebels of the Feliciana District" and to charge them to "admonish and reprimand Reuben Kemper." Mississippi officials must, Casa Calvo wrote, "have him secured in jail."[38]

Claiborne declined to involve American forces in the capture of the Kempers, though he did offer to speak with Reuben Kemper as they were both in Pinckneyville. Claiborne further denied any American involvement. "I therefore presume it is scarcely necessary for me to repeat to your Excellency that the insurgents in West Florida have never received any encouragement or countenance in any shape from the American Government or its officers," Claiborne replied.[39]

Throughout his correspondence with Spanish officials, Claiborne focused on two things. First, he adamantly denied American involvement in the filibusters' actions. Second, he refused to involve American resources, including labor, to capture the filibusters residing in US territory. But when discussing the Kempers with American officials, the governor's priorities changed. In an 1804 letter to President Thomas Jefferson, for example, Claiborne expressed concern. "I find Kemper's Riot, for it cannot be called an Insurrection, is viewed to the northward [i.e., the United States government], as an important affair, and that it has been used by the Spanish minister among others, as a pretext for calumniating our administration," Claiborne reported. He assured Jefferson that his response had been firm. "The Marquis [Casa Calvo] was assured by me, that Kemper was not encouraged by any officer of the United States, and that my Government would hear with regret of the disturbances at Batton-Rouge."[40]

Claiborne's unwillingness to aid Spain in its attempts to quell the rebellion can be attributed to his political status and the belief that it was inevitable that the Spanish Floridas would eventually be taken over by Americans. Claiborne wanted to be held in high regard as a leader, to serve the president in whatever manner requested, and further to assure the president his region was well managed. This is evident in the closing of his October 27 letter to President Jefferson. "I again repeat, that I earnestly desire to see the United States at Peace with all the world," Claiborne wrote. "But if a war, should arise, I shall esteem myself particularly fortunate to be placed in a situation to render some service to my Country." Claiborne was a recognized leader in the region and was willing to serve the president's agenda in whatever manner was necessary. He wanted to make it clear he would not act without the Jefferson's approval, yet he was willing and able to take on more responsibility, especially military responsibility, at any time.[41]

While Jefferson valued the Mississippi River and the Gulf Coast, the success of his administration relied on his ability to balance the good of the whole nation against what a potential war with Spain over a specific region might do. Considering the United States had recently acquired the Louisiana territory in 1803, it is understandable that Jefferson was not willing to wage an official war, regardless of how it might benefit a particular region. While the Gulf Coast was valuable, it did not offer much that the United States had not already acquired in the Louisiana Purchase. A war, even with a declining Spanish Empire, was too high a price to pay.

Despite the Kemper brothers' attempts to hasten West Florida's acquisition, US leaders were unwilling to comply. In the end, Jefferson (and his successors Madison and Monroe) each relied on expansionist Americans, such as the Kempers, to apply pressure to the region through occupation and the deterioration of the Spanish Empire's hold of the region.[42]

Even though the Kempers attempted rebellion was unsuccessful, it mattered to the United States and not just to their local area. The 1804 rebellion was the first in a string of filibustering attempts by the Kempers, including the subsequent West Florida Rebellion (1810) and the Magee-Gutierrez Expedition (1812–1813). The Kempers can be considered a case study in the Virginia Dynasty's filibustering attempts, an early example of how Jefferson, Madison, and Monroe each turned to American expansionists instead of the official military to implement their agenda on the Gulf Coast.

Despite the Kempers' best efforts, when the United States did obtain the Floridas in 1819, it happened just as Jefferson had intended—without official military action. Ultimately, the US acquisition of Florida had little to do with the Kemper Raids, and instead was the result of the Spanish Crown's diminishing ability to maintain their colony amongst the consistent pressure of expansionist Americans. Though Jefferson never officially supported any American expansionism, the policy he initiated led to the many filibustering events in the Gulf South, including, but not limited to, that of the unscrupulous Kemper brothers—Reuben, Nathan, and Samuel.

★ ★ ★

Regardless of how they presented themselves in government documents, the Kemper brothers were not well-mannered Anglo-American residents of Spanish West Florida. Nor were they victims of circumstances orchestrated by the villainous Spanish government. They were scoundrels, motivated by their own personal vendettas; their loyalty lay with whichever power could help them achieve their own goals. They worked to undermine Spanish authority, hoping that by demonstrating Spanish weakness they would gain followers for their anti-Spanish crusade. They raided local Spanish communities, stole enslaved people, cattle, and other property. Then they escaped to American soil to avoid Spanish justice.[43]

Nor were the brothers representative of the larger Anglo-American population's views. Instead, the brothers served their own interests while exacting vengeance against the Spanish government, which they felt had mistreated them. Reuben was hurt when Spain sided with Smith in the court case over their failed business, Nathan and Samuel resented the failure of their raid of Baton Rouge. Though the brothers' actions served the larger purpose of gaining the Floridas, the motivations behind those actions were much more of a scoundrel's nature than an American patriot.

WILLIAM AUGUSTUS BOWLES, THE PRETENDER: A TORY ADVENTURER AS NATIVE AMERICAN LEADER

DAVID NARRETT

★ ★ ★

William Augustus Bowles was a risk-taker from his earliest years. Born to an English family in Maryland in 1763, he put his life on the line for the king as a teenage Tory soldier in Pennsylvania. By the vagaries of war, his life changed in unforeseen ways after his unit was transferred to British West Florida in 1778. Stationed in Pensacola, he got into a row with an officer, deserted, and found shelter in the household of Perryman, a Creek chief of Anglo-Native parentage who lived by the Chattahoochee River above the Gulf Coast. He soon fell in love with his host's daughter, Mary, and probably had at least one child with her.[1]

Bowles's residence on the Chattahoochee gave him a glimpse of a complex Native American world. The Chattahoochee was the site of many Indigenous towns whose inhabitants were collectively known to the British as Lower Creeks. The Upper Creeks lived to the northwest in villages by the Tallapoosa and Coosa Rivers. While the Muskogees were the predominant ethnicity throughout the region, smaller

Native groups collaborated with them for security and leverage vis-à-vis colonials and other Indigenous nations. Creek diplomacy rested on consultation between regions, towns, ethnicities, and the kin-based clans that were their heartstrings. Authority at nearly all social levels depended on custom and persuasion rather than coercion. Indigenous respect for tradition did not mean stasis. As Stephen C. Hahn has written, eighteenth-century Creek social bonds were subject to "periods of decline and renewal, fission, fusion, and factionalism."[2]

The American Revolutionary War was radically disruptive to Creek communities. Many Creeks sided with the British against the Americans, but others oscillated between neutrality and pro-British military involvement as seemed most opportune. The war entered a new phase when Spain entered hostilities against Britain in 1779. Madrid's objectives had immediate relevance for the Creeks since Spain aimed at regaining Florida, which it had lost to Britain during the Seven Years' War.[3]

While residing with the Perryman family, William Augustus Bowles saw that southern Indians cared deeply about Anglo–Spanish warfare for control of the Gulf Coast. In 1780–1781, the Creeks showed a decided preference for continued British possession of Pensacola—the main port through which the English supplied them with munitions and trade goods. In early 1781, Bowles joined Creek and Choctaw fighters in battle against the Spanish east of Mobile. He then returned to Loyalist military ranks at Pensacola, only to be present when a large Spanish amphibious force cannonaded the British garrison, forcing its surrender on May 10, 1781. The Creeks fought gamely on the British side in this climactic battle. Bowles was himself fortunate to survive a Spanish blast that hit near his station, igniting an ammunition pile and setting off a huge explosion. Only eighteen years old at the time, he could have scarcely imagined that he would aspire within a decade to be head of the Creek Nation and, after further travails, proclaim an independent "State of Muskogee."[4]

The British Loyalist world was in ferment when Bowles moved to Nassau in the Bahamas in 1783 after a brief residence in New York. Exile bred resentment without arresting ambition. Jousting for place and prestige with other Tories was nearly constant in Bowles's post-war endeavors. His restless soul and vibrant imagination did not rest quietly on small isles where the sea beckoned outward. He pursued stage acting and portraiture for a few shillings in Nassau, all the while dreaming of a broader stage and canvas. The British cession of Florida to Spain in the imperial peace settlement of 1783 was fresh in his mind and hurt badly. Bowles did not accept the curtailment of independence for himself. His feelings were not dissimilar to Britain's Native allies that experienced collective loss and betrayal at the war's outcome.[5]

The international scene was far from settled despite the peace treaties of 1783. The United States had achieved independence but had not yet cohered as a nation. Spain's position in Florida was tenuous. The Spanish had to rely on Alexander McGillivray, the single most influential Creek leader after the war, to obtain cooperation in the struggle to hold American settlers at bay. Madrid endowed a British Loyalist merchant firm—Panton, Leslie & Company—with a virtual monopoly on Florida's Indian trade from St. Augustine to Pensacola by 1785. The company lobbied for more privileges over time, becoming a force and earning Bowles's enmity for lording over southern Indians. William Panton, a native Scotsman, was assertive on the political front, pledging conditional loyalty to the Spanish monarch while keeping his British nationality and freedom of maneuver at his Pensacola residence and storehouse.[6]

Great Britain had yielded Florida to Spain, but Britons and their progeny had considerable weight as traders and property-holders in Creek country. Since the Creeks were a matrilineal society, the children of Indigenous women by British traders were themselves considered Native by blood. As historian Claudio Saunt has argued, "a new order of things" was emerging in Creek society in the late eighteenth century, an order headed by a relatively small but disproportionately influential "mestizo" elite—men of mixed ethnic ancestry who had private landholdings and sizable numbers of enslaved Blacks. McGillivray, himself a leader of Scots-Native heritage, conducted diplomacy with Spanish and US officials as if he spoke for all Creeks. Bowles learned from McGillivray's example before coming to challenge him for power and conceiving of a Creek national state under his guidance.[7]

Recent historians are of different minds about Bowles. Two starkly contrasting interpretations by Eliga Gould and Gilbert Din are valuable to set the stage for debate. Gould views Bowles as a true revolutionary, the herald of a new "postcolonial nation," and a champion of Indigenous sovereignty who fought boldly, if not always consistently, to achieve worthy aims against Spanish and US opposition. Din takes a nearly opposite view, seeing Bowles as an egotist whose "haughty and deceptive promises" and "self-serving schemes" brought "more misery" to Indigenous people "than the relief they anxiously sought."[8]

Certainly Bowles often lied in his quest to become a supreme Creek leader. The more challenging question is whether he fibbed and fenagled for honorable purposes and with Indigenous interests genuinely at heart. Paradox abounds in his story. He despised the American Revolution, but the war liberated him to chart his own course. The war's unresolved issues, especially white settler–Indian conflict, lingering imperial rivalries, and a turbulent Indigenous landscape from the Gulf Coast to Canada spelled opportunity. Although a Tory, Bowles was inspired by US nationals such as James Wilkinson and others who acted outside official channels of authority to shape contested frontier regions where the balance of power appeared up for grabs. To be an "adventurer" in this sense might appear honorable to one's friends, though it was lawless, roguish, and scurrilous to those who felt threatened by disruptive change.[9]

Bowles was a man of words as much as deeds. An irrepressible publicist, he tailored messages to impress high-ranking imperial and colonial authorities—and he went so far as to write lengthy missives to the British and Spanish monarchs. Comparatively little is known about how he conversed with Creeks and other Indigenous people apart from what he wrote himself. Indigenous perspectives on Bowles may be inferred from British, Spanish, and US documentary sources. Native opinion, itself variable and diverse, was the critical test of Bowles's pretensions, which changed over time from being a deputy of a "United Creek and Cherokee Nation" to calling himself "Director" and "General" of the State of Muskogee. Bowles was not a pretender in the sense of being a simple fake, but rather a man who pretended to great things and acted as if his declamations would have power to transform social and political realities. Though he finally failed—and died in a Spanish prison in Havana in 1805—his story invites fresh analysis, to be rediscovered not only for its intrinsic drama but for what it tells us about a Tory adventurer and the Native peoples among whom he lived, schemed, and dreamed.[10]

★ ★ ★

It would be a mistake to think that Bowles had a clear and consistent design to establish a State of Muskogee from the beginning of his post-war maneuvers. If there was a constant in his plans, it was the desire for open trade with Florida's Indigenous peoples. In this respect, he acted by the standard colonial assumption that Natives would necessarily incline toward individuals and nations that had the wherewithal to manage commercial exchange, which for the Creeks involved the bartering of deerskins for European cloth, munitions, metalware, and a wide array of goods. Bowles got a firsthand view of the shipment of these articles once he set foot in the Bahamas. Nassau was an important way station for Panton, Leslie, and their associates—nearly all of whom were British Loyalists by background. Other Nassau merchants resented the company's monopoly, courtesy of Spain, on both the import and export sides of Florida's Indian commerce. The challengers found a champion in John Murray, Earl of Dunmore, who became royal governor of the Bahamas in 1786. Given to intrigue, Dunmore found the young Bowles much to his liking. Bowles knew little of commerce but was the type of fellow who ached to prove his mettle beyond the theater roles he had played.[11]

In the late summer of 1788, Nassau was abuzz with talk of conspiracy. A young man named Bowles had just embarked as the head of fifty armed volunteers who sailed in two schooners for Florida's Atlantic shore. The smart talk had it that the entourage, consisting of freebooters rather than soldiers, had the backing of Dunmore and his merchant friends John Miller and Broomfield Bonnamy. Indeed, this was the case. Bowles told his men that their mission was to seize John Leslie's trading storehouse near St. Augustine. The recruits would divvy up plunder while Dunmore and his Nassau allies would achieve an entry point for commerce with the region's Native peoples. This was supposed to be done with the aid of Florida Indians and without attacking the Spanish in the vicinity!

Bowles prepared the way, or so he thought, by consulting with McGillivray at Coweta in Lower Creek country a few months before the invasion. He believed he had McGillivray's tacit consent and the prospect of assistance. Contrary to Bowles's expectations, only about fifteen Native men joined his foray once the invaders put ashore south of their target. Spanish troops were soon on the ready but there was no attack. Bowles's men, a ragtag group, collapsed under the strain of fatigue and hunger. At least a dozen desperate recruits deserted and surrendered to the Spanish at St. Augustine's doorstep.[12]

Recovering from the fiasco, Bowles relocated to the Chattahoochee River and Florida's Gulf Coast by early 1789. Bowles knew the region. It was where he had lived with the Perryman family during the Revolution—and he spoke Muskogee fluently. The Tory adventurer eyed the lightly manned Spanish fort of San Marcos and William Panton's nearby Wakulla River storehouse just above Apalachee Bay. This obscure maritime zone could be an opening to the continent's Native peoples and a lifeline to the British imperium.[13]

Bowles maneuvered in a fluid Indigenous environment by the Florida Gulf Coast. Lower Creeks mixed freely with Seminoles, most of whom had deep historic connections to the Muskogees and affiliated groups. Many Seminoles were stoutly pro-British during the American Revolution, and consequently disturbed by the English military evacuation in 1783–1784. While cultivating Seminole allies, Bowles looked northward, too. Pan-Indian resistance to US expansionism was a potent force in Cherokee country, the Ohio Valley, and by the Great Lakes. The Chickamaugas were the most intrepid Cherokee militants, with towns proliferating on the northern margins of Creek country. Allied with the British during the American Revolutionary War, they networked with Ohio Indians and the British in Canada. Like the Creeks, the Chickamaugas relied on Tory agents and traders to supply them with munitions and goods from the Gulf Coast.[14]

Bowles took the initiative as a putative Native leader when he attended a conference of Creek and Cherokee headmen at Coweta, a prestigious Chattahoochee town, in early May 1789. After deliberations, Bowles drafted two petitions to George III, one in the name of the Creeks, the other on behalf of the Cherokees. While tailored to each nation's circumstances, both petitions called for English support in free trade and the supply of goods and munitions.[15]

The Coweta conference had an impressive array of Native attendees whose names Bowles carefully inscribed at the close of each document according to the chiefs' nationality. In all, twenty Creek headmen and thirteen Cherokees, largely of the Chickamauga region, attended the consultation, at least if Bowles's record is taken as entirely genuine. Unlike many documents of this kind, his copy did not bear the marks of Native headmen. As one might expect, Bowles was particularly knowledgeable of Creek leaders, nine of whom he identified as *micos* or civil chiefs—men whose foremost responsibility lay in social order and diplomacy. He identified four chiefs as head warriors. Of the towns he listed, most were in the Lower Creek region, his core area of support. That point is credible as is Creek–Chickamauga collaboration.

We simply cannot know if the conference involved all the specified individuals.[16]

Bowles presented himself as a British Loyalist at Coweta. One can imagine him wearing a military redcoat with a silver gorget to impress Native men. He doubtless kept mum on the fact that he was a "reduced" or retired officer who had not attained a rank above ensign (a junior position). As draftsman of the petitions, Bowles wrote of Creeks and Cherokees honoring him as "the Beloved Warrior." The Muskogee were effusive in praise, telling the British king of "our Beloved Warrior [Bowles] one of your Warriors that came back to us after you [the King] left our Land & he has lived with us ever since . . . he knows what we say to be true."[17]

In a pattern that would recur time and again, Bowles deliberately magnified his current influence in Creek country. He did not shrink from inventing facts—such as writing that he had been continually present among the Creeks since the war, though he had actually resided in the Bahamas for much of that period. Bowles meanwhile encouraged Creek and Cherokee men to voyage with him to England and put their case directly to the king. The idea of crossing "the Great Water" to England for diplomatic consultation was not new in Indian country, but it was still unusual. Cherokees had made notable visits to England in 1730 and 1762.[18]

In truth, Bowles needed at least some Native men with him to validate his own credentials as a genuine Indigenous leader to the British. Two Creeks and three Cherokees eventually decided to accompany him on the voyage, which proved far more circuitous and arduous than they would have desired. Two of the Cherokee voyagers were notable, if not principal individuals. One was Moses Price (Wosseo), a man of Cherokee British ancestry, who was fluent and literate in English. Another was Richard Justice (Uwenahi), shaman of Lookout Mountain town in the Chickamauga heartland.[19]

Interestingly, Bowles did not sign the first two petitions that he drafted to King George on behalf of the Creeks and Cherokees. In subsequent memorials to British and Spanish officials, he invariably signed as William Augustus Bowles or Wm. A. Bowles. I have found no extant document in which he wrote his Creek name—Eastajoca. The fact that Bowles retained his English name in correspondence indicates how he preserved his place in the European and Anglo-American world even while he spoke for Indigenous peoples. William C. Sturtevant, the distinguished anthropologist, has offered an intriguing translation of "Eastajoca," which may have derived from Muskogees who called Bowles *isti•co ka* ("writing person"). If so, the name would certainly have been appropriate given Bowles's highly active pen.[20]

Bowles initially desired to sail from the Bahamas directly to Britain but eventually decided, with Dunmore's advice, to voyage first to Canada where he could sound out British officials on the prospect of royal support and alliance between southern and northern Native peoples. In July 1790, Bowles took charge in presenting Native views in conference with Lord Dorchester, governor of Quebec. The Cherokee and Creek visitors had relatively little to do with this interchange apart from placing their trust in Bowles.[21]

Dorchester was rather dubious about backing the Native men's voyage to Britain, but finally lent assistance. Bowles was intent on putting his case to the highest levels of government. He played up Creek and Cherokee military strength as an English asset, especially since Britain and Spain were then on the brink of war over possession of Nootka Sound off Vancouver Island in the Pacific Northwest. Bowles's written presentations to Dorchester were imaginative and not short on fiction. He told of a "united" Creek and Cherokee Nation whose "residence is in Florida and whose force is 20,000 enrolled Warriors or fighting men" loyal to his Britannic Majesty. Bowles's geography was a bit loose here as the Cherokees dwelt in southern Appalachian valleys, not in Florida. More glaring is his tale of a formally "enrolled" Indian military force, which simply did not exist in the centralized manner he stated. Far from united among themselves, the Cherokees had fewer than 2,000 men of fighting age—and the more populous Creeks, quite as disparate, had some 5,000 warriors.[22]

Bowles was only getting started in the art of political fabrication and hyperbole while in Canada. In subsequent proposals of January 1791 to George III and foreign secretary William Wyndham, Lord Grenville, he again identified himself as deputy of the "United Nation of Creeks and Cherokees," which he claimed was governed by a Supreme Council of seventy-two men responsible for appointing a "Generalisimo" for the whole. This was his invention. While Lower Cherokee Towns (the Chickamaugas) frequently cooperated with the Creeks and Shawnees, there was no such united nation as Bowles asserted, let alone one with a single council or military leader.[23]

Bowles had a penchant for big-time braggadocio. He informed Grenville that he was ready, as soon as he returned to the Gulf Coast, to head a joint Creek–Cherokee army that would seize control of the Floridas, New Orleans, and even march on Mexico and liberate it from Spanish rule. An indefatigable self-promoter, he set the stage by sending word to London newspapers of his plan for "the reduction of Mexico." What would be considered absurd if declared in Florida did not necessarily appear that way to a British public with scant knowledge of North American geography or its Native peoples. Bowles meanwhile played on the commonplace view in British government circles that Spanish America was on the verge of internal upheaval and revolution.[24]

Bowles's discourse had its own style, a blend of plausible assumptions and principle interspersed with inflated rhetoric and bluffs. There was also ambiguity; the unanswered question was whether his main fight was to bolster the Creeks via-à-vis Spaniards or to resist the Americans. His diplomacy was double-edged, marked by appeals to high Spanish as well as British officialdom. In August 1789, only a few months before embarking for Canada, he forwarded letters, which amounted to political manifestos, to José de Ezpeleta, Captain General of Cuba, and to Conde de Floridablanca, the Spanish king's first minister. In the letter to Ezpeleta, Bowles harped on the Spanish policy of giving "exclusive privilege" in Florida's Indian trade to Panton, Leslie & Company. After describing the harm done under the current policy, he declared it "absolutely needful to give permission to another Commercial house to supply the Indians." Native leaders should decide on those whom they would entrust with the responsibility. Moreover, the state of trade should revert to what Indians "were accustomed to when the Country was in the possession of his Britannic Majesty." This was "the only means," Bowles added, to preserve peace.[25]

Bowles ingratiated himself with the Spanish even while he conveyed muted threats. His Catholic Majesty, Spanish King Carlos I, should know of anti-Spanish plotting in the western United States. The Creek and Cherokee Indians, he wrote Floridablanca, had received overtures from several unnamed parties conspiring to invade Louisiana. Thus far, both nations had refused these entreaties, but they could change their minds if Madrid denied them a commodious port in Florida. Spain would do well, Bowles advised, to accede to Native requests consonant with "the rights of humanity" ("*derechos de humanidad*"). The spirit of the age demanded no less from a benevolent monarch who wished to remedy the plight of Indian Nations now reduced to "nakedness" by dependency on a single trading house.[26]

Bowles's diplomacy was revolutionary. Though a mere commoner by European standards, he admonished high-ranking Spanish officials as if the playing field were level between all parties. Writing Floridablanca, he announced his plan to visit England with Native emissaries, reputably "principal men" of their nations. He also declared his intent to call on the Spanish ambassador in London. Bowles remarked that he might travel to Madrid, too, notwithstanding "the distance, costs, and inconvenience." This was one nervy fellow.[27]

Bowles's diplomatic persona was no more conventional than his dress. While going about London in 1790–1791, he projected the image of a Native leader, as would seem plausible to the English public. During his stay, he posed for artist Thomas Hardy whose portrait wonderfully captures the dashing protagonist. Bowles wears an elaborate headdress—a turban about his forehead with colored plumes above. The overall design is a collage of cultural styles, singular and individualistic, not unlike Native men of the late 1700s who used European cloth, leather, earrings, and other ornaments in their own manner. In the portrait, Bowles's brownish eyebrows stand out; a smidgen of similarly colored hair protrudes from the turban close by his right ear. As we gaze below that point, we see a finely woven neck collar bedecked with purplish wampum, and lower still a British's officer's silver gorget sits at chest level, held by a string about the neck. Bowles's beautifully flowing white shirt is cusped by a silver band on the right arm, and no doubt on left, too, though the latter is not visible in the subject's three-quarter pose.[28]

While cutting through the ordinary in dress, Bowles did the same in diplomatic discourse. He was an actor, now performing on a greater stage than he had once done in Nassau's amateurish theater. His manifestos for George III and Grenville amounted to "performative utterances"—a term employed by the twentieth-century English philosopher J. L. Austin to indicate a type of "speech act," essentially a promise, pledge, or assertion made with the intent of creating a bond between the speaker and the recipient audience. Bowles's "speech acts" were guarantees, *namely*, that what he expressed in the present would become true in the future.[29]

In a discourse of twenty-six pages to George III, Bowles portrayed the Creeks and Cherokees as "a portion of the original inhabitants of North America" who had known little but "the miseries of continual warfare," and "the diminution, & decay" associated with "a rude, & savage life," but were newly "resolved" on "Measures for their future conduct" that "would retrieve, & firmly establish their Affairs." They were nations committed to giving up hunting and "the hardships of a wandering life." They wished instead to rely on "plantation & farmyard" as "the best resources for the supply of a family." One fiction built on another in Bowles's paean to progress. The Creeks and

Cherokees "are now become a people, that live in a fixed society; have their Town, & their country life; are Mechanics & farmers," he wrote. "They have stemmed the course of waste & decay; their population encreases; individuals have property, & the blessings of civil Society Multiply every day." Loyalist refugees, who presently enjoyed the protection of Creeks and Cherokees, would repay their Indian benefactors by helping them to advance "in the light of European improvements to naturalize their skill, their arts, & their Manners."[30]

There were snippets of truth in Bowles's portrayal of Creek society, which had an increasingly influential propertied elite. However, the overwhelming portion of the Muskogees and closely affiliated groups depended on customary traditions in which men were hunters and women the foremost horticulturists. The Native way of life was not "wandering," as Bowles described. For hundreds of years, towns had been the foundation of Creek and Cherokee society, the place for councils and ceremonial rites besides much else.[31]

Bowles's climactic "performative utterance" came at the close of his Creek–Cherokee memorial to the king. Here he spoke directly for himself, reviewing his service to Britain in wartime at the risk of life and property. Bowles wrote that the king "sees" him, a loyal subject, "becoming the adviser, & the leader of an independent & populous Nation, presenting to your Majesty their devotion & services as Allies, both in peace & War." This was a futurist vision—a pledge of things to be. Though not gaining a royal audience, Bowles wrote as if he physically stood before the monarch who "sees" and trusts him. That is the bond imagined on Bowles's part.[32]

Skeptical of Bowles's pronouncements, Grenville placated him without encouraging the adventurer's military schemes. The Creeks and Cherokees were to be permitted, by Grenville's judgment, to traffic in British Caribbean ports, should "they [the Indians nations] find themselves in a situation to avail themselves of this indulgence." This favor came after the British war-scare with Spain had died down, lessening the value of adventurist gambits. Bowles trumpeted Grenville's limited endorsement as triumph. In an anonymous piece, written for the London press in February 1791, Bowles was heralded as "uniting in himself great beauty and strength of person, with great force and reach of mind, great intrepidity and great conduct." He was no less than a Roman hero: *"Vir magna vi corporis & animi praeditus"* ("A great man endowed with strength of body and spirit").[33]

A month later, Bowles addressed a memorial under his own signature to Carlos IV of Spain. The theme of progress again rushed from his pen. The Creeks and Cherokees, since their union, were leaving the state of hunting for agriculture, building a disciplined military establishment—signs of "their advances in Civilization." And yes, they had 20,000 men united in arms with another 20,000 through alliance with the Chickasaws and Choctaws. It would be "cruel" for any European monarch to deny a "free people" the use of their own coastline. Bowles's conception of Indigenous sovereignty was consistent with Creek understandings. Less than a year after the adventurer's pronouncement, a group of Lower Creek headmen told a Spanish official that his nation possessed only a few limited points along the Florida coast—St. Augustine, San Marcos de Apalache, and Pensacola—garrisons and ports that sat within Native lands.[34]

Bowles bluntly announced a Muskogee agenda to the Spanish monarch. The Creeks were determined to open two ports of their own—one at the mouth of the Apalachicola River and the other at Cape Florida, off what is Miami today. If the king refused to approve, the Creek–Cherokee Nation would immediately declare war on Spain! Bowles reminded the monarch that his hold in the Floridas was threatened not simply by rival empires, but by private "adventurers" ("*aventureros particulares*") acting for their own gain and power. He did not, of course, name himself as within that group. Bowles's bluster hardly endeared him to Spanish officials who were profoundly distrustful of British interlopers seeking coastal bases to exploit the contraband trade to Hispano-American colonies. Madrid tolerated Panton, Leslie & Company out of necessity, not by imperial preference.[35]

Before dispatching his most recent ultimatum to Madrid, Bowles requested an audience with Bernardo del Campo, Spanish ambassador to Britain. Campo, a veteran diplomat, granted the favor. He was curious, since Bowles and his Native companions had been traipsing about London for more than five months enjoying city sights and entertainments. The ambassador listened carefully to Bowles and invited him to a second interview before passing a scathing judgment to Madrid. Bowles might be "well studied" in speech, but he was essentially a "daring rascally rogue," deceiving Native friends to promote his claim to Indian leadership, whipping up English war fever, and lining his pockets in the process.[36]

Campo faced the knotty problem of distinguishing between truth and fiction in Bowles's presentations. The ambassador doubted the existence of a "general union" of powerful Indian nations, as Bowles represented. Campo correctly discerned that Bowles had Dunmore's backing, but little weight with his Britannic Majesty's government. The ambassador still worried about English influence exerted by "some hundreds of American Loyalist [Tory] Families," besides British nationals, among the Creeks and Cherokees. What Campo saw as danger was Bowles's hope, provided such persons could be won to his standard.[37]

★ ★ ★

Bowles and his five Native friends embarked from London in April 1791 and docked in Nassau one month later. The chief adventurer relied once more on Dunmore and merchant John Miller to procure a ship, provisions, and arms for a voyage later that summer to the Gulf Coast. Once in Florida, Bowles's Native companions went their own ways. By all accounts, Richard Justice and Moses Price of the Cherokees believed in Bowles. When an American officer visited Justice's home in March 1792, he was astonished by a painting showing Bowles in a standing pose, flanked by a Native chief on each side. The painting bore the title, "General Bowles, commander-in-chief of the Creek and Cherokee nations." The same officer heard Price describe Bowles as "a very great man" who could obtain a free port in "East Florida" and procure an open British trade. Price discredited the idea that Britain had ceded Cherokee or Creek lands to the United States by the Treaty of Paris of 1783. In his view, Bowles's campaign augured the flow of English arms and the arrival of British soldiers to hold back the Americans.[38]

While Bowles boasted of a "united" Creek–Cherokee nation, his Cherokee adherents had little interest in contending with the Spanish in Florida. Creek views toward Spain were decidedly mixed, with lukewarm support alternating with discontent. In Lower Creek and Seminole country, headmen and villagers fondly recalled English support during the war with the Americans. To say that Spain's reputation suffered by comparison would be an understatement. Bowles emboldened his Indian supporters by telling them that Panton was "no Englishman, but a Damned Spaniard."[39]

Bowles's return to the Gulf Coast in September 1791 came at a politically fortuitous time. The adventurer badly wanted to unseat McGillivray, whose prestige in Creek country diminished after he reached a controversial peace treaty with the United States. The agreement, signed in New York City in August 1790, was at best a mixed bag for the Creeks who obtained a federal annuity of $1,500 but ceded hunting grounds along the Oconee River (in present-day Georgia) to the United States. McGillivray meanwhile negotiated secret treaty articles by which he gained a US brigadier general's commission with an annual stipend of $1,200. President George Washington and Secretary of War Henry Knox believed they made a good investment; they saw McGillivray as the sole Creek leader capable of establishing stability on the tempestuous Georgia frontier. The administration's approach, while quite logical at the time, failed badly.[40]

US commissioners were anxious to mark the new treaty boundary line but were hampered by clashes between the Creeks and Georgia's intruding settlers. Bowles seized on this situation. Publicity mattered, as always. On October 28, 1791, he issued a declaration, which found its way into the English press and US newspapers, in which he identified himself as "Gen. Wm. Bowles, Director of Affairs, Creek Nation." He was then at Usiche, a few miles below Coweta on the Chattahoochee. Purportedly speaking in the name of "Indian Chiefs, in Council Assembled," he warned US commissioners *not* to execute the boundary line. McGillivray's treaty was invalid, Bowles averred, because it ceded Creek lands without "the concurrence of the Legislative Council of the Nation." The Creeks were "an independent and free people" who wished for peace but would fight rather than yield. Bowles again sold himself to Indians as an officer with the English king's commission. His new flag had British colors and an Indigenous flair in the form of a human-faced sun in the upper left quadrant.[41]

Bowles opposed McGillivray's treaty out of both ambition and conviction. He doubtless held a grudge against McGillivray for failing to support him during his previous Florida incursion of 1788. Most important, he believed himself destined to lead the Creeks to economic and political independence. Bowles cared little that Creek tradition made no place for a commander in chief's role as he envisioned it. True, there were honored Creek civil chiefs and head warriors in particular towns, but no single figure who directed what might be called an "army" in English or European usage. Not even McGillivray was quite so powerful in the political arena as was commonly assumed by Spaniards, Americans, and Britons.[42]

Bowles the pretender needed to project command, as much as wield it, to intimidate foes. His position in Lower Creek country in the fall of 1791 was not nearly so secure as implied by proclamation. The Spanish were out to capture him. Panton, his most implacable enemy, wanted him dead and urged McGillivray to see to the business. McGillivray hired three Creek warriors to kill Bowles, but the plot failed. One wonders if the prospective assassins truly wanted to carry out their mission, which could incite conflict within their nation. Bowles's old benefactor Perryman shielded him while the adventurer stayed with Philatouche, an influential Creek headman of Chehaw.[43]

By December 1791, Bowles had evaded his enemies but his position was still precarious. His supply of munitions diminished after his schooner left the Gulf shore for Nassau that September. There was no inflow of Loyalist colonists as he had hoped. Considering his shortfall, Bowles altered his approach by proposing a Creek–Cherokee alliance with Spain. He made his pitch to Arturo O'Neill, commandant at Pensacola and an Irish veteran in the Spanish service. The dispatch to O'Neill enclosed a copy of Bowles's previous missive to Floridablanca. The Spanish first minister had not yet replied, but Bowles had not given up.[44]

Exaggerating his military strength, Bowles stated that he had 500 Native men in possession of coastal harbors. He announced himself ready to march in their support with another 150 fighters. Bowles then offered a deal. Spain would recognize the Creek and Cherokee right to "free Navigation of the Sea that borders on their Native Country." In return, his Indian nation would safeguard the Spanish monarch's possessions against the United States. As proof of good will, Bowles forwarded the published plans of American land companies to engross southern Indian territories as far west as the Mississippi. The adventurer stood his ground on his most critical demand: Spain should not interfere with any vessels "going to or from our ports & wearing our Flag." If any Creek ships were assailed, there would be a hostile response. Not one for subtle diplomacy, "Director" Bowles stated that his Native nation would then be obliged to "unite with the Americans" against Spain. His fighting words were flung hither and yon with reckless abandon.[45]

Bowles was impatient for action. Feeling under threat by Panton and Leslie, he resolved to take the initiative. On the night of January 16, 1792, he gave the go-ahead for the capture of Panton and Leslie's practically unguarded storehouse near Apalachee Bay. Nine Indian men led the way under Bowles's confederate, "Major-General" William Cunningham, himself a Tory exile. Bowles followed with about seventy Creek and Seminole men. No person was killed in the affair. The heist was considerable—at least $10,000 worth of goods were taken, which gave Bowles the wherewithal to build Native loyalty.[46]

Native respect for Bowles rose through the capture, though some Creeks, including his adoptive kinsman Thomas Perryman, loathed him for interrupting business and sowing chaos. An uncertain interval followed the seizure. Bowles chose not to attack the Spanish fort of San Marcos. He evidently believed his negotiating leverage was at a height and he could achieve his goals without the sword. A new Spanish governor of Louisiana, Barón de Carondelet, was just taking charge at New Orleans. His purview included all of West Florida and its coastline. While Carondelet wanted Bowles dead or alive, he finally resorted to deception to capture his foe. His prime tactic was to appeal to Bowles's vanity—the desire to be recognized on a par with imperial statesmen.[47]

Carondelet ordered naval Ensign José de Hevia, whose armed schooner carried twenty-four soldiers, to sail from New Orleans to Apalachee Bay. The governor dispatched a letter to Bowles, via Hevia's ship, intended to put the adventurer off guard. Carondelet wished to speak privately to Bowles of confidential affairs and offered him safe passage on Hevia's ship on its return to Louisiana's capital. With Carondelet's implicit blessing, Hevia enhanced the bait, stating that he would show Bowles a letter from Floridablanca and promising to treat his guest with all "esteem and affection." This was an irresistible offer to Bowles, no less convincing for being an artful lie that played on his pride. The adventurer accepted the invitation to Louisiana, telling his Creek supporters to remain quiet until he returned to them within forty days by Spanish guarantee.[48]

On the morning of March 12, 1792, William Augustus Bowles arrived in New Orleans. He was politely received by Carondelet who ordered his guest imprisoned in the city's military barracks. The governor was quite pleased with his coup. Over the next four days, Bowles wrote Carondelet three letters, pleading why a Creek alliance was in Spain's interest in common cause against the Americans. His tone was sober, apart from his execration of McGillivray as a traitor worthy of death. By his fourth day in prison, Bowles warned of "catastrophy" unless Carondelet paid heed. The Americans had to be stopped. If Bowles was kept prisoner, the governor should know that "the Whole Creek Nation may be turned against you, from resentment. What will then happen you may judge."[49]

Carondelet spent some time in conversation with Bowles and remarked that his prisoner was an "extraordinary young man," who though in "savage" Indian dress spoke ably "with an animated and resolute spirit." The governor now understood how Bowles had won a following among the Creeks. Carondelet was not, however, swayed by the prisoner's words. Bowles was an Englishman, after all, a natural enemy of Spain. The governor ordered a halt to all communication between Nassau, where Dunmore remained troublesome, and Bowles's Creek partisans. He meanwhile sent Bowles to Havana, where Luis de las Casas, Cuba's Captain General, would decide the adventurer's fate. Casas, who happened to be Carondelet's brother-in-law, believed Bowles a dangerous character—a "bold audacious, and shrewd" man liable to be used by the English government against Spain or the United States. In the Spanish colonial bureaucracy, officials tended to push especially difficult cases up the line to Madrid. Bowles was soon put on board the king's ship *Mississippi* bound for Cádiz.[50]

On the long ocean voyage, Bowles was befriended by Esteban Miró, Louisiana's outgoing governor, and his wife, Celeste Macarty. Enjoying a certain freedom on board, Bowles painted Celeste's portrait at her request. He also wrote a roughly ten-page, highly revealing account of his life for Miró. A certified Spanish translation of the autobiography was made in 1793; the English original may be lost. Downplaying his loyalty to Britain, Bowles claimed that he had visited England in 1790 primarily to obtain seals to validate official acts in the name of the Creek Nation. The prisoner did not divulge that he also wished to bring a printing press from England to Indian country. To control the news was no small thing.[51]

Bowles gladly answered Miró's query of how someone who had grown up among Indians, "a people in a state of simple nature," could have gained knowledge of mankind and the arts. A self-taught man, Bowles calibrated progress in idealized stages as if he were a philosophe of the Enlightenment. Studying agriculture in youth, he came to acquire books through travel in "civilized countries." While reading history, he was most interested in science, mathematics, and the means of putting knowledge to practice. He discussed his love of painting and music. Then came some disarming candor. Bowles admitted that he was no expert and saw "a thousand difficulties" when he reflected on "man's imperfections." His studies necessarily included warfare. Knowledge in military affairs was essential to defeat enemies and protect "the [Creek] people." As for religion, Bowles was squarely in the rationalist camp. He expressed trust in a Supreme Being within the limits of human reason and understanding.[52]

There was one omission in Bowles's account of his endeavors in the arts and sciences. He made no mention of stage-acting and theater. Perhaps he did not wish to give the impression of being a mere player and not a serious man. Miró was worth impressing. He might moderate the Spanish court's deliberations on the prisoner's fate. But that proved wishful thinking. Bowles was imprisoned in Spain for two years before transported in 1795 for confinement in the Philippines. His opportunity for freedom finally came when he was a prisoner on the high seas a few years later, this time ostensibly bound from Manila to Spain. Put aboard a Spanish vessel and then transferred to an allied French frigate, he jumped ship during a battle with a British cruiser off the West African coast in May 1798, swam to a nearby American vessel, and put ashore in Sierra Leone. This was drama befitting the intrepid adventurer. Once a free man, Bowles thought immediately of gaining passage to the Bahamas and another venture to Creek country. There was much to do to catch up with all that had transpired in his adopted Indigenous nation in his absence.[53]

★ ★ ★

Bowles's impact on Creek society did not arise from titles of "Director" or "General" displayed to European officials, but from bold acts that answered Indigenous needs. Many Creeks and Seminoles had welcomed his arrival via the Apalachicola River in 1791 because it appeared to herald an unrestricted infusion of English goods and a renewed British military commitment. Madrid's colonial officers understandably feared a Creek backlash after Carondelet snared Bowles through deception. The governor and his subordinates quickly moved to assuage a feared uprising by distributing gifts to the Muskogees. Creeks meanwhile showed that their cooperation was not to be taken for granted. In May 1792, a group of headmen told Pedro Olivier, Spanish commissary, that Bowles had volunteered to lead them in war against the Americans, and that Creek forces were to be supported by 600 English troops arriving in ships loaded with presents. That summer, chiefs at Coweta sent a written talk to Governor Manuel de Zéspedes at St. Augustine in which they described "General Bowles as their beloved friend and Father." Their hearts were "heavy" since his departure. They vowed not to heed Spanish talks until they saw him again. The English were their true "Fathers" and Spanish officials should not interfere with British vessels that brought goods to Native shores. Panton and Leslie's monopoly continued to rouse discontent. By early 1793, 400 to 500 Lower Creeks and Seminoles were building a storehouse by the mouth of the Ochlockonee River to receive English wares out of Nassau. George Welbank, Bowles's loyal confederate, actively supported this venture, which the Spanish impeded as best they could.[54]

While hostile to interlopers like Bowles, Carondelet initiated his own plan of countering the Americans by promoting a southern Indian confederation under Spanish auspices. McGillivray, who was himself disillusioned with unfulfilled US pledges, renewed his alliance with Spain in July 1792 on meeting Carondelet in New Orleans. The governor was the driving force, increasing the flow of arms to Creeks and

Cherokees for attacks on American frontier settlements. Chickamauga leaders visited Pensacola later that summer to receive generous quantities of munitions. Carondelet was optimistic, building on successive northern Indian victories over American forces in the Wabash region, notably the crushing defeat inflicted on General Arthur St. Clair's army in 1791. Bowles had talked broadly of unifying southern and northern Native nations, and he made a start toward that end before his arrest. The Little Prince (Tustanagee Hopoy) of Broken Arrow, one of Bowles's staunchest supporters among the Lower Creeks, was part of a far-reaching network of Native militants. In March 1792, he carried reports of Bowles's maneuvers to the Cherokees for conveyance to the British in Canada.[55]

Disparate ethnic and tribal loyalties were an obstacle to grand plans of a pan-Indian confederation. McGillivray could not, for example, impose his will on pro-US Chickasaws, though he resorted to violence to do so well before his death in February 1793. Imperial Spain's support for southern Indians proved far less effective and sustainable than Carondelet hoped. Absorbed in war with France (1793–1795), Madrid pulled back from arming the Cherokees in 1794. The next year brought the Treaty of San Lorenzo by which Madrid recognized the US right of free navigation on the Mississippi and ceded its claims to a broad swath of territory to the American Republic. The cession, which encompassed a large portion of Creek lands, extended along the 31st parallel from the Mississippi to the Chattahoochee. Seeing the balance of power tilt against them, Creek chiefs reached a peace accord—the Treaty of Coleraine—with US commissioners in 1796. A Creek national council soon developed under US agent Benjamin Hawkins's guidance, but its authority was not fully accepted among the Muskogees and affiliated peoples. The council's rulings sparked internal dissent, with the most intense opposition arising in southerly villages bordering Seminole country. Centralized governance, exercising coercive power, was a quite new and controversial phenomenon in Creek country.[56]

★ ★ ★

Bowles operated in a time warp once a free man on the West African coast in May 1798. His ambition to be director and general of a unified Indigenous nation was unabated, but much had changed in Creek country during his long absence. US influence was far more pronounced among the Creeks than it had been a half-dozen years earlier. Bowles meanwhile remained fixated on Anglo-Spanish conflict, and that seemed perfectly logical on the surface. After all, Great Britain and Spain had been at war since 1796. Surely the British government would support his efforts to oust the Spanish from Creek country and the Floridas—or so he thought.[57]

Given the international scene, Bowles's first course of action in Sierra Leone was to write Grenville, still foreign secretary, and win his backing before setting sail for the Bahamas and Florida. Besides discoursing on wrongs suffered under Spanish confinement, he described his treatment as an insult to Creek sovereign rights. His betrayal by Carondelet was itself a "violation of all good faith and the sacred Laws of Nations." Eager to return to America, Bowles requested Grenville's advice on whether the Creeks, whom he described as "an original American Nation," should negotiate with the Spanish or assume the role of English "allies" against them. By a quirk of fate, the adventurer had to forego a transatlantic ocean passage from Sierra Leone when high seas lashed his outbound ship and forced it back to harbor. He next set his course to England, arriving in London in November 1798.[58]

Bowles's stay in Britain was very different than his first visit eight years before. His Majesty's government then footed the bill for him and his Native friends. He was now a solo act, ill at times, and as hard up for money as ever. The British were at war with Spain, but republican France was the foremost enemy. Absent official backing, Bowles attempted a strategy of winning private adventurers to his cause. He knew that Panton, Leslie, & Company were formidable enemies. His old friend George Welbank had been clubbed to death by an unknown

Native man in 1794 while traveling in Creek country. Bowles did not have sufficient clout to gain recruits in England. He won a few kindred spirits during his transatlantic passage of 1799, first putting into Barbados and Jamaica before returning to his old haunt of Nassau.[59]

In a well-worn pattern, Bowles operated without imperial license but with sufficient British assistance to take passage on a navy schooner from the Bahamas to the Florida Gulf Coast in September 1799. Though his ship ran aground on St. Georges Island off Apalachee Bay, he received timely aid from Andrew Ellicott, US commissioner, who happened to be in the region while surveying the new boundary line, set by the Treaty of San Lorenzo, between Spanish and US territories. Though Bowles believed the US–Spanish accord a gross infringement of Creek sovereignty, he enjoyed Ellicott's company and used the commissioner to spread word of his political agenda to US and Spanish officials. He would declare his aims and then proceed to fuse word and deed.[60]

Seminoles in the Gulf region generally welcomed Bowles's return. So, too, did some Lower Creeks, though others were wary of aiding a man who aroused US and Spanish opposition. Bowles did what he could to attract followers by distributing munitions to Native men. Camped by the Apalachicola River in late October, he issued a proclamation with an august opening ("We the Chiefs of Muskugan in Special Council assembled"), calling on Bowles to "direct the Affairs of our Nation and support our Dignity." This pronouncement was false on its surface because there was no general Creek gathering that bestowed such authority. Bowles simply inscribed the headmen's names to give the appearance that he held legitimate power. The proclamation was intended for US and Spanish officials rather than for the Creeks themselves. In fact, a number of the allegedly witnessing chiefs, notably Efau Hadjo (Mad Dog) of Tukabatchee, were then rallying Creek opinion against the adventurer. The heading on Bowles's proclamation, "God Save the State," tells us of his relentless ambition to fashion his own national government in Creek country.[61]

Bowles wanted to make his presence known and felt. In a letter of late October 1799 to President John Adams, he blasted the US "thirst for dominion" over Indians, while stating his openness for negotiations if held in Muskogee territory. Bowles was haunted by the American Revolution, which he castigated for spawning "licenciousness" and "a spirit of speculation in Land" raging among "men of every class." The fact that Bowles was a revolutionary in his own way is an ironic twist on this judgment. His plan for Indigenous nationhood had a kingly air, along with an emphasis on state-building through maritime and commercial independence. Bowles even took on the royal "we" in one edict: "We the Director General of Muskogee." By this directive, he announced the establishments of three ports—Apalachicola, Ochlockonee, and Tampa—open to all nations not at war with Muskogee, with provision for import duties. Certainly, Native peoples wanted open trade. The question was how ports could be made functional and defensible.[62]

Following through on long-held ideas of colonization, Bowles announced the Creek policy of admitting "worthy European families," including political exiles, into a "large tract" of "unoccupied" national lands—with newcomers having "the Rights of Citizens of Muskogee." The director general's stated intent was to further "Arts, Manufactures, and a well-regulated Commerce . . . to better the situation of all our beloved people." Bowles had an inchoate vision of incorporating colonials into Native territories in a manner that would work, at least in his thinking, for the good of the whole. He was mum on the issue of African slavery, neither openly encouraging it nor ruling it out. His authority was quite limited in this area since the propertied Creek elite commonly possessed enslaved Black workers. The Seminole situation was stunningly variegated, with its growing space for African freedom alongside degrees of Black subordination and slavery.[63]

Bowles never truly became "Director General" of an *Indigenous* "State of Muskogee" during his tumultuous Florida venture of 1799–1803. The minimal state power that he exercised was largely confined to the maritime sphere where he licensed privateers that seized Spanish ships and strived to keep open his critical lifeline to Nassau. The handful of ship captains who answered his call were British and Anglo-American adventurers with a hankering for lucre. Under Bowles's regime, captains and crews were entitled to keep two-thirds of their prizes, with one-third claimed by the State of Muskogee. Native men served on privateers. On one occasion, Indian sailors brought captured enslaved Blacks on board a Muskogee vessel to exchange for munitions in Nassau. Seminole raids on East Florida plantations yielded a bounty in Black laborers, some of whom were sold while others adopted.[64]

Kinache, Seminole chief of Miccosukee, was the most potent headman who leagued with Bowles in 1800–1801. He was one of many Seminoles and Lower Creeks who hungered for an open trade and broad British connections. Kinache and allies did not take well to Spanish coastal vessels and river galleys that impeded Bowles's supply ships and the promise of presents and exchange on favorable terms. In late February 1800, headmen balked when Tomas Portell, Spanish commandant at San Marcos, offered a large bribe for Bowles's arrest. To deliver a brave guest such as Bowles would violate Native customs of hospitality, besides dimming the prospect of a renewed British presence.[65]

Bowles was a more capable politico in Indian country than either Spanish or US officials believed. They saw him as liar, impostor, and renegade. Portell told headmen that Bowles wanted to cheat them and sell their land to white colonists. Bowles won the propaganda battle for the moment by showing courage and cultivating Native bonds built on mutual respect and strength. Perhaps he did speak for the English king and could wrest the region from the Spaniards. By late April 1800, several hundred Lower Creek and Seminole warriors besieged Fort San Marcos. Bowles urged all on. He had only a few white and black armed supporters in assistance. Indian control of nearby river passages was critical to the siege's success. Portell formally surrendered his post on May 19.[66]

Bowles made it clear that the battle was far from over. On June 22, he issued a written declaration of war against his Catholic Majesty. It was a benevolent ruler's pronouncement, airing indignation at wrongs and expressing a collective will to wage war as "necessary to defend our sacred Rights, to defend the Honor of this State, and procure reparation and satisfaction to our injured Citizens." The declaration announced the right to seize Spanish ships and goods on "the high Seas" and bring them to "our Ports . . . that they may be legally adjudged and Condemned in our Court of Admiralty according to the Law." "Free trade or die" would have been an apt motto for Bowles's vision of a Muskogee state.[67]

Bowles played to win. In June 1800, he sought an alliance with Richard Lang and other Georgia settlers who nursed grievances against Spain and had launched a freebooting invasion into East Florida in 1795. The director was also eager to enlist General Elijah Clarke of Georgia, though the latter was notorious for aggressively fighting the Creeks over years. Bowles enticed these prospective allies with pledges of East Florida lands should his army triumph. It is not at all clear in this instance how Bowles planned to reconcile settler ambitions with his commitment to Native sovereignty. Lang seriously considered Bowles's proposition, but backtracked after word leaked of the plan, which met opposition from Georgia's governor, James Jackson. US policy was adamantly anti-Bowles. The adventurer was fingered as a British agent stirring frontier instability, harboring runaway slaves, and undercutting American territorial gains and future Creek land cessions to the United States. Benjamin Hawkins, federal agent to the Creeks, was aghast when the Spanish appeared befuddled and at wit's end about Bowles. If chaos erupted in Creek–Seminole lands south of the 31st parallel, it could ignite trouble north of the line where the United States was titular sovereign.[68]

While Hawkins and Bowles were bitter adversaries, they shared somewhat similar ideas of transforming the Creeks toward "civilization." Hawkins lobbied Indian men on the benefits of adopting plow agriculture, cotton-planting, and ranching in Anglo-American style rather than hunting for sustenance. He encouraged Creek women's domesticity in the realm of fashioning cloth. The Creeks meanwhile struggled with a declining deerskin trade and destabilizing violence between white settlers and Native men. Hawkins was in a difficult position. While he wanted the Creek national council to punish Indians for stealing settlers' horses and absconding with enslaved Blacks, the federal government was powerless to bring whites to justice for assaulting or even murdering Creeks.[69]

Bowles's perspective was radically different from Hawkins's, even though he, too, believed in Native American "progress" based on European mores. For all his writing on this theme, he did not pressure Creeks or Seminoles to change their mode of life. If such developments were to occur, they would implicitly take time to carry out. His ideal Creek regime would be open to European and Anglo-American immigration—with special encouragement to British Loyalists. But he had little chance to try the experiment. His first task was to show strength, obtain Creek support, and open ports for trade and defense.

Bowles's prospects suffered a great blow when Britain entered an armistice with Spain and France in 1802. Without sure connections to the Bahamas or the British Caribbean, he had precious little in resources to offer Creeks and Seminoles. In truth, his position was weakening even before news of the European armistice reached America. The Spanish augmented their defensive capabilities in naval galleys and troops along the Gulf Coast. Then, too, Bowles was a general in name only. He did not really control the several hundred Seminole and Lower Creek fighters who ranged about Fort San Marcos, which the Spanish had recaptured in the summer of 1800. The warriors eschewed a frontal assault on the garrison in favor of guerilla strikes, seizing Spanish supplies and killing or capturing soldiers who ventured outside the fort.[70]

★ ★ ★

Bowles was fond of historical painting, among his many interests and diversions. What might he have painted along the Gulf Coast if he had time to display the unfolding history? Some of the scenes would not have been of the traditional heroic kind. In one episode of February 1800, Bowles escaped so hurriedly at night from a Spanish patrol that his wife Mary was captured at his camp with three white followers, a Black man, and a mulatto woman. Mary was released, but the others kept under custody. The adventurer's exploits intersected with a myriad of individuals—the obscure as well as the powerful, women and men, free and enslaved.[71]

Bowles's grand game was all too real and dangerous for Creeks and Seminoles. Their lives and land were at stake, and something else, too, namely their cohesion as a people, gravely threatened not only by US expansionism but their own internal divides under rapid social change and stress. Bowles wanted to direct the Creeks, but he was not quite of them. He certainly had supporters, but there were many who doubted him. In early 1800, Potato King, a Lower Creek chief, sent Bowles some tough advice courtesy of James Burgess, a veteran trader who was fluent in Muskogean language and wrote a colloquial English that rendered Native speech in unadorned words. The chief encouraged Bowles, whom he called "my friend," to get to his "[own] C[o]untrey," whether by land or water, and "Out of the way of wors[e] Misch[i]ef." Potato King feared harm would come to his community while the Spanish battled Bowles and the "Red" people who were his partisans. If Bowles went to his own "Land," he might bring relief from there or stay away. Of course, Bowles was not done—and Burgess knew it. He sent the adventurer paper, ink, and coffee with the wish, "Much Good may it Doe you."[72]

Bowles's undoing was the product of many forces, not least the Creek desire to stave off disorders that presented great risk and threatened internecine conflict. The adventurer had scarcely any pull in Upper Creek country where Efau Hadjo of Tukabatchee was among the most influential chiefs attempting to uphold Native rights by opposing

Bowles and securing peace with "the White people." This was music to Benjamin Hawkins's ears. The US agent moved his residence from the Chattahoochee to Tukabatchee in early 1801 to be closer, in his words, "to the center of the [Creek] nation."[73]

Hawkins knew what he was about. In June 1802, Efau Hadjo headed a group of forty Upper and Lower Creek headmen that entered a treaty with the United States, represented by Hawkins and General James Wilkinson. The agreement, which involved Creek land cessions with supposedly secure boundaries, was sealed with handsome annuities to principal headmen and $10,000 worth of merchandise. Efau Hadjo did his part by openly appealing to the Seminoles to cast away "talks, which have misled you"—a clear reference to Bowles's declarations.[74]

Native diplomacy was an intricate affair in which consensus was all important to decisive action across regional bounds. Efau Hadjo wished to do away with Bowles but could not do so without Seminole cooperation. Kinache and friends moved by their own pace, distancing themselves from Bowles according to their own interests. The adventurer's weakening position was evident when Seminole and Lower Creek headmen entered a truce with Spanish officials at San Marcos in August 1802. Fourteen hundred Native men, women, and children gathered near the treaty site, receiving their due in presents from his Catholic Majesty. The peace terms showed Native tenacity. Kinache did not come to San Marcos until the Spanish released militant chief Mislogue, whom they had taken captive with the aim of pressuring the Seminoles into surrendering Bowles. There was no give in the Seminole position on this last score. The Spanish had offered a reward of 4,500 pesos for Bowles's capture and delivery for two years but to no avail.[75]

It took a great deal of planning by Hawkins to corner Bowles the next spring, and then only with widespread Native consent and collaboration. Through painstaking diplomacy, the US agent induced a number of Cherokee, Chickasaw, and Choctaw headmen to join a large

Native gathering in late May 1803 at the Hickory Ground in Upper Creek country. Hawkins was present as well as a Spanish representative, and John Forbes, the late William Panton's associate who angled for a large Lower Creek–Seminole land cession. To say that there was a plot to snare Bowles would be a simplification. The Hickory Ground gathering, which took place near the site of present-day Montgomery, Alabama, was a cabal of many interested parties. Two factors were critical to the climactic drama. First, Kinache and Seminoles, with Lower Creek allies, decided to attend the conference. Second, Bowles made a free choice to journey with that group to state his cause. He would not bow to Hawkins. Tired of running about in Seminole country, he would face opponents and win over Native headmen with a courageous "speech act"—a performative utterance that would reverse all against him.

John Forbes shook with fear and delight when he heard that "lower towns chiefs," along with Bowles and Kinache and his "Mickasooky gang," were on the path to Hickory Ground towards evening on May 23. He could hardly predict what would transpire. As hosts at the Hickory Ground conference, Efau Hadjo and other Upper Creek leaders provided quarters to visiting participants. After consultations, Aleck Cornells, a well-to-do Creek chief, offered his house, where Cherokee guests lodged, for use by Bowles and Seminoles as well. On the evening of the 24th, Bowles told the Cherokees that "all talks would be straight now & that he expected to be made *King of the four Nations*," i.e., the Creeks, Cherokees, Chickasaws, and Choctaws. The next night, a Cherokee headman asked Bowles if he carried any commission. In reply, Bowles stated that "he came from a Great Prince, King George, to preserve all the red people from having their lands taken from them as the Americans & Spaniards intended to do." This declamation failed. The Cherokee chief believed that Bowles should have papers with a "Big Seal" if he spoke the truth. Native peoples were long accustomed to European diplomatic protocol and expected certain forms to be followed in official proceedings. In truth, Bowles's lack of a "Big Seal" was but a symbol of his demise, not its actual cause. The adventurer was isolated and could not credibly pretend to be what he claimed over years. His Native foes detested him for creating disturbances while his allies deserted him upon seeing his weakness. Significantly, Kinache acquiesced in Bowles's capture but did not openly criticize him. On the night of May 27, 1803, several Upper Creek men bound and tied Bowles. The next day, the adventurer's closest Seminole and Lower Creek friends cried over what they had lost.[76]

Bowles was outwardly calm though disturbed when handcuffs were riveted on him on his second day in captivity. This was done at US and Spanish insistence. He said that he had never suffered that indignity before—a revealing statement for a man who had suffered Spanish imprisonment for six years, at times more in the situation of a gentleman prisoner than a common criminal. Bowles still had some fight left in him. Several days after being bound, he escaped his Creek guards while camped by the Alabama River but was soon recaptured. During the next few weeks, he was brought to Mobile, New Orleans, and from there shipped to Havana's Morro fortress. His plight in Morro prison was horrific, and he died there on December 23, 1805, expiring in the castle's military hospital at age forty-two.[77]

We can only speculate how Bowles might have responded to the convulsions in Creek society in the dozen years after his death. While he might have identified with the Creek militants ("the Red Sticks") in their battle to drive out the Americans in 1813–1814, one doubts he would have found common ground with a movement steeped in Nativist mystical prophesies that propelled the Creeks into a terrible civil war and countenanced the destruction of cattle, plows, and other signs of "civilization." If we move forward a few years, we can see Bowles rallying beside British forces that entered the Apalachicola in 1814 with the intent of rousing Native and Black fighters for the crown. He would have shared in their setback when the British withdrew from the Gulf Coast yet again.[78]

Bowles's vision of founding a Muskogee state open to European settlement under British protection seemed possible for a time. Perhaps his greatest flaw was to underrate his enemies and exaggerate his breadth of Indigenous support. Many Creeks and Seminoles wished to believe in Bowles. They were patient to a point. Truth was not simply an absolute in their thinking. It depended on what made sense and appeared right at a given time and place. The adventurer's grand talk became a lie when what he said for so long did not become true. Bowles the pretender aimed high, remained courageous up to the end, but could not realize a Muskogee state as a vehicle for Native self-rule.

DIEGO DE GARDOQUI: FROM HERO OF THE REVOLUTION TO SCOUNDREL OF THE EARLY REPUBLIC

TYSON REEDER

★ ★ ★

From the Bay of Biscay north of Spain, the River Nervión (known in the local Basque language as Ybaiçabal) slipped south past the small Spanish port town of Portugalete. The water glided by high mountainsides six miles inland, snaking around a couple of bends until the bustling city of Bilbao emerged in a small valley in the Biscay region of northern Spain. In the second half of the eighteenth century, a crewmember approaching by ship would have spied a respectable population of about 1,200 houses, mostly hugged between the river's east bank and the mountains behind them.[1]

Smaller villages peppered Bilbao's countryside. Their people enjoyed a reputation for ironworks, and the Nervión famously provided excellent water for quenching and hardening hot iron. Tradition held that the ancient inhabitants of the region had no use for weapons not forged with water from the river. By the mid-eighteenth century, therefore, Bilbao developed as a major exporter of swords and firearms.[2]

Like most Spanish cities, Bilbao breathed Catholicism. By the end of the eighteenth century, it boasted five parishes and twelve monasteries or convents. The imposing Santiago Church stood at the middle of the city. On November 13, 1735, that church hosted a one-day-old baby, baptized Diego María de Gardoqui y Arriquibar.[3]

The city, port, and commerce of Bilbao shaped Gardoqui's future impact on the early United States. From the earliest stages of the Revolutionary War until the ratification of the US Constitution, Gardoqui helped chart the destiny of the young republic. During his career, his reputation alternated between a savior of the Revolution and scoundrel of the Spanish court, depending on the time and region. As Spain swung from an indirect ally of the United States to a potential adversary, Gardoqui embodied the foreign danger that threatened to disunite the US confederation. Most Americans viewed Britain as the greatest foreign threat to their sovereignty throughout the 1780s, but no single foreign agent had a stronger influence on how the US Constitution addressed international relations than Gardoqui. His volatile relationship with Americans reveals the fine lines between hero and villain, fidelity and treachery, and ally and enemy that characterized the revolutionary period.[4]

★ ★ ★

Gardoqui traced his roots to the surrounding Biscay regions. His family had enjoyed prominence at least since the days of his grandfather. His father, José Gardoqui y Meceta, was born several miles east in Guernica but moved to Bilbao and married Simona de Arriquibar y Mezcorta. They jumped into a lucrative mercantile business by 1726. Over the next ten years, they became one of the most prominent families in the city. When one observer noted Bilbao's elite merchant class could "fit out three or four vessels at their own expense," he spoke of people like José Gardoqui, who owned three vessels by the time his son Diego was three years old in 1758. As José's four sons grew, he expanded his business with the three of them that followed him into the merchant class.[5]

Diego joined the firm José Gardoqui & Sons at twenty-three years old. By the time he joined his father in business, he had gained important mercantile education in London at the feet of eminent British merchant George Hayley and Simona's brother, Nicolás de Arriquibar. By the time of the American Revolution, Gardoqui's friendship with Hayley associated him with one of Parliament's fiercest opponents of war with the colonies. He also befriended Hayley's America-friendly brother-in-law, John Wilkes. Gardoqui's sojourn in Britain gave him not only important business experience but a mastery of English, and it introduced him to London's foremost British-American sympathizers. It would all prove vital to his future career.[6]

At José's death, Diego, his mother, and his brothers continued the business, targeting British North America and trading common goods of the Biscay region such as wool and iron. As business expanded, Gardoqui seized official influence. By 1763, he was vice-prior of the Bilbao consulate. Five years later, he occupied a prestigious post as a council member in Bilbao's municipal government. By the mid-1770s, he had advanced as principal prior of the consulate. His family had held such positions for generations by that time.[7]

Business boomed in the 1760s and 1770s as the firm created close ties with British-American codfish and rice merchants and the colonists started to chafe against British rule. A 1771–1772 voyage typified the Gardoqui's trade patterns with North America. They imported a cargo of cod from Salem, Massachusetts, loaded the ship with iron bars, sent the bars to Cádiz, loaded the ship with salt, and returned it to Salem. The process made them a fortune and facilitated their near-monopoly of the Salem–Bilbao trade. They also showed their devious side with smuggling ventures, on at least one occasion helping a North American firm transport contraband flour to Havana. Advantageous marriages also helped. Diego married Brígida de Orueta Uriarte and his brother married her sister Higinia, bringing healthy dowries into the family coffers. With their combination of legal and illegal trade, the Gardoquis began to amass family wealth that became the equivalent of about $50 million today. By the early 1770s, José Gardoqui & Sons was a preeminent merchant firm in Bilbao.[8]

At the beginning of the American Revolution, Diego de Gardoqui was a wealthy, influential merchant specializing in the British–American trade, unafraid to undertake risky or illegal ventures from a city known for its arms exports. He stood in a prime position to capitalize on the American Revolution for personal gain and Spanish glory. Other Bilbao merchants had similar ties to British America, but in the 1760s and 1770s, Gardoqui had made a crucial, fortuitous shift in his trade networks to Salem. In the early stages of the Revolution, the region adopted an important role in importing arms and supplies for the fight against Britain. Gardoqui became the point man for Spanish help to the rebellious colonists.[9]

At the outset of the American Revolutionary War, Spain and the United States seemed unlikely collaborators. For decades, British Americans defined themselves against Spain and their French allies. Northern European Britons against southern European Spanish. Protestants against Catholics. A constitutional monarchy against an absolute monarchy. Older colonists would have remembered wars between the British and Spanish of the 1740s. Almost all colonists lived through the recent Seven Years' War (or French and Indian War, as it became known) that lasted from 1756–1763, when many British Americans fought France, Spain, and several Native American nations. The colonists had helped the British Empire sweep the French out of North America and claim French land in Canada and west beyond the Appalachians to the Mississippi River. During the same war, Spanish allies lost East Florida and West Florida, a strip of land along the coast of the Gulf of Mexico from Mississippi into the current Florida panhandle.[10]

The purpose of the American rebellion aggravated Spain's distrust. With vast dominions in North and South America, King Carlos III of Spain hesitated to support an anti-monarchical revolt in overseas colonies. One Spanish official put it succinctly: "A civil war in the English colonies would be a bad example in ours." Besides, Carlos had good reason to suspect that independent Americans would trouble his empire beyond the Mississippi more than the British did. To mitigate colonial–Native friction, King George III had issued the Royal Proclamation of 1763, meant to restrain colonists' westward expansion beyond the Appalachian Mountains. If the Spanish king helped British Americans break their colonial bands, he might just unleash them to overrun his own North American dominions and those of his Native allies. Perceiving that concern, American negotiators awkwardly tried to convince Spain of Americans' weakness, even as they tried to tell them they could win a war against Britain. "You may believe," Charles Lee wrote one Spanish official, "that the independent colonies will become a dangerous neighbor due to their strength, but you must consider, sir, that it will be impossible for a long time for them to be in a situation to count on a fleet in position to disturb any power."[11]

Despite his concerns about American independence, Carlos III and American rebels now had a common enemy in Britain. The Spanish king might recover the Floridas and, more importantly, Spain's southern tip of Gibraltar and the Mediterranean Island of Minorca. Gibraltar lay at the head of the Mediterranean and Minorca at its heart, making them vital geostrategic targets disproportionate to their size. The British and Spanish had disputed the two strongholds for most of the eighteenth century. Carlos III did not overlook the Floridas, though. If the Spanish failed to act preemptively, the British might use its position in the Floridas to expand west into Spanish Louisiana and south to Spain's colonies in the Caribbean. Less importantly, American negotiators offered some trade enticements worth considering, but such commerce meant more to Americans than to Spain. If Spain wanted to regain lost territory and protect its holdings, Americans presented the ideal opportunity with their revolution.

With those incentives, combined with French pressure, Carlos III moved haltingly toward a union with France against Britain.[12]

While Carlos III pondered and negotiated, Gardoqui acted. "We see with the utmost concern the difficulties You labour under," he sympathized with colonist Jeremiah Lee. In October 1774, Lee joined Massachusetts Committee of Public Supplies, charged with procuring cannon, arms, and ammunition for potential hostilities with British Regulars. He wrote to Gardoqui late that year asking for weaponry, Bilbao's trade specialization. With some difficulty, Gardoqui's firm procured three hundred muskets and bayonets along with about six hundred pairs of pistols.[13]

Gardoqui would ship the order in secrecy, he assured Lee, for the Spanish minister had told the British government that officials would seize such cargoes bound for rebel colonies. Though Spain had little interest in enforcing that promise, British agents nosed about Spanish ports looking for contraband. Fortunately for Gardoqui, the British lacked a robust consular presence at Bilbao, making it easier to arm the American patriots, as British Americans in favor of independence styled themselves. By mid-year, with fighting underway, the Committee of Supplies was distributing Spanish guns to its recruits, almost certainly those furnished by Gardoqui. Grateful for the shipment, the Committee of Supplies asked Gardoqui "how fully You can supply Us with Military Stores of every kind in future." In 1776, Gardoqui apparently followed up with a shipment of 430 barrels of gunpowder and 300 arms. A thriving partnership had begun.[14]

In early March 1777, Gardoqui attended a secret meeting with American commissioner Arthur Lee and Spanish minister Pablo Jerónimo Grimaldi y Pallavicini. Lee had intended to meet Grimaldi in Madrid, but the Spaniard worried about the appearance of a rebel envoy in the Spanish capital. He used Gardoqui, with his bona fides among Americans and excellent English, to divert Lee to Burgos instead. There, Lee begged for direct money from Spain. The Iberian power still recoiled from war with Britain, but the Crown wanted to help American revolutionaries humiliate their mutual enemy. Since 1776, the Spanish government had funneled money to France to assist the cause. Grimaldi had helped establish Roderigue Hortalez & Co.—what would now be called a shell corporation—with the French foreign minister Count de Vergennes. They gave its charge to Pierre Augustin Caron de Beaumarchais and used it to fund and supply American insurgents without inviting the wrath of Britain. The company name carried a Spanish valence, which (along with Beaumarchais's position on the board of an important Spanish company) allowed it to operate in both French and Spanish Empires. Lee wanted to streamline the aid, receiving goods and money from the government rather than through a corporate front. He also wanted it made public to lend legitimacy to US independence. Grimaldi still refused. Instead, they agreed that Gardoqui would supply American patriots their needs on his private account. In Spain, Gardoqui's firm would mirror the role of Roderigue Hortalez & Co. in France. With the new arrangement, Spain and Gardoqui escalated their involvement in the war.[15]

Merchants and politicians worked with Gardoqui to supply the ill-equipped, ill-clad Continental Army. No longer just a sporadic supplier, Gardoqui would clear all war supplies shipped from Spain to the United States. From there, the orders grew. One request included 100,000 musket flints, 20 tons of lead, 1,000 blankets, 5,000 yards of ticklenburg for tent-making, and more muskets and bayonets. Gardoqui also provided medicines, shoes, stockings, cloth, and salt (a wartime necessity for preserving meat rations). General George Washington prized the clothing, stockings, shoes, and blankets even more than the firearms. In return, Americans sent Gardoqui codfish, tobacco, and rice. In 1777, Gardoqui's firm sent at least ten shipments of war supplies to the needy Americans. According to one estimate, Spain shoveled 4 million *reales* worth of goods and money to American insurgents during the war. The total included 425 large and small field artillery, 600,000 pounds of gunpowder, several thousand tents, and tens of thousands of uniforms, grenades, muskets, and ammunition.[16]

Until 1779, Spain kept out of the war, preferring to fight their British enemies with treasure and diplomacy rather than blood. Hoping to conclude hostilities without entering the fight, Spanish negotiators had tried to convince Britain to grant the colonies independence. They threatened to join the war if Britain refused, almost ensuring British defeat. Britain did refuse, a self-destructive move Washington could only attribute to its "obstinacy," even "insanity." In June 1779, Spain declared war on Britain, joining France, which had made a formal alliance with the United States a year earlier. Spain joined the war as ally of France, not of the United States. Though that distinction made little practical difference in the fighting, it made a significant difference to the US image, as Americans desired legitimacy on the world stage. In the meantime, the war raged, and battlefronts opened in the Mediterranean, Caribbean, and North American Gulf Coast.[17]

In 1780, diplomat John Jay traveled to Madrid as an accredited minister, and Gardoqui again facilitated contact between American and Spanish negotiators. Congress sent Jay to connect Spain and the United States through treaties and to secure a new loan. The Spanish prime minister, Count Floridablanca, recruited Gardoqui to negotiate with Jay and insist on Spain's exclusive control of the lower Mississippi River after they achieved peace. In 1782, Jay's mission ended with a whimper. He obtained no treaty, no loan, and no guarantee of US access to the Mississippi. Gardoqui signed the missive that notified Jay that Spain would not give more loans to Congress. Jay returned to Paris. He and Gardoqui had fired the opening salvos in a diplomatic fight that would divide Spain and the United States for decades. The fight also turned Spain—and Gardoqui by extension—from savior to suspect in the eyes of many Americans.[18]

★ ★ ★

Signed in 1783, the Peace of Paris ended the war, but it left peace incomplete. During the war, a combined force of Spaniards and Native

Americans ousted the British from the Gulf region, including from Natchez and Baton Rouge along the Mississippi to Pensacola. The victories secured Spanish control of the lower Mississippi and gave the empire bargaining power for the region during the peace talks. Spain had failed to secure its main target of Gibraltar, making the Floridas an even more important prize. However, the 1783 treaty left over one hundred thousand square miles in dispute between the United States, Spain, and Indigenous nations. The region extended from the Flint River to the Mississippi River on the east and west and from the Tennessee River to the 31st parallel on the north and south. With control of the Mississippi mouth, Spain closed navigation of the river to Americans in 1784.[19]

Many Americans, especially those in the southern states, believed the dispute posed a security risk to their young confederation. Westerners depended on access to the Gulf of Mexico to export their products. Without the Mississippi River, Mobile River, and other water routes in the area, they would languish in poverty. If a distant Congress could not secure that access for them, Westerners might pledge loyalty to a foreign power that could. As George Washington put it, Westerners stood "upon a pivot—the touch of a feather, would turn them any way."[20]

Few Americans felt more anxious about the Mississippi and Western loyalty than James Madison. "The ideas of America and Spain irreconcilably clash," the Virginian griped after he learned that Spain had closed the Mississippi. Madison had little doubt that the United States would one day possess the population and power to force Spain to terms. At the time, however, Americans suffered from "the Complexity of our fœderal Govt. and the diversity of interests among the members of it," as Madison put it. The United States could only challenge Spain with a united front, something it lacked under the Articles of Confederation.[21]

The Articles of Confederation bound the states in an allied confederation rather than a united nation. The compact amounted to a "diplomatic assembly," to use John Adams's phrase. The Confederation Congress possessed few powers beyond waging war and overseeing diplomacy. Plagued by division, debt, and debility, the states struggled to assert force even on issues that Congress controlled. Britain, France, Spain, and Indigenous nations waited for the confederation's collapse, when they could repartition North America.[22]

Gardoqui planned to exploit those weaknesses when he stepped onto Philadelphia's docks on May 20, 1785, after a tortuous seven-month voyage. In the fall of 1784, Carlos III had named him chargé d'affaires in the United States. The Crown had considered appointing Gardoqui as an envoy to the United States since at least 1780. By 1784, Gardoqui had further burnished his diplomatic credentials by serving as Spain's Consul General in London in 1783 and 1784. He combined diplomatic experience, excellent English, and high esteem among US leaders.[23]

Learning that Congress had relocated to New York, Gardoqui headed for the new capital, where he met John Jay, by then Congress's secretary of foreign affairs. New York reflected the confederation's physical and economic pain. Burnt buildings still reminded residents of the recent war. Like other cities, it suffered from the economic collapse that accompanied independence. Gardoqui took "the finest house in the city" at the head of Broadway as part of a quest to awe Americans into reverence for Spain's wealth and power.[24]

Gardoqui arrived in the city with a four-part mission. The Spanish court wanted him to negotiate the disputed boundaries between the two nations, increase US commerce to Spain, prevent US commerce in the Empire's American dominions, and halt US demands for access to the lower Mississippi. He enjoyed some flexibility on the first two points, but he could not budge on the final two. The Floridas and the Mississippi meant little to Spain by themselves, but they provided a buffer between the United States and the Viceroyalty of New Spain. Gardoqui's instructions butted with Jay's mandate to accept no treaty that sacrificed access to the Mississippi.[25]

The cagey Gardoqui launched a two-pronged strategy to convince Americans to fold on the Mississippi question. First, he hoped to flatter or bribe influential leaders to his side. "There are many needy in the government body," he smirked. Some fancy dinners, "good wines," and effective bribes masquerading as loans, he hoped, would cajole influential leaders to his side. John and Sarah Jay were his main target; eventually John received a fine horse as a gift with Congress's permission. His targets also included men like Virginian Henry Lee, a congressional delegate to whom he gave at least two loans of 5,000 pesos during his time in the United States. "He is very much mine," bragged Gardoqui.[26]

For the second part of his strategy, Gardoqui depended on the northern commercial community. He knew Northerners cared more about Atlantic trade than access to the Mississippi. He had spent his career doing business with Massachusetts merchants, and he witnessed the importance of Spain's markets for grain and fish to US traders. The trade provided Americans with one of their few supplies of coveted specie. He offered Jay the chance to reassert North American trade in Spain (though not in Spain's American colonies) if he would abandon the Mississippi some three decades. If Jay refused, Gardoqui threatened to close the valuable markets to Americans. Jay could not withstand the temptations of personal gifts much less a treaty that could help Americans escape their post-war economic depression.[27]

The proposed treaty embittered Southerners and Westerners, who counted more on westward migration and access to the Gulf Coast. Many Southerners complained that Jay was abandoning Westerners, leaving them to join a foreign power. They rose in fury and convinced Northerners that the union would collapse if the treaty passed by the bare majority of seven out of thirteen states. If the confederation split, Westerners would turn to Britain for protection, they warned. Congress agreed that nine states must consent to the treaty—an impossible threshold for Gardoqui, no matter how many "guises and talents" he mustered to "bolster the majority." Acrimony festered until some Northerners discussed splitting the union and making their own treaty with Spain. They discussed the plan with Gardoqui, but it never materialized. Gardoqui only cared about Northern commerce as a bargaining chip to protect the Mississippi. He needed to convince Northerners to forswear the Mississippi on behalf of the union, not form a separate body.[28]

Though apparently unimpressed by Northern separatists, Gardoqui was intrigued by their Western counterparts. On August 26, 1786, while Congress feuded over the treaty, Congressman James White of western North Carolina stepped into Gardoqui's mansion on Broadway. White assumed that Spain would win the Mississippi debate, leaving Westerners only one option to access the river and protect their livelihoods: side with Spain.[29]

Westerners clamored for statehood for their new settlements in the Tennessee River Valley, such as Kentucky, Franklin, and Cumberland. Congress had ignored their pleas, stoking the anti-union sentiment of many of White's constituents. As White explained to Gardoqui in their meeting, if Spain granted independent Westerners access to the Mississippi, the empire could "win them forever." Gardoqui listened without committing his government, but White had introduced a tempting alternative to a treaty with the United States.[30]

Months later, on March 13, 1787, Congressmen James Madison and William Bingham of Pennsylvania met Gardoqui in his home. A leading proponent of US access to the Mississippi, Madison believed that Gardoqui deliberately promoted disunion among the East, West, North, and South. He feared Great Britain even more than Spain, convinced that Westerners would recruit British support if the Atlantic states abandoned them. Inside Gardoqui's mansion, Madison and Bingham tried to convince Gardoqui that a Western alliance with Britain would spell disaster for Spain. The participants waded through a long meeting on fine points of international legal custom as the Americans tried to convince Gardoqui of their right to navigate the river.[31]

"Spain never would give up" its claim to exclusive control of the lower Mississippi, Gardoqui told his visitors. He quipped that "the people of Kentucky would make good Spanish subjects." They would submit to the Empire for the privilege of using the Mississippi. He said it as a lighthearted gibe, but it caught Madison's attention.[32]

As for their warning that Westerners would turn to the British for help, Gardoqui insisted that "Spain had it in her power to make G[reat] B[ritain] bend to her views." He chose not to elaborate, making Madison think he must have been bluffing. Whether he was or not, as the meeting concluded and they rose to leave, he reminded them of "the inflexibility of Spain on the point of the Mississpi."[33]

Just over two weeks later, on March 29, Madison again conversed with Gardoqui, this time with others of Virginia's congressional delegation by his side. They called on the Spaniard on a matter unrelated to the river negotiations, but "a free conversation on the Western Country & the Mississpi" followed. They repeated the same arguments that Madison and Bingham had made earlier that month, and Gardoqui repeated his replies.[34]

Toward the end of the conversation, Gardoqui returned to his joke from a week earlier that Westerners might become Spanish subjects. This time, however, Gardoqui sobered his tone and told the Virginians that "some person connected with the Western Country" had suggested such a plan. He meant White, but he withheld the name. Carlos III's "dignity & Character" would never allow him to adopt such a scheme, Gardoqui reassured the delegates. Maybe not, but they wanted more assurance than the "dignity & Character" of a monarch. They protested that Spain should treat Westerners as "friendly neighbours" rather than adopt them as "refractory subjects." They had little more with which to argue. They knew that Westerners lived closer to Spain's orbit than the union's, with the Appalachian Mountains as a natural barrier and the Mississippi as a natural draw.[35]

With his half-joking threats that Westerners would join Spain, Gardoqui crystallized Madison's concern for the US confederation.

Nearly a week after the first conference, he described the encounter to Jefferson and complained that Spanish policy would "foment distrusts" among the states and invite British meddling. Three days after the second meeting, Madison alerted his father that a "partition of Union" would ensue if the states failed to find an alternative at the planned Constitutional Convention.[36]

By that spring, Gardoqui considered Madison a friend. Madison retained some suspicion of Gardoqui, but he believed that the diplomat might have budged on the Mississippi question if his court had let him. Although Madison refused to hold Gardoqui personally responsible for the friction, Gardoqui was the face of the Spanish policy.[37]

In the quarrel over the Mississippi, Madison thought he spied the elements that had destroyed confederations throughout history. A year earlier, he had undertaken an arduous study of past confederations to understand their vulnerabilities and steer the United States away from them. He noticed a common pattern. Internal discord divided members of the confederation. The quarrelling regions allied or colluded with stronger foreign powers. Foreign powers asserted gradual power over the confederation until they stole its sovereignty or the confederation dissolved.[38]

Madison fumed to Jefferson that some Americans would make "fit instruments of foreign machinations." To Madison, Northerners betrayed a worrisome impulse to sacrifice the West for a treaty with Spain that only benefited their region. The United States was edging into the second step of the process that seemed the downfall of so many earlier confederations. If Northerners completed that step, Westerners would break from the union and pledge allegiance to Spain or Britain, nearly concluding the disastrous course. As the Constitutional Convention approached, Madison labored to devise a system that could accommodate America's political diversity while withstanding foreign meddling and foreign collusion.[39]

Madison carried his lessons to the Constitutional Convention, currently getting underway at Philadelphia. When William Paterson presented his so-called "New Jersey Plan" to counter the "Virginia Plan," Madison questioned whether Paterson's proposal could "secure the Union agst. the influence of foreign powers." He escorted his audience through the history he had imbibed the prior year. The powerful Philip of Macedon intrigued against the Amphyctionic League, Rome did the same against the Achaeans, Austria and France against the Swiss cantons, and Europe's great powers against the German and Belgian confederations. Madison referred to the theme of foreign meddling throughout the rest of the convention's debates.[40]

Madison denied that he alluded to any specific episode of foreign meddling, but he had been a leading voice in the Mississippi dispute since 1784. Weeks prior to leaving for the convention, Gardoqui had confirmed that Westerners were indeed considering throwing their loyalty to a foreign power. When Madison worried about foreign meddling and foreign collusion, the Mississippi conflict would have come foremost to his mind. Examining Gardoqui's influence on the US Constitution, historians have emphasized the requirement for a two-thirds Senate approval for all treaties. The Framers agreed on the rule to prohibit a simple majority of states from sacrificing the interests of the minority, as nearly happened during the Jay–Gardoqui negotiations. The clause grew straight from the controversy. In a less direct way, Gardoqui contributed to an even more fundamental purpose of the Constitution, at least as conceived by Madison: the desire to strengthen the union against foreign powers that would exploit internal divisions to usurp US sovereignty.[41]

As a testament to Gardoqui's effective informant network, he sent his government an accurate description of the US Constitution eleven days before its signing, despite the Framers' pledges of secrecy. Almost a week after the signing, he dispatched a copy and translation to Madrid. At first, he expected it to pass with some nominal opposition. As the ratification debates raged for months, however, he began to wonder if the feud might yet dissolve the United States and benefit Spain.[42]

"The opposition is greater than was believed," Gardoqui wrote to Madrid in April 1788. He witnessed with sardonic pleasure the "disgust over the new government, which if not adopted may result in confusion, or, what is better, in two confederations." Westerners still doubted whether a national government would secure the Mississippi for them. Separatist movements had only strengthened since the ratification debates began. Gardoqui began to maneuver to bring Westerners under Spanish influence.[43]

Separatists and schemers started to slip through Gardoqui's Broadway mansion doors with proposed projects to exploit the discontent. Gardoqui renewed his connection with James White and recruited him as an informant. White traveled to a disaffected region in the Tennessee River Valley known as the state of Franklin to promote an alliance with Spain.[44]

In June 1788, New Hampshire ratified the Constitution, making it operative and dampening disunionist spirits. That July, Gardoqui hosted John Brown of Virginia's Kentucky region. Infuriated that Congress refused Kentucky statehood, Brown agreed with Gardoqui to advocate a Western–Spanish alliance. In Kentucky, Brown learned that he had misgauged public opinion. That December, he informed Gardoqui that Kentuckians would gamble on the United States rather than on Spain.[45]

At the same time, White's Franklin project was unraveling. Earlier in the fall, the breakaway state had sent James Sevier with secret dispatches to Gardoqui to plead for Spanish support. In the meantime, North Carolina forces arrested the governor of the rogue state (Sevier's father, John) for treason. Gardoqui sent the younger Sevier to New Orleans for aid and White sped to Cuba under the alias Jacques Dubois to recruit help from Captain General José de Ezpeleta. White then continued to New Orleans to support Sevier's negotiations with Governor Esteban Miró.[46]

The talks collapsed around the same time Brown informed Gardoqui that Kentucky would not ally with Spain. Franklinites had grown suspicious of Spain, and Miró grew more cautious about promoting disorder in Franklin. His superiors directed him to support Western separatists on condition that they had gained actual independence. In February 1789, Franklin's overwhelmed leadership swore allegiance to North Carolina.[47]

On April 30, 1789, fireworks shattered the evening sky above Gardoqui's mansion, ignited by troops at the nearby fort to celebrate the inauguration of President George Washington. The explosions illuminated Gardoqui's brilliant display of transparent paintings on the façade of his house, along with statues and flowers designed to commemorate the day. The paintings included thirteen stars (two slightly opaque to signify the two states yet to ratify the Constitution), the sun, the Greek figure Pheme holding a trumpet, and a Spanish flag. The Castile and León coat of arms ornamented the doorway just above the crossed flags of the United States and Spain emblazoning the motto "Natural Union."[48]

The display belied the tension that had prevailed for years between the two powers. The festivities inaugurated the new Constitution along with Washington, which meant that the two-thirds Senate approval requirement for treaties became active. Gardoqui would not get his treaty. His time in America dwindled to near-uselessness.[49]

Less than six months later, Gardoqui boarded the *San Nicolás* and departed the United States. To those who knew of his aid, he had arrived as a hero of the Revolutionary War. He left as the face of an acrimonious struggle for continental power that would last another three decades. His mission encapsulated the shifting alliances, interests, and tensions of the early republic that so often blurred the lines between heroes and scoundrels. On November 13, he wound along the River Nervión, past Portugalete, drifted along the mountainsides of the Biscay region, and stepped onto the docks of Bilbao.[50]

AN AMERICAN SCOUNDREL ON TRIAL: AARON BURR AND HIS FAILED INSURRECTION, 1805–1807

TIMOTHY C. HEMMIS

★ ★ ★

Around midnight on February 18, 1807, near present-day McIntosh, Alabama, two gentlemen rode into town and asked how to find Major John Hinson, who lived "7 or 8 miles" outside of town. One of the newcomers inquired with Federal Land Registrar Nicolas Perkins, Sheriff Theodore Brightwell, and Thomas Malone about directions to Hinson's residence. Perkins sensed trouble. These men, he feared, "had a bad design upon Hinson or his property." Or, maybe, they were up to something more dramatic. Perkins wondered if it might be one of America's most wanted men: "'Colonel [Aaron] Burr' making his escape through that country."

Perkins, Brightwell, and Malone formed a posse and decided to follow the mysterious men to Hinson's homestead. Once they arrived, Perkins got a good look at the "extraordinary gentlemen." There stood a man wearing a broad brimmed white hat and a checkered handkerchief around his neck. On his belt he carried a tin cup, and he had a large butcher knife strapped to his side. Immediately Perkins suspected this man was the former vice president of the United States, Aaron Burr, now a fugitive from justice.[1]

Perkins left immediately for Fort Stoddert to alert Lieutenant Edmund P. Gaines of the whereabouts of Colonel Burr. Sheriff Brightwell remained at Hinson's house with the suspect. While Perkins was gone, Brightwell and Burr talked about going to Mr. Mimms, who operated the ferry on the Mobile delta, and Brightwell agreed to guide him to the ferry. Meanwhile, Perkins arrived at Fort Stoddert and notified an army officer of the suspicious gentlemen he had met the night before. Gaines, along with a sergeant and three privates, went with Perkins to apprehend Burr. As they approached the Hinson's residence, Colonel Burr met the posse on the road a few miles away from the major's house. Gaines announced his intent to arrest Burr, and the suspect questioned the officer's authority to make the apprehension. After a long conversation, Burr agreed to go with the posse to Fort Stoddert to sort the matter out.[2]

The next day, Burr's accomplice Major Robert Ashley, a known associate of Philip Nolan who also worked with General James Wilkinson, was temporarily arrested by militia Colonel James Callier. According to Perkins, Ashley openly discussed Burr's intentions with the Spanish. Ashley was, according to Wilkinson, "a most Desperate Villain & a great Woodsman." Perkins and Ashley become embroiled in war of rhetoric in the newspapers. Ashley later countered Perkins's newspaper account by taking his own version of events to the printer and defending himself and Burr. He said he really did not know Burr or his plans and believed he was on his way to Washington not Florida. Ashley's defense of Burr in the newspapers tried to paint a counternarrative to his arrest. Despite Ashley's defense, it did little to persuade Burr's enemies. Nonetheless, Burr's arrest and subsequent return to Virginia to stand trial became the obsession of the country. Burr's arrest shook the young republic and tested the foundations of the Constitution. The Burr court case threatened to tear the nation apart and was undoubtedly the trial of the young nineteenth century. Neither the hit Broadway musical, *Hamilton*, nor the 1993 "Who Shot Hamilton?" Got Milk commercial mention Burr's extraordinary activities after the duel. However dramatic the death of Hamilton was, the treasonous actions of Burr in 1806–1807 might surpass his misdeeds in New Jersey on that morning in 1804.[3]

★ ★ ★

Burr's 1807 arrest and subsequent treason trial highlighted the political and cultural fractures within the American Republic. Burr's frustration with the American political system launched him on a course to exploit the regionalism that existed in the early republic. After the death of Hamilton, the former vice president toured the western part of the United States. Burr recognized that there was a societal divide between the East and the West. The regionalism came to the surface during the 1794 Whiskey Rebellion in Western Pennsylvania and Virginia. The people of the west often were skeptical of the new federal government and still wanted to believe in the ideals of the 1776 Revolution. When the federalized militia arrived in the west in October 1794, the leaders of the insurrection fled or were captured. The Whiskey Rebellion ended with a whimper and showed the strength of the new Constitution. However, Burr recognized the attitudes of the insurrectionists did not fully disappear and wanted to manipulate those divisions for his own ends. During Burr's western tour, he sought out individuals he believed would favor his cabal.

News of Burr's activities in the West prompted President Thomas Jefferson to issue an arrest warrant for his former vice president. In January, Jefferson wrote to Congress about his concerns, telling the body he had instructed civil authorities in the West "to arrest the persons concerned, & to suppress effectually the further progress of the enterprize." When Gaines and Perkins captured Burr in present-day Alabama, it was not a conclusion of the episode but just a turning point in the American political crisis. Burr peacefully remained in custody, but there were many curious events that happened during his journey to Virginia where he stood trial for treason against the United States of America.[4]

During Burr's first night as prisoner, a Spanish officer approached Fort Stoddert, seeking to see the captive. Though skeptical of the Spanish officer's intent, Gaines allowed him into the American outpost and even granted him permission to speak (through an interpreter) with Burr. According to Perkins, Burr scratched out a note sending his "compliments to Morales and his daughter" and asking for some wine and other items. Morales was believed to be Don Juan Ventura Morales, a former Spanish official in New Orleans and alleged associate of the Burr Conspiracy. The Spanish officer's visit spooked Gaines. Burr escaping or, just as bad, using his confinement as a rallying point for his followers was a real concern, and Gaines dispatched express letters to Major General James Wilkinson and Mississippi Territorial Governor Robert Williams asking for help. "I am convinced," Gaines wrote, "if he [Burr] had remained here a week longer, the consequences would have been of a most serious nature." The populist Burr had strong backing along the frontier and many friends in Spain who might also intervene. If Burr were to stand trial, Gaines needed to get him out of the Mississippi Territory fast.[5]

Encouraged by a reward of two thousand dollars offered by the president, Nicholas Perkins and seven men escorted Burr from Alabama to Virginia. The journey was fraught with danger: from the natural elements, from possible hostile Native Americans, and also from Burr eyeing every opportunity to escape. Despite the bad weather typical for a southern spring, Perkins delivered Burr to Virginia with little incident—except one. Near Chester, South Carolina, Burr leapt from his horse and tried to get help from the local magistrate. He was being kept against his will, the victim of an illegal arrest, Burr claimed. However, his escort was able to restrain Burr before he could persuade the people of Chester to help him. Perkins tightened control of Burr as a result. According to a report in the Richmond *Enquirer*, the party had given their prisoner a healthy supply of "tea, coffee, wine, and brandy" and he was "permitted to wear his pistols and a large knife." Those courtesies disappeared after his attempted escape in South Carolina.[6]

Prior to Burr's arrest, he had openly recruited men, mostly from the western states and territory, who were disgruntled with the federal government. He recruited men like Harmon Blennerhassett. His homestead on Blennerhassett Island in the middle of the Ohio River became the base of operations for the Burr Conspiracy until December 1806, when the Virginia militia raided and occupied the island. Fortunately for Burr, he was not at the island, having already moved south to recruit others. Blennerhassett and his men were stockpiling weapons and provisions for an expected expedition. Burr's account of his plans varied depending on who was listening. Some options included an expedition to take land from Spain, sometimes specifically targeting New Orleans and launching a filibuster campaign into Mexico. Other Burr plans called for carving out western lands to create a new independent nation separate from the United States, marching on Washington City, and waging war on the United States and the federal government. Burr probably told different tales on purpose to keep his true intentions a mystery.

Eventually, Burr and his escort arrived in Richmond, Virginia, on March 25—twenty days after they had left Alabama. Originally the group headed to Washington City, but they were redirected to Richmond because Jefferson believed that because of the alleged activities at Blennerhassett Island, which was technically in Virginia, the trial needed to be in the state capital, not Washington. Once secured in Richmond, tales of Burr's exploits began to circulate around the nation, especially in the newspapers. The line between truth and fiction often becomes blurred, but tales of Burr's plot, arrest, and trial became the talk of the country, which made the truth difficult to sort out. Even before he had his trial, many Americans had already made up their minds to hate or support Burr. Predictably, the divisions usually fell along political party lines.

★ ★ ★

Federal officials had been wary of Burr since late August 1806 when Colonel George Morgan, formerly an Indian agent for the Continental Congress at Fort Pitt, sounded the alarm in a letter to his friend President Jefferson. Morgan had just received a visit from Burr, who knew Morgan from their army days. Living on an estate called "Morganza" in Canonsburg, Pennsylvania, just south of Pittsburgh, Morgan had, like Burr, experience with the Spanish along the frontier and with the people of the West. Also like Burr, Morgan had many issues with the American government. In the 1780s, before the ratification of the Constitution, Morgan had flirted with the Spanish as he set up the colony of New Madrid in present-day Missouri. He encouraged Americans to emigrate to the new settlement. Possibly his involvement with the Spanish government was more extensive—and less friendly to the United States. Though Burr thought he had found a fellow traveler, he underestimated Morgan's loyalty to his country and to the Jefferson administration.

Unfortunately, no copy of Morgan's letter informing Jefferson about Burr exists, but Jefferson did reference it in his reply to Morgan a few weeks later. Jefferson thanked Morgan for his information and noted that "it coincides with what has been learned from other quarters." Years later in a note to Morgan's daughter, Jefferson confided it was her father's letter that first alerted him to Burr's activities on the borderlands and his treasonous intentions.

In his reply, Jefferson also mentioned that he dined with Judge Samuel Roberts and Pennsylvania Militia General Presley Neville to discuss Burr, and in October, Roberts and Neville penned a joint letter to Secretary of State James Madison warning of Burr's exploits. Though hoping the rumors were false, Roberts and Neville relayed Morgan's concern about "A separation of the Western country, from that part of the United States, which borders on the Atlantic." Additionally, they said, Burr openly recruited "men of talents, and enterprize, and especially for Military men" and sought out people instrumental in the late Whiskey Rebellion. Burr spoke "of the strength and military spirit of the *western* country; and derided the weakness and pusillanimity of the country bordering on the Atlantic." Morgan, not satisfied with contacting the president and the secretary of state, also voiced his concerns to Pennsylvania Chief Justice William Tilghman so that local officials would be prepared.[7]

Morgan was not the only one trying to direct the government's attention to Burr. General William Eaton, for example, was another high-ranking official raising red flags. General Eaton, known for his role in the Barbary Wars, sent a letter through Postmaster Gideon Granger to Jefferson. Burr, said Eaton, was bent "on a scheme of separating the Western from the Atlantic states, & creating the former into an independent confederacy." The ultimate goal? Burr would appoint himself leader of this new western nation.[8]

Jefferson and his cabinet discussed Burr in an October 22, 1806, meeting. Guided by Morgan and Eaton's warnings, Jefferson urged his administration to contact "the governors of Ohio, Indiana, Missisipi & Orleans," and send word "to the district attorney of Kentucky, of Tennissee, of Louisiana" to keep an eye on Burr and his associates. He also recommended that if Burr committed "any overt act unequivocally, to have him arrested & tried for treason, misdemeanor, or whatever other offence the act may amount to; and in like manner to arrest & try any of his followers committing acts against the laws."[9]

Burr moved from being a person of interest to a fugitive thanks to an affidavit from another western general, one who came with baggage of his own: General James Wilkinson. In a December 26, 1806, statement, Wilkinson outlined Burr's plot to raise an army of frontiersmen and lead them to attack the Spanish provinces in Mexico. Wilkinson was in an excellent position to know, since he was a paid Spanish informant. Known to the Spanish secret service as Agent 13, he had been recruited by Burr to be the expedition's second-in-command. Flipping on Burr, most likely to protect his lucrative position as a spy, Wilkinson recalled a meeting in which Burr suggested an opportunity. "This Territory [the west] would be revolutionized," Burr reportedly said, "throughout the western Country where the People were ready to join them, and that there would be Some Seizing he Supposed at New Orleans." Burr and his followers "expected to be ready to embark about the first of February," Wilkinson revealed, "and intended to land at vera cruz and to march from there to Mexico." Burr preyed on East–West regionalism along with the hard feelings prevalent among politically alienated military officers. According to Wilkinson, an unnamed navy captain, likely Thomas Truxtun, "and the Officers of our own Navy, were So disgusted with the Government that they were ready to join." Wilkinson continued raising the alarm. "Similar disgusts prevailed throughout the western Country where the People were zealous in favor of the enterprize."[10]

Also included in Wilkinson's affidavit was a cipher letter he had received from Samuel Swartwout in October 1806. Swartwout, a land speculator from New York and a strong Burr ally, suggested that Burr had secured funds for his expedition and convinced Commodore Thomas Truxtun to sail to Jamaica to get help from the British Navy. A filibuster expedition to take Spanish provinces would follow. According to Swartwout, Burr was to meet Wilkinson in Natchez in December with 500 to 1,000 men and then decide whether to move against Baton Rouge. "Burr guarantees," Swartwout wrote, "the result with his life and honor, the lives, the honor and fortunes of hundreds, the best blood of the country."[11]

Though Swartwout had privately met Wilkinson in Natchitoches, Louisiana, where he slipped the general the infamous cipher letter, Wilkinson arrested him and two other men for misprision of treason on December 26, 1806, in New Orleans. Wilkinson claimed the meeting in Natchitoches was a sting: he wanted to lull Swartwout into a false sense of loyalty and draw out his plot. "Tho' determined to deceive him if possible," Wilkinson swore, "I could not refrain telling Mr. Swartout, it was impossible that I could ever dishonor my

Commission, And I believe I duped him, by my admiration of the Plan, and by observing 'that although I could not join in the expedition, the engagements which the Spaniards had prepared for me in my front might prevent my opposing it.'" Wilkinson sprung his trap. "[Once] I had deciphered the letter," Wilkinson recorded, "[I] put it into the hands of Colo. Cushing, my Adjutant and Inspector, making the declaration that I should oppose the lawless enterprize with my utmost force." Wilkinson closed in full furor. "I do believe," he said, that Swartwout and two associates "have been parties to, and have be[en] concerned in the insurrection formed or forming in the States & Territories on the Ohio and Mississippi Rivers, against the Laws and constitution of the United States." By swearing out his deposition and ordering the arrest of Swartwout, Wilkinson protected his own interests and preserved his cover as a Spanish spy. Six months later in Richmond, the process Wilkinson had set in motion—the arrest and trial of the former vice president of the United States on charges of treason—was about to begin.[12]

★ ★ ★

After being brought to Richmond, Burr did not exactly languish in a medieval dungeon. He stayed at the Eagle Tavern under the supervision of a federal marshal. Still, Burr needed a strong legal team to keep him from the gallows. He found it in former United States Attorney General Edmund Randolph, former Maryland Attorney General Luther Martin, John Wickham (a close friend to John Marshall) and young rising attorney Benjamin Gaines Botts, who together formed Burr's superb defense team. And, of course, Burr himself was a brilliant legal mind. He had more than a fighting chance against the treason charges. On the other side were federal prosecutors George Hays and Alexander McRae, and presiding over the trial was Chief Justice John Marshall, taking a turn, as was common at the time for Supreme Court justices, sitting as a trial judge in a federal court.

On March 30, 1807, Burr appeared before Marshall, who indicted Burr on charges of organizing an invasion of a foreign country during a time of peace, but he did not proceed with treason charges at that time. Later, the prosecution indicted Burr for treason on charges of exciting an insurrection against the United States. The grand jury proceedings started May 22 with the contentious selection of the jury. Here Burr and his legal team worried that the jury would be biased against him. Many men for jury duty admitted they already had preconceived opinions of Burr because of newspaper reports they had read and rumors they had heard. Burr complained that "he was really afraid they should not be able to find any man without such prepossessions." After some dismissals and lengthy discussions, the jury was empaneled, and the trial was scheduled to begin later that summer.[13]

Burr's team wasted no time maneuvering for an advantage. They attempted to subpoena President Jefferson for the documents he had received from Morgan and others who had reported on Burr the previous year. Jefferson ignored the subpoena. On the positive side, Burr's lawyers did secure his release on $10,000 bail.[14]

The next phase of the trial began August 2 in Richmond's Hall of Delegates. Burr and his team opened by reminding the court of the subpoena to Jefferson and consistently tried to delay the trial in legal maneuvers. Burr even suggested that "the court should meet at as early and adjourn at as late an hour as possible." His tactic was based on English precedent, but the hot Virginia climate would make the conditions of the courtroom unbearable. Chief Justice Marshall ignored the defendant's request.[15]

The substance of the trial turned on whether Burr had committed an overt act of treason. Marshall's definition of treason hinged on whether an overt act had occurred. It was a narrow interpretation of treason based on his reading of Article III, Section 3, Clause 1 of the Constitution. For Marshall, the overt act required was waging war against the Federal government. Given that up to the point of his arrest, Burr and his confederates had not yet levied war against the United

States government, the prosecution faced an enormous challenge to prove Burr's activities were overtly treasonous.

The prosecutors called witnesses before the grand jury, many of them military men, to reveal Burr's many treacherous acts. The two key witnesses were Wilkinson and Eaton. According to Washington Irving, the famed writer who was present as a reporter, "Wilkinson strutted into Court, and took his stand in parallel line with Burr on his right hand. Here he stood for a moment swelling like a turkey-cock." Irving also noted that as soon as Wilkinson's testimony ended he left the court. Wilkinson only testified during the grand jury proceedings and not in the actual trial.[16]

When Eaton took the stand during the trial portion, he told the court of Burr's intention "to erect an empire in the West, and seize New Orleans." Eaton said Burr expressed his desire to "organize a military expedition to be moved against the Spanish provinces on the south-western frontiers of the United States" in the winter of 1805–1806. Eaton surmised that Burr confided in him because he also nursed a resentment of the federal government, which had slighted him when he served as consul in Tunis during the Tripoli War. Trusting Eaton, Burr revealed his plan of "revolutionizing the territory west of the Alleghany" and "establishing an independent empire" with New Orleans as the capital city and himself the leader of that new state. From there, Burr said he would go filibustering in Mexico. Eaton admitted he initially pledged his support to Burr because he believed that war with Spain was inevitable and wanted to defend the United States.[17]

Burr understood there was a regional divide within the United States, and it was only a matter of time before it broke open. According to Eaton, Burr "talked of this revolution as a matter of right, inherent in the people, and constitutional." In doing so, Burr invoked the spirit of 1776, the rhetoric and imagery of the Revolution often deployed by people frustrated with their government and hoping to overthrow what is imagined as the government's corruption and tyranny. It was the animating spirit of the Whiskey Rebellion of the 1790s and other acts of resistance throughout US history, and it stands in distinction from the spirit of 1787, the ideals of the Constitution, centralization, and order. Burr's invoking the spirit of 1776 made him popular among many people including the western population. Knowing that people in the West often resented the East and suspected its 1787-style centralization, Burr exploited the regional and cultural differences for his own benefit.[18]

Following Eaton, Commodore Thomas Truxtun, a retired naval officer, took the stand. Truxtun met Burr in the winter of 1805–1806 when Burr visited Philadelphia after his western tour. At first, the commodore recalled ignoring Burr's interest in the West. His plans "were not interesting to me in the least," Truxtun testified. The two continued their conversation over several occasions, and in July 1806, Burr tried to persuade Truxtun to join his expedition against the Spanish. Truxtun asked "if the executive of the United States was privy to or concerned in the project." No, Burr responded, the president knew nothing about his plan to take Mexico. Truxtun responded that he was not interested in participating. Burr persisted. He told Truxtun that "he intended to establish an independent government in Mexico," Wilkinson would be the top general, and "the army, and many officers of the navy would join." Burr offered Truxtun a position as admiral under his command. "Thousands to the westward would join," Burr promised, and "many greater men than Wilkinson would join" as well. Truxtun's testimony portrayed Burr as eager to secretly take over the Southwest.[19]

The prosecutors continued building their case. On August 19, 1807, George Morgan, the man who had first tipped off the president about Burr, and his sons John and Thomas took their turn. John went first. An adjutant general in the New Jersey State Militia, John, the oldest of three Morgan sons, had served in the regular army during the late Northwest Indian War. Burr apparently thought John's bitter experience in the army made him a likely convert to his scheme. In 1791, Morgan had openly criticized General Arthur St. Clair for the defeat during the Battle of the Wabash. He was court-martialed and cashiered out of the army. Morgan's testimony dwelled on Burr's visit to Morganza in August 1806. While escorting Burr and his traveling companion, a man named Colonel Dupiester, to the house, Morgan said Burr had commented "that the union of the states could not possibly last." The result? "A separation of the states must ensue as a natural consequence." Burr peppered Morgan with questions about Washington County. He was especially interested in its militia and its officers. Morgan also recalled running into one of the farmhands on their ride. "He wished he had ten thousand such fellows," Morgan recalled Burr remarking in reference to the young laborer.[20]

When George Morgan took the stand, he provided details about the conversation that ensued over dinner and into the evening. At one point, Morgan said, the conversation became heated when Morgan reminisced about how much the country had grown, particularly in Western Pennsylvania. When he first arrived in Western Pennsylvania shortly after the end of the Seven Years' War in 1763, Morgan recalled saying, "there was not a single family between the Allegheny mountains and the Ohio." Over a glass of wine, Morgan jested "that by and by we should have congress sitting in this neighborhood or at Pittsburgh." Burr thought an independent national capital might really be built nearby, "for in less than five years," retorted, "you will be totally divided from the Atlantic states." Burr's comment worried Morgan.[21]

The debate began to escalate as Burr argued that the eastern states were exploiting the western states. Land speculation, he said, only benefited the East. "The people to the west should not be tributary" to the eastern states, Burr maintained. Turning to the heavy taxes imposed on Westerners by leaders from the East, Burr played up the rhetoric of the spirit of 1776. "Our taxes were very heavy," Morgan recalled Burr complaining. He "demanded why we should pay them to the Atlantic parts of the country?" Burr knew the region's history of resistance to the excise tax in the 1790s that became known as the Whiskey Rebellion. He knew the people of western Pennsylvania and Virginia understood his perspective. However, Colonel Morgan vehemently disagreed with Burr on this point. "God forbid!" the elder Morgan exclaimed. "I hoped that no such things would ever happen, at least in my time." Morgan politically was probably a Jeffersonian Republican and did not want to see his country torn apart, as he worked hard to build his estate, family, reputation, and status in society.[22]

The conversation then took a disturbing turn, which led Morgan "to think that all was not right." Speaking of "the weakness and imbecility of the federal government," Burr went on a tirade. "With two hundred men he could drive congress, with the president at its head, into the river Potomac," Morgan recalled. Burr derided the weakness of Eastern people; a small force would easily conquer them. "With five hundred men," Burr boasted, "he could take possession of New York." However, Thomas Morgan, the middle Morgan brother, took offense, saying "he would be damned if they could take our little town of Canonsburg with that force." Always quick witted, Burr made a concession to the younger man. "Confine yourself to this side of the mountain, and I'll not contradict you." Burr then left the room, but he motioned for Thomas to follow.[23]

Thomas Morgan's testimony picked up the story. The two left for a short walk. Thomas thought the moment was ripe to share his aspiration to be a lawyer. George Morgan encouraged his son to seek out Burr for his connections and mentorship to further his career. But Burr was in no mood to help. "Colonel Burr inquired what my pursuits were," Thomas testified. "I informed him that I was studying the law." Burr poured cold water on his plans. "He was sure I could not find employment for either body or mind," Thomas said, because, according to Burr, "under our government there was no encouragement for talents." Virginia Congressman John Randolph had said so openly, declaring "on the floor of congress that men of talents were dangerous to the government." The reference to Randolph must have caught the attention of everyone at the trial because Randolph was present in court—as foreman of the jury! Burr told Thomas he had a better idea than a career at the bar. He wondered if Thomas had any desire to join a military expedition. "It would entirely depend," Thomas replied, "upon the object or cause for which I was to fight." That was not a "no," and so Burr continued to pressure Thomas Morgan to join him. He also turned to the youngest Morgan brother, George Jr., saying "he was a fine, stout-looking fellow," and he "would like to see him at the head of a corps of grenadiers." Hearing these comments and concerned about his brothers, John Morgan informed their father about Burr's enticements.[24]

After the heated dinner conversation, Burr retired to his bedroom, but he was not done probing for information. Around 11:00 P.M. he returned downstairs to speak to the elder George Morgan about Francis Vigo of Fort Vincent (Vincennes), a figure with his own scandalous past on the American frontier. In 1788, Vigo had been part of a rumored conspiracy to seed discontent in the western United States. According to Morgan, Vigo "was deeply involved in the British conspiracy in 1788, as I supposed, the object of which was to separate the states." One can speculate that Burr either wanted to learn more about Vigo or to recall a time when Morgan had been no stranger to western plots so as to broach the topic of him joining a new scheme. Morgan would not take the bait. "I called it a nefarious thing to aim at the division of the states," Morgan testified. "I was careful to put emphasis on the word 'nefarious.'" Morgan's strong words gave Burr pause and he stopped his inquiry. The next morning Burr and Dupiester left before breakfast with John Morgan, who gave them a tour of Washington, Pennsylvania. Given the previous night's events, Burr's stealthy departure did not surprise George Morgan.

Washington, Pennsylvania, was the focal point of the Whiskey Rebellion, and during the tour Burr inquired about the kinds of men who lived there. Burr particularly hoped to meet David Bradford, a local leader of the rebellion, but he had since moved to Baton Rouge, Louisiana. When Burr heard that Bradford's son was still in the area, he insisted on meeting him instead. That morning, Burr also told John

Morgan that "he had met with several who had been concerned in the western insurrection, and particularly a major in the Northwestern Territory." Morgan could not remember the major's name, but the words Burr attributed to him were unforgettable. "If he was ever engaged in another business of the kind," the major told Burr, "he pledged himself it should not end without bloodshed." Worried about what Burr had planned, when he returned home John Morgan urged his father to write to President Jefferson.[25]

★ ★ ★

The prosecution's witnesses painted a damning picture of the former vice president. He plotted to divide the nation's West against the East, detach the western states from the nation, and set himself up as the leader, enjoying the kind of power his political career in the US government had denied him. As the testimony unfolded, several cozy relationships emerged among some of the principal figures in the trial. For example, John Randolph's role on the jury. In addition to being mentioned in testimony, he was also the nephew of Burr's lead attorney, Edmund Randolph. Burr and the Randolphs had similar views of Thomas Jefferson: pure hatred. In addition, Chief Justice John Marshall attended a dinner party during the proceedings hosted by one of Burr's other lawyers, John Wickham—which Burr also attended. Rumors spread. Conspiracy theories blossomed. The "Feast of Treason," the Republican press screamed. Regardless of the true events of Wickham's dinner party, many people believed there was some wickedness afoot.[26]

During the trial, Burr's legal strategy focused on attacking the character of the witnesses against him, with Burr himself leading the charge. For example, Burr conducted a crucial cross-examination of George Morgan. Burr knew of Morgan's 1788 New Madrid scheme in which he had worked with the Spanish in present-day Missouri. "Did you not once live on the Mississippi, or go to that country with a design to settle there?" Burr asked Morgan. Of course, the answer was yes. Morgan maintained that he had US approval to help the Spanish in New Madrid. He openly recruited Americans to move to New Madrid, he worked with Spanish diplomat Don Diego de Gardoqui to build a Spanish colony west of the Mississippi River, and in return the Spanish promised Morgan a large tract of land, a commission in the Spanish Army, and free education for his daughters as rewards for his service. He never received any of his incentives, however, because after about forty days, Morgan returned to the United States disgruntled over political squabbling with the Spanish governor and what he perceived as personal slights. Morgan's dreams for his Spanish New Madrid were relatively quickly dashed.[27]

Though Morgan never concealed his involvement with the Spanish, many American leaders were concerned. Arthur St. Clair, governor of the Northwest Territory and target of John Morgan's earlier recriminations, reported the elder Morgan's activities to President George Washington. "It is strongly suspected," St. Clair wrote, that Gardoqui "has an Understanding with some leading Characters, and that thro' them, the desire to throw off all Connection both with Virginia and the Union, is spread among the People." Morgan was one of those "leading characters." Morgan's brief flirtation with the Spanish gave him a reputation of being a scoundrel by many of his rivals and being forced to admit to his own Spanish intrigues on the record discredited Morgan's character more widely.[28]

Burr also made an issue of how Morgan's advanced age of sixty-three might have hindered his memory. Cross-examining John Morgan, Burr asked about his father's health and state of mind. "He had lately had a fall, which had done him considerable injury," John admitted. John continued to tell the court that his father was "old and infirm, and like other old men told long stories, and was apt to forget his repetitions." Burr's legal maneuvering put the Morgans' testimonies into question. But the Morgan testimonies were not the only ones that swung the trial in Burr's favor.[29]

Between August 17 and 21, fourteen witnesses took the stand, and Burr and his legal team successfully cross-examined each person. Burr and his attorneys picked apart each witness, including the Morgan family. The closing arguments of both the prosecution and defense became a grueling competition of endurance as both teams spoke for over seven hours straight each day. Once the courtroom performances had concluded, Marshall handed down his opinion that, by his strict reading of the Constitution, the law required a narrow definition of treason. Following Marshall's reasoning, the jury voted to acquit Burr on the charges of treason due to the lack of evidence, especially since when Blennhassett's Island was raided, the vice president was absent.

Seemingly the verdict brought a conclusion to the Burr saga, but the prosecution wanted to continue to press other charges against the defendant, especially the charge of treason in other states and territories. Historian James E. Lewis Jr. argues that this often-forgotten next round of hearings were "the longest and most interesting stages of the trial," because it dealt with the legal definition of double jeopardy. After another six weeks, Burr remained in Richmond, and on October 20, Marshall finally decided that a new trial would be futile because there was no overt treason conducted by Burr or his men. Although there could have been another misdemeanor trial in Ohio or Kentucky for insurrection, the case seemed doubtful.[30]

Despite all the accusations against Burr, the jury rendered a not guilty verdict largely because of Marshall's strict definition of treason as an overt act of violence. But Burr's cunning should not be overlooked. He was involved in so many purported schemes—filibustering in Spanish territories, taking over New Orleans, creating an independent western state, or even taking over Washington City with a western army—that it was hard to take them seriously, especially when no scheme came to fruition. Burr and his legal team outsmarted the prosecution.

★ ★ ★

Although Burr saved his life, the trial left a stain on his reputation just like the stain of his duel with Alexander Hamilton. In many

Jeffersonian Republican circles, Burr was undoubtedly guilty of treason. But in Federalist circles, Burr was unfairly made a target of Jefferson's hatred. The results of the Burr trial sparked mob protests across the country. Burr was a free man, but he was still entangled in several legal cases, including complications lingering from his duel with Hamilton. Hoping to lie low, Burr embarked on a tour of Europe.

The Burr Conspiracy and subsequent trial showcased a wide variety of Americans with scurrilous characters. From Burr, Wilkinson, and Swartwout to Eaton, Truxtun, and Morgan, each of these Americans had some blemish in their public reputation that made them scoundrels. Wilkinson, in fact, was one of the most self-interested public men in the early republic. Nonetheless, it was his affidavit that prompted Jefferson to ask for the arrest of Burr. Wilkinson's actions were more to protect his own position and life than it was his love for country. During the Burr trial, Wilkinson challenged a variety of individuals to duels to protect his own honor, but none ever happened. In the end, Burr and his associates, even the ones who turned on him, were all men that had something in common: they were self-interested men, who felt disgraced or passed over—and some would call them scoundrels.

The Burr court case lay bare the political frailties of the American Republic, and the self-interested men who struggled to lead the state. Despite Burr's acquittal, there was substantial evidence that he and his associates plotted and conspired to divide the nation, possibly even to start a civil war. It is entirely possible that the state's prosecution team failed to bring the correct charges because Jefferson had already been convinced of Burr's guilt. Unfortunately, the partisan politics of the republic intervened in the trial and left a bad taste in many people's mouths. Burr disappeared from the political stage when he toured Europe, and his name forever became associated with being an American scoundrel. However, Burr's populist politics and filibustering schemes would inspire the next American generation of politics, starting with the rise of Andrew Jackson and the age that bears his name.

CONCLUSION

DAVID HEAD

★ ★ ★

The men profiled in the foregoing pages reveal the many ways to be a scoundrel in the early republic. There were scoundrel traitors like Benedict Arnold and, nearly, Aaron Burr. There were land- and money-hungry scoundrels like William Blount, Thomas Green, and Philip Nolan. Provocateur scoundrels such as Don Diego de Gardoqui stirred up trouble. Scoundrels on the wrong side of politics, such as Charles Lee and Matthew Lyon, suffered because of the trouble enemies stirred up against them. Jason Fairbanks and the Kemper brothers violated community expectations—and perpetrated violence—and became known as scoundrels along the way. Scoundrel adventurers, like the big-talking William Augustus Bowles, had grand dreams and possibly noble intentions, but little success in the end. And then there was scoundrel-at-large James Wilkinson, who seemed to have a hand in every scheme plotted west of the Appalachian Mountains.

The contributors make clear that the term "scoundrel" was complex. It fits more easily in some cases than others. Lee and Lyons, for example, appear more sympathetic when it's pointed out that their scoundrel reputations came more from their opponents than any dire moral failing of their own. Meanwhile, Wilkinson, who is often trotted out to give histories of the period a splash of scheming color, was trusted by four presidents, sharp political operators all, because, as Samuel Watson notes, Wilkinson was effective as a commander and diplomat. He was useful to others as he served himself. Even Arnold, the arch-traitor, chose his treason in no small part because of the frustration he felt with the military and civilian scoundrels around him who repeatedly thwarted the recognition he deserved. As James Kirby Martin writes, Arnold's misfortune was failing to understand that his treason would revive the patriot cause, covering over the scandalous conduct of his peers long enough to inspire an American victory.

★ ★ ★

Arnold's story reminds us that although he may have been the greatest scoundrel of the era, he was not alone. Look across early America and scoundrels start popping up everywhere. For example, George Morgan appeared in the Burr chapter as one witness against Burr and his testimony revealed the threat posed by the former vice president. But Morgan was easily a scoundrel all his own. By the time of the American War for Independence, Colonel Morgan already had a reputation as a rascal because of his shrewd, sometimes unethical business dealings. His close relationships with Native Americans also invited suspicion. His most infamous scheme unfolded when he worked with Don Gardoqui to create a Spanish colony, called New Madrid, in present-day Missouri on the western side of the Mississippi River. Gardoqui envisioned New Madrid as a buffer against US encroachment, and handpicked Morgan, who had traded nearby as a merchant in British-controlled Illinois in the 1760s and knew the region intimately. Morgan believed he could encourage hundreds if not thousands of American families to emigrate to Spanish New Madrid. Unfortunately for Morgan, Wilkinson (of course) had a competing scheme with the Spanish in Kentucky. Currying favor with Governor Esteban Miró, Wilkinson blocked Morgan's plans for New Madrid. Morgan arrived on the banks of New Madrid in 1789. He was disappointed with its progress. About forty days later, he left, disgusted with the Spanish.[1]

Morgan may have been done with the Spanish, but his reputation for intrigue remained intact, which is why Burr sought him out in August 1806. Arriving at Morganza, the family homestead in Pennsylvania, Burr thought he had his man to lead his frontier neighbors, who, after all, had welcomed the Whiskey Rebellion, for a new uprising. Unfortunately for Burr, Morgan was a friend of Thomas Jefferson and informed him of the insurrection plot. Today a small monument in Canonsburg, Pennsylvania, highlights Morgan's role raising the alarm about Burr. But he had a long career as a scoundrel before that redeeming moment.

The list of scoundrels is a long one and, as with Morgan, Wilkinson, and Burr, scoundrels frequently crossed paths. For example, in 1788 Dr. John Connolly, a Pennsylvania loyalist during the American Revolution, calculated a way to seize New Orleans for the British. George Morgan learned of the plot and offered to capture Connolly—to prove his loyalty not to the United States but to Spain. Other international intriguers include Edmund Genet, who created a popular commotion—and a diplomatic headache for President Washington—when he arrived in America in 1793 and demanded the United States honor its treaty to fight alongside France in its war with Britain. Genet forgot the US alliance was with the king of France, who had inconveniently lost his head, ending the commitment.[2]

Founding a new state on the frontier was another popular goal for scoundrels who saw opportunity in the West—the opportunity to pursue their own interests, free from the scrutiny of a distant government and the policies that served others. For example, two North Carolinians, Richard Henderson and John Sevier, tried to establish their own western states. In 1775, Richard Henderson led the purchase of an enormous tract of land in what would become Kentucky and Tennessee in hopes of building Transylvania, an inviting home for ambitious farmers. The American Revolution intervened, dashing his plans. About a decade later, Sevier launched the state of Franklin, taking over land North Carolina had ceded to the central government. He was Franklin's first and only governor. Conflicts with Natives, failed talks with the Spanish, and rivalry with North Carolina proved too much for the young state to bear, and Franklin collapsed before the new federal government could begin.[3]

★ ★ ★

Why were there so many scoundrels in the early republic? Taken together, the prior chapters suggest three answers.

First, the prevalence of so many self-interested men in the 1780s, 1790s, and 1800s was one unintended result of the American Revolution. The Founding Fathers may have expected the best sort of men to rule and cultural leaders trumpeted the importance of virtue, self-sacrifice, and patriotism, but once free to make their own economic and political decisions, many men decided they had their own ideas about what was most important, and it wasn't the virtue, self-sacrifice, and patriotism defined by elites. Blount was probably the most egregious example of someone who knew what the leaders of the new republic deemed essential and then ignored it as he amassed his own private kingdom of land. Blount cheated Revolutionary War veterans out of their land bounties and finagled an appointment as governor of the Southwest Territory so he could bully Native Americans, forge land titles, and arrange favorable terms for his purchases. His office existed for his private emolument. And Blount did all this after signing the Constitution as a delegate from North Carolina.

On the opposite side of the war but no less benefiting from the Revolution's result was William Augustus Bowles. Though a Tory who during the war certainly didn't want the Revolution to succeed, the American victory freed Bowles to pursue his life's work: founding an independent State of Muskogee, a place where Natives could live under British protection but outside US control. Bowles's Muskogee adventure took him around the world, willingly to the Bahamas, Canada, and England, unwillingly to the Philippines, Africa, and Cuba. None of it would have been possible if the Floridas remained in British hands. He had no path to prominence until the Revolution opened the way.

Second, the sheer number of schemes in the borderlands highlights the vital importance of the American West as a zone of territorial expansion, economic opportunity, and foreign intrigue. The United States shared a border with the Spanish empire until 1821, when the Transcontinental Treaty settled the boundary between the two and, later that year, Mexico threw off Spanish rule and took over its North American territory. That's forty-five years after 1776—a fact that's not well appreciated in popular memory of the early United States.

The West didn't just fall into US hands, either. Nor was it peacefully purchased from France one day. The western border was contested all along the Mississippi River with the outcome very much in doubt. With the United States relatively weak internationally and a global conflict between France and Britain brewing in the 1790s, the nation's map could have easily ended up with fewer pieces than it did. Or the nation could have broken apart altogether. Scoundrels like Burr, Gardoqui, Green, and Wilkinson knew it, and tried to manipulate those circumstances to their advantage.

Their zeal for pushing westward sometimes pulled the United States along with them. Green, for example, tried to force his way into Spanish Natchez by getting Georgia to annex the land to the new state. He knew the Spanish feared US expansion, and he played on those fears to get what he wanted. Green was an example of a private citizen forcing the US government's hand. Though US officials wanted to expand, they wanted control over how it happened and what the costs, both in money and in conflict, would be. No one could restrain Green, however, and he ended up, as Christian Pinnen writes, an example of the "individual adventurers" who "drove foreign policy in the lower Mississippi valley."

Though they never lacked for boldness, western schemers did not always succeed. US expansion was never a straightforward American march westward. Nolan and the Kemper brothers learned the limitations of US expansion. Nolan saw opportunity not just across the border in Spanish Texas, but because of the border itself: he could gain access to the land by manipulating Spanish fears of US incursions. The game worked, until it didn't, and Nolan was killed by the Spanish while searching for ponies on the Texas plains.

The Kempers, too, miscalculated their place in the geopolitics of the borderlands. They thought they could instigate a general uprising in Spanish West Florida by promising political independence. It turned out, however, that many Anglo-Americans were happy under Spanish rule. They took Spain's side, seeing through the Kempers lofty rhetoric for what it was: a fig leaf for their personal vendetta. The West beckoned to scoundrels, calling them to break it open for their own benefit, but that call could be silenced by the complexity of relationships in the borderlands.

Finally, the existence of so many scoundrels in the nation's early days makes a point that is so obvious it is easy to miss: early America was simply a time and a place for scoundrels. Winning independence, surviving the aftermath of the Revolution, and securing a firm footing for the new nation were Herculean labors that required not only a handful of demi-gods with names like Washington, Jefferson, Madison, and Hamilton, but a host of mere mortals, many of whom were out for themselves. Blount making possible Tennessee statehood and Wilkinson helping build Kentucky are only two examples of scoundrels also playing the role of founders.

Documenting the lives of men such as Blount, Wilkinson, and the rest provides a refreshing way to consider the full, contradictory story of America's origins beyond the giants in ruffled shirts and breeches we call Founding Fathers. The America they built and the America the scoundrels built were the same country. The early United States was truly a republic of scoundrels.

ACKNOWLEDGMENTS

A Republic of Scoundrels began as an idea during a research trip to the American Philosophical Society in Philadelphia in 2018. While reading through Benjamin Franklin's papers, I noticed there were many schemers and scoundrels he corresponded with and wrote about. These self-interested men had been largely overlooked in the larger narrative of early America. I considered the topic as a solo project, but only a few of the most infamous characters had their own biographies and many primary sources are scattered across various archives. Research and writing for a project of this scope would have been a monumental task. When the global Covid pandemic of 2020 hit, research became even more difficult. However, the possibility of a book on scoundrels of the early republic became a fun exchange on Twitter, and that gave me hope that there would be interest in an edited volume. Eventually, David Head and I took the conversation offline and further developed the idea from innovative concept to a full-blown book project.

Together, we would like to thank our wonderful contributors. They are the foundation of projects like *A Republic of Scoundrels*, and their hard work, scholarship, and professionalism made this volume possible. I am privileged to have worked with a great group of scholars and people. Our literary agent, Roger Williams, believed in the book early on and guided us through the publishing process. Claiborne Hancock and the team at Pegasus, especially Maria Fernandez, produced a beautiful book. University of Central Florida graduate student Cole Taylor did invaluable work wrangling the notes.

Additionally, my colleagues at Texas A&M University-Central Texas in Killeen, Texas, have been extremely supportive. I want to thank Jerry W. Jones, Bruce Bowles, Amber Dunai, Allen Redmon, Luke Nichter, Cadra McDaniel, Christine Jones, Lynn Greenwood, Roslyn Fraser, Miene Roberts, and many others for listening to my constant obsession with the project. Thanks, also, to the TAMUCT Library and Archive staff for their help obtaining a ton of interlibrary loan materials for the project during a pandemic.

For my chapter on Aaron Burr, I want to thank Adrienne Sharp of Yale University's Beinecke Rare Book and Manuscript Library, who scanned and sent valuable primary source letters. I am also grateful for the staff at the University of Virginia Special Collection Library who helped track down some letters. Clay Kilgore of the Washington County Historical Society in Washington, Pennsylvania, helped me track down the only portrait of George Morgan, which hangs in the LeMoyne House.

Finally, I want to thank David for his advice, mentorship, and sage guidance throughout the project. When this project was just an idea, he helped move it to where it is today.

I could not have completed this without my friends and family. Thank you Jared Runkel, Dan Vogel, Tim Trimmer, and my Mississippi "family" the Lazenbys for all the support along the way. Lastly, I want to thank Vicky Eastes for her encouraging words and prayers through this project. I am sure you are tired of me talking about Aaron Burr and George Morgan, but I cannot promise I will stop.

—Timothy C. Hemmis

★ ★ ★

In addition to the people mentioned above, I'd like to express my gratitude to Tim for bringing me onto the project and providing its intellectual vision. I appreciated his patience to talk while I drove my kids to the YMCA or gave them breakfast. He always offered a calming perspective when things got crazy. I could not have completed the book without my family: my wife, Andrea, and our children, Carolina, Camila, and Andrew, who were willing to let a dozen scoundrels into our lives.

—David Head

CONTRIBUTORS

David Head is associate lecturer of history at the University of Central Florida and distinguished faculty fellow in history at Kentucky Wesleyan College. His most recent book is *A Crisis of Peace: George Washington, the Newbury Conspiracy, and the Fate of the American Revolution* (Pegasus Books, 2019).

Timothy Hemmis is associate professor of history at Texas A&M University—Central Texas. He is the history book review editor for *The Presidential Studies Quarterly*.

Mark Edward Lender is professor emeritus of history at Kean University. His books include *Cabal!: The Plot Against General Washington* (Westholme Publishing, 2019) and, with Garry Wheeler Stone, *Fatal Sunday: George Washington, the Monmouth Campaign, and the Politics of Battle* (University of Oklahoma Press, 2017).

Shira Lurie is an assistant professor of history at Saint Mary's University, in Halifax, Nova Scotia. She is the author of *The American Liberty Pole: Popular Politics and the Struggle for Democracy in the Early Republic* (University of Virginia Press, 2023).

Christopher Magra, a professor of history at the University of Tennessee, is the author of *The Fisherman's Cause: Atlantic Commerce and Maritime Dimensions of the American Revolution* (Cambridge University Press, 2009) and *Poseidon's Curse: British Naval Impressment and Atlantic Origins of the American Revolution* (Cambridge University Press, 2016).

James Kirby Martin is the Hugh Roy and Lillie Cranz Cullen University Professor Emeritus of History at the University of Houston. His most recent books included *Insurrection: The American Revolution and Its Meaning* (Westholme Publishing, 2019) and *Surviving Dresden: A Novel about Life, Death, and Redemption in World War II* (Permuted Press, 2021).

David Narrett is professor of history at the University of Texas at Arlington. His most recent book is *Adventurism and Empire: The Struggle for Mastery in the Louisiana–Florida Borderlands, 1763–1803* (University of North Carolina Press, 2015).

Jackson Pearson is a PhD candidate at Texas Christian University. His dissertation examines the Neutral Ground Agreement and the Spanish–American contest for sovereignty in the Louisiana–Texas Borderland following the Louisiana Purchase.

Christian Pinnen is a professor of history and co-director of African American Studies at Mississippi College. He is the author of *Complexion of Empire in Natchez: Race and Slavery in the Mississippi Borderlands* (University of Georgia Press, 2021) and, with Charles Weeks, *A Borrowed Land: A History of Colonial Mississippi* (University of Mississippi Press, 2021).

Jane H. Plummer is a doctoral student in history at Texas Christian University. She received her MA in history from the University of West Florida.

Tyson Reeder is assistant professor of history at Brigham Young University. He is the author of *Smugglers, Pirates, and Patriots: Free Trade in the Age of Revolution* (University of Pennsylvania Press, 2019) and *Serpent in Eden: Foreign Meddling and Partisan Politics in James Madison's America* (Oxford University Press, forthcoming 2024).

Craig Bruce Smith is a historian and author of *American Honor: The Creation of the Nation's Ideals during the Revolutionary Era* (University of North Carolina Press, 2020).

Samuel Watson, a professor of history at the United States Military Academy, is the author of *Jackson's Sword: The Army Officer Corps on the American Frontier, 1810–1821* (University Press of Kansas, 2012) and *Peacekeepers and Conquerors: The Army Officer Corps on the American Frontier, 1821–1846* (University Press of Kansas, 2013).

NOTE ON SOURCES

The papers of figures such as George Washington, Thomas Jefferson, Alexander Hamilton, and James Madison have been published as books and made available through the National Archives' Founders Online website: https://founders.archives.gov/. Since online is most accessible to readers, we've cited the digital versions, without volume and page numbers. When you see *Founders Online*, go to the website, search the author, recipient, and date, and you'll quickly locate any document.

Abbreviations

AGI	Archivo General de Indias
AGI, PPC	Archivo General de Indies, Papeles de Cuba. Microfilm Copy at Historic New Orleans Collection, New Orleans, LA.
AHN	Archivo Histórico Nacional, at Library of Congress and The Historic New Orleans Collection, New Orleans, LA.
BA	Bexar Archives, Briscoe Center of American History, University of Texas at Austin
BCAH	Dolph Briscoe Center for American History, University of Texas, Austin
FHQ	*Florida Historical Quarterly*
FO	Foreign Office, National Archives, Kew, Great Britain
HNF	Historic Natchez Foundation, Natchez, MS
LOC	Library of Congress
NONA	New Orleans Notarial Archives, New Orleans, LA
PLC	Papers of Panton, Leslie and Company, microfilm edition at Mary Couts Burnett Library, Texas Christian University, Fort Worth, TX
PNP-Morrow	Philip Nolan Papers, William H. Morrow Collection, Briscoe Center of American History, University of Texas at Austin
PNP-LSU	Philip Nolan Papers, Louisiana and Lower Mississippi Valley Collections, Louisiana State University Libraries, Baton Rouge, LA
THNOC	The Historic New Orleans Collection, New Orleans, LA

SOURCES

Introduction

1 Andro Linklater, *An Artist in Treason: The Extraordinary Double Life of General James Wilkinson* (New York, 2009), 84–85; James Wilkinson, Wilkinson's Second Memorial, September 17, 1789, in "Papers Bearing on James Wilkinson's Relations with Spain, 1787–1816," *The American Historical Review*, 9 (1904), 751.

2 Wilkinson to Esteban Miró, Sept. 18, 1789, in "Papers Bearing on James Wilkinson's Relations with Spain," 764–766; Wilkinson to Miró, Sept. 17, 1789, James Wilkinson Letters to Miró and Related Documents (Yale University Beinecke Library, New Haven, CT).

3 Thomas Marshall to George Washington, Feb. 12, 1789, *Founders Online.*

4 Samuel Johnson, "Scoundrel, n.s." *A Dictionary of the English Language*, 1755, Johnsonsdictionary.com. For discussions of scoundrels that emphasizes financial misdeeds, see *Southern Scoundrels: Grifters and Graft in the Nineteenth Century*, ed. Jeff Forret and Bruce E. Baker (Baton Rouge, LA, 2021); *Capitalism by Gaslight: Illuminating the Economy of Nineteenth-Century America*, ed. Brian P. Luskey and Wendy A. Woloson (Philadelphia, 2015).

"Your Best Friends Are Not Your Countrymen"

1 Benedict Arnold to George Washington, Sept. 25, 1780, *Founders Online.*

2 Arnold (alias "J. Moore") to John André (alias "John Anderson"), July 12, 1780, quoted in Carl Van Doren, *Secret History of the American Revolution* (New York, 1941), 463–464.

3 Samuel Frost Orderly Book (United States Military Academy Library, West Point, NY). These words appeared in many orderly books. See, for example, the Orderly Book of Col. Philip Van Cortlandt, 2nd New York Regiment, Sept. 23–Oct. 1, 1780 (New-York Historical Society, New York, NY).

4 Alexander Scammell to Meschech Weare, Oct. 1, 3, or 4? 1780, Weare Papers (Massachusetts Historical Society, Boston, MA).

5 Words that appeared on a woodcut drawing of the Philadelphia float featuring Arnold and Beelzebub, Sept. 30, 1780. See the Philadelphia *Pennsylvania Packet*, Oct. 3 and 7, 1780.

6 Marquis de Lafayette to Comte de Vergennes, Oct.4, 1780, *Facsimiles of Manuscripts In European Archives Relating to America, 1773–1783*, ed. Benjamin F. Stevens (26 vols., London, 1889–1895), 17: no. 1627. For other negative descriptions of Arnold by his contemporaries, see J. K. Martin, *Benedict Arnold, Revolutionary Hero: An American Hero Reconsidered* (New York, 1997), 7–10.

7 Nathanael Greene to Elihue Greene, Oct. 2, 1780, *The Papers of Nathanael Greene*, ed. R. K. Showman, et al. (13 vols., Chapel Hill, NC, 1976–2005), 6: 327.

8 Merrill Jensen (1905–1980) was a stickler about his graduate students at the University of Wisconsin, Madison, conducting archival research based on a working hypothesis rather than predetermined conclusions. Among his books are these highly respected volumes: *The Articles of Confederation* (1940), *The New Nation* (1950), and *The Founding of a Nation* (1968). He emphasized the importance of not prejudging subjects, a dominant and misleading characteristic of virtually all Arnold related commentary.

9 Jared Sparks (1789–1866) was a prolific historian of his era and even served briefly as the president of Harvard College. He was innovative in his storytelling, including in engaging in a form of oral history. For instance, he wrote acquaintances in Connecticut who claimed to have familiarity with Arnold's childhood and young adulthood. These sources were good at making up Arnold tales. See James Lanman to Sparks, Apr. 7, 1834, and James Stedman to Sparks, Apr. 8, 1834, Sparks Papers (Houghton Library, Cambridge, MA). For a complete discussion of the Arnold myth stories, see Martin, *Benedict Arnold*, 11–15.

10 Many biographies implicate Peggy Shippen as the Eve-like force behind Arnold's decision to return his allegiance to the British. Samples attempting some balance in this causation debate include, among others, James Thomas Flexner, *The Traitor and the Spy: Benedict Arnold and John André* (Boston, 1973), and Nancy Rubin Stuart, *Defiant Brides: The Story of Two Revolutionary-Era Women and the Radical Men They Married* (Boston, 2014).

11 This intentionally derogatory handbill by John Brown appeared in Apr. 1777 and repeated many of the charges made in Brown's earlier charges against Arnold. Brown sent this handbill to the Continental Congress, again demanding action, but the delegates ignored the matter. Brown had recently resigned his Continental officer's commission, which did not enhance his credibility as a committed patriot to members of that body. For Brown's

actual words, see J. E. A. Smith, *The History of Pittsfield (Berkshire County), Massachusetts, . . . 1734 to the Year 1800* (Boston, 1869), 272–274.

12 Martin, *Benedict Arnold*, 64–73.

13 The traditional belief that the colonists overwhelmingly favored independence and were fully united in purpose from beginning to end does not square well with the actual historical record. See J. K. Martin and M. E. Lender, *"A Respectable Army": The Military Origins of the Republic, 1763–1789* (3rd ed., Malden, MA, 2015), 1–28, and J. K. Martin, "The Reluctantly Rebellious Insurgents Who Started the Revolution" *SAR Magazine*, Spring 2022, 22–23.

14 John Adams to Abigail Adams, May 22, 1777, *Founders Online.*

15 Martin, *Benedict Arnold*, 80–91.

16 Brown arrived in Philadelphia on May 17, where he lied and claimed that he was a courier from Arnold. For the proceedings, see *Journals of the Continental Congress*, May 18, 1775, ed. W. C. Ford, et al. (34 vols., Washington, DC, 1904–1937), 2: 55–56.

17 Allen has many admirers, but his service record does not support claims to heroic status. See John J. Duffy and H. Nicholas Muller, *Inventing Ethan Allen* (Lebanon, NH, 2014).

18 For the complex story of Arnold's dismissal from command at West Point, see Martin, *Benedict Arnold*, 87–99.

19 Martin, *Benedict Arnold*, 104–114. Northern Department commander Philip Schuyler helped convince Washington that Arnold was a worthy candidate to lead a detached force though the Maine wilderness in an attempt to capture Quebec City.

20 For a claim that Brown did not rifle through and possibly steal from the British officers' baggage, see Ennis Duling, *Thirteen Charges against Benedict Arnold: The Accusations of Colonel John Brown Prior to the Act of Treason* (Jefferson, NC, 2021), 51–52. To Brown's credit, he did lead one of the diversionary columns in the failed attempt to capture Quebec City on Dec. 31, 1775. But Arnold had no reason to believe that the late General Richard Montgomery, killed in the Quebec assault, had promised Brown a colonelcy or anything else. See Martin, *Benedict Arnold*, 194–196.

21 Arnold to John Hancock, Feb. 1, 1776, *March to Quebec: Journals of the Members of Arnold's Expedition*, ed. K. Roberts (New York, 1938), 119–120.

22 For a copy of Brown's charges, see Duling, *Thirteen Charges*, 199–202; see also, Adams to Abigail Adams, May 20, 1777, *Founders Online.*

23 Arnold to Schuyler, June 10 and June 13, 1776, *American Archives*, 4th series, ed. P. Force (6 vols., Washington, DC, 1836–1846), 6: 976–977, 6: 1038–1039. For assessments of Hazen, see Holly A. Mayer, *Congress's Own:*

A Canadian Regiment, the Continental Army, and American Union (Norman, OK, 2021), and Martin, *Benedict Arnold*, 186–187, 419–420.

24 For a summary of the court-martial proceedings relating to Hazen, see Martin, *Benedict Arnold*, 241–245. Brown's condemnation of Arnold may be found in Duling, *Thirteen Charges*, 200–201.

25 Horatio Gates to Hancock, Sept. 2, 1776, *American Archives*, 5 series, ed. P. Force (3 vols., Washington, DC, 1848–1853), 1: 1268. This letter was written while Arnold and Gates were working together and the latter had not yet turned against Arnold.

26 William Maxwell to William Livingston, Oct. 20, 1776, ibid., 2: 1143.

27 Lewis Beebe, June 1, 7, 10, 13, 1776, "Journal of a Physician on the Expedition Against Canada, 1776," *Pennsylvania Magazine of History and Biography*, 59 (1935), 331–334.

28 For Congress's actions, see Martin, *Benedict Arnold*, 231–233. To this point, Brown had performed scant military service.

29 Samuel Chase to Arnold, Aug. 7, 1776, *Letters of Delegates*, 4: 633.

30 See Brown's list of complaints against Arnold and correspondence relating to the transmission of this document to the Continental Congress in Dec. 1776. The letters include Gates's agreement to lay the accusations before that body, contained in Duling, *Thirteen Charges*, 199–202.

31 For the story of how Gates turned against Arnold and became an implacable enemy, see Martin, *Benedict Arnold*, 292–296. The New Englanders were especially pleased that Gates had joined them. For various reasons, these delegates thought of Gates as some sort of military genius, which he was not. Wrote Samuel Adams, "General Gates is here. How shall we make him head of that [northern] army?" Samuel to John Adams, Jan. 7, 1777, *Letters of Delegates*, 6: 65. For the New England delegates, their goal was to sack Schuyler in favor of Gates, and they would succeed in Aug. 1777.

32 Arnold to Gates, Sept. 7, 1776, *American Archives*, 2: 354.

33 For Arnold being passed over for a promotion to major general, see Martin, *Benedict Arnold*, 303–315.

34 Washington to Richard Henry Lee, Mar. 6, 1777, *Founders Online*.

35 Washington to Arnold, Mar. 3, 1777; and Arnold to Washington, Mar. 26, 1777, *Founders Online*.

36 On the British Danbury raid and battles at Ridgefield and Compo Hill, see Martin, *Benedict Arnold*, 316–322.

37 Adams to Nathanael Greene, May 9, 1777, *Founders Online*. Throughout the war the Continental Congress issued only seven gold medals. One of them recognized Gates as the hero of Saratoga, an honor that actually belonged to Arnold, based on who led the American troops to victory in the two Saratoga

battles. That Congress favored their preferred general, Gates, should come as no surprise, given that they had removed Schuyler in favor of him just before the Saratoga battles took place. Gates was never near the actual fighting.

38 Washington to Richard Henry Lee, Mar. 6, 1777, *Founders Online*; Arnold to Hancock, July 11, 1777, Papers of the Continental Congress, microfilm reel 179, item 162: 106–107 (National Archives and Records Administration, Washington, DC).

39 Washington to Hancock, July 10, 1777, *Founders Online*.

40 For Arnold's sortie up the Mohawk River, see Martin, *Benedict Arnold*, 361–368, and J. Glatthaar and J. K. Martin, *Forgotten Allies: The Oneida Indians and the American Revolution* (New York, 2006), 170–178.

41 Many studies of the campaign, looking backward through Arnold's treason, have ignored many of Arnold's vital actions, or, more recently, have concluded that Arnold and Gates were getting along, especially at the time of the second battle. The evidence strongly suggests otherwise. See Martin, *Benedict Arnold*, 369–409. While recovering from his wounded leg shortly after the second battle, Arnold even referred to Gates as a "poltroon," or coward, hardly a term of cooperative respect.

42 Covert assistance from France before the formal 1778 alliance proved essential to keeping the patriot cause going. Many of the weapons and related supplies used to help defeat and capture Burgoyne's army came from France, an important element in understanding the crucial Saratoga campaign victory.

43 Chase to Arnold, Phila., Aug. 7, 1776, *Letters of Delegates*, 4: 633.

44 Washington to Arnold, Jan. 20, 1778, *Founders Online*. Congress voted for the restoration of Arnold's seniority on Nov. 29, 1777, then told Washington to inform Arnold, as if such an assignment was beyond their responsibility. So pressed by business on so many fronts, including settling the army into Valley Forge, Washington apologized for not getting this news to Arnold sooner.

45 Arnold to Washington, Mar. 12, 1778, *Founders Online*.

46 For Arnold's growing disillusionment, see Martin, *Benedict Arnold*, 403–432.

47 This denunciation of Arnold reads as follows:
Mothers Shall Still Their Children, and say—Arnold!—
Arnold shall be the bugbear of their years.
Arnold!—vile, treacherous, and leagued with Satan.
See also the anti-Arnold acrostic in Martin, *Benedict Arnold*, 20.

Charles Lee

1 For the historiography of Lee, see Mark Edward Lender, "The Ever Controversial General Charles Lee," *Journal of Military History*, 78 (2014), 1395–1406.

2 This sketch of Lee is based on John R. Alden, *General Charles Lee: Traitor or Patriot?* (Baton Rouge, 1951); John Shy, "Charles Lee: The Soldier as Radical," in *George Washington's Generals*, George Athan Billias, ed. (New York, 1964), 22–53; Phillip Papas, *Renegade Revolutionary: The Life of General Charles Lee* (New York, 2014).

3 *Collections of the New York Historical Society for the Year 1872: The Lee Papers* (4 vols., New York, 1872–1875), 1: 3–5; Alden, *General Charles Lee*, 14.

4 Burgoyne to Lord North, 1775, in Edward Barrington De Fonblanque, *Political and Military Episodes in the latter Half of the Eighteenth century Derived from the Life and Correspondence of the Right Hon. John Burgoyne, General, Statesman, Dramatist* (London, 1876), 174, 176.

5 Charles W. Snell, "General Charles Lee House, 'Prato Rio,'" National Register of Historic Places Inventory—Nomination Form, National Park Service, July 27, 1972; Papas, *Renegade Revolutionary*, 4.

6 Shy, "Charles Lee," 23; Papas, *Renegade Revolutionary*, 93–113. For a contrary view—that Lee's radicalism was self-serving opportunism—see Dominick Mazzagetti, *Charles Lee: Self before Country* (New Brunswick, NJ, 2013).

7 Burgoyne to Lord North, 1775, in De Fonblanque, *Burgoyne Correspondence*, 174.

8 Joseph Reed to Lee, Nov. 21, 1776, in *Life and Correspondence of Joseph Reed*, ed. William B. Reed (2 vols., Philadelphia, 1847), 1: 255–256; Reed to Lee, Nov. 21, 1776, *Lee Papers*, 2: 293–294; Lee to Horatio Gates, Dec. 12–13, 1776, ibid., 348; Washington to Lee, Dec. 3, 1776, and Dec. 7, 1776, *Founders Online*; Arthur S. Lefkowitz, *The Long Retreat: The Calamitous American Defense of New Jersey, 1776* (Metuchen, NJ, 1998), 107–111; Shy, "Charles Lee," 39; Lee to Washington, Dec. 4, 1776, *Founders Online*.

9 The insinuation is in James Flexner, *George Washington in the American Revolution, 1775–1783* (Boston, 1968), 167; Christian M. McBurney, *Kidnapping the Enemy: The Special Operations to Capture Generals Charles Lee and Richard Prescott* (Yardley, PA, 2014), chapter 2.

10 Parole, Apr. 5, 1778, *Lee Papers*, 2: 382; Samuel Adams to James Warren, Jan. 8, 1777, *Letters of Delegates to Congress, 1774–1789*, Paul H. Smith and Ronald M. Gephart (26 vols., Washington, DC, 1976–2000), 6: 49; Samuel Adams to John Adams, Jan. 9, 1777, ibid., 64; Thomas Burke's Notes of Debates, Feb. 20, 1777, ibid., 327–328; Richard Peters to Washington, Feb. 21, 1777, *Founders Online*; Lee's correspondence from December 1776 and April 1778 is found in *Lee Papers*, 2: 356–382; Thomas Burke's Notes of Debates, Feb. 21, 1777, *Letters of Delegates to Congress*, 6: 336. These are the surviving letters; there probably were others. Richard Henry Lee to Charles Lee, Feb. 1777, *Letters of Delegates to Congress*, 6: 337n2; Lee to Giuseppe Minghini, Apr. 4, 1777, *Lee Papers*, 2: 367–368; Caroline Cox, *A Proper Sense*

of Honor: Service and Sacrifice in George Washington's Army (Chapel Hill, NC, 2004), 199–200, 224.

11 "Scheme for Putting an End to the War, Submitted to the Royal Commissioners, Mar. 29, 1777," *Lee Papers*, 2: 361–366; George H. Moore, "The Treason of Charles Lee, Major General," ibid., 4: 339–427.

12 George H. Moore, *The Treason of Charles Lee, Major General, Second in Command of the American Army of the Revolution* (New York, 1860). This short book (115 pages) is the published version of Moore's 1858 paper; Alden, *General Charles Lee*, 175–179; Mazzagetti, *General Charles Lee*, 139–147; Christian M. McBurney, *George Washington's Nemesis: The Outrageous Treason and Unfair Court-Martial of Major General Charles Lee during the Revolutionary War* (El Dorado Hills, CA, 2020), 1–63.

13 *The Henry Strachey Papers*, 1768–1802 (Ann Arbor, MI) contain no references to Lee's plan.

14 Shy, "Charles Lee," 40–41; Otway Byrd to Lee, June 1, 1778, *Lee Papers*, 2: 396.

15 Charles Thomson to Washington, July 21, 1777, *Letters of Delegates to Congress*, 7: 358–359; ibid., 7: 377n1; Parole, Apr. 5, 1778, *Lee Papers*, 2: 382.

16 U.S. Coast Guard, "Situational Awareness," *Team Coordination Training Student Guide* (August 1998), chap. 5.

17 Elias Boudinot, *Journal or Historical Recollections of American Events during the Revolutionary War* (Philadelphia, 1894), 78.

18 Henry Laurens to John Laurens, July 6, 1778, *Letters of Delegates to Congress*, 10: 230, 323n3; Alden, *General Charles Lee*, 191; Lee to Henry Laurens, Apr. 17, 1778, *Lee Papers*, 2: 390; Henry Laurens to John Laurens, June 17, 1778, *Letters of Delegates to Congress*, 10: 126.

19 Thomas Burke to Richard Caswell, Apr. 9, 1778, ibid., 9: 393; Charles Pettit to Thomas Bradford, May 19, 1778, *Lee Papers*, 2: 393–394; Nathanael Greene to William Greene, May 25, 1778, and to Griffin Green, May 25, 1778, in *The Papers of Nathanael Greene*, ed. Richard K. Showman, et. al. (8 vols., Chapel Hill, 1976–), 2: 408, 2: 406.

20 Lee to Benjamin Rush, June 4, 1778, *Lee Papers*, 2: 397.

21 Lee to Henry Laurens, May 13, 1778, ibid., 2: 392–293; Washington to Lee, June 15, 1778, *Founders Online*.

22 "Plan of an Army, Etc.," Apr. 13, 1778, *Lee Papers*, 2: 383; unless noted otherwise, all references to Lee's plan are from this document; Lee to Washington, Apr. 13, 1778, ibid.

23 Washington to Lee, Apr. 22, 1778, *Founders Online*.

24 "Plan of an Army," *Lee Papers*, 2: 384, 388.

25 Mercy Otis Warren, *History of the Rise, Progress and Termination of the American Revolution. Interspersed with Biographical, Political and Moral Observations* (3 vols., Boston, 1805), 2: 95; Shy, "Charles Lee," 42.

26 Washington to Lee, June 15, 1778, *Founders Online.*

27 Paul Lockhart, *The Drillmaster of Valley Forge: The Baron de Steuben and the Making of the American Army* (New York, 2008), 132–133; James Varnum to Washington, May 5, 1778, *Founders Online*; Alexander Hamilton to Elias Boudinot, July 26, 1778, *Founders Online.*

28 Papas, *Renegade Revolutionary*, 237; Alden, *General Charles Lee*, 202. Recently, Thomas Fleming has suggested that Lee intended the remark as a jab at the commander in chief—that perhaps Lee obliquely referred to the tendency of British opposition politicians to rally to the prince when they disagreed with the king. The implication is that Lee saw Washington as the king; Thomas Fleming, *Washington's Secret War: The Hidden History of Valley Forge* (New York, 2005), 301. Papas, *Renegade Revolutionary*, 237, cautiously agrees Lee may have intended a dig at Washington. This interpretation seems strained; but there is little doubt the commander-in-chief failed to appreciate Lee's conduct.

29 Boudinot, *Journal*, 78; Lee to Gates, Apr. 4, 1778, *Lee Papers*, 3: 321.

30 Marquis de Lafayette, *Memoirs*: *Correspondence and Manuscripts of General Lafayette* (London, 1837), 50–51; Jared Sparks, "Life of Charles Lee, Major-General in the Army of the Revolution," *Lee Papers*, 4: 302; Theodore B. Thayer, *The Making of a Scapegoat: Washington and Lee at Monmouth* (Port Washington, NY, 1976), 29; Greene to Washington, June 24, 1778, *Papers of Nathanael Greene*, 2: 447.

31 Testimony of Charles Scott and Anthony Wayne, in Charles Lee, defendant, *Proceedings of a General Court Martial . . . for the Trial of Major-General Lee* (New York, 1864), 5–8.

32 Testimony of Lee and John Brooks, ibid., 169, 215, 218–219.

33 Lafayette and Scott quoted in Mark Edward Lender and Garry Wheeler Stone, *Fatal Sunday: George Washington, the Monmouth Campaign, and the Politics of Battle* (Norman, OK, 2016), 290. For a full discussion of the Washington–Lee encounter, see ibid., 288–291.

34 Boudinot to Hamilton, July 8, 1778, *Letters of Delegates to Congress*, 10: 238.

35 Shy, "Charles Lee," 45; *Proceedings of a General Court Martial*, 4.

36 David Ramsay, *The History of the American Revolution* (Philadelphia, 1789), 85–86; Henry Laurens to Rawlins Lowndes, Aug. 18, 1778, *Letters of Delegates to Congress*, 10: 478; Gouverneur Morris to Washington, Oct. 26, 1778, ibid., 11: 127; Lender and Stone, *Fatal Sunday*, 400.

37 Copy of Lee's Will, Sept. 10, 1782, *Lee Papers*, 4: 29–33.

38 Samuel Johnson, *A Dictionary of the English Language* (2 vols., London, 1766), 2: 576.

39 Shy, "Charles Lee," 22.

40 Bilby and Jenkins, *Monmouth Court House*, 200, have described Lee's retreat as "the inevitable result of Lee's haphazard battle preparation and lack of terrain knowledge"; but they advanced no explanation of how Lee might have planned any differently given the circumstances of the run-up to the battle. As to the matter of "terrain knowledge:" Lee had the advice of local guides, and he clearly understood the terrain favored the oncoming British.

Blount's Bunko

1 Thomas Jefferson to William Blount, Aug. 1, 1790, *Founders Online*. Washington nominated Blount on June 7, 1790. See Washington to the United States Senate, June 7, 1790, *Founders Online*. The Senate immediately approved Washington's nomination. Blount's commission was officially dated June 8, 1790. Secretary of State Thomas Jefferson sent Blount the commission on June 15, 1790. Blount acknowledged receiving the commission from Jefferson on July 7, 1790.

2 William Blount to John Gray Blount, June 6, 1790, *John Gray Blount Papers, 1706–1900* (State Archives of North Carolina, Raleigh). William Blount to John Steele, July 10, 1790, in *The Papers of John Steele*, ed. Henry Wagstaff (2 vols., Raleigh, N.C., 1924), 1: 67–70. Blount not only knew about the plum position well in advance, he also used all of his contacts and called in all of his favors to secure the nomination.

3 Blount left North Carolina to take up residence in the Southwest Territory on Aug. 24, 1790. See Blount to Jefferson, Aug. 20, 1790, *Founders Online*.

4 Gregory Ablavsky does discuss Blount's role in westward expansion in his *Federal Ground: Governing Property and Violence in the First U.S. Territories* (New York, 2021), 33–40 and 212–221. Ablavsky focuses on contested laws regarding property rights and the right to use violence. He is especially interested in the westward spread of federal authority in northern and southern borderlands. Blount is an important figure in this narrative. However, Ablavsky is not much interested in Blount's chicanery. For Ablavsky, "much of the scramble for lands under indiscriminate location reflected, not outright fraud, but the multiple ways that the powerful and well-connected could tilt the poorly supervised land system in their favor." Ablavsky, *Federal Ground*, 33. Deliberately tilting any system in one's favor does constitute outright fraud, in my estimation. And I think this sort of intention deserves scrutiny. What is more, Blount engaged in a host of more direct chicaneries such as falsifying documents and resorted to lies and

bribery, which even Ablavsky would call outright fraud. Recent histories of westward expansion include, for example, Matthew Karp, *This Vast Southern Empire: Slaveholders at the Helm of American Foreign Policy* (2016; rep., Cambridge, MA, 2018); Walter Johnson, *River of Dark Dreams: Slavery and Empire in the Cotton Kingdom* (2013; rep., Cambridge, MA, 2017); and Paul Frymer, *Building an American Empire: The Era of Territorial and Political Expansion* (Princeton, 2017). Academic overviews of westward expansion do not discuss Blount. See Ray Allen Billington and Martin Ridge, *Westward Expansion: A History of the American Frontier* (1949; 6th ed.,Albuquerque, NM, 2001). Popular histories do not even mention Blount. For example, see David McCullough, *Pioneers: The Heroic Story of the Settlers Who Brought the American Ideal West* (New York, 2019). Tennessee histories have discussed Blount's land speculation. See Paul Bergeron, Stephen V. Ash, and Jeanette Keith, *Tennesseans and Their History* (Knoxville, TN, 1999), 47–67; and Thomas Perkins Abernethy, *From Frontier to Plantation in Tennessee: A Study in Frontier Democracy* (Chapel Hill, NC, 1932), 51–60. However, these books do not focus on Blount's chicanery. Buckner F. Melton Jr. does have a lot to say about Blount's lack of scruples. Buckner F. Melton Jr., *The First Impeachment: The Constitution's Framers and the Case of Senator William Blount* (Macon, GA, 1998). But, this book is mostly focused on the time after Tennessee became a state. For Blount's biography, see William H. Masterson, *William Blount* (Baton Rouge, LA, 1954).

5 Quotes: William Blount to John Gray Blount, Jan. 7, 1782, and William Blount to unknown, Mar. 9, 1784, *John Gray Blount Papers*; Blount to John Donelson, Joseph Martin, and John Sevier, May 31, 1784, in *John Gray Blount Papers*, ed. Alice Barnwell Keith (4 vols., Raleigh, NC, 1952–1982), 1: 167–169; Thomas Hart to Blount, Jan. 25, 1780, in ibid., 1: 8–9.

6 Masterson, *William Blount*, 43.

7 Jefferson, "Report on Public Lands," Nov. 8, 1791, *Founders Online*; Masterson, *William Blount*, 68–70.

8 Masterson, *William Blount*, 70.

9 Ablavsky, *Federal Ground*, 33; Masterson, *William Blount*, 171.

10 Masterson, *William Blount*, 71–73, 79, 81, and 99; Blount to unknown, Mar. 9, 1784; Blount to James McIntosh, Stephen Heard, John Morrell, and William Downes, May 31, 1784, *John Gray Blount Papers*.

11 Masterson, *William Blount*, 57; James C. Mountflorence, "A Short Sketch of the Public Life of Major J. C. Mountflorence" (n.p. 1817), 5.

12 Hugh Williamson to John Gray Blount, Apr. 6, 1790, *John Gray Blount Papers*.

13 *The Territorial Papers of the United States*, ed. Clarence E. Carter (28 vols., Washington, D.C., 1934–1975), 4: 18–19.

14 Masterson, *William Blount*, 176.

15 Ibid.

16 Hugh Williamson to Washington, May 28, 1790, in *Territorial Papers*, 4: 19–20.

17 Quotes: Hugh Williamson to John Gray Blount, June 15, 1790; John Steele to John Gray Blount, July 10, 1790; and William Blount to John Gray Blount, June 6, 1790, *John Gray Blount Papers*.

18 Masterson, *William Blount*, 183–184.

19 William Blount to John Gray Blount, Nov. 10, 1790, *John Gray Blount Papers*.

20 Henry Knox to Washington, Mar. 10, 1791, *Founders Online*.

21 For more on the events of the Treaty of Holston, see Masterson, *William Blount*, 203–205.

22 Proclamation on the Treaty of Holston, Nov. 11, 1791, *Founders Online*.

23 *American State Papers: Indian Affairs*, 1: 203–204.

24 William Blount to Thomas Jefferson, July 17, 1791, *Founders Online*.

25 Quotes: Knox to Washington, Mar. 10, 1791; Blount to Jefferson, Aug. 12, 1791; Jefferson, "Report on Public Lands," Nov. 8, 1791; Jefferson to Blount, Aug. 17, 1791, *Founders Online*. Articles eight and nine of the Treaty of Holston specifically made it illegal for settlers to hunt or settle on lands reserved for the Cherokee people.

26 Jefferson to Blount, Mar. 26, 1791; Jefferson to Blount, Mar. 26, 1791, *Founders Online*. George Hammond, a British agent, reported to the British foreign minister Lord Grenville in 1792 that he had spoken with Jefferson about "the claims, which the United States asserted over the soil and internal regulation of the Indians occupying lands within the American territory. Mr. Jefferson replied that the nature of the sovereignty of the United States was not yet precisely defined, but that in regard to the soil they claimed the right of pre-emption, by which the Indians were understood to be precluded from disposing of any part of their land except with the consent of the United States—that in respect to the internal regulation of the Indians the United States have not hitherto exercised any other jurisdiction over them than that of prohibiting them from allowing any person to inhabit their country, who were not provided with licenses from the government of the United States. On the validity or justice of these arguments it is unnecessary for me to make any comment, but your Lordship will perceive from them that as this government asserts this sort of paramount sovereignty over the soil actually occupied by the Indians, it would naturally regard any grant of that soil in perpetuity not only as a dereliction of right, but also as a sacrifice of a part of its territory." See Jefferson, "Report on Public Lands," Nov. 8, 1791, *Founders Online*. See

also Drew R. McCoy, *The Elusive Republic: Political Economy in Jeffersonian America* (Chapel Hill, N.C., 1980), 13–16.

27 Jefferson to Knox, Aug. 26, 1790, *Founders Online*. In this same letter, Jefferson explained that Indigenous people did not own land. Congress reserved lands for them. He phrased it thus: Indigenous people "were entitled to the sole occupation of the lands within the limits guaranteed to them." And Congress was the sole authority that could guarantee these limits.

28 Blount to Jefferson, July 17, 1791, *Founders Online*; Blount to John Steele, Nov. 8, 1792, in *Papers of John Steele*, 1: 85. See also Jefferson to Blount, Aug. 17, 1791, in which Jefferson wrote: "On conversing with this gentleman, I find he cannot inform me whereabouts the S. Carolina Indian boundary, will strike the Southern boundary of N. Carolina, from which point you know the North line of your treaty is to set out and meet the line which crosses Holston. I will therefore still ask your information of this point." Also, see Blount to Jefferson, Aug. 12, 1791, *Founders Online*. Jefferson's frustrations can be seen in the letters he sent to Blount on Mar. 26, Aug. 12, Aug. 17, and Aug. 22, 1791, *Founders Online*.

29 Blount to James Robertson, Apr. 29, 1792, *James Robertson Papers* (Vanderbilt University Special Collections, Nashville, TN); Masterson, *William Blount*, 214, 218.

30 Quotes: Blount to Robertson, Dec. 7, 1793, in *James Robertson Papers*; Blount to Robertson, Jan. 19, 1794, in "Correspondence of Gen. James Robertson," *The American Historical Magazine* 3 (1898), 283. See also Masterson, *William Blount*, 250. For more on Morris, see Charles Rappleye, *Robert Morris: Financier of the American Revolution* (New York, 2011).

31 *John Gray Blount Papers*, drawer numbers 881 and 884; Masterson, *William Blount*, 261–262.

32 Blount to Robertson, Jan. 19, 1794, in "Correspondence of Gen. James Roberts," 283.

33 Quotes: Blount to James Robertson, Nov. 22, 1794, and Dec. 4, 1794, *James Robertson Papers*.

34 Masterson, *William Blount*, 298.

"The Spitting Lyon"

1 While the party's full name was the "Democratic-Republicans," early Americans more often used the shorter "Republicans."

2 William Goddard, *The Prowess of the Whig Club, and the Manoeuvres of Legion* (Baltimore, 1777), 7; Aleine Austin, *Matthew Lyon: "New Man" of the Democratic Revolution, 1749–1822* (University Park, PA, 1981), 1; See, for example, Gordon Wood, *The Creation of the American Republic, 1776–1787*

(Chapel Hill, NC, 1969), 476–483, 506–518; Gordon Wood, *Empire of Liberty: A History of the Early Republic, 1789–1815* (New York, 2009), 227–230; Alan Taylor, "From Fathers to Friends of the People: Political Personas in the Early Republic," *Journal of the Early Republic*, 11 (1991), 465–491.

3 Robert Yates's Version of Hamilton's Speech to the Constitutional Convention, June 18, 1787, *Founders Online*. For more on the Federalists and their ideology, see, for example, James Roger Sharp, *American Politics in the Early Republic: A New Nation in Crisis* (New Haven, CT, 1993); Stanley Elkins and Erik McKitrick, *The Age of Federalism: The Early American Republic, 1788–1800* (New York, 1974); Doron Ben-Atar and Barbara B. Oberg, ed., *Federalists Reconsidered* (Charlottesville, VA, 1998).

4 Austin, *Matthew Lyon,* 7–44; Matthew Lyon to Armisted C. Mason, Jan. 16, 1817, in J. Fairfax McLaughlin, *Matthew Lyon: The Hampden of Congress, A Biography* (New York, 1900), 498–501; John Crossley Morgan and Richard Lyon Morgan, *Resisting Tyranny: The Story of Matthew Lyon, Early American Patriot* (Eugene, OR, 2018), 4–5.

5 Lyon to Mason in *The Hampden of Congress*, 500–501; Andrew N. Adams, *A History of the Town of Fair Haven, Vermont. In Three Parts* (Fair Haven, 1870), 419; Austin, *Matthew Lyon*, 45–75.

6 Lyon to Mason, in *The Hampden of Congress*, 501; *Farmers' Library* (Fair Haven, VT), Feb. 17, 1794; Austin, *Matthew Lyon*, 76–89.

7 *Farmers' Library* (Fair Haven, VT), Aug. 14, 1794, June 10, 1793; See also *Farmer's Library* (Fair Haven, VT), July 8, 1794; Adams, *A History of the Town of Fair Haven,* 419; Austin, *Matthew Lyon,* 64–75.

8 *Annals of Congress*, 5th Cong., 1st sess., 234–235; Austin, *Matthew Lyon*, 91–94; Adams, *A History of the Town of Fair Haven*, 419–420. Jefferson later abolished the practice, see McLaughlin, *The Hampden of Congress,* 225. For more on Federalists' ceremony and cult of Washington, see David Waldstreicher, *In the Midst of Perpetual Fetes: The Making of American Nationalism, 1776–1820* (Chapel Hill, NC, 1997), 117–126; Simon P. Newman, *Parades and the Politics of the Street: Festive Culture in the Early American Republic* (Philadelphia, 1997), 44–68; Jeffrey L. Pasley, *The First Presidential Contest: 1796 and the Founding of American Democracy* (Lawrence, KS, 2013), 132–181.

9 William Cobbett, *Porcupine's Works: Containing Various Writings and Selections, exhibiting a faithful picture of the United States of America* (12 vols, London, 1801), 6: 17–18; *Life of Gallatin,* quoted in McLaughlin, *Hampden of Congress,* 229.

10 *Annals of Congress*, 5th Cong., 2nd sess., 961–962; Austin, *Matthew Lyon*, 96–97.

11 *Annals of Congress*, 5th Cong., 2nd sess., 1007, 962, 975, 982, 974, 962–1029; Austin, *Matthew Lyon*, 97. Lyon also submitted a letter to the speaker making the same point regarding the House not being in order. See Austin, *Matthew Lyon*, 97.

12 William Cobbett, *Porcupine's Works*, 3: 87–89; *Gazette of the United States* (NY), Nov. 14, 1798; *Rutland Herald* (VT), Aug. 13, 1798; James McHenry to George Washington, Feb. 1, 1798, *Founders Online*; *Federal Gazette* (Philadelphia), Mar. 19, 1798; *Western Star* (Stockbridge, Mass.), Feb. 12, 1798; *Annals of Congress*, 5th Cong., 2nd sess., 1008–1009; Austin, *Matthew Lyon*, 97–98. See also Abigail Adams to Mary Smith Cranch, Feb. 21, 1798, *Founders Online*; Isaacson to Unknown, Feb. 19, 1798, Matthew Lyon Letters (Vermont Historical Society, Barre, VT).

13 Roger Griswold to unknown, Feb. 25, 1798, quoted in Austin, *Matthew Lyon*, 100; *Annals of Congress*, 5th Cong., 2nd sess., 1034; Austin, *Matthew Lyon*, 100.

14 *Northern Centinel* (Salem, NY), Mar. 5, 1798; Rutland (VT) *Herald*, Mar. 26, 1798; Manisha Sinha, "The Caning of Charles Sumner: Slavery, Race, and Ideology in the Age of the Civil War," *Journal of the Early Republic*, 23 (2003), 245.

15 *Annals of Congress*, 5th Cong., 2nd sess., 1036, 1036–1067; *Life of Gallatin*, quoted in McLaughlin, *Hampden of Congress*, 230.

16 *Farmer's Weekly Museum* (Walpole, NH), Apr. 17, 1798; *The Bee* (New London, CT), Mar. 14, 1798; *Columbian Centinel* (Boston), Feb. 24, 1798. Others preferred a more humorous approach and a number of songs and poems describing the event flooded both the Republican and Federalist presses. See, for example, "Lyon and Griswold. Battle of the Wooden Sword!!," Rutland (VT) *Herald*, Apr. 30, 1798; "The Spunkiad: or Heroism Improved" (Newburgh, NY, 1798); "Lord Save Us, the Congress are Fighting! A New Song" (Alexandria, 1798); Geoffrey Touchstone, "The House of Wisdom in a Bustle: A Poem, Descriptive of the Noted Battle Lately Fought in C-ng-ss" (New York, 1798).

17 Matthew Lyon to John Adams, Mar. 4, 1801, *Founders Online*; Austin, *Matthew Lyon*, 102–103; Sharp, *American Politics*, 164–176; Elkins and McKitrick, *The Age of Federalism*, 537–588; Carol Sue Humphrey, *The Press of the Young Republic, 1783–1833* (Westport, CT, 1996), 57–58. In his newspaper *The Scourge of Aristocracy*, Lyon called the Sedition Law "a refinement upon Despotism" and warned that it "present[ed] an image of the utmost fearful Tyranny." See *Scourge of Aristocracy* (Stonington-Port, CT), Oct. 20, 1798, quoted in Morgan, *Resisting Tyranny*, 8.

18 *Spooner's Vermont Journal* (Windsor, VT), May 29, 1798.

19 Ibid., July 31, 1798.

20 Joel Barlow, "Copy of a Letter from an American Diplomatic Character in France, to a Member of Congress in Philadelphia," (Fairhaven, VT, 1798); Francis Wharton, *State Trials of the United States During the Administrations of Washington and Adams: With References, Historical and Professional, and Preliminary Notes on the Politics of the Times* (Philadelphia, 1849), 334; Austin, *Matthew Lyon*, 109–110.

21 *Annals of Congress*, 16th Cong., 2nd sess., 480–484; Wharton, *State of Trials,* 333–334; Austin, *Matthew Lyon*, 110–111; Morgan, *Resisting Tyranny*, 8.

22 Wharton, *State of Trials,* 334–335; Austin, *Matthew Lyon*, 111–116.

23 Wharton, *State of Trials,* 336–337; *Greenleaf's New York Journal* (New York), Nov. 14, 1798; Austin, *Matthew Lyon*, 116–117.

24 *Greenleaf's New York Journal* (New York), Nov. 14, 1798.

25 *The Bee* (New London, CT), Dec. 12, 1798; *Commercial Advertiser* (New York), Dec. 7, 1798; *Massachusetts Mercury* (Boston), Dec. 25, 1798; *Gazette of the United States* (Philadelphia), Dec. 5, 1798; See also, *Daily Advertiser* (Philadelphia), Dec. 12, 1798.

26 *Aurora General Advertiser* (Philadelphia), Feb. 8, 1799.

27 Norwich (CT) *Courier*, Jan. 9, 1799; *Gazette of the United States* (Philadelphia), Jan. 31, 1799; *Spectator* (New York), Dec. 29, 1798; *Political Repository* (Brookfield, MA), Jan.1, 1799; *Oracle of the Day* (Portsmouth, NH), Jan. 12, 1799; Vergennes (VT) *Gazette*, Jan. 17, 1799.

28 *Aurora General Advertiser* (Philadelphia), Jan. 14, 1799; Thomas Jefferson to James Madison, Jan. 3, 1799, *Founders Online*; *Centinel of Freedom* (Newark, NJ), Mar. 5, 1799; Austin, *Matthew Lyon*, 124–125.

29 *Vermont Gazette* (Bennington, VT), Feb. 14, 1799; *Independent Chronicle* (Boston), Feb. 25, 1799; *Courier of New Hampshire* (Concord, NH), Apr. 20, 1799; Austin, *Matthew Lyon*, 126–127; Morgan, *Resisting Tyranny,* 19; McLaughlin, *Hampden of Congress,* 377–380.

30 *Annals of Congress*, 5th Cong., 3rd sess., 2960, 2972, 2959– 2973; Austin, *Matthew Lyon*, 127–128.

31 Lyon to Mason, in *Hampden of Congress*, 503–504; Austin, *Matthew Lyon*, 128.

32 Austin, *Matthew Lyon*, 129.

The Devil from Dedham

1 Nathaniel Ames, August 6–7, 1801, in *The Diary of Dr. Nathaniel Ames of Dedham, Massachusetts, 1758–1822*, ed. Robert Brand Hanson (2 vols., Camden, ME, 1998); *Columbia Minerva* (Dedham), Aug. 11, 1801; Boston *Gazette*, Aug. 24, 1801; Ebenezer Fairbanks Jr., *The Solemn Declaration of the Late Unfortunate Jason Fairbanks* (Dedham, MA, 1802), 14, 19–21; "A Mournful Tragedy," Boston or Dedham?, 1801.

2 Robert Brand Hanson, *Dedham, Massachusetts, 1635–1890* (Dedham, 1976), 176–177; Daniel A. Cohen, "The Beautiful Female Murder Victim: Literary Genres and Courtship Practices in the Origins of a Cultural Motif, 1590–1850," *Journal of Social History*, 31 (1997), 277–306; *Columbia Minerva* (Dedham), Mar. 21, 1799, and Feb. 20, 1800; Ebenezer Fairbanks Jr., *The Solemn Declaration of the Late Unfortunate Jason Fairbanks* (Dedham, 1801), 20; J. M. Opal, *Beyond the Farm: National Ambitions in Rural New England* (Philadelphia, 2008), 82; *Report of the Trial of Jason Fairbanks, on an Indictment for the Murder of Miss Elizabeth Fales* (Boston, 1801), 7.

3 *Report of the Trial of Jason Fairbanks*, 6, 8–9, 14–16, 32, 66–67, 71, 77; E. Fairbanks, *Solemn Declaration*, 6, 45.

4 *Report of the Trial of Jason Fairbanks*, 6, 14, 15, 18, 22, 77; Boston *Gazette*, Sept. 7, 1801; Fales Family Papers (Dedham Historical Society); Martha J. McNamara, "Nearest a Kin to Fisher," *Common-Place*, 2 (2002), 13; David Cressy, "The Seasonality of Marriage in Old and New England," *Journal of Interdisciplinary History*, 16 (1985), 13; Boston *Gazette*, May 1801; *Report of the Trial of Jason Fairbanks*, 6, 67.

5 David H. Flaherty, "Crime and Social Control in Provincial Massachusetts," *The Historical Journal*, 24 (1981), 345–346; Kenneth A. Lockridge, *A New England Town: The First Hundred Years: Dedham Massachusetts, 1636–1736*, (New York, 1970), 93–94, 118, 148; David Hackett Fischer, *Albion's Seed: Four British Folkways in America* (New York, 1989), 190–193; Roger Lane, "Murder in America: A Historian's Perspective," *Crime and Justice*, 25 (1999), 198–199; James Morton Smith, "The Federalist 'Saints' versus 'The Devil of Sedition': The Liberty Pole Case of Dedham, Massachusetts, 1798–1799," *New England Quarterly*, 28 (1955), 199; Doron S. Ben-Atar and Richard D. Brown, *Taming Lust: Crimes Against Nature in the Early Republic* (Philadelphia, 2014), 156–157n20, 172n12; Salem (MA) *Impartial Register*, Nov. 23, 1801; Joy Wiltenburg, "True Crime: The Origins of Modern Sensationalism," *American Historical Review*, 109 (2004), 1377–1404; *New York Times*, Feb. 19, and June 14, 1880; *Saturday Evening Post* (Indianapolis, IN), June 15, 1929; Opal, *Beyond the Farm*, 49; Vergennes (VT) *Gazette*, Aug. 27, 1801.

6 John Adams to Abigail Adams, Apr. 12, 1778, *Founders Online*. Craig Bruce Smith, *American Honor: The Creation of the Nation's Ideals during the Revolutionary Era* (Chapel Hill, NC, 2018); Bertram Wyatt-Brown, *Southern Honor: Ethics and Behavior in the Old South* (New York, 2007); Joanne B. Freeman, *Affairs of Honor: National Politics in the New Republic* (New Haven, CT, 2002); Sari Altschuller and Cristobal Silva, "Early American Disabilities Studies," *Early American Literature*, 52 (2017), 2; Thomas A. Foster, *Sex and the Eighteenth-Century Man: Massachusetts and the History of*

Sexuality in America (Boston, 2006), 9; *Report of the Trial of Jason Fairbanks*, preface, 69.

7 Dale H. Freeman, "'Melancholy Catastrophe!': The Story of Jason Fairbanks and Elizabeth Fales," *Historical Journal of Massachusetts*, 26 (1998); Norman Dain and Eric T. Carlson, "Social Class and Psychological Medicine in the United States, 1789–1824," *Bulletin of the History of Medicine*, 33 (1959), 454–465; Daniel A. Cohen, *Pillars of Salt, Monuments of Grace: New England Crime Literature and the Origins of American Popular Culture, 1674–1860* (New York, 1993); Cohen, "The Beautiful Female Murder Victim," *Journal of Social History*, 31 (1997); Constance B. Schulz, "'Of Bigotry in Politics and Religion': Jefferson's Religion, the Federalist Press, and the Syllabus," *Virginia Magazine of History and Biography*, 91 (1983), 73–91; "The Village, a Poem" in *The American Monthly Magazine and Critical Review*, 1 (1817), 117–120; Craig Bruce Smith, "Claiming the Centennial: The American Revolution's Blood and Spirit in Boston, 1870–1876," *Massachusetts Historical Review*, 15 (2013), 7–53.

8 *Supplement to the Massachusetts Gazette* (Boston), Sept. 15, 1774; Herman Mann, *Historical Annals of Dedham* (Dedham, 1847), 30–36; Frank Smith, *A History of Dedham, Massachusetts* (Dedham, 1936), 434–466; Walter Austin, *Tale of a Dedham Tavern: History of the Norfolk Hotel, Dedham, Massachusetts* (Cambridge, MA, 1912), 3, 9; Erastus Worthington, *The History of Dedham: From the Beginning of its Settlement, in September 1635* (Boston, 1827), 64–74; Kenneth Lockridge, "Land, Population, and the Evolution of New England Society, 1630–1790," *Past & Present*, 39 (1968), 62–80; Numbers and percentage are based on Mann's *Historical Annals*, and *A List of Revolutionary Soldiers Who Served Dedham in the Revolution* (Dedham, 1917), which lists 656 men who fought. Smith's *A History of Dedham* (449) records 678; David Hackett Fischer, *Paul Revere's Ride* (New York, 1994), 158; Richard Frothingham, *History of the Siege of Boston, and of the Battles of Lexington, Concord, and Bunker Hill* (Boston, 1851), 71–72n3.

9 Robert A. Gross, *The Minutemen and Their World* (New York, 1976), 71; "Revolutionary Muster Rolls" in Smith, *A History of Dedham*, 450–466.

10 Israel Evans, *A Discourse . . .* (Philadelphia, 1781), 31; Frank Warren Coburn, *The Battle of April 19, 1775* (Lexington, MA, 1912), 54–60, 135; Edward Field, *Manual of the Rhode Island Sons of the American Revolution* (Providence, 1900), 124; *A List of Revolutionary Soldiers Who Served Dedham in the Revolution*; Fischer, *Paul Revere's Ride*, 147; Smith, *A History of Dedham*, 466–467; Robert A. Gross, "A Yankee Rebellion?: The Regulators, New England, and the New Nation," *The New England Quarterly*, 82 (2009), 112–135; John A. Ruddiman, *Becoming Men of*

Some Consequence: Youth and Military Service in the Revolutionary War (Charlottesville, VA, 2014), 182.

11 Lorri Glover, *Founders as Fathers: The Private Lives and Politics of the American Revolutionaries* (New Haven, CT, 2014), 245. See also Peter Charles Hoffer, *Revolution and Regeneration: Life Cycle and the Historical Vision of the Generation of 1776* (Athens, GA, 1983). For more on post-Revolutionary generations: Joyce Appleby, *Inheriting the Revolution: The First Generation of Americans* (Cambridge, MA, 2000); Sarah J. Purcell, *Sealed With Blood: War, Sacrifice, and Memory in Revolutionary America* (Philadelphia, 2002); Rodney Hessinger, *Seduced, Abandoned, and Reborn: Visions of Youth in Middle-Class America, 1780–1850* (Philadelphia, PA, 2005); Glenn Wallach, *Obedient Sons: The Discourse of Youth and Generations in American Culture, 1630–1860* (Amherst, MA, 1997).

12 Mann, *Historical Annals of Dedham*, 38; Militia Act of 1792, May 8, 1792; *Laws for Regulating and Governing the Militia of the Commonwealth of Massachusetts* (Boston, 1803), 4.

13 *The Biography of Mr. Jason Fairbanks and Miss Eliza Fales* (Boston, 1801); "Deed, Feb. 16, 1764," in Lorenzo Sayles Fairbanks, *Genealogy of the Fairbanks Family in America, 1633–1897* (Boston, 1897), 85–86; John Adams to Students of Harvard College, July 1798; Abigail Adams to Thomas Boylston Adams, June 10, 1796, *Founders Online.* See also S. E. Morison, "Squire Ames and Doctor Ames," *New England Quarterly*, 1 (1928), 5–31; Elisha P. Douglass, "Fisher Ames, Spokesman for New England Federalism," *Proceedings of the American Philosophical Society*, 103 (1959), 693–715; Smith, *American Honor*, chaps. 2 and 6.

14 Smith, *A History of Dedham*, chapter 8; Jordan D. Fiore, *Wrentham, 1673–1973: A History* (Wrentham, MA, 1973), chapter 7; Lane, "Murder in America: A Historian's Perspective," 212; Edward M. Cook Jr., "Social Behavior and Changing Values in Dedham, Massachusetts, 1700 to 1775," *William and Mary Quarterly*, 34 (1977), 566; Worthington, *History of Dedham*, 89, 91; Mann, *Historical Annals*, 93; Opal, *Beyond the Farm*, 57; Tom Cutterham, *Gentleman Revolutionaries: Power and Justice in the New American Republic* (Princeton, NJ, 2017), 44–45, 54–63.

15 Gross, *Minutemen*, 18; Edward M. Cook Jr., "Local Leadership and the Typology of New England Towns, 1700–1785," *Political Science Quarterly*, 86 (1971), 596–597; Fischer, *Albion's Seed*, 167; J.M. Opal, "Exciting Emulation: Academies and Transformation of the Rural North, 1780s–1820s," *Journal of American History*, 91 (2004), 453; L. Fairbanks, *Genealogy*, 11, 31; Smith, *A History of Dedham*, 45; Robert Blair St. George, "Style and Structure in the Joinery of Dedham and Medfield, Massachusetts, 1635–1685," *Winterthur*

Portfolio, 13 (1979), 37; B. Katherine Brown, "Puritan Democracy in Dedham, Massachusetts: Another Case Study," *William and Mary Quarterly*, 24 (1967), 378–396; E. Fairbanks, *Solemn Declaration*, 20, 34; Nathaniel Ames, Nov. 6, 1798, "The [Nathaniel] Ames Diary," *Dedham Historical Register*, 10 (1899), 27; Mark Boonshoft, *Aristocratic Education and the Making of the American Republic* (Chapel Hill, NC, 2020), 68.

16 There are questions regarding the authenticity of *The Biography of Mr. Jason Fairbanks and Miss Eliza Fales*. This account is exaggerated in the style of early republican fiction. However, it's the only source allegedly from a classmate. The tone is reflective of an educated author, and is comparable to works by academy students, such as "The Village, a Poem" in *The American Monthly Magazine and Critical Review*, which was probably published (possibly written) by printer Nathaniel Coverly Jr. See also Cohen, *Pillars of Salt*, 178–180; Greta Lafleur, "Defective in One of the Principle Part of Virility: Impotence, Generation, and Defining Disability in Early North America," *Early American Literature*, 52 (2017), 80, 87, 98; *A Mournful Tragedy: Giving an Account of the Shocking and Unprecedented Catastrophe, which Happened at Dedham* (Boston or Dedham?, 1801); E. Fairbanks, *Solemn Declaration*, 18, 21–22; Opal, *Beyond the Farm*, 127; Thomas Green Fessenden, *Original Poems* (Philadelphia, 1806), 141; *Biography of Mr. Jason Fairbanks and Miss Eliza Fales*.

17 Anne S. Lombard, *Making Manhood: Growing Up Male in Colonial New England* (Cambridge, MA, 2003), chap. 5; *Report of the Trial of Jason Fairbanks*, 30, 34–35.

18 "The Village, a Poem," 117–118; *Report of the Trial of Jason Fairbanks*, 7; *Columbia Minerva* (Dedham), Nov. 11, 1796, and May 9, 1797; Opal, *Beyond the Farm*, 61, 107; Michael Hattem, *Past and Prologue: Politics and Memory in the American Revolution* (New Haven, CT, 2020), 145.

19 Hansen, *Dedham*, 176–177; Cohen, "Beautiful Female Murder Victim"; *Columbia Minerva* (Dedham), Mar. 21, 1799, Feb. 20, 1800; E. Fairbanks, *Solemn Declaration*, 20; Opal, *Beyond the Farm*, 82; Halttunen, *Murder Most Foul*, 100; Mary Caroline Crawford, "A Historic Tragedy, Which Added a Given Chapter to Story of the Fairbanks House in Dedham," *The New England Magazine* (Boston) 1901, Jason Fairbanks folder (Dedham Historical Society); *Report of the Trial of Jason Fairbanks*, 17, 32; E. Fairbanks, *Solemn Declaration*, 2, 19–21; *Biography of Mr. Jason Fairbanks and Miss Eliza Fales*.

20 E. Fairbanks, *Solemn Declaration*, 4; Richard D. Brown, "The Emergence of Urban Society in Rural Massachusetts, 1760–1820," *Journal of American History*, 61 (1974), 33; Fischer, *Albion's Seed*, 78–79; Hessinger, *Seduced, Abandoned, and Reborn*, 2, 27–28.

21 *Independent Chronicle* (Boston), Nov. 8–12, 1798; *Columbian Centinel* (Boston), Mar. 30 and Nov. 10, 1798; *Massachusetts Mercury* (Boston), June 21, 1799; Smith, "The Federalist 'Saints' versus "The Devil of Sedition," 198–2105; Leonard L. Richards, *Shays's Rebellion: The American Revolution's Final Battle* (Philadelphia, 2014); *The Debate on the Constitution: Federalist and Antifederalist Speeches, Articles, and Letters During the Struggle over Ratification*, ed. Bernard Bailyn (New York, 1993); Fisher Ames, *Works of Fisher Ames* (2 vols., Boston, 1809), 2: xi-xii, 1–19; Morison, "Squire Ames and Doctor Ames," 13, 31; Smith, *A History of Dedham*, 466–467; David Hackett Fischer, *The Revolution of American Conservatism: The Federalist Party in the Era of Jeffersonian Democracy* (New York, 1965), 95; Charles Warren, *Jacobin and Junto: Or, Early American Politics as Viewed in the Diary of Dr. Nathaniel Ames* (Cambridge, 1931), chap. 4; Rachel Hope Cleves, "'Jacobins in this Country': The United States, Great Britain, and Trans-Atlantic Anti-Jacobinism," *Early American Studies*, 8 (2010), 410–445.

22 Only three Sprague men were married in New York within two years of 1798: Benjamin, Roger, and William. Benjamin was two years older than Jason Fairbanks, making him the most likely suitor based on age. Roger Sprague (born 1767) was a captain in the Continental Army. William Sprague (born 1763) was also a militia officer during the War of 1812. All three men were fourth cousins once removed of Dr. Sprague. See *The Sprague Project*, https://www.sprague-database.org/; Warren Vincent Sprague, *Sprague Families in America* (Rutland, VT, 1913); Mrs. Chester Pratt, "Stories of Dedham," *New England Historical and Genealogical Register*, April 1909, 158; *Year Book of the Society of Sons of the Revolution in the State of New York* (New York, 1899), 562; Francis William Sprague, *The Brothers Ralph and William Sprague and Some of Their Descendants* (Boston, 1909), 11; *Report of the Trial of Jason Fairbanks*, 7, 19, 34–35, 61, 17, 22, 19; E. Fairbanks, *Solemn Declaration*, 19–21; *Biography of Mr. Jason Fairbanks and Miss Eliza Fales*; Smith, *A History of Dedham*, 365; Richards, *Shays's Rebellion*, 75.

23 *Report of the Trial of Jason Fairbanks*, 32, 22, 25, 26; E. Fairbanks, *Solemn Declaration*, 27; Lombard, *Making Manhood*, 129; Fischer, *Albion's Seed*, 111–116; Fairbanks had also made a made a similar threat in front of his friend Isaac Whiting in December 1800.

24 *A Correct and Concise Account of the Interesting Trial of Jason Fairbanks for the Barbarous and Cruel Murder of Elizabeth Fales* (Boston, 1801), 2; *A Deed of Horror!: Trial of Jason Fairbanks* (Salem, MA, 1801), 2.

25 For themes of seduction and death in novels, see Samuel Richardson's *Clarissa, Or, The History of a Young Lady* (1748), Frances Brooke's *The History of Lady*

Julia Mandeville (1763), William Hill Brown's *The Power of Sympathy: or, The Triumph of Nature* (1789), and Hannah Webster Foster's *The Coquette or, The History of Eliza Wharton* (1797); Cohen, *Pillars of Salt*, 167; David A. Copeland, "Virtuous and Vicious: The Dual Portrayal of Women in Colonial Newspapers," *American Periodicals*, 5 (1995), 59–85; *Columbia Minerva* (Dedham), July 14, 1801; James L. Parr, *Dedham: Historic and Heroic Tales from Shiretown* (Charleston, 2009), chap. 3; Ann Brandwein, "An Eighteenth-Century Depression: The Sad Conclusion of Faith Trumbull Huntington," *Connecticut History Review*, 26 (1985), 19–32; Maggie Meahl, "Faith Trumbull Huntington: An Eighteenth-Century Woman Encounters War," *Connecticut History Review*, 58 (2019), 3–34; Ed Hatton, "'He Murdered Her Because He Loved Her': Passion, Masculinity, and Intimate Homicide in Antebellum America," in *Over the Threshold: Intimate Violence in Early America*, ed. Christine Daniels and Michael V. Kennedy (New York, 1999), 111–133.

26 Diaries and "Charges to Grand Juries," Aug. 1801, Robert Treat Paine Papers (Massachusetts Historical Society, Boston); Robert Treat Paine to John Adams, July 27, 1799, *Founders Online.*

27 "Maxims," Dana Family Papers (Massachusetts Historical Society, Boston); Hessinger, *Seduced, Abandoned, and Reborn*, chapters 1 and 2; *Report of the Trial of Jason Fairbanks*, 11.

28 Alvan Lamson, *A History of the First Church and Parish in Dedham* (Dedham: H. Mann, 1839); Thomas Boylston Adams, *Daybook,* 1801 summary from Bartleby's Books, https://www.bartlebysbooks.com/pages/books/61467/thomas-boylston-adams/daybook-of-thomas-boylston-adams-for-the-year-1801; Thomas Boylston Adams to Abigail Adams, Sept. 14, 1798, and July 19, 1800; Abigail Adams to John Adams, May 27, 1794, *Founders Online*; John Ferling, *John Adams: A Life* (New York, 1992), 297, 322, 388–389, 406, 420–421.

29 Arthur Scherr, *Thomas Jefferson's Imagine of New England: Nationalism Versus Sectionalism in the Young Republic* (Jefferson, NC, 2016), 125; Alan Rogers, *Murder and the Death Penalty in Massachusetts* (Amherst, MA, 2008), 64–65.

30 Thomas C. Amory, *Life of James Sullivan* (2 vols., Boston, 1859), 1: 19–22, 2: 20; James Sullivan, *The History of the District of Maine* (Boston, 1795), vi-viii; *Report of the Trial of Jason Fairbanks,* 71.

31 *Correct and Concise Account of the Interesting Trial of Jason Fairbanks,* 2.

32 *Report of the Trial of Jason Fairbanks,* 48–49, 56, 59; Ferris Greenslet, *The Lowells and Their Seven Worlds* (Boston, 1946), 96–111.

33 *Report of the Trial of Jason Fairbanks,* 48–49.

34 Amory, *Life of James Sullivan,* 2: 20. Six years earlier, Sullivan's ideas on education were included in *The History of the District of Maine,* iii, 292. See also

Report of the Trial of Jason Fairbanks, 68–71. For more, see Johann N. Nemm, *Democracy's Schools: The Rise of Public Education in America* (Baltimore, 2017).

35 *Report of the Trial of Jason Fairbanks,* 7, 71, 74, 75, 77; Sharon Bock, "Rape without Women: Print Culture and the Politicization of Rape, 1765–1815," *Journal of American History*, 89 (2002), 852–855, 868; Foster, *Sex and the Eighteenth-Century Man*, 65; Alexander Smyth and Randal L. Hall, *A Rape in the Early Republic: Gender and Legal Culture in an 1806 Virginia Trial* (Lexington, KY, 2017).

36 *Report of the Trial of Jason Fairbanks,* 72; Robert Treat Paine, Aug. 8, 1801, Diary, Robert Treat Paine Papers (Massachusetts Historical Society, Boston); Richard Bell, *We Shall Be No More: Suicide and Self-Government in the Newly United States* (Cambridge, MA, 2012), 129.

37 Andrew N. Adams, *A Genealogical History of Henry Adams* (Rutland, VT, 1898), 527; Simon Elliot to Caleb Strong, c. 1800, viewable at https://www.auctionzip.com/auction-lot/2nd-MA-Maj.-Timothy-Whiting-Accused-of-Dishonorab_A004BA4B29/.

38 Paine, Diary, Aug. 8, 1801; Ava Chamberlain, "The Execution of Moses Paul: A Story of Crime and Contact in Eighteenth-century Connecticut," *New England Quarterly*, 77 (2004), 450; Louis P. Masur, *Rites of Execution: Capital Punishment and the Transformation of American Culture, 1776–1865* (New York, 1989), 5, chap. 2; Gordon S. Wood, *Empire of Liberty: A History of the Early Republic, 1789–1815* (New York, 2009), 491–495.

39 George N. Thomson, *Confessions, Trials, and Biographical Sketches of the Most Cold Blooded Murderers, who Have Been Executed in this Country from Its First Settlement Down to the Present Time* (Boston, 1841), 68.

40 Smith, *A History of Dedham*, 466–467; Worthington, *The History of Dedham*, 76–77; [Meeting of 1840], *Proceedings of the Massachusetts Historical Society*, Vol. 2 (1835–1855), 162; Ann-Marie Szymanski, "Stop, Thief!: Private Protective Societies in Nineteenth-Century New England," *New England Quarterly*, 78 (2005), 413.

41 Proceedings of the Massachusetts Historical Society, 2 (1835–1855), 162; Ann-Marie Szymanski, "Stop, Thief!: Private Protective Societies in Nineteenth-Century New England," *New England Quarterly*, 78, (2005), 413; *Federal Galaxy* (Brattleborough, VT), Aug. 31, 1801.

42 Thomson, *Confessions, Trials, and Biographical Sketches*, 68; Ames, August 6–7, 20, 1801, *Diary of Dr. Ames*; Appendix, *Report of the Trial of Jason Fairbanks*, 83; "One Thousand Dollars Reward" [wanted poster], Aug. 18, 1801, Dedham Historical Society.

43 *Columbia Centinel* (Boston), Aug. 29, 1801; Freeman, "The Melancholy Catastrophe," 15, 20–22; Boston *Gazette*, Aug. 24, Aug. 31, and Sept. 10, 1801; Thomson, *Confessions, Trials, and Biographical Sketches,* 69.

44 "From an Address to the Members of the Bar of the Counties of Hampshire, Franklin, and Hampden, Sept. 1862, by George Bliss, Esq," Caleb Strong Papers (Massachusetts Historical Society, Boston); Ben-Atar and Brown, *Taming Lust*, 129–136; *Biographical Directory of the United States Congress, 1774–Present*, s.v. "Mattoon, Ebenezer."

45 Freeman, 20–22; Boston *Gazette*, Aug 31, and Sept. 10, 1801; Ames, Aug. 29, 1801, *Diary of Dr. Ames*.

46 *Report of the Trial of Jason Fairbanks*, 77; E. Fairbanks, *Solemn Declaration*, 3, 4–9, 14; Boston *Gazette* (Boston), Aug. 24, 1801. Although the *Gazette* article claims it to be an "original Manuscript, composed and signed by himself, and attested by his Counsel," the veracity of this account is questionable. Was it dictated to his cellmate John Rowe as alleged or even composed by Jason Fairbanks, or is it Ebenezer Jr.'s creation? It was similar to Otis and Lowell's version of events with the major differences being Fales's chastity—a tale undoubtedly told to Ebenezer Jr. These were probably Fairbanks's sentiments, if not his exact words, or at least what he wanted the public to believe.

47 Boston *Gazette*, Sept. 10, 1801; *Biography of Mr. Jason Fairbanks and Miss Eliza Fales*; Clough Map, State Street Property Lines, ca. 1798 (Massachusetts Historical Society, Boston); E. Fairbanks, *Solemn Declaration*, 8; Robert Hanson, "The Fairbanks–Fales Case, 1801," *The Homestead Courier*, Fall 1997, 7; Freeman, "Melancholy Catastrophe!," 15; Ames, Sept. 4, 1801, *Diary of Dr. Ames*; Gross, "A Yankee Rebellion?," 131; Richards, *Shays's Rebellion*, 117.

48 W. H. Sumner to John Adams, May 3, 1823, *Founders Online;* William Blake Trask, "Memoir of Rev. Elias Nason, M.A.," *The New England Historical and Genealogical Register*, 43 (1889), 22; Fales Family Papers (Dedham Historical Society, Dedham).

49 Cohen, "In Defense of the Gallows," 157; Dwight Conquergood, "Lethal Theatre: Performance, Punishment, and the Death Penalty," *Theatre Journal*, 54 (2002), 339–367.

50 Mary Caroline Crawford, "A Historic Tragedy," *The New England Home Magazine*, c. 1901 in Fairbanks, Jason folder, Dedham Historical Society.

51 "Jason Fairbanks," Sept. 19, 1801, *United States Oracle* (Portsmouth, NH), Sept. 19, 1801; Ames, Sept. 10, 1801, *Diary of Dr. Ames*; *Dedham Transcript*, 1862, in Crimes Folder, Dedham Historical Society; *Columbian Centinel* (Boston), Sept. 12, 1801; Boston *Gazette*, Sept. 14, 1801; Crawford, "A Historic Tragedy," *Weekly Museum* (New York), Sept. 12 and 19, 1801; *Constitutional Telegraph* (Boston), Sept. 12, 1801; *Columbia Minerva* (Dedham), Dec. 15, 1801.

52 Ames, Sept. 16, 1801, *Diary of Dr. Ames*; Greenslet, *The Lowells and Their Seven Worlds*, 132.

53 Thatcher, *The Danger of Despising the Divine Counsel*, 5, 15.
54 Ibid., 24; Harris, *A Sermon Preached in the First Parish in Dedham*, 23.
55 Ibid.; Cohen, *Pillars of Salt*, 182; *Biography of Mr. Jason Fairbanks and Miss Eliza Fales;* Joshua Hett Smith, *An Authentic Narrative of the Causes which Led to the Death of Major Andre* (New York, 1809), 92; Alexander Hamilton to John Laurens, Oct. 11, 1780, *Founders Online*; Henry Phelps Johnston, *Nathan Hale, 1776: Biography and Memorials* (New York, 1901), 120–126; Virginia DeJohn Anderson, *The Martyr and the Traitor: Nathan Hale, Moses Dunbar, and the American Revolution* (New York, 2017); Hannah Adams, *A Summary History of New-England* (Dedham, 1799), 359–360.
56 Thatcher, *The Danger of Despising the Divine Counsel*, 18.
57 E. Fairbanks, *Solemn Declaration*, 10–11, 33–34, 55; Cohen, *Pillars of Salt*, 188—speculates Sarah Wentworth Morton helped write it.
58 E. Fairbanks, *Solemn Declaration*, 10–11.
59 Daniel E. Williams, "Rogues, Rascals, and Scoundrels: The Underworld Literature of Early America," *American Studies*, 24 (1983), 5–19; Ava Chamberlain, "The Execution of Moses Paul: A Story of Crime and Contact in Eighteenth-century Connecticut," *New England Quarterly*, 77 (2004), 430-431; Ben-Atar and Brown, *Taming Lust,* 140; Thomas Boylston Adams to William Smith Shaw, Apr. 11, 1802, Thomas Boylston Adams to John Quincy Adams, Nov. 10, 1802, *Founders Online.*
60 John R. Byers Jr. "Further Verification of the Authorship of the Power of Sympathy," *American Literature*, 43 (1971), 424n11; "The 1788 Scandal of Fanny Apthorp Never Dies," *New England Historical Society,* https://newenglandhistoricalsociety.com/1788-scandal-of-fanny-apthorp-never-dies/; Walter Muir Whitehill, "Perez Morton's Daughter Revisits Boston in 1825," *Proceedings of the Massachusetts Historical Society,* third series, 82 (1970), 26–27; Cathy N. Davidson, *Revolution and the Word: The Rise of the Novel in America* (New York, 1986), 85, 101–102, 105, 289 n33; Thomson, *Confessions, Trials, and Biographical Sketches,* 69.
61 Crawford, "A Historic Tragedy"; Hanson, "The Fairbanks-Fales Case, 1801," 1.

James Wilkinson

1 Thomas Robson Hay and M. R. Werner, *The Admirable Trumpeter: A Biography of General James Wilkinson* (New York, 1941); Royal Shreve, *The Finished Scoundrel: General James Wilkinson, Sometime Commander-In-chief of the Army of the United States, Who Made Intrigue a Trade and Treason a Profession* (Indianapolis, IN, 1933); Arno Linklater, *An Artist in Treason: The Extraordinary Double Life of General James Wilkinson* (New York, 2010). Wilkinson attempted to justify his career in his *Memoirs of My Own Times* (3 vols., Philadelphia, 1816).

2 See above in addition to Howard W. Cox, *General James Wilkinson: Treason and Betrayal in the New American Republic* (Washington, D.C., 2023), the best legal analysis of Wilkinson's behavior and the investigations into it after 1806; James Ripley Jacobs, *Tarnished Warrior: Major General James Wilkinson* (New York, 1938), the best exploration of Wilkinson and the U.S. Army. My interpretation here is most akin to (though less positive than) that of John Thornton Posey, "Rascality Revisited: In Defense of General James Wilkinson," *Filson Club History Quarterly*, 74 (2000), 309–351. See also William E. Foley, "James Wilkinson: Pike's Mentor and Jefferson's Capricious Point Man in the West," in *Zebulon Pike, Thomas Jefferson, and the Opening of the American West*, ed. Matthew L. Harris and Jay H. Buckley (Norman, OK, 2012). Unfortunately, Cox is the only biography that provides consistent and clear citations.

3 David E. Narrett, "Kentucky and the Union at the Crossroads: George Rogers Clark, James Wilkinson, and the Danville Committee, 1786–1787," *Ohio History*, 16 (2016), 3–23.

4 The essence of Wilkinson's "first memorial" to the Spanish can be conveniently found in William R. Shepard, "Wilkinson and the Beginnings of the Spanish Conspiracy," *American Historical Review*, 9 (1904), 490–506 (quotations from 497).

5 Wilkinson, "Second Memorial," Sept. 17, 1789, in "Papers Bearing on James Wilkinson's Relations with Spain, 1787–1816," *American Historical Review*, 9 (1904), 751–64; Jacobs, *Tarnished Warrior*, 90.

6 Ibid., 102, 104; Colton Storm, ed., "Up the Tennessee in 1790: The Report of Major John Doughty to the Secretary of War," *East Tennessee Historical Society Publications*, 17 (1945), 119–132. Jacobs notes that Wilkinson found out about the intended survey and advised the Spanish to send Indians to stop it. This did not necessarily mean attacking the surveying party but was a likely consequence that Wilkinson could easily anticipate.

7 George Washington to Alexander Hamilton, June 25, 1799, *Founders Online*.

8 Posey, "Rascality Revisited," 326.

9 Wilkinson to Peyton Short, Dec. 28, 1791, in Jacobs, *Tarnished Warrior*, 182; Wilkinson to Esteban Miró, Dec. 4, 1791, in Linklater, *An Artist in Treason*, 115.

10 Samuel J. Watson, "Surprisingly Professional: Trajectories in Army Officer Corps Drawdowns, 1783–1848," in *Drawdown: The American Way of Postwar*, ed. Jason W. Warren (New York, 2016), 73–106.

11 Note that the rumor of Wilkinson trying to assassinate Wayne, when a tree limb fell on Wayne's tent in 1794, is not present in any of the standard Wilkinson biographies. See Richard H. Kohn, *Eagle and Sword: The Federalists and the Creation of the Military Establishment in America, 1783–1802* (New York, 1975); Richard H. Kohn, "General Wilkinson's Vendetta

with General Wayne: Politics and Command in the American Army, 1791–1796," *Filson Club History Quarterly*, 45 (1971), 361–372; and Paul David Nelson, *Anthony Wayne: Soldier of the New Republic* (Bloomington, IN, 1985), the standard biography of Wayne. Hugh T. Harrington argues that Wayne's death, usually attributed to gout and malaria combining to rupture an ulcer, may have been due to arsenic delivered by Wilkinson ("Was General Anthony Wayne Murdered?" *Journal of the American Revolution*, Aug. 20, 2013, https://allthingsliberty.com/2013/08/was-general-anthony-wayne-murdered/). The argument relies entirely on Wilkinson's interest in gaining command and his fear of exposure, but it exaggerates Wilkinson's medical knowledge (his training had been more than twenty years before), is inconsistent with his tendency to avoid irreversible physical commitment, and assumes that he or some agent could ply Wayne with poison over an extended period.

12 Posey, "Rascality Revisited," 321.

13 See Samuel J. Watson, "The Army Secures the Mississippi Valley: Officers, Filibusters, and Spain, 1793–1798," *Southern Studies: An Interdisciplinary Journal*, 20 (2013–2014), 33–63.

14 See Kohn, *Eagle and Sword*; Lawrence Delbert Cress, *Citizens in Arms: The Army and Militia in American Society to the War of 1812* (Chapel Hill, NC, 1982); and Theodore J. Crackel, *Mr. Jefferson's Army: Political and Social Reform of the Military Establishment, 1801–1809* (New York, 1987) for this acceptance. For a later, similar dynamic, see Samuel J. Watson, "How the Army Became Accepted: West Point Socialization, Military Accountability, and the Nation-State during the Jacksonian Era," *American Nineteenth Century History* 7 (2006), 217–249.

15 Posey, "Rascality Revisited," 328–329; Isaac J. Cox, "General Wilkinson and His Later Intrigues with the Spaniards," *American Historical Review*, 19 (1914), 800.

16 Stephen King, *Everything's Eventual: 14 Dark Tales* (New York, 2002); Joseph Fichtelberg, "The Devil Designs a Career: Aaron Burr and the Shaping of Enterprise," *Early American Literature*, 41 (2006), 495–513.

17 James E. Lewis Jr., ""The Strongest Government on Earth' Proves Its Strength: The Jefferson Administration and the Burr Conspiracy," in *Jeffersonians in Power: The Rhetoric of Opposition Meets the Realities of Governing*, ed. Joanne B. Freeman and Johann N. Neem (Charlottesville, VA, 2019), 222–241; William B. Skelton, *An American Profession of Arms: The Army Officer Corps, 1784–1861* (Lawrence, KS, 1992), 78–83.

18 Jefferson to Madison, Apr. 7, 1811, *Founders Online*. For the best exploration of Wilkinson's views about Mexico, see David E. Narrett,

"Geopolitics and Intrigue: James Wilkinson, the Spanish Borderlands, and Mexican Independence," *William and Mary Quarterly*, 69 (2012), 101–146. Wilkinson's biographers often note that he warned the Spanish about the Lewis and Clark expedition, but it was public knowledge, Wilkinson did not know its route, and he surely knew how unlikely the Spanish were to find the explorers amid the vast space of the West. Zebulon Montgomery Pike's southwestern expedition (1806–1807) presents similar ambiguities: it was suggested to the president by Pike's mentor, Wilkinson (who does not seem to have warned the Spanish about it), and like most of his efforts could serve multiple purposes, as a military reconnaissance in case of war with Spain, as a provocation to try to spur such a conflict, or for Wilkinson's private benefit, helping to open trade with Santa Fe, or perhaps in conjunction with his discussions with Burr. His warning to the Spanish about the 1806 Red River (Freeman and Custis) exploring expedition was more treacherous, in that a Spanish military force could easily intercept the party, but Jefferson had ordered the explorers to avoid conflict with Spanish forces, which they did by retreating when Spanish troops confronted them.

19 John R. Maass, "'Humanity Mourns over Such a Site': The Army's Disaster at Terre aux Boeufs, 1809," *Army History*, 85 (2012), 7–25.

20 See Cox, *General James Wilkinson,* chap. 8, for allegations that Wilkinson took bribes from supply contractors at New Orleans. Cox notes that these allegations were not investigated.

"The Mexican Traveler"

1 Cleburne (TX) *Times-Review*, Apr. 16, 1954.

2 Edward Everett Hale, "The Man without a Country," *The Atlantic Monthly*, Dec. 1863, 665–679; Edward Hale, *Philip Nolan's Friends: A Story of the Change of Western Empire*, (Boston, 1910).

3 Maurine T. Wilson and Jack Jackson, *Philip Nolan and Texas: Expeditions to the Unknown Land, 1791–1801* (Waco, TX, 1987), vii, 1–76. John Edward Weems published a three-part biography that combined the stories of Nolan, James Wilkinson, and Ellis P. Bean. His story, while grounded in some historical research, took liberties in expanding on Nolan's patriotism and scoundrel plotting with Wilkinson. See John Edward Weems, *Men without Countries: Three Adventurers of the Early Southwest* (Boston, 1969). Several authors place Nolan within a filibuster framework, see Noel Loomis, "Philip Nolan's Entry into Texas in 1800" in *The Spanish in the Mississippi Valley, 1762–1804*, ed. John Francis McDermott (Urbana, IL, 1974), 120–132, and Noel Loomis and Abraham Nasatir, *Pedro Vial and the Roads to Santa Fe* (Norman, OK, 1967).

Other scholarship on filibusters highlights the perception of Spanish officials toward Nolan but does not portray him as a filibuster intent on American expansion. See Frank Lawrence Owsley Jr., and Gene Allen Smith, *Filibusters and Expansionists: Jeffersonian Manifest Destiny, 1800–1821* (Tuscaloosa, AL, 1997), 32–34; and Ed Bradley, *"We Never Retreat": Filibustering Expeditions into Spanish Texas, 1812–1821* (College Station, TX, 2015), 1–28. Roger G. Kennedy placed Nolan within the framework of cotton expansion, but his study relied solely on Weems, Jackson, and Wilson for his interpretation of Nolan. See Roger G. Kennedy, *Cotton and Conquest: How the Plantation System Acquired Texas* (Norman, OK, 2014), 167–222.

4 Nacogdoches Census, Dec. 1794, Bexar Archives, BCAH; Jackson and Wilson, *Philip Nolan and Texas*, 3; James Wilkinson to Manuel Gayoso de Lemos, Feb. 6, 1797, in Daniel Clark, *Proofs of the Corruption of General James Wilkinson* (Philadelphia, 1809), 42; Wilson and Jackson, *Nolan and Texas*, 2; Nolan to Wilkinson, June 10, 1796, in Wilkinson, *Memoirs*, 2: 588–589; Wilkinson to Messrs. Clark and Rees, May 20, 1790. *Memoirs*, 2: 692–693; Grace King, "The Real Philip Nolan," *Louisiana Historical Society Publications*, 10 (1917), 112. For the best example of Nolan's prose, see Nolan to Bernard Lintot, Feb. 26, 1796, PNP-LSU; Wilkinson to Manuel Gayoso, May 10, 1790, AGI, PPC, legajo 2373 (Historic New Orleans Collection, New Orleans, LA); Wilson and Jackson, *Nolan and Texas*, 2. For photocopies of Philip Nolan miniature painting, see PNP-Morrow. For discussion of the portrait's ownership, see Wilson and Jackson, *Philip Nolan*, 3, 116–117. For Andrew Ellicot's description of Nolan, see Andrew Ellicott, *The Journal of Andrew Ellicott* (Philadelphia, 1803), 29–30. For an account of Nolan's ability on a horse, see Francis Baily, *Journal of a Tour in Unsettled Parts of North America in 1796 & 1797* (London, 1856), 310–312. For the statement on Nolan's strength, see Evan Jones to Daniel Clark, Feb. 16, 1809, in *Memoirs*, 2: 657.

5 For the most complete biography of Wilkinson, see James Ripley Jacobs, *Tarnished Warrior: Major-General James Wilkinson* (New York, 1938), 78–80. For an analysis of Wilkinson and his times, see Andro Linklater, *An Artist in Treason: The Extraordinary Double Life of General James Wilkinson* (New York, 2009); Arthur Whittaker, *The Spanish–American Frontier, 1783–1795* (Lincoln, NE, 1927); Thomas Marshall Green, *The Spanish American Conspiracy* (1891; rep., Gloucester, MA, 1967); and David Narrett, *Adventurism and Empire: The Struggle for Mastery in the Louisiana-Florida Borderlands, 1763–1803* (Chapel Hill, NC, 2015). For Wilkinson's agreement, see Jacobs, *Tarnished Warrior*, 81. For the partnership's beginning and end, see James Wilkinson and Daniel Clark Sr., agreement, Apr. 24, 1788, Pedro Pedesclaux Notary Book, 3:

559–561, NONA. For the partnership's dissolution, see James Wilkinson and Daniel Clark Sr. Dissolution of Partnership, Sept. 15, 1789, Raphael Perdomo Notary Book, 14: 441–442, NONA. For Nolan's position as primary agent, see James Wilkinson to Messrs. Clark and Rees, May 20, 1790. *Memoirs*, 2: 692–693. James Wilkinson to Manuel Gayoso, May 10, 1790, AGI, PPC, legajo 2373. For Nolan's sale of the tobacco cargo, see Clark, *Proofs*, 38. For more information on Spanish Louisiana, see James Pitot, *Observations on the Colony of Louisiana, from 1796 to 1802* (Baton Rouge, 1979), Daniel H. Usner, *Indians, Settlers, & Slaves in a Frontier Exchange Economy: The Lower Mississippi Valley before 1783* (Chapel Hill, NC, 1992), Sophie Burton and F. Todd Smith, *Colonial Natchitoches: A Creole Community on the Louisiana-Texas Frontier* (College Station, TX, 2008), and Gilbert C. Din, ed., *The Spanish Presence in Louisiana, 1763–1803* (Lafayette, LA, 1996).

6 James Wilkinson to Philip Nolan, Mar. 17, 1791, PNP-LSU. For Nolan's plan to begin horse trading in Texas, see Philip Nolan to James Wilkinson, Apr. 6, 1791, in Wilkinson, *Memoirs*, 2: 587–588.

7 Agreement between Philip Nolan and John Ballinger, Aug. 7, 1791, in *The Natchez Court Records, 1767–1805: Abstracts of Early Records*, ed. May Wilson McBee (2 vols., Ann Arbor, MI, 1953), 2: book B: 519–520. For the promissory notes, Nolan later stated that he was a debtor making it likely that he acquired trade goods via this method. See Philip Nolan to James Wilkinson, June 10, 1796, *Memoirs*, 2: 588–589. For Nolan's loss of goods in Nacogdoches, see Philip Nolan to James Wilkinson, June 10, 1796, *Memoirs*, 2: 588–589. For more information on Spanish Texas, see Donald Chipman and Harriett Denise Joseph, *Spanish Texas, 1519–1821* (Austin, TX, 2010), David J. Weber, *The Spanish Frontier in North America* (New Haven, CT, 1992), and Juliana Barr, *Peace Came in the Form of a Woman: Indians and Spaniards in the Texas Borderlands* (Chapel Hill, NC, 2007).

8 F. Todd Smith, *The Wichita Indians: Traders of Texas and the Southern Plains, 1540–1845* (College Station, TX, 2000); Pekka Hämäläinen, *The Comanche Empire* (New Haven, CT, 2008), 145–183. Dan Flores identified this trader as John Lucas Talapoon, who lived near Natchitoches. Nolan later brought Talapoon with him to Natchez where William Dunbar and Daniel Clark Jr. both met him and later informed Jefferson of his abilities. Daniel Clark Jr. to Thomas Jefferson, Nov. 12, 1799, *Founders Online*. For Flores's identification, see Flores, *American Serengeti*, 72–78. Dan Flores argues that Talapoon, a mestizo who lived in Louisiana, probably represented the source of Nolan's ability to communicate in Indian sign language. Flores, *American Serengeti*, 63–78. Ellicott, *Journal*, 30.

9 Baily, *Journal of a Tour*, 310–312. Flores, *American Serengeti*, 75–77.

10 For Nolan's description of his return to New Orleans and reasons for doing so, see Philip Nolan to James Wilkinson, June 10, 1796, *Memoirs*, 2: 588–589.

11 Philip Nolan Passport from Baron de Carondelet, Sept. 9, 1794, Bexar Archives, microfilm, reel 24, 949–951, BCAH; "Testimonies regarding Gertrudis de los Santos, Juan Cook, Peter Longueville, and others at Nacogdoches, 1801," in Philip Nolan Papers, 1797–180, box 2Q241, folder 796, BCAH. For Nolan's return to New Orleans, see Nolan to Wilkinson, June 10, 1796, *Memoirs*, 2: 588–589. For the relationships between Bernard Lintot, Stephen Minor, and Manuel Gayoso de Lemos, see Manuel Gayoso de Lemos to Stephen Minor, Dec. 23, 1797, and Manuel Gayoso de Lemos to Stephen Minor, Dec. 24, 1797, Manuel Gayoso de Lemos Papers, Louisiana and Lower Mississippi Valley Collections (Louisiana State University Libraries, Baton Rouge, LA). For Nolan's request to court Fanny, see Philip Nolan to Bernard Lintot, Feb. 25, 1796, PNP-LSU. Grace King, "The Real Philip Nolan," *The Louisiana Historical Society Publications*, 10 (1917), 106–107; Wilson and Jackson, *Philip Nolan and Texas*, 2–8.

12 Nolan to Wilkinson, Jan. 6, 1796, and Apr. 24, 1797, *Memoirs*, 2: 117–118, 588–589; Clark, *Proofs*, 22–25, 42, 59–60. For Wilkinson's testimony, see Wilkinson, *Memoirs*, 2: 76–77.

13 For Nolan's arrival in Frankfort with 42 horses, see Nolan to Wilkinson, June 10, 1796, *Memoirs*, 2: 588–589. Wilkinson referred to Nolan as the "mexican traveler" in a letter to Jefferson, see Wilkinson to Jefferson, May 22, 1800, *Founders Online*.

14 John Girault and Philip Nolan Agreement with Richard Terrell, Oct. 15, 1796, and Nov. 5, 1796, in Francis Hegan Miller Collection, 1780–1950, mss. A M647, folders 7 and 8 (Filson Historical Society, Louisville, KY); "Account of the administration of Abijah Hunt, Administrator of all and singular the goods and chattles, rights and accounts of Philip Noland, deceased," June 10, 1803, PNP-Morrow; Abijah Hunt to John Hunt, Feb. 28, 1800, John Wesley Hunt Papers, 1772–1849, mss. A H941, box 1, folder 3, FHS; Ellicott, *Journal*, 29–35; Nolan to James Wilkinson, Apr. 24, 1797, *Memoirs*, 2: 589; Andrew Ellicott to Clark, Jan. 21, 1808, in *Proofs*, 69–70.

15 Manuel Gayoso de Lemos, "Political Condition of the Province of Louisiana," July 5, 1792, and Baron de Carondelet, "Military Report on Louisiana and West Florida," Nov. 24, 1794, in Robertson, *Louisiana under the Rule*, 1: 287–288, 298–299; Nolan to Gayoso de Lemos, Mar. 13 and 14, 1797, AGI, PPC, legajo 188B, reel 20, Historic New Orleans Collection; Nolan to Wilkinson, Apr. 24, 1797, *Memoirs*, 2: 589–590.

16 For Nolan's passport, see testimony of Philip Nolan, June 20, 1797, Notarial Book of Pedro Pedesclaux, 30: 362–364, NONA; "Agreement between Philip Nolan and John Murdoch, Apr. 2, 1797," in King, "The Real Philip Nolan," 100–101. For Nolan's technique in transporting goods, see Baily, *Tour in Unsettled Parts*, 311; Nolan to Wilkinson, July 21, 1797, *Memoirs*, 2: 589–600; Clark to Jefferson, Nov. 12, 1799, *Founders Online*; Wilson and Jackson, *Philip Nolan and Texas*, 32–35; Loomis, "Nolan's Entry" in *Spanish in the Mississippi Valley*, 123–125.

17 Jefferson to Nolan, June 24, 1798; Jefferson to Clark, June 23, 1799, and Jan. 16, 1800; Clark to Jefferson, Feb. 12, 1799, and May 29, 1800; Wilkinson to Jefferson, May 22, 1800, and Sept. 1, 1800, *Founders Online*.

18 Loomis, "Nolan's Entry," in *Spanish in the Mississippi Valley*, 120–122. For the birth of Nolan's first child, Maria Josefa, see copy of baptismal record in PNP-Morrow; Wilson and Jackson, *Philip Nolan and Texas*, 83–86. For the marriage of Nolan and Fanny Lintot, see Marriage of Philip Nolan and Francis (Fanny) Lintot, Dec. 19, 1799, B: 9, *Records of Natchez Book B, Commencing 29th March 1798*, HNF. For the marriage and dowry between Samuel Steer and Maria Lintot, see marriage between Samuel Steer and Maria Lintot, McBee, *Natchez Court Records*, 2: D: 125. For Nolan's ranch, see King, "The Real Philip Nolan," 107–108.

19 "Brand and Mark of Philip Nolan," B: 33, *Records of Natchez Book B*, HNF; "Philip Nolan and William Lintot Proposal, Apr. 27, 1800," in King, "Real Philip Nolan," 101. For data on increased cotton production and the development of Natchez, see Robert V. Haynes, *The Mississippi Territory and the Southwest Frontier, 1795–1817* (Lexington, KY, 2010), 12–14. For Nolan's sale, see "Sales of Horses and Mares the Property of Philip Nolan on Saturday, the 24th May 1800," PNP-LSU.

20 Loomis, "Nolan's Entry" in *Spanish in the Mississippi Valley*, 123–126; Wilson and Jackson, *Philip Nolan and Texas*, 33–36; Gilbert C. Din, *An Extraordinary Life: Sebastián Nicolás Calvo de la Puerta y O'Farrill, Marqués de Casa-Calvo* (Lafayette, LA, 2016); Pedro Nava to Governor of Texas, Aug. 8, 1800, Bexar Archives, reel 30, 628–630, BCAH; Loomis, "Nolan's Entry" in *Spanish in the Mississippi Valley*, 124–126.

21 "Account of the administration of Abijah Hunt, Administrator of all and singular the goods and chattles, rights and accounts of Philip Noland [*sic.*], deceased," June 10, 1803, PNP-Morrow. For note with Samuel Moore, see *Abijah Hunt (Administrator Philip Nolan)* v. *Samuel P. Moore*, Aug. 1801, Record of Judgements, 1802–1811, Superior Court, Judgements Book B, HNF. For note given to Francis Chabus, see *Francis Chabus* v. *Abijah Hunt Executor of Philip Nolan Estate, Adams County Court of Common Pleas*, Aug.

1801 term, PNP-Morrow. For Fero's commission, see "Agreement between Philip Nolan and David Fero," Oct. 4, 1800, *Records of Natchez Book B*, HNF; Wilson and Jackson, *Philip Nolan and Texas*, 40–46.

22 For Richards testimony, see Wilson and Jackson, *Philip Nolan and Texas*, 44–46. For Richard's land grant on the Homochitto River in the Natchez district from Spanish authorities, see *Records of Natchez Book B*, page 160. "Land Grant Mordecai Richards, Apr. 1, 1801," HNF. For Vidal's trust in Richards' testimony, see Wilson and Jackson, *Philip Nolan and Texas*, 77–78.

23 Henderson King Yoakum, *History of Texas* (New York, 1855), Appendix 2; Wilson and Jackson, *Philip Nolan and Texas*, 44–68.

24 "Diary of Músquiz Expedition against Nolan," Mar. 4, 1801–Apr. 3, 1801, *Philip Nolan Papers, 1797–1804*, BCAH; Wilson and Jackson, *Philip Nolan and Texas*, 66–74.

25 "Diary of Músquiz Expedition against Nolan," Mar. 4, 1801–Apr. 3, 1801, *Philip Nolan Papers, 1797–1804*, BCAH; Wilson and Jackson, *Philip Nolan and Texas*, 66–74. There are conflicting reports on who initiated the firefight. Ellis Bean testified that Spanish soldiers fired the first shot, while Spanish officers reported that Nolan fired first. For Bean's account, see Appendix 2 in Henderson King Yoakum, *History of Texas*.

26 *The Paladium* (Frankfort, KY), June 9, 1801; Fanny Lintot obituary, PNP-Morrow; Bernard Lintot Family Bible with genealogical sketch, ibid.

27 "Account of the administration of Abijah Hunt, Administrator of all and singular the goods and chattles, rights and accounts of Philip Noland, deceased," June 10, 1803, PNP-Morrow; *Abijah Hunt (Administrator Philip Nolan)* v. *Samuel P. Moore*, Aug. 1801, Record of Judgements, 1802–1811, Superior Court, Judgements Book B, HNF; *James Wilkinson* v. *Philip Nolan Administrators*, Index of Cases, Nov. 1802–Feb. 1805; Abijah Hunt to John Hunt, Feb. 28, 1800, *Francis Chabus* v. *Abijah Hunt Executor of Philip Nolan Estate*, Adams County Court of Common Pleas, Aug. 1801 term, PNP-Morrow.

28 *Hunt* vs. *Philip Absalom Gray*, 1801, Adams County Court House Records, Folder 24-68, HNF; *Abijah Hunt* v. *Dayton Ebenezer*, 1801, Adams County Court House Records, folder 24-68, HNF; *Philip Nolan* v. *Benjamin Kitchen*, June 1802, Adams County Court House Records, Folder 24-167, HNF. Other cases may be found in Jefferson Country Chancery Clerk's Office in Fayette County, Mississippi, PNP-Morrow; "Account of the administration of Abijah Hunt, Administrator of all and singular the goods and chattles, rights and accounts of Philip Noland, deceased," June 10, 1803, PNP-Morrow.

American Adventurers in the Mississippi Borderlands

1 Francisco Bouligny to Esteban Miró, Aug. 22, 1785, in *Spain in the Mississippi Valley, 1765–1794*, ed. Lawrence Kinnaird (4 vols., Washington, 1949), 3: 138–139. For Green, see David E. Narrett, *Adventurism and Empire: The Struggle for Mastery in the Louisiana–Florida Borderlands, 1762–1803* (Chapel Hill, NC, 2014), 121.

2 See Mike Bunn, *Fourteenth Colony: The Forgotten Story of the Gulf South During America's Revolutionary Era* (Montgomery, AL, 2020).

3 Declaration of the State of Georgia, Feb. 17, 1783, "Mississippi Provincial Archives Spanish Dominion" (9 vols., unpublished manuscript, Mississippi Department of Archives and History, Jackson, MS), 2: 151–152; D. Clayton James, *Antebellum Natchez* (Baton Rouge, LA, 1968), 54–55; David J. Weber, *The Spanish Frontier in North America* (New Haven, CT, 1992), 278–279; George Edward Milne, *Natchez Country: Indians, Colonists, and the Landscapes of Race in French Louisiana* (Athens, GA, 2015), 15.

4 Walter Johnson, *River of Dark Dreams: Slavery and Empire in the Cotton Kingdom* (Cambridge, MA, 2013); Shannon Lee Dawdy, *Building the Devil's Empire: French Colonial New Orleans* (Chicago, 2008); Narrett, *Adventurism and Empire*. For more on slavery specifically in Natchez, see Christian Pinnen, *Complexion of Empire in Natchez: Race and Slavery in the Mississippi Borderlands* (Athens, GA, 2021).

5 Bouligny to Miró, Aug. 22, 1785, in *Spain in the Mississippi Valley*, 138–139.

6 Pinnen, *Complexion of Empire in Natchez*, chaps. 4 and 5; Christian Pinnen and Charles A. Weeks, *Colonial Mississippi: A Borrowed Land* (Jackson, MS, 2021); James, *Antebellum Natchez*, chap. 1; Narrett, *Adventurism and Empire*, chap. 5; Jack David Lazarus Holmes, *Gayoso: The Life of a Spanish Governor in the Mississippi Valley, 1789–1799* (Baton Rouge, LA, 1965), 18.

7 Lot sales, Natchez, Sept. 14, 1782, and Natchez, Apr. 8, 1784, in May Wilson McBee, *The Natchez Court Records, 1767–1805: Abstracts of Early Records* (Baltimore, MD, 1979), 16, 25. For various court appearances, see *Thomas Green* v. *His Creditors*, Feb. 8, 1783; *William Smith* v. *Thomas Green*, Feb. 4, 1783; *Richard Bacon* v. *Thomas Green*, Feb. 13, 1783, all in McBee, *Natchez Court Records*, 302. For Green's suit, see Thomas Green versus Adam Bingaman, Mar. 28, 1783, in McBee, *Natchez Court Records*, 307. For Green's arrival in Natchez see Pinnen, *Complexion of Empire in Natchez*, 87; Narrett, *Adventurism and Empire*, 121.

8 James, *Antebellum Natchez*, 57; Weber, *Spanish Frontier*, 279.

9 Narrett, *Adventurism and Empire*, 123; loyalty oath, Jan. 4, 1787, Archivos General des Indies, Papeles de Cuba, legajo 13 (Seville, Spain). All

translations are by the author unless otherwise noted. Tacitus Gaillard, for example, never signed the oath but was still allowed to stay.

10 Bouligny to Miró, Aug. 22, 1785, in Kinnaird, *Spain in the Mississippi Valley*, 3: 139.

11 Bouligny to Miró, Aug. 22, 1785, in Kinnaird, *Spain in the Mississippi Valley*, 3: 140. For Spanish militia systems and benefits derived from it, see Kimberly S. Hanger, *Bounded Lives, Bounded Places: Free Black Society in Colonial New Orleans, 1769–1803* (Durham, NC, 1997), chap. 4; Elena Andrea Schneider, *The Occupation of Havana: War, Trade, and Slavery in the Atlantic World* (Chapel Hill, NC, 2018), 294–303.

12 Bouligny to Miró, Aug. 22, 1785, in Kinnaird, *Spain in the Mississippi Valley*, 3: 142.

13 Miró to Conde de Galvez, June 20, 1785, in "Mississippi Provincial Archives Spanish Dominion," 2: 126. On Native American diplomacy in the area, see James Taylor Carson, *Searching for the Bright Path: The Mississippi Choctaws from Prehistory to Removal* (Lincoln, NE, 2003), 39–48. Green was the stereotypical rogue colonialist as defined by Shannon Dawdy. See Dawdy, *Building the Devil's Empire*.

14 "Mississippi Provincial Archives Spanish Dominion," 2: 126. Thomas Green alone produced a sizeable tobacco crop within two years of his arrival. See surety for tobacco by Cato West and Thomas Marston Green (son), Jan. 3, 1784, McBee, *Natchez Court Records*, 22.

15 Act Organizing Bourbon County, Feb. 7, 1785, in Edmund C. Burnett, "Papers Relating to Bourbon County, Georgia, 1785–1786," *The American Historical Review*, 15 (1909), 70.

16 Instructions to the justices of Bourbon County, Feb. 11, 1785, in Burnett, 71–72.

17 Green to Felipe Trevino, June 1785; Ellis, Gaillard, and Banks to the citizens of Natchez, June 1785, in Burnett, "Papers Relating to Bourbon County," 76–77; James, *Antebellum Natchez*, 56.

18 Trevino to Miró, June 15, 1785, in "Mississippi Provincial Archives Spanish Dominion," 2: 147–151.

19 Narrett, *Adventurism and Empire*, 124–125.

20 Trevino to Miró, June 15, 1785, "Mississippi Provincial Archives Spanish Dominion," 2: 150–151.

21 Gilbert C. Din, "War Clouds on the Mississippi: Spain's 1785 Crisis in West Florida," *The Florida Historical Quarterly*, 60 (1981), 59; Trevino to Miró, June 15, 1785, "Mississippi Provincial Archives Spanish Dominion," 2: 151; James, *Antebellum Natchez*, 56.

22 Miró to Green, June 19, 1785, in Burnett, "Papers Relating to Bourbon County," 90–91; Pinnen, *Complexion of Empire in Natchez*; Narrett, *Adventurism and Empire*, 122.

23 Miró to Conde de Galvez, June 20, 1785, and Miró to Joseph de Galvez, June 25, 1785, in Burnett, "Papers Relating to Bourbon County," 94, 96. Translations by the author unless otherwise noted. Bouligny immediately persecuted Gaillard, Ellis, and Banks. According to Gilbert Din, Bouligny quickly sent troops to arrest the three, but only Banks was apprehended. Gaillard and Ellis had both managed to flee before the troops could get ahold of them. Benjamin Farrar, Gaillard's son-in-law, as well as John Ellis, the oldest son of the fugitive Richard Ellis, appeared quickly before Bouligny and expressed their allegiance to Spain. At the same time, both pleaded the cases of their relatives. Bouligny agreed to place Gaillard and Ellis under house arrest if they would surrender. Both Farrar and the younger Ellis had to vouch for their relatives and argued that both men were too old and sick to escape into the wilderness. Only Banks was retained in jail, where he would remain for three months; he also had to pay a fine of fifty pesos; Din, "War Clouds on the Mississippi," 65.

24 Trevino to Miró, July 4, 1785; William Daveport to Samuel Elbert, Fort Panmure, July 17, 1785, in Burnett, "Papers Relating to Bourbon County," 98–100, 105–106.

25 Statment of Stephen Minor, July 10, 1785, Burnett, "Papers Relating to Bourbon County," 100–101.

26 William Davenport to Samuel Elbert, July 17, 1785; Miró to Bouligny, July 19, 1785, Burnett, "Papers Relating to Bourbon County," 105–106, 106.

27 Bouligny to Miró, Aug. 28, 1785, in Kinnaird, *Spain in the Mississippi Valley*, 3: 143–145.

28 Ibid., 3: 144–145. The unfettered desire of the United States, and the fervent belief of Southerners, in the westward expansion of slavery foreshadows Johnson's argument in *River of Dark Dreams*.

29 Sameul Elber to Green, Nov. 9, 1785, in Burnett, "Papers Relating to Bourbon County," 341; J. F. H. Claiborne, *Mississippi, as a Province, Territory and State, with Biographical Notices of Eminent Citizens* (Jackson, MS, 1880), 228n; Green Brothers to Manuel Gayoso de Lemos, Dec. 1792, Archivo General des Indies, Papeles de Cuba, legajo 41 (Seville, Spain).

30 Gayoso de Lemos to Baron the Carondelet, Dec. 18, 1792, Archivo General des Indies, legajo 41 (Seville Spain).

31 On the politics of family migrations, and the difficulties of establishing a business vis-à-vis a political career in American territories, see Edward E. Baptist, "The Migration of Planters to Antebellum Florida: Kinship and Power," *The Journal of Southern History*, 62 (1996), 527–554; Edward E. Baptist, *Creating an Old South: Middle Florida's Plantation Frontier before the Civil War* (Chapel Hill, NC, 2002).

32 Burnett, "Papers Relating to Bourbon County," 298; Miró to Davenport, Christmas, and Long, Nov. 10, 1785; Miró to Bouligny, Nov. 10, 1785, in Burnett, "Papers Relating to Bourbon County," 342–343, 46–47.

33 Din, "War Clouds on the Mississippi," 71, 73–74.

34 David Smith to Colonel Tacitus Gillyard, July 25, 1786, *Natchez Trace Collection: Provincial and Territorial Records* (Center for American History, University of Texas, Austin); Burnett, "Papers Relating to Bourbon County," 352n, 207.

35 On concepts of periphery and center, see Lauren A. Benton, *A Search for Sovereignty: Law and Geography in European Empires, 1400–1900* (New York, 2010); Lauren A. Benton and Richard Jeffrey Ross, *Legal Pluralism and Empires, 1500–1850* (New York, 2013). On the American land ordinances, see Peter S. Onuf, *The Origins of the Federal Republic: Jurisdictional Controversies in the United States, 1775–1787* (Philadelphia, 1983), 149–172.

Troubled Trio

1 William Horace Brown, *The Glory Seekers: The Romance of Would-Be Founders of Empire in the Early Days of the Southwest* (Chicago, 1906), 165–166, 172, 173; Charles Carroll Griffin, *The United States and the Disruption of the Spanish Empire 1810–1822: A Study of the Relations of the United States with Spain and with the Rebel Spanish Colonies* (New York, 1968), 25; William C. Davis, *The Rogue Republic: How Would-Be Patriots Waged the Shortest Revolution in American History* (Boston, 2011), 1.

2 Thomas P. Abernethy, *The South in the New Nation, 1789–1819* (Baton Rouge, LA, 1989), 333; Gilbert C. Din, "A Troubled Seven Years: Spanish Reactions to American Claims and Aggression in 'West Florida,' 1803–1810," *Louisiana History: The Journal of the Louisiana Historical Association*, 59 (2018), 409–410; Andrew McMichael, "The Kemper 'Rebellion': Filibustering and Resident Anglo-American Loyalty in Spanish West Florida," *Louisiana History: The Journal of the Louisiana Historical Association*, 43 (2002), 133–134.

3 Lewis, *American Union*, 31. Throughout the late 1700s to the early- to mid-1800s, the United States shared its southern border with the Spanish Empire's colonies of East and West Florida. Matters were only further complicated by the United States's purchase of Louisiana (1803), resulting in the region being contested among the Spanish Empire and the United States as well as the French, British, Indigenous populations, and runaway American slave and maroon communities. All inhabited the region for various amounts of time and with varying degrees of permanence. The culmination of these influences resulted in an ideal atmosphere for insubordinate and/or autonomous frontiersmen such as the Kemper brothers to create financial and administrative opportunities for themselves. In

addition to the overlapping and contrasting influences, the inconsistent official authority allowed those like the Kemper brothers to maximize their impact on the region's history. Even with the Louisiana Purchase, the Virginia Dynasty presidents did not feel the region was secure because the United States did not have unfettered access to the Mississippi River. Therefore, President Madison instructed Secretary of State Monroe to ensure American ownership of this trade route by attempting to procure both East and West Florida from Spain. See James E. Lewis Jr., *The American Union and the Problem of Neighborhood 1783–1829: The United States and the Collapse of the Spanish Empire* (Chapel Hill, NC, 1998), 31. While every president inherits the policies of their predecessor, each of the Virginia Dynasty presidents served as secretary of state prior to becoming president, and Madison and Monroe both moved directly from secretary of state to president. In their role as secretary of state, Jefferson, Madison, and Monroe (especially the latter two) were intimately involved in negotiations for the Floridas. Each came to see how vital the Floridas were to the overall agenda of the United States, especially commerce in the West and American expansionism. See Frank L. Owsley Jr., and Gene A. Smith, *Filibusters and Expansionists: Jeffersonian Manifest Destiny, 1800–1821* (Tuscaloosa, AL, 1997); Andrew McMichael, *Atlantic Loyalties: Americans in Spanish West Florida, 1785–1810*; J. C. A. Stagg, *Borderlines in Borderlands: James Madison and the Spanish American Frontier, 1776–1821* (New Haven, CT, 2009); Robert V. Haynes, *The Mississippi Territory and the Southwest Frontier, 1795–1817*; John Sledge, *The Mobile River* (Columbia, SC, 2015); and William S. Belko, "The Origins of the Monroe Doctrine Revisited: The Madison Administration, the West Florida Revolt, and the No Transfer Policy," *Florida Historical Quarterly*, 90 (2011), 157–192; Two of the major points of contention in the area were the access to the Mississippi River and the borders of the Louisiana Purchase. One of the British's primary reasons for acquiring Florida in 1763 was to eliminate the Anglo–Spanish border along the modern Florida–Georgia state border, in addition to the trade opportunities it offered. See Mike Bunn, *Fourteenth Colony: The Forgotten Story of the Gulf South During America's Revolutionary Era* (Montgomery, AL, 2020), 5–6. Since the British established colonies close enough for their slaves to run away to Spanish Florida the New World powers consistently struggled against each other. See J. Leitch Wright Jr., *Anglo–Spanish Rivalry in North America* (Athens, GA, 1971) for details.

4 Brown, *The Glory Seekers*, 220–221.

5 While analyses of the Kemper brothers' filibustering activities are sparse, two authors have covered the brothers in depth: Stanley Clisby Arthur, *The Story*

of the Kemper Brothers: Three Fighting Sons of a Baptist Preacher Who Fought for Freedom When Louisiana Was Young (St. Francisville, LA, 1933), and William C. Davis, *Rogue Republic*. Arthur also included the brothers in his *The Story of The West Florida Rebellion* (St. Francisville, LA, 1935). Both authors focus heavily on Reuben, incorporating Nathan and Samuel to a lesser extent, as Reuben left the most written documents and arguably instigated most of the brothers' activities.

6 Davis, *Rogue Republic*, 3–4, 8.

7 Ibid., 7–8.

8 Ibid., 9.

9 McMichael, "The Kemper 'Rebellion,'" 144–145; Davis, *Rogue Republic*, 9.

10 Davis, *Rogue Republic*, 12; Abernethy, *The South in the New Nation*, 334; James Padgett, "The West Florida Revolution of 1810, As Told in the letters of John Rhea," *Louisiana Historical Quarterly*, 21 (1938), 77.

11 McMichael, "The Kemper 'Rebellion,'" 145–147; Davis, *Rogue Republic*, 13.

12 McMichael, "The Kemper 'Rebellion,'" 147; Isaac J. Cox, *The West Florida Controversy, 1798–1813; A Study in American Diplomacy* (Baltimore, 1918); Davis, *Rogue Republic*, 22; Abernethy, *The South in the New Nation*, 334.

13 Davis, *Rogue Republic*, 22.

14 Ibid., 22–23. Though Spanish officials would have preferred Spanish colonists, Florida was not a desirable destination within the Spanish Empire and recruiting colonists would have been too costly in time and money. Having Anglo-American occupants, many of whom at moved to the region during Florida's British period (1763–1783), was ultimately better for Spain than leaving the colony unoccupied. As a result the Spanish were accustomed to Anglo residents and as early as August 1787, Spain opened West Florida for land grants to Americans who were willing to take "oaths of allegiance" to the Spanish colonial government. Due to the lack of resources in the Spanish Floridas, the colonial government relied heavily on its citizens, another reason the colonial government accepted that their colony would be occupied by foreigners. See McMichael, "The Kemper 'Rebellion,'" 136–137; Davis, *Rogue Republic*, 7, 22–23; Richmond F. Brown, *Coastal Encounters: The Transformation of the Gulf South in the Eighteenth Century* (Lincoln, NE, 2007), 213; Abernethy, *The South in the New Nation*, 334.

15 Davis, *Rogue Republic*, 24.

16 Davis, *Rogue Republic*, 24.

17 McMichael, "The Kemper 'Rebellion,'" 147–148.

18 Ibid., 149.

19 McMichael, "The Kemper 'Rebellion,'" 148–149; Davis, *Rogue Republic*, 27–28; Carlos de Grand Pré to Vincente Pintado, June 25, 1804, Pintado Papers, LOC.

20 Thomas D. Clark and John D. W. Guice, *Frontiers in Conflict: The Old Southwest, 1795–1830* (Albuquerque, NM, 1989), 48; McMichael, "The Kemper 'Rebellion,'" 147–148, 153; Cox, *West Florida Controversy*, 154; Davis, *Rogue Republic*, 23–26.

21 Many people in the region assumed the United States would ultimately take over, since it was only getting stronger while the Spanish Empire declined. See Davis, *Rogue Republic*, 27–29.

22 Cox, *West Florida Controversy*, 154; Davis, *Rogue Republic*, 27–29; McMichael, "The Kemper 'Rebellion,'" 150, 154.

23 W. C. C. Claiborne to Julien Poydras, Aug. 6, 1804, *Official Letter Books of W. C. C. Claiborne, 1801–1816*, ed. Rowland Dunbar (6 vols., 1917; reprint, London, 2016), 2: 293–295.

24 Ibid., 154.

25 Ibid., 151, 154; Davis, *Rogue Republic*, 27–32.

26 Davis, *Rogue Republic*, 33.

27 Cox, *West Florida Controversy*, 155–156. This proclamation was published in the Charleston (SC) *Courier*, Sept. 2, 1804. See also Abernethy, *The South in the New Nation 1789–819*, 334; Davis, *Rogue Republic*, 35–39; Clark and Guice, *Frontiers in Conflict*, 48.

28 Davis, *Rogue Republic*, 34, 40–43; Washington (DC) *National Intelligencer*, June 8, 1804. It is important to note that by taking a Spanish official captive, the Kempers elevated their actions to an international incident. If they had apprehended only Americans living in Spanish West Florida, while serious, the gravity of the event would be entirely different. See Cox, *The West Florida Controversy*, 155–156; McMichael, "The Kemper 'Rebellion,'" 154; Clark and Guice, *Frontiers in Conflict*, 47.

29 Davis, *Rogue Republic*, 42–43.

30 Ibid., 34–35; Casa Calvo to W.C.C. Claiborne, Aug. 11, 1804, *Official Letter Books of W. C. C. Claiborne*, 2: 308–309.

31 McMichael, "The Kemper 'Rebellion,'" 155; Davis, *Rogue Republic*, 44–45.

32 Abernethy, *The South in the New Nation*, 336–337; Casa Calvo to W.C.C. Claiborne, Sept. 13, 1804, *Official Letter Books of W. C. C. Claiborne*, 2: 331–332; McMichael, "The Kemper 'Rebellion,'" 156.

33 Affidavit of Nathan Kemper, Sept. 5, 1805, *American State Papers: Foreign Affairs*, 2: 684.

34 Affidavit of Reuben Kemper, Sept. 5, 1805, *American State Papers: Foreign Affairs*, 2: 684–685.

35 Affidavit of Samuel Kemper, Sept. 5, 1805, *American State Papers: Foreign Affairs*, 2: 684; Davis, *Rogue Republic*, 75.

36 Abernethy, *The South in the New Nation*, 337–338; Brown, *The Glory Seekers*, 168; Clark and Guice, *Frontiers in Conflict*, 48; Noble E Cunningham Jr., *Circular Letters of Congressmen to Their Constituents, 1789–1829* (Chapel Hill, NC, 1978), 457–461; Davis, *Rogue Republic*, 73–76.

37 Ibid., 70–80.

38 Casa Calvo to W.C.C. Claiborne, Aug. 11, 1804, *Official Letter Books of W.C.C. Claiborne*, 2: 308–309.

39 W.C.C. Claiborne to Casa Calvo, Aug. 27, 1804, *Official Letter Books of W.C.C. Claiborne*, 2: 309–310.

40 William C. C. Claiborne to Thomas Jefferson, Oct. 27, 1804, *Founders Online*.

41 Ibid.

42 Owsley and Smith, *Filibusters and Expansionists*, 30–31.

43 Gene A. Smith and Sylvia L. Hilton, *Nexus of Empire: Negotiating Loyalty and Identity in the Revolutionary Borderlands, 1760s–1820s* (Gainesville, FL 2011), 6; Andrew McMichael "Maintaining Loyalty in the West Florida Borderlands: Land as Cause and Effect in the West Florida Revolution of 1810," in *Coastal Encounters: The Transformation of the Gulf South in the Eighteenth Century*, ed. Richmond F. Brown (Lincoln, NE, 2007), 210–230. McMichael, "The Kemper 'Rebellion,'" 133; Davis, *Rogue Republic*, 31–33. In *Nexus of Empire*, Smith and Hilton summarized Gulf South occupants' national ideology as displaying loyalty as "the practical side of national identity, or the rational expression of patriotic solidarity" (6).

William Augustus Bowles, the Pretender

1 J. Leitch Wright Jr., *William Augustus Bowles: Director General of the Creek Nation* (Athens, GA, 1967), 1, 12–13. Perryman's first name may have been "William." See Gilbert C. Din, *War on the Gulf Coast: The Spanish Fight Against William Augustus Bowles* (Gainesville, FL, 2012), 22–23.

2 Stephen C. Hahn, *The Invention of the Creek Nation, 1670–1763* (Lincoln, NE, 2004), 7–8; Robbie Ethridge, *Creek Country: The Creek Indians and Their World* (Chapel Hill, NC, 2003), 94–96.

3 Gonzalo M. Qunitero Saravía, *Bernardo de Gálvez: Spanish Hero of the American Revolution* (Chapel Hill, NC, 2018), 144–146; J. Leitch Wright Jr., *Anglo-Spanish Rivalry in North America* (Athens, GA, 1971), 106–111, 127–133.

4 Wright, *William Augustus Bowles*, 14–15. For Bowles's wartime exploits, as relayed by a close English friend, see Benjamin Baynton, *Authentic Memoirs of William Augustus Bowles, Esquire, Ambassador from the United Nations of Creeks and Cherokees, to the Court of London* (London, 1791), 1–8, 12–13, 21–23, 28–36. See also Jack D. L. Holmes, "Alabama's Bloodiest Day of the American Revolution: Counterattack at the Village, January 7, 1781," *Alabama Review*,

29 (1976), 208–219; James H. O'Donnell III, "Hamstrung by Penury: Alexander Cameron's Failure at Pensacola," in *Anglo-Spanish Confrontation on the Gulf Coast During the American Revolution*, ed. William S. Coker and Robert R. Rea (Pensacola, FL, 1982), 76–89; Quintero Saravía, *Bernardo de Gálvez*, 216–227. For the broader scene, see Jim Piecuch, *Three Peoples, One King: Loyalists, Indians, and Slaves in the Revolutionary South, 1775–1782* (Columbia, SC, 2008).

5 Britain lost West Florida to Spain by military defeat and ceded East Florida, too, by the Treaty of Paris of 1783. See David Narrett, *Adventurism and Empire: The Struggle for Mastery in the Louisiana-Florida Borderlands, 1762–1803* (Chapel Hill, NC, 2015), 92–112. For the postwar situation, see Maya Jasanoff, *Liberty's Exiles: American Loyalists in the Revolutionary World* (New York, 2011), 96–109; Kathleen DuVal, *Independence Lost: Lives on the Edge of the American Revolution* (New York, 2015).

6 For McGillivray's connection to Panton and Leslie, see William S. Coker and Thomas D. Watson, *Indian Traders of the Southeastern Spanish Borderlands: Panton, Leslie and Company and John Forbes and Company, 1783–1847* (Pensacola, FL, 1986), 69–72, 101–110, 129; David Narrett, "William Panton, British Merchant and Politico: Negotiating Allegiance in the Spanish and Southern Indian Borderlands, 1783–1801," FHQ, 96 (2017), 135–173.

7 Claudio Saunt, *A New Order of Things: Property, Power, and the Transformation of the Creek Indians, 1733–1816* (Cambridge, UK, 1999), 62–63, 98–101. For McGillivray's diplomacy, see DuVal, *Independence Lost*, 246–262; Kevin Kokomoor, *Of One Mind and of One Government: The Rise and Fall of the Creek Nation in the Early Republic* (Lincoln, NE, 2018), 84–86, 107–117, 130–135.

8 Eliga H. Gould, "Independence and Interdependence: The American Revolution and the Problem of Post-Colonial Nationhood, circa 1802," *William and Mary Quarterly*, 75 (2017), 731 (quotation), 751; Din, *War on the Gulf Coast*, ix ("haughty and deceptive promises" and "self-serving schemes"), 227 ("more misery than . . . relief"). Another critic writes that Bowles's "long-term vision for an independent Creek political entity was complete fantasy." See Kokomoor, *Of One Mind*, 144. A far more sympathetic account of Bowles as a "quirky advocate" of "Pan-Indianism" is in Robert M. Owens, *Red Dreams, White Nightmares: Pan-Indian Alliances in the Anglo-American Mind, 1763–1815* (Norman, OK, 2015), 190. See also Saunt, *A New Order of Things*, 86; Jane G. Landers, *Atlantic Creoles in the Age of Revolutions* (Cambridge, MA, 2010), 100–101.

9 The political and cultural meanings of "adventurer" in English, Anglo-American, and Spanish usage is discussed in Narrett, *Adventurism and Empire*, 4–6, 65–66, 131–132, 185–191, 217–218, 259.

10 The Representation of Wm. Augustus Bowles on behalf of himself and Unatoy, Kuahtekiske, Sepouejah, Tuskeniah, [and] Wosseo Deputed from the United Nation of Creeks and Cherrokees [sic] to His Britannic Majesty, in Bowles to Grenville, Jan. 3, 1791, FO 4/9.

11 While residing in Nassau, Bowles traveled on occasion to the continent and visited his Creek family before he appears more fully in the historical record from 1788 and onward. See Wright, *William Augustus Bowles*, 20–23; Baynton, *Authentic Memoirs,* 45–49. For Bowles's connection to Dunmore, see James Corbett David, *Dunmore's New World* (Charlottesville, VA, 2013), 161–164. For trade, see Kathryn E. Holland Braund, *Deerskins and Duffels: The Creek Indian Trade with Anglo-America, 1685–1815* (1993; 2d ed., Lincoln, NE, 2008), 61–72, 121–128.

12 The deserters offered an account of the expedition to Spanish authorities. See Substance of a Voluntary declaration made by Sundry fellow Banditti at St. Augustine, Nov. 21, 1788, Archivo Nacional de Cuba, Fondos Floridas, legajo 1. See also Coker and Watson, *Indian Traders*, 113–121; Din, *War on the Gulf Coast*, 27–29.

13 Din, *War on the Gulf Coast*, 9–11, 17–21.

14 The Chickamuagas were Cherokees who relocated to more secure ground in the wake of American militia invasions of 1776. See Tyler Boulware, *Deconstructing the Cherokee Nation: Town, Region, and Nation among Eighteenth-Century Cherokees* (Gainesville, FL, 2011), 158–169; Gregory Evans Dowd, *A Spirited Resistance: The North American Indian Struggle for Unity, 1745–1815* (Baltimore, MD, 1992), 90–115.

15 For the Seminoles, see Saunt, *A New Order of Things*, 35–36, 129–135; J. Leitch Wright Jr., *Creeks and Seminoles: The Destruction and Regeneration of the Muscogulge People* (Lincoln, NE, 1986), 5–16; Colin G. Calloway, *The American Revolution in Indian Country: Crisis and Diversity in Native American Communities* (Cambridge, UK, 1995), 257–266. Cherokee and Creek petitions to King George III, May 6, 1789, FO 4/7.

16 Creek petition to George III, May 6, 1789, FO 4/7. For the Cherokee and Creek leaders who endorsed the petitions, see William C. Sturtevant, "The Cherokee Frontiers, the French Revolution, and William Augustus Bowles," in *The Cherokee Nation: A Troubled History*, ed. Duane H. King (Knoxville, TN, 1979), 74–75. Dragging Canoe (Tsi-yuginsini) was the most influential Chickamauga leader listed as at the conference.

17 Creek petition to George III, May 6, 1789, FO 4/7. For Bowles as a courier for Native peoples, see James L. Hill, *Creek Internationalism in an Age of Revolution, 1763–1788* (Lincoln, NE, 2022), 92–96.

18 Wright, *William Augustus Bowles*, 37–43. See also Alden T. Vaughan, *Transatlantic Encounters: American Indians in Britain, 1500–1776* (Cambridge,

UK, 2006); Nancy Shoemaker, *A Strange Likeness: Becoming Red and White in Eighteenth-Century North America* (New York, Oxford, 2004), 34–43, 50–58; Kate Fullagar, *The Warrior, the Voyager, and the Artist; Three Lives in an Age of Empire* (New Haven, CT, 2020), chap. 3. For the "great Water" as a Cherokee phrase, see the account of Sir Alexander Cuming, "West Indies," *The Historical Register,* 61 (1731), 4.

19 Wright identifies Richard Justice as of mixed Cherokee-British ancestry, but some historians believe he was entirely Cherokee by heritage. See Wright, *William Augustus Bowles*, 42. The name "Justice" may reflect a Cherokee notion of a "just" man as rendered in English. See Cephas Washburn on "Dick Justice," in *Cherokees "West": 1794 to 1839* (Claremont, OK, 1910), 101.

20 I have only found one written reference to "Eastajoca"—a friendly use in Dunmore to Bowles, [1798], AGI, PPC, 2371. For the translation, see Sturtevant, "Cherokee Frontiers," 87.

21 Wright, *William Augustus Bowles*, 39–45.

22 Bowles to Dorchester, July 7, 1790, Colonial Office 42/68 (National Archives, Kew, Great Britain). Robbie Ethridge estimates the Creek population of 15,000–20,000 persons in the late eighteenth century. See Ethridge, *Creek Country*, 31. For Cherokee and Creek fighting strength relative to population, see Peter H. Wood, "The Changing Population of the Colonial South: An Overview by Race and Region, 1685–1790," in *Powhatan's Mantle: Indians in the Colonial Southeast*, ed. Gregory A. Waselkov, Peter H. Wood, and Tom Hatley (Lincoln, NE, 2006), 86. The Cherokee population seems to have ranged from 7,500 to perhaps 10,000 in 1790. See Paul Kelton, *Cherokee Medicine, Colonial Germs: An Indigenous Nation's Fight Against Smallpox, 1518–1824* (Norman, OK, 2015), 173, 181.

23 The Representation of Wm. Augustus Bowles on behalf of himself and Unatoy, Kuahtekiske, Sepouejah, Tuskeniah, [and] Wosseo Deputed from the United Nation of Creeks and Cherrokees [sic] to His Britannic Majesty, in Bowles to Grenville, Jan. 3, 1791, FO 4/9. For Chickamauga contacts with British agents in Canada, see Alexander McKee to the Dragging Canoe, July 22, 1791, in Philip M. Hamer, "The British in Canada and the Southern Indians, 1790–1794," *East Tennessee Historical Society Publications*, 2 (1930), 114.

24 Within three days of Bowles's arrival in England—and roughly two months before his memorandum to Grenville—one newspaper reported that six Cherokee chiefs, including Bowles, had the purpose of forming "a connection with the English Government, in order to attempt the reduction of Mexico, near which place they have 20,000 men in arms, and can raise 30,000 more in a short time." See *General Evening Post* (London), Oct. 28–30,

1790. The London press identified Bowles as the leader of Cherokee deputies for two months before one newspaper notice indicated that he was a Creek chief. See *Gazetteer and Newly Daily Advertiser* (London), Jan. 15, 1791. He was "Generalissimo" of the Creeks in the *Diary or Woodfall's Register* (London), Feb. 11, 1791; The Representation of Wm. Augustus Bowles . . . to His Britannic Majesty, in Bowles to Grenville, Jan. 3, 1791, FO 4/9. For British and US ideas of Hispano-American revolution, circa 1790, see J. Leitch Wright Jr., *Britain and the American Frontier, 1783–1815* (Athens, GA, 1975), 53–56. See also Karen Racine, *Francisco de Miranda: A Transatlantic Life in the Age of Revolution* (Wilmington, DE, 2003), 106–112, 133–144, 150–159. For historical context and important primary documents bearing on Bowles's mission, see Frederick J. Turner, "English Policy toward America in 1791," *American Historical Review*, 7 (1902), 706–735.

25 Bowles to Ezpeleta, Aug. 21, 1789, AGI, PPC, legajo 1425. See also Bowles's Aug. 21, 1789, letter to Vicente Manuel de Zéspedes, Governor of East Florida, PPC, legajo 1425, Lockey Transcripts. Bowles's letter of Aug. 30, 1789, to Floridablanca, in Spanish translation, is in AHN, Estado, legajo 3889 bis., LOC.

26 Bowles to Floridablanca, Aug. 30, 1789, AHN, legajo 3889 bis., LOC.

27 Ibid.

28 The original portrait belongs to the National Trust, Upton House and Gardens, Warwickshire, England. For Creek men's use of turbans, which seem to have become widespread by the late 1700s, see Charles Hudson, *The Southeastern Indians* (Knoxville, TN, 1976), 262–264. Bowles did not follow Indigenous customs of either fashioning the hair on the crown of his head into a scalplock or fastening strands of hair with feathers and ornaments. The scalplock is described in William Bartram, *Travels* (Philadelphia, 1791), 501.

29 J. L. Austin, *How to Do Things with Words* (Oxford, UK, 1962), 6 "performative utterance"), 147 ("speech act"). Bowles's "utterances" combined three types: 1) "verdicitive," involving "a verdict" or "an estimate, reckoning, or appraisal"; 2) "exercitive" by "the exercising of powers, rights, or influence"; 3) and "commissive" by "declarations or announcements of intention." See Austin, *How to Do Things*, 150–151. For Austin's theory and philosophical critiques of his work, see Lars Bernaerts, "Interactions in 'Cuckoo's Nest': Elements of a Narrative Speech-Act Analysis," *Narrative*, 18 (2010), 276–299.

30 The Representation of Wm. Augustus Bowles . . . to His Britannic Majesty, in Bowles to Grenville, Jan. 3, 1791, FO 4/9. For Bowles's geopolitical vision, see his letter to Grenville, Jan. 13, 1791, FO 4/9.

31 For the importance of towns, see Ethridge, *Creek Country*, 27–31; Boulware, *Deconstructing the Cherokees*, 11–25.

32 The Representation of Wm. Augustus Bowles . . . to His Britannic Majesty, in Bowles to Grenville, Jan. 3, 1791, FO 4/9.

33 For the newspaper article on "General Bowles" as hero, see *Public Advertiser* (London), Feb. 9, 1791. Grenville's concession to Bowles is quoted from the foreign secretary's letter to Dorchester, Mar. 7, 1791, Colonial Office 42/73.

34 Bowles also mentioned Mobile as one of four Spanish garrisons in the Floridas. See Memorial a S.M.C. [his Catholic Majesty] de William Augustus Bowles, Mar. 25, 1791, AHN, Estado, 3889 bis., LOC. Bowles wrote the names of his five Indian companions below the heading with his name. Creeks and Seminoles believed that the Spanish resided at St. Augustine, San Marcos, and Pensacola only by Native gift, which could be withdrawn if circumstances warranted. See Talk of Kings, Chiefs, and Warriors of the Lower Creeks [Talapuches de abaxo] to Pedro Olivier, July 3, 1792, AHN, Estado, 3898, THNOC.

35 Memorial a S.M.C. [his Catholic Majesty] de William Augustus Bowles, Mar. 25, 1791, AHN, Estado, 3889 bis., LOC. For the issue of contraband, see Coker and Watson, *Indian Traders*, 87–92, 127–134, 205–212.

36 Campo to Floridablanca, Apr. 15, 1791, AHN, Estado, 3889 bis., LOC. Like several Spanish officials, Campo had grave doubts about Panton and Leslie's monopoly and considered it potentially dangerous to imperial interests.

37 Campo to Floridablanca, Apr. 15, 1791, AHN, Estado, 3889 bis., LOC. In response to Campo's complaints, Grenville maintained that Bowles had not received any royal commission or encouragement. See Grenville to Campo, AHN, Estado 3889 bis., LOC.

38 Bowles's vessel arrived at Nassau on May 25, 1791. See his certified statement, of June 11, 1791, Colonial Office 23/15. For Dunmore and Miller's aid to Bowles, see Wright, *William Augustus Bowles*, 56–57. For the picture in Justice's home and Moses Price's views, see Report of Major David Craig to William Blount, Mar. 15, 1792, *American State Papers, Indian Affairs*, 1: 264. Price maintained contact with the British in Canada and by the Gulf. See Price to Alexander McKee [1793], in Hamer, "The British in Canada," 122–123.

39 For Bowles's support among the Lower Creeks, see Arturo O'Neill to the Marqués de Bajamar, AHN, Estado, legajo 3889 bis., LOC. One Spanish officer commented that "Simonoles" or "savages," did not listen to McGillivray and threatened to harass Spaniards at Fort San Marcos unless given provisions. See Luis Bertucat to O'Neill, Sept. 26, 1791, PLC, reel 6. For the insult of Panton as "a Damned Spaniard," see McGillivray to Panton, Mar. 12, 1792, Fondos Floridas, legajo 1, THNOC.

40 The Washington administration's policy is discussed in Colin G. Calloway, *The Indian World of George Washington: The First President, The First Americans, and the Birth of the Nation* (New York, 2018), 367–374.

41 Bowles's protest or "Remonstrance" of Oct. 26, 1791, to US boundary commissioners was printed in the *General Evening Post* (London), Apr. 14–17, 1792. US newspapers carried extracts of this protest as filtered by McGillivray or one of his anonymous allies who alleged that Creeks called Bowles the "lying captain," and warned that McGillivray's "importance and life probably depend on Bowles being driven out of the nation." See "Authentic Intelligence of fresh Disturbances among the Creek Indians," *Maryland Journal* (Baltimore), Dec. 9, 1791. There were several Muskogee flags, as designed by Bowles in the period ca. 1791–1792 and 1799–1803. For images of Bowles's flags, see AHN, Estado, 3889, LOC. One Eduardo Londres (Edward London?) informed Spanish Captain Carlos Howard at St. Augustine that Bowles had a flag of "new invention" and official seals for an "Indian Nation." See deposition of Aug. 9, 1791, AGI, PPC, legajo 151 B, LOC. For digitized, color images of two of Bowles's flags in Spanish archives, see "Diseño de las Banderas de los Corsarios de Bowles," Aug. 15, 1802, AGI, MP-Banderas-13 and 14, PARES.

42 For historians' varying perceptions of McGillivray's power, see DuVal, *Independence Lost*, 246–255, 295–304; Saunt, *A New Order of Things*, 78–89; Kokomoor, *Of One Mind*, 107–125, 143–158. Creek political and social structure are discussed in Ethridge, *Creek Country*, 102–03; Hudson, *Southeastern Indians*, 232–243, 325–327; Hill, *Creek Internationalism*, 68–73.

43 See McGillivray to Panton, Oct. 28, 1791; McGillivray to O'Neill, Oct. 28, 1791, PLC, reel 6.

44 Bowles to O'Neill, Dec. 4, 1791, AHN, Estado 3889 bis, LOC. That same day, a similar but differently worded letter was addressed by Bowles to Carondelet, PLC, reel 6. Bowles had asked his schooner's captain to carry "English Subjects" with him when next sailing from Nassau to Florida. See undated note from Bowles to Captain Young [1791], AHN, Estado 3889 bis., LOC. (This document was captured by Spanish soldiers at one of Bowles's camps.)

45 See Bowles to O'Neill, Dec. 4, 1791, AHN, Estado 3889 bis., LOC. For the Yazoo companies, which troubled Spanish officials at the same time as Bowles's incursions, see Narrett, *Adventurism and Empire*, 184–191.

46 Coker and Watson, *Indian Traders*, 151–152; Lawrence Kinnaird, "The Significance of William Augustus Bowles' Seizure of Panton's Apalachee Store in 1792," FHQ, 9 (1931): 156–192. The precise number of Bowles's Creek and Seminole followers is unknown. One Spanish report stated that

Bowles had 74 Native followers who collaborated in seizing the store and rifling goods. See Eduardo de la Puente to Quesada, Jan. 25, 1792, East Florida Papers, reel 47 (Mary Couts Burnett Library, Ft. Worth, TX).

47 For Carondelet's policy, see Din, *War on the Gulf Coast*, 45–54. Bowles had quite substantial support in the Lower Creek Towns, though some headmen opposed him there. See Kokomoor, *Of One Mind*, 146–147.

48 Carondelet to Bowles, Feb. 2, 1792, PLC, reel 6. By Carondelet's implicit order, Hevia (also spelled Evia) offered to show Bowles a letter from the Spanish Minister of the Treasury [Hacienda], an evident reference to Floridablanca who was Minister of State. See Hevia to Bowles, Feb. 24, 1792, which followed Hevia's letter to Bowles of Feb. 22, which spoke of "esteem and affection," and in which Floridablanca's alleged missive was used as bait. Bowles replied favorably. See Bowles to Hevia, Feb. 22, 1792. The correspondence is in PLC, reel 6. For Bowles's pledge to return in forty days, see his letter [to his associate George Welbank], Feb. 29, 1792, AGI, PPC, legajo 2371. Bowles signed the letter as "Director [of] Affairs, C.N" [Creek Nation].

49 Before departing San Marcos, Bowles issued a written statement to Creek chiefs in which he purposefully mentioned the Spanish promise that he would return safely in forty days. See statement, Feb. 29, 1792, AGI, PPC, legajo 2371. See also Bowles to Carondelet, letters of Mar. 13, Mar. 14, and Mar. 17, 1792, PPC, legajo 2371. For additional details on Bowles's capture and imprisonment, see Din, *War on the Gulf Coast,* 48–54, and Wright, *William Augustus Bowles*, 73–77, 80–82.

50 Carondelet to Floridablanca, Mar. 22, 1792, PLC, reel 7; Casas to conde del Campo de Alange, Mar. 28, 1792, Archivos General de Simancas, GM, legajo 6916, PARES (Portal del Archivo Españoles). For Bowles's passage to Cuba and then Spain, see Din, *War on the Gulf Coast,* 52–57.

51 For Bowles's friendly relations with Miró and his wife, see Wright, *William Augustus Bowles*, 76–77. For the brief autobiography, see "Manifesto o Vida de Guillermo Aug. Bowles," May 26, 1792, in Spanish translation, certified Apr. 12, 1793, PLC, reel 6. For Bowles's interest in acquiring a printing press in London, see *E. Johnson's British Gazette and Sunday Monitor* (London), Feb. 27, 1791.

52 "Manifesto o Vida de Guillermo Aug. Bowles," PLC, reel 6. Bowles joined a Masonic lodge while in London. See London notice, Dec. 11, 1791, in the Portsmouth *New-Hampshire Spy*, Mar. 16, 1791.

53 "Manifesto o Vida de Guillermo Aug. Bowles," PLC, reel 6.; Wright, *William Augustus Bowles*, 87–95.

54 Olivier to Carondelet, May 29, 1792, AHN, Estado 3898; Talk of the Kings, Chiefs, and Warriors of the Lower Creeks (Talapuches de abaxo),

July 3, 1792, in Olivier to Carondelet, AHN, Estado 3898, THNOC. For the Lower Creek and Seminole struggle for open trade, see Capt. Francisco Montreuil to Juan Nepomuceno de Quesada, Jan. 19, 1793; Quesada (governor of East Florida) to Montreuil, Feb. 9, 1793, East Florida Papers, reel 43. Chief Philatouche and a few companions voyaged on a British merchant vessel to Nassau in late 1792 and were welcomed by Governor Dunmore. Spanish officers seized the ship on its return to the Gulf Coast, which elicited Philatouche's protest. Seminoles and nearby Creeks vented their anger by seizing six horses, 30 to 40 cattle, and 800 fowl from Robert Leslie, manager at Panton and company's Apalachee store. See Robert Leslie to John Leslie, Mar. 17, 1793, East Florida Papers, reel 43.

55 Carondelet to Floridablanca, Feb. 25, 1792 (no. 9, reservado), (Biblioteca Nacional, Madrid, Spain), "Documentos de la Louisiana," THNOC. For the new treaty of alliance, July 6, 1792, see John Walton Caughey, *McGillivray of the Creeks* (1959; 2nd ed., Norman, OK, 2012), 329–330. For the Little Prince, see George Welbank to Genl. Wm. A. Bowles, Mar. 6, 1792, in Welbank to Carondelet, AGI, PPC, legajo 152A.

56 For the pullback from the Cherokees, see Aranda to Casas, Mar. 5, 1794, in Casas to Carondelet, June 14, 1794, AGI, PPC, 152B. For the changing geopolitical situation, see Coker and Watson, *Indian Traders*, 158–172, 198–202; Elena Sánchez-Fabrés Mirat, *Situation histórico de las Floridas en la segunda mitad del siglo XVII (1783–1891)* (Madrid, ES, 1977), 74–86. For the national council, see Saunt, *A New Order of Things*, 179–185, 217–221; Hill, *Creek Internationalism*, 135–139; Kokomoor, *Of One Mind*, 240–257.

57 James Seagrove to Henry Knox, May 24, 1792, *American State Papers, Indian Affairs*, 1: 296.

58 Bowles to Grenville, June 5, 1798, AGI, PPC, legajo 2371, LOC. For Bowles's escape and return to England, see Wright, *William Augustus Bowles*, 93–101; Din, *War of the Gulf Coast*, 60–64.

59 Wright, *William Augustus Bowles*, 83–84, 107–114. From 1789 until his murder, Welbank sought to build a pro-British Native network from Creek and Cherokee country to Canada. During his last days, spent in Upper Creek country, he feared that Panton had put a price on his head. See Welbank to Alexander McKee, Apr. 12, 1794; John McDonald to McKee, Dec. 26, 1794, in Hamer, "The British in Canada," 129–134.

60 Bowles to Ellicott, Sept. 22, 1799, AGI, PPC, 2371, LOC. Ellicott sagely observed that Bowles "speaks in the style of a King; 'my nation', and 'my people,' are his common expressions." See Ellicott to Benjamin Hawkins, Oct. 9, 1799, in *The Journal of Andrew Ellicott* (Philadelphia, 1803), 232.

61 Bowles's declaration in the name of "Muskugan" chiefs, Oct. 26, 1799, AGI, PPC, 2371. Efau Hadjo declared before Hawkins that Bowles was "an imposter and liar" and that Creeks and other southern Indians "never had a White Chief." See Talk of Efau Hadjo, Nov. 25, 1799, in "A Talk of the Creek Nation Respecting William Augustus Bowles," FHQ, 11 (1932), 34.

62 Bowles's declaration, Oct. 26, 1799, AGI, PPC, 2371. Bowles to John Adams, Oct. 31, 1799, *Founders Online*. Bowles's individualism and lack of deference are reflective of the American revolutionary era. See Gordon S. Wood, *The Radicalism of the American Revolution* (New York, 1992), 305–310. For the boundary issue, see Jack D.L. Holmes, "The Southern Boundary Commission, the Chattahoochee River, and the Florida Seminoles, 1799," FHQ, 44 (1966), 312–341; Bowles's proclamations are in AGI, PPC, 2371, LOC. Both appear to be dated Nov. 26, 1799 (though the one concerning trade may read Nov. 16 instead of 26). These proclamations are reprinted in the *City Gazette and Daily Advertiser* (Charleston, SC), Mar. 11, 1800.

63 On immigration, see Bowles's proclamation, Nov. 26, 1799, AGI, PPC, 2371. The line between free and enslaved Black status in Creek country, and especially in Seminole villages, was commonly blurred, dependent on understandings between Native masters and individual Blacks. See Daniel F. Littlefield Jr., *Africans and Creeks: From the Colonial Period to the Civil War* (Westport, CT, 1979), 36–51; Kathleen E. Holland Braund, "The Creek Indians, Blacks, and Slavery," *Journal of Southern History*, 57 (1991), 601–637 (especially pp. 618–631).

64 For the shipment of some enslaved Blacks to Nassau, see Saunt, *A New Order of Things*, 211–212. For Bowles's naval force, see Lyle N. McAlister, "The Marine Forces of William Augustus Bowles and His 'State of Muskogee'," FHQ, 32 (1953), 3–27; Lyle N. McAlister, "William Augustus Bowles and the State of Muskogee," FHQ, 40 (1962), 317–328.

65 For the rejection of Portell's proposal, see conference of Feb. 22, 1800, in report of Manuel Garcia, Mar. 4, 1800, Archivo Nacional de Cuba, Florida, legajo 1, Transcript, Ayer Collection (Newberry Library, Chicago). See also Din, *War on the Gulf Coast*, 104–113.

66 Conference record of Feb. 22, 1800, in report of Manuel Garcia, Mar. 4, 1800, Archivo Nacional de Cuba, Florida, legajo 1, Ayer Collection (MS 1076), Newberry Library (Chicago). See also Din, *War on the Gulf Coast*, 104–113, 117–124. At this time, there was a Spanish price of 4,500 pesos on Bowles's head. See Wright, *William Augustus Bowles*, 128.

67 The declaration of war was issued in the name of "His Excellency William Augustus Bowles Director General of Muskogee," AGI, PPC, legajo 2372.

68 Wright, *William Augustus Bowles*, 140–141. For US policy, see Coker and Watson, *Indian Traders*, 239–241.

69 For Hawkins, see Calloway, *Indian World of George Washington*, 369, 468–474; Saunt, *A New Order of Things*, 179–185; Ethridge, *Creek Country*, 12–20, 177–194. Bowles knew that Hawkins was urging his capture, and he responded in kind, stating he would seize Hawkins if possible. See Bowles to Little Prince of Broken Arrow, Nov. 30, 1799, AGI, PPC, legajo 2371.

70 Din, *War on the Gulf Coast*, 175–86; Coker and Watson, *Indian Traders*, 238–242; Lyle N. McAlister, "William Augustus Bowles and the State of Muskogee," FHQ, 40 (1962), 317–328.

71 For Bowles's love of historical painting, see John Devereux DeLacy to Thomas Jefferson, Dec. 18, 1801, *Founders Online*. For the capture of Mary, see Din, *War on the Gulf Coast*, 106.

72 Potato King ("Wackegithy") to Bowles, Feb. 14, 1800 (postscript by James Burgess), AGI, PPC, legajo 2372.

73 Hawkins to Thomas Jefferson, Mar. 1, 1801, *Founders Online*. See also "A Talk of the Creek Nation," 33.

74 Talk of Efau Hadjo, June 17, 1802, *American State Papers, Indian Affairs*, 1: 680.

75 For Kinache's reluctance to meet with Efau Hajo and allied Creek chiefs, see the Talk of Efau Hadjo and the Hollowing [Hallooing] King of Coweta to Kinache in the presence of Benjamin Hawkins and interpreters Timothy Barnard and Alexander Cornells, in Burgess to Bowles, July 17, 1802 [?], PPC, legajo 2372. For Spanish treaty negotiations with the Seminoles and Lower Creeks, see Din, *War on the Gulf Coast*, 196–200.

76 See "A Journal of John Forbes, May, 1803: The Seizure of William Augustus Bowles," FHQ, 9 (1931), 283; "A Journal of John Forbes," 285–287; Din, *War on the Gulf Coast*, 211–212. For the sorrow of Bowles's closest Indian supporters, see entry of May 28, 1803, in "A Journal of John Forbes, Part 2: The Continuation of a Journal of Talks with the Four Nations Assembled at Hickory Ground May & June 1803," ed. Kohn Kelly Innerarity and Kathryn H. Braund, FHQ, 94 (2016), 516.

77 Din, *War on the Gulf Coast*, 211–213.

78 My assessment, admittedly speculative, is based on a reading of Saunt, *A New Order of Things*, 250–269, 275–281; Gregory A. Waselkov, *A Conquering Spirit: Fort Mims and the Redstick War of 1813–1814* (Tuscaloosa, AL, 2006), 78–95; Kokomoor, *Of One Mind*, 342–362; Eliga H. Gould, *Among the Powers of the Earth: The American Revolution and the Making of a New World Empire* (Cambridge, MA, 2012), 197–209.

Diego de Gardoqui

1 John Seally, *A Complete Geographical Dictionary, or Universal Gazetteer of Ancient and Modern Geography* (2 vols., London, n.d.), 1: "Bilbao"; Don Juan Alvarez de Colmenar, *Annales D'Espagne et de Portugal* (4 vols, Amsterdam, 1741), 3: 95–97, 3: 127–131.

2 Colmenar, *Annales D'Espagne*, 3: 96–97, 127–131; Seally, *Complete Geographical Dictionary*, "Bilbao."

3 Seally, *Complete Geographical Dictionary*, "Bilbao"; Colmenar, *Annales D'Espagne*, 3: 128–129 (see map insert); *Relaciones Diplomaticas Entre España y los Estados Unidos Segun los Documentos del Archivo Historico Nacional*, ed. Miguel Gómez del Campillo (2 vols., Madrid, 1944), 1: xxiv.

4 Colmenar, *Annales D'Espagne*, 3: 129; Francisco Murillo Ferrol, *Don Diego de Gardoqui y la Constitucion Norteamericana* (Granada, 1950), 3–21.

5 Campillo, *Relacions Diplomaticas*, 1: xxiv; Reyes Calderón Cuadrado, "La casa Gardoqui. Las claves del éxito de una familia de empresarios," *Bidebarrieta* 17 (2006), 201–203; Colmenar, *Annales D'Espagne*, 3: 129.

6 Cuadrado, "Casa Gardoqui," 203–204; Reyes Calderón Cuadrado, *Empresarios españoles en el proceso de independencia norteamericana: La Casa Gardoqui, e hijos de Bilbao* (Madrid, 2004), 125–126; Campillo, *Relaciones Diplomaticas*, 1: xxiv; Larrie D. Ferreiro, *Brothers at Arms: American Independence and the Men of France and Spain Who Saved It* (New York, 2016), 41; Jonathan Eacott, *Selling Empire: India in the Making of Britain and America, 1600–1830* (Chapel Hill, NC, 2016), 193.

7 Cuadrado, "Casa Gardoqui," 203–206; Cuadrado, *Empresarios españoles*, 127; Alfonso Carlos Saiz Valdivielso, *Diego de Gardoqui: Esplendor y Penumbra* (Bilbao, 2014), 17–18; María Jesús Cava and Begoña Cava, *Diego María de Gardoqui: Un Bilbaino en la diplomacia del siglo XVIII* (Bilbao, 1991), 18–20.

8 Cuadrado, "Casa Gardoqui," 203–206; James G. Lydon, *Fish and Flour for Gold, 1600–1800: Southern Europe in the Colonial Balance of Payments* (Philadelphia, 2008), 71–72, 87, 89, 95, 95n47, 165; Ferreiro, *Brothers at Arms*, 40.

9 Buchanan Parker Thomson, *Spain: Forgotten Ally of the American Revolution* (North Quincy, MA, 1976), 241–248; Cuadrado, *Empresarios españoles*, 192–200.

10 Jonathan R. Dull, "Diplomacy and Independence," in *The Routledge History of U.S. Foreign Relations*, ed. Tyson Reeder (New York, 2022), 108–109; Colin G. Calloway, *The Scratch of a Pen: 1763 and the Transformation of North America* (New York, 2006), 112–132, 152–157.

11 Calloway, *Scratch of a Pen*, 92–100; María Pilar Ruigómez de Hernández, *El Gobierno Español del Despotismo Ilustrado Ante la Independencia de los Estados*

Unidos de América: Una Nueva Estructura de la Política Internacional (1773–1783) (Madrid, 1978), 177, 187, 202.

12 Dull, "Diplomacy and Independence," 117; James Falkner, *Fire Over the Rock: The Great Siege of Gibraltar, 1779–1783* (South Yorkshire, UK, 2009), 1–18; Ruigómez, *Gobierno Español*, 183, 201–202; Thomas E. Chávez, *Spain and the Independence of the United States: An Intrinsic Gift* (Albuquerque, NM, 2012), 54–55; Lydon, *Fish and Flour*, 95, 132–133, 235–237, 242.

13 Joseph Gardoqui & Sons to Jeremiah Lee, Feb. 15, 1775, *Naval Documents of the American Revolution*, ed. William Bell Clark (Washington, 1964), 401; Thomas Amory Lee, *Colonel Jeremiah Lee, Patriot* (Salem, MA, 1916), 13; Cuadrado, *Empresarios españoles*, 197–205.

14 Lydon, *Fish and Flour*, 233–234; Joseph Gardoqui & Sons to Jeremiah Lee, Feb. 15, 1775, and Elbridge Gerry to Joseph Gardoqui and Sons, July 5, 1775, in Clark, *Naval Documents*, 401, 818; Ferreiro, *Brothers at Arms*, 41–42; Cuadrado, *Empresarios españoles*, 200–210.

15 Cuadrado, *Empresarios españoles*, 200–210, 238–244; Thomson, *Spain*, 23–25; Chávez, *Spain and the Independence of the United States*, 49, 60–62; Michael A. Otero, "The American Mission of Diego de Gardoqui" (PhD diss., University of California, Los Angeles, 1948), 28–41; Ferreiro, *Brothers at Arms*, 49–50.

16 Cuadrado, *Empresarios españoles*, 200–235, 242–245; Otero, "American Mission," 41; Larry G. Bowman, "The Scarcity of Salt in Virginia During the American Revolution," *Virginia Magazine of History and Biography* 77 (Oct. 1969), 464–466; José Luciano Franco, *Diego de Gardoqui y las negociaciones entre España y Norteamerica, 1777–1790* (Havana, 1957), 9.

17 Chávez, *Spain and the Independence of the United States*, 126–136, esp. 132; Eliga Gould, *Among the Powers of the Earth: The American Revolution and the Making of a New World Empire* (Cambridge, MA, 2012), 1–4.

18 Otero, "American Mission," 44–47; Thomson, *Spain*, 75–93; Benjamin C. Lyons, "Law in early modern diplomacy: The Jay–Floridablanca negotiations of 1780," in *Spain and the American Revolution: New Approaches and Perspectives*, ed. Gabriel Paquette and Gonzalo M. Quintero Saravia (London, 2019), 147, 151–155.

19 Ferreiro, *Brothers at Arms*, 161–162, 253–254, 288–290; Dull, "Diplomacy and Independence," 117; David J. Weber, *The Spanish Frontier in North America* (New Haven, 2009), 204–206; Otero, "American Mission," 60–61; David Narrett, *Adventurism and Empire: The Struggle for Mastery in the Louisiana–Florida Borderlands, 1762–1803* (Chapel Hill, 2015), 126–127, 210–211; Providence (RI) *Gazette*, Aug. 14, 1784; Arthur Preston Whitaker, *The Spanish–American Frontier: 1783–1795: The Westward Movement and the Spanish Retreat in the Mississippi Valley* (New York, 1927), 65.

20 Drew R. McCoy, *The Elusive Republic: Political Economy in Jeffersonian America* (Chapel Hill, NC, 1980), 123–124; George William Van Cleve, *We Have Not a Government: The Articles of Confederation and the Road to the Constitution* (Chicago, 2017), 142.

21 McCoy, *Elusive Republic*, 123–24; Martin Öhman, "The Mississippi Question in Jeffersonian Political Economy," in *Jeffersonians in Power: The Rhetoric of Opposition Meets the Realities of Governing*, ed. Joanne B. Freeman and Johann N. Neem (Charlottesville, 2019), 44–45; Madison to Jefferson, Sept. 7 and 15, and Aug. 20, 1784, *Founders Online*.

22 Van Cleve, *We Have Not a Government*, 1–3; Alan Taylor, *American Revolutions: A Continental History, 1750–1804* (New York, 2016), 338–339, esp. 338.

23 Valdivielso, *Diego de Gardoqui*, 113–116, 119; Campillo, *Relaciones Diplomaticas*, 1: xli–xlii; Otero, "American Mission," 64–65.

24 Valdivielso, *Diego de Gardoqui*, 119–120; Otero, "American Mission," 233; Gardoqui to Floridablanca, June 30, 1785, in Campillo, *Relaciones Diplomaticas*, 486–487: Valdivielso, *Diego de Gardoqui*, 119–120; Diego de Gardoqui to Washington, July 24, 1789, *Founders Online*.

25 Campillo, *Relaciones Diplomaticas*, 1: xxxvi–xxxvii; Lydon, *Fish and Flour*, 239; Otero, "American Mission," 187.

26 Van Cleve, *We Have Not a Government*, 165; Gardoqui to Floridablanca, Aug. 27, 1784, and May 12, 1787, both in Campillo, *Relaciones Diplomaticas*, 1: xxxv, 518; John Jay to Gardoqui, Oct. 4, 1785, and Mar. 1, 1786, and Jay to Charles Thomson, Mar. 3, 1786, all in *The Selected Papers of John Jay Digital Edition*, ed. Elizabeth M. Nuxoll (Charlottesville, VA, 2014–); Garoqui to Floridablanca, Dec. 6, 1787, Estado, legajo 3893, AHN—Madrid.

27 Lydon, *Fish and Flour*, 238–240; Gardoqui to Floridablanca, June 30, 1785, Estado, legajo 3884 bis, AHN; Campillo, *Relaciones Diplomaticas*, 1: xlv–xlvi; Lydon, *Fish and Flour*, 240.

28 James Monroe to Madison, May 31, 1786, *Founders Online*; Campillo, *Relaciones Diplomaticas*, 1: li–liii, esp. liii; Lydon, *Fish and Flour*, 240.

29 Kevin T. Barksdale, *The Lost State of Franklin: America's First Secession* (Lexington, KY, 2008), 147.

30 Barksdale, *Lost State*, 3–4, 146–148, esp. 147; José Navarro Latorre and Fernando Solano Costa, *Conspiración Española? 1787–1789: Contribución al Estudio de las Primeras Relaciones Históricas Entre España y los Estados Unidos de Norteamérica* (Zaragoza, Spain, 1949), 45, 57; Kathleen DuVal, *Independence Lost: Lives on the Edge of the American Revolution* (New York, 2015), 310–311, 315–316; Gardoqui to Floridablanca, May 12, 1787, in Campillo, *Relaciones Diplomaticas*, 376.

31 Madison, "Notes on Debates," Mar. 13, 1787, and Madison to Jefferson, Aug. 12, 1786, both in *Founders Online.*

32 "Notes on Debates," Mar. 13, 1787, *Founders Online.*

33 Ibid.

34 "Notes on Debates," Mar. 29, 1787, *Founders Online.* Though a Virginia delegate, Henry Lee was not at the meeting with Gardoqui, not having arrived in New York until Apr. 19. Madison seems unaware of the relationship between Gardoqui and Lee, though he did note Lee's "heterodoxy touching the Mississpi [*sic*]." Washington to Jeremiah Wadsworth, Feb. 20, 1787, and Madison to Jefferson, Dec. 4, 1786, *Founders Online.*

35 "Notes on Debates," Mar. 13 and 29, 1787, *Founders Online.*

36 Madison to Jefferson, Mar. 19, 1787, and Madison to James Madison Sr., Apr. 1, 1787, *Founders Online.* To Jefferson, Madison misrepresented his meeting as an "accidental conversation," though he had obviously premeditated it. He likely wanted to conceal that he had gone above Jay's head to negotiate with Spain, though he justified his decision by complaining of Jay's lack of transparency.

37 Gardoqui to Floridablanca, May 12, 1787, in Campillo, *Relaciones Diplomaticas*, 1: 374–375; "Notes on Debates," Mar. 29, 1787, *Founders Online.*

38 "Notes on Ancient and Modern Confederacies," Apr.–June 1786, *Founders Online.*

39 Madison to Jefferson, Mar. 18, 1786, *Founders Online.*

40 For instances that Madison assessed foreign meddling during the Constitutional Convention, see "Reply to the New Jersey Plan," June 19, 1787, "Revisionary Power of the Executive and the Judiciary," June 6, 1787, "Rule of Representation in the Legislature," July 5, 1787, "Method of Appointing the Executive," July 25, 1787, "Impeachment of the Executive," July 20, 1787, and "Citizenship Qualifications for Senators," Aug. 9, 1787, *Founders Online.*

41 "Reply to the New Jersey Plan," June 19, 1787, *Founders Online*; Lydon, *Fish and Flour*, 240; Ferrol, *Don Diego de Gardoqui*, 19–21; Otero, "American Mission," 209–10, 219–223.

42 Ferrol, *Don Diego de Gardoqui*, 15.

43 Gardoqui to Floridablanca, Apr. 18, 1788, in Campillo, *Relaciones Diplomaticas*, 532.

44 Narrett, *Adventurism*, 143–144; Gardoqui to Floridablanca, Apr. 18, 1788, in Campillo, *Relaciones Diplomaticas*, 531–532; Barksdale, *Lost State*, 149–151.

45 Narrett, *Adventurism*, 165–166; Gardoqui to Floridablanca, July 25, 1787, in John Mason Brown, *The Political Beginnings of Kentucky* (Louisville, 1889),

146–148; Brown to Gardoqui, Sept. 15, 1788, Dec. 17, 1788 [misdated by Gardoqui in his translation as 1789], and Jan. 15, 1789, all in Estado, legajo 3894, AHN—Madrid; Gardoqui to Floridablanca, Nov. 22, 1788, Estado, legajo 3894, AHN—Madrid.

46 Barksdale, *Lost State*, 151–52; Narrett, *Adventurism*, 167.

47 Barksdale, *Lost State*, 153–161; Narrett, *Adventurism*, 167, 169; *Conspiración Española*, Latorre and Costa, 79, 144n28, 323–325; DuVal, *Independence Lost*, 320.

48 "Relación de las ceremonias y funciones que se celebraron el día de la proclamación del President General de lost Estados Unidos, Ilustre Jorge Wáshington," May 1, 1789, in Campillo, *Relaciones Diplomaticas*, 1: 546–547.

49 Otero, "American Mission," 279–280.

50 Otero, "American Mission," 281.

An American Scoundrel on Trial

1 Stuart Stumpf, ed., "The Arrest of Aaron Burr: A Documentary Record," *Alabama Historical Quarterly*, 42 (1980), 118–119.

2 Ibid., 120.

3 The musical sparked more discussions on Hamilton. See *Historians on Hamilton: How a Blockbuster Musical Is Restaging America's Past*, ed. Renee Christine Romano and Claire Bond Potter (New Brunswick, NJ, 2018). The 1993 "Who Shot Hamilton?" Got Milk Commercial can be found on youtube.com.

4 Thomas Jefferson to United States Congress, Jan. 22, 1807, *Founders Online*.

5 Edmund Gaines to Wilkinson, Mar. 4, 1807, Records of the Office of the Secretary of War 1791–1948 (National Archives, Washington, DC), RG-107, M221, W-261(3); Stumpf, "Arrest of Aaron Burr," 122.

6 Natchez (MS) *Gazette*, Feb. 18, 1807; Richmond (VA) *Enquirer*, Apr. 17, 1807.

7 Presley Neville and Samuel Roberts to James Madison, Oct. 7, 1806, *Founders Online*; Thomas Jefferson to George Morgan, Sept. 19, 1806; Katherine Duane Morgan to Jefferson, Jan. 10, 1822; Neville and Roberts to Madison, Oct. 7, 1806, *Founders Online*.

8 Notes on a Cabinet Meeting, Oct. 22, 1806, *Founders Online*.

9 Ibid.

10 Deposition of James Wilkinson, Dec. 26, 1806, *Founders Online*.

11 Ibid.

12 Ibid.; James E. Lewis Jr., *The Burr Conspiracy: Uncovering the Story of an Early American Crisis* (Princeton, NJ, 2017), 329.

13 Argument of Aaron Burr in David Robertson, ed., *Trial of Aaron Burr for Treason* (New York, 1875), 12.

14 Ruling of John Marshall, *Trial of Aaron Burr*, 85; David O. Stewart, *American Emperor: Aaron Burr's Challenge to Jefferson's America* (New York, 2012), 229.

15 Argument of Burr, *Trial of Aaron Burr*, 508.
16 Pierre Munroe Irving, *The Life and Letters of Washington Irving* (4 vols., New York, 1862–1864), 1: 158.
17 Testimony of William Eaton, *Trial of Aaron Burr*, 538.
18 Ibid., 540.
19 Testimony of Thomas Truxtun, *Trial of Aaron Burr*, 549–550.
20 Testimony of John Morgan, *Trial of Aaron Burr*, 561–562.
21 Testimony of George Morgan, *Trial of Aaron Burr*, 566.
22 Ibid.
23 Ibid., 566–568.
24 Testimony of Thomas Morgan and John Morgan, *Trial of Aaron Burr*, 569–571, 562.
25 Ibid., 563.
26 Lancaster (PA) *Intelligencer*, May 5, 1807.
27 Testimony of George Morgan, *Trial of Aaron Burr*, 563.
28 Arthur St. Clair to George Washington, Aug. 1789, *Founders Online*.
29 Testimony of John Morgan, *Trial of Aaron Burr*, 569.
30 James Lewis, *The Burr Conspiracy: Uncovering the Story of An Early American Crisis* (Princeton, NJ, 2017), 301; John Marshall, *The Papers of John Marshall* (12 vols., Chapel Hill N.C, 1993) 7: 163.

Conclusion

1 For Morgan, see Max Savelle, *George Morgan Colony Builder* (New York, 1932); Timothy Hemmis, "Under the Banner of War: Frontier Militia and Uncontrolled Violence," *Journal of the American Revolution*, March 29, 2022, online: https://allthingsliberty.com/2022/03/under-the-banner-of-war-frontier-militia-and-uncontrolled-violence/.
2 For Connolly, see John Connolly, *A Narrative of the Transactions, Imprisonment, and Sufferings of John Connolly, an American Loyalist and Lieutenant-Colonel in his Majesty's Service in which are Shewn the Unjustifiable Proceedings of Congress, in his Treatment and Detention* (London, 1783); Clarence Monroe Burton, *John Connolly: A Tory of the Revolution* (Worcester, MA, 1909); Arthur St. Clair to John Jay, Dec. 13–15, 1788, *Founders Online*. For Genet, see Lindsay M. Chervinsky, *The Cabinet: George Washington and the Creation of an American Institution* (Cambridge, MA, 2020).
3 For Sevier and the State of Franklin, see Kevin Barksdale, *The Lost State of Franklin: America's First Secession* (Lexington, KY, 2009). For Henderson, see Susan Fowles and Susan S. Toules. "Col. Richard Henderson of The Famous Transylvania Company," *Register of Kentucky State Historical Society*, 7 (1909), 37–45.

INDEX